About the Author

ALEXIS DE TOCQUEVILLE was born in 1805 in Verneuil, France. At the age of twenty-five, a historian and political scientist, Tocqueville visited the United States in 1831 to report on the prison system, and his experiences there later would become the basis for his classic study *Democracy in America*. He died in 1859.

◆

About the Abridger

SCOTT A. SANDAGE is the author of *Born Losers: A History of Failure in America* (Harvard University Press, 2005). He graduated from the University of Iowa and holds a doctorate in history from Rutgers University. He teaches American cultural history at Carnegie Mellon University in Pittsburgh, Pennsylvania.

DEMOCRACY IN AMERICA

Alexis de Tocqueville

DEMOCRACY IN AMERICA

Abridged Edition

Edited by
J. P. MAYER

Translated by George Lawrence
Abridged by Scott A. Sandage

HARPER**PERENNIAL** ● MODERN**CLASSICS**

NEW YORK ● LONDON ● TORONTO ● SYDNEY

HARPER**PERENNIAL** ● MODERN**CLASSICS**

HarperCollins books may be purchased for educational, business, or sales promotional use. For information please write: Special Markets Department, HarperCollins Publishers, 10 East 53rd Street, New York, NY 10022.

FIRST EDITION

Designed by Jaime Putorti

Library of Congress Cataloging-in-Publication Data is available upon request.

ISBN: 978-0-06-000873-4
ISBN-10: 0-06-000873-3

07 08 09 10 11 ❖/RRD 10 9 8 7 6 5 4 3 2 1

CONTENTS

A Succinct Introduction to the Abridged Edition   vii
Foreword by J. P. Mayer (1966 Edition)   xv
Tocqueville's Preface to the Twelfth Edition (1848)   xvii

VOLUME ONE

Contents of Volume One   3
Tocqueville's Introduction   9
Democracy in America: Volume One   17

VOLUME TWO

Contents of Volume Two   225
Tocqueville's Preface to Volume Two   231
Democracy in America: Volume Two   233

Appendix: Excerpt from Tocqueville's Travel Diary   403
A Note on the Abridgement   407
Index   411

A SUCCINCT INTRODUCTION
TO THE ABRIDGED EDITION

"THEY LIKE BOOKS WHICH are easily got and quickly read," Alexis de Tocqueville observes of democratic readers and their taste for works that "plunge them . . . into the middle of the subject." The Frenchman who toured the United States in 1831 and 1832 was not that kind of writer. The first edition of *De la démocratie en Amérique* totaled nearly 1,000 pages. The first English translation ran almost 1,500. Some modern editions top 900 pages, weighing in at three pounds or more. Tocqueville spent nine years writing his masterpiece, but it shouldn't take that long to read.

An abridgement surely would have exasperated the author, except for the chance to gloat that it proves him right about us, again. But it would add insult to injury, having subtracted 400 pages from Tocqueville's book, to add many new ones. If Americans today are as busy as those he met and observed, few readers will pick up this book hoping for a lengthy introduction.

What you need to know, before finally tackling this famous book, is who wrote it and why it is so important.

Nobody put it more bluntly than Kurt Vonnegut. "I consider anybody a twerp who hasn't read *Democracy in America* by Alexis de Tocqueville," he writes in chapter 2 of *A Man Without a Country* (Seven Stories Press, 2005). "There can never be a better book than that one on the strengths and vulnerabilities inherent in our form of government."

If we are still a nation of twerps, the punchline is that we are still a nation at all, 175 years after Tocqueville's visit. He wrote for Europeans in an era when democratic revolutions against monarchy and aristocracy usually ended in terror or anarchy. He wondered why the democratic experiment in the United States had endured peacefully and prosperously for more than half a century.

Democracy in America is an elaborate hypothesis about whether (and if so, how) democracy could endure anywhere. How are freedom and equality different, and what is the relationship between them? What is the proper balance between liberty and power? Does individual ambition threaten or advance society? What does it mean to say that "the people" are sovereign? What are the consequences if "the people" really means "the majority"? What happens if prosperity makes people forget about politics?

These were urgent and unsolved questions not only because modern democracy was still in its infancy, but because the seemingly irresistible momentum of it posed the greatest problem of the age. Tocqueville examined his test case neither as a cynic nor as a romantic. Although he came to believe that American-style republics were the wave of the future, he remained leery that such a future might lead to despotism rather than to freedom—as it had, in his view, after the French Revolution.

Inquiring into the United States, Tocqueville did not always draw the right conclusions, yet he posed timeless questions about "the strengths and vulnerabilities inherent in our form of government." Even now, only a twerp could shrug off Tocqueville's hopes and fears as being outdated or irrelevant.

This is not to anoint him as a prophet. It does seem miraculous that a twenty-five-year-old Frenchman could spend 271 days here and write the American *I Ching*. Open to any page, it seems, and you find quotable wisdom, unchanging truths for an always changing society.

But Tocqueville misjudged much of what he saw in Jacksonian America, as many scholars have noted; here and there, his logic reads like a Monty Python sketch. He overgeneralized about national politics from what he observed at the local level. He mistook New England for the American norm rather than the exception. He thought states' rights always would outweigh federal power. He swallowed what factory owners told him about workers and what slave owners told him about Negroes, while showing little interest in speaking directly to either. He believed that most citizens were middle class and rose to that status as self-made men. He presumed that strivers always and easily bounced back from failure.

In short, he homogenized Americans and their destinies, as if an unprecedented mix of peoples could ever be of one mind about what democracy meant or who it profited.

Some of his lapses reveal Alexis-Charles-Henri-Maurice-Clérel de Tocqueville as the young aristocrat he was, hardly callow but with an inbred contempt for the "poor and ignorant." Born in Paris in 1805, he was the third son in a minor noble family. His father (descended from old Norman landowners) and his mother (from one of the châteaux of the Loire Valley) narrowly escaped the guillotine; his mother's father, a minister of state who volunteered to defend King Louis XVI at trial, did not. After the fall of Napoleon in 1814 and the subsequent restoration of the monarchy, Tocqueville's father garnered a series of administrative appointments. Alexis was educated by a private tutor before attending secondary school and the royal college at Metz, where he majored in rhetoric and philosophy. He studied law in Paris, and after he turned twenty-one, a junior magistrate's position was created for him at Versailles.

Come the "July Revolution" of 1830, Tocqueville secured a comparable appointment under the new constitutional monarchy, but soon he began to envision a transatlantic excursion. With his friend and legal colleague Gustave de Beaumont, he finagled eighteen months' leave of absence from the Ministry of Justice— ostensibly to study prisons in the United States. The future author of *Democracy in America* got here on a bureaucratic junket.

Beginning with a five-week voyage from Le Havre, the adventure lasted ten months and covered more than 7,384 miles of the United States, by every available mode of transportation. The Frenchmen landed at Newport, Rhode Island, on May 9, 1831. Two days later, they sailed down the coast to New York City (where they spent nearly two months over several stints). In July, a Hudson

River sloop carried them upstate to Albany, a stagecoach got them to Syracuse, and they continued on horseback. They went by steamboat from Buffalo to Detroit and by canoe from Sault Sainte Marie upriver to Lake Superior.

Few Americans then, or now, saw so much of the country, top to bottom. Niagara Falls, Montréal, and Québec City. Three weeks in Boston. Two weeks in Philadelphia, one in Baltimore. They rode a stage over the Alleghenies to Pittsburgh and a paddle-wheeler down the Ohio River to Cincinnati. Icebound, the party disembarked and walked twenty-two miles into Louisville. Ten days in Nashville and Memphis. Stranded on a Mississippi sandbar for two days, they reached New Orleans on New Year's Day 1832. On across Alabama, Georgia, and the Carolinas to Norfolk and the Chesapeake Bay, they headed up the Potomac River. During two weeks in Washington, D.C., they met President Andrew Jackson— who plied them with Madeira wine. Returning to New York City for two final weeks, they sailed for home on February 20, 1832.

Beaumont and Tocqueville's 1833 report, *On the Penitentiary System of the United States and Its Application in France,* attracted moderate attention, but *Democracy in America* was what we now call "a publishing event." Volume 1 (1835) sold out seven editions in four years. Many Europeans had published books after visiting the United States, but Tocqueville eschewed travelogue in favor of political philosophy, producing a work of extraordinary breadth, depth, and originality.

Democracy in America emphasized how culture—"habits of the heart"—was as important as law and politics in determining the overall direction and stability of a society. John Stuart Mill's review hailed it as "the beginning of a new era in the scientific study of politics." By 1840, when volume 2 was published in French and English simultaneously, the author was an international celebrity. Elected to national office in 1839, Tocqueville served in the Chamber of Deputies until the revolution of 1848. Elected to the new Constituent Assembly, he helped to frame the new French constitution. He traveled and wrote throughout the next decade, while his health failed. He died at age fifty-four in 1859.

If Alexis de Tocqueville had never lived, modern-day political speechwriters and news commentators would have had to invent him—and in a way, they did.

Surprisingly, *Democracy in America* was largely forgotten by the early twentieth century. After 1899, no new edition appeared in English for almost fifty years. From 1900 to 1935, the book rated only twenty mentions in the *New York Times*—some of them advertisements for secondhand books. The 1935 centennial of *Democracy in America* renewed scholarly interest and generated new editions of Tocqueville's works. But a more general revival took hold in the postwar decades, when liberals and conservatives began to spin Tocqueville's Big Book on all sides of the cold war and the culture wars. Between 1950 and 2000, more than two hundred books about Tocqueville were published in English.

Just as Benjamin Franklin's *Autobiography* became a classic when nineteenth-century readers adopted it as the bible of self-made manhood, *Democracy in America* became "something that everybody wants to have read and nobody wants to read" (Mark Twain's definition of a classic) only when it was finally dusted off by twentieth-century ideologues.

Both sides talked up a single word epitomized by Franklin and coined, evidently, by Tocqueville: *individualism.*

In French, *l'individualisme* meant extreme selfishness with antisocial or even anarchic consequences, but Tocqueville redefined the word because no other quite described the American way of life. The first translator of *Democracy in America,* Henry Reeve, imported the unfamiliar word into English for the same reason.

"Individualism is a calm and considered feeling," Tocqueville wrote, which leads the citizen to "withdraw into the circle of family and friends," leaving "the greater society to look after itself." Although he warned that apathy and anarchy posed omnipresent dangers, Tocqueville explained how "the doctrine of self-interest properly understood" (as practiced in the United States) might make the world safe for individualism, and hence safe for democracy.

Whether you consider Tocqueville—"properly understood"—

to be an icon of libertarianism, as Michael A. Ledeen's *Tocqueville on American Character* (St. Martin's Press, 2000) suggests, or an icon of communitarianism, as Robert N. Bellah and his coauthors would have it in *Habits of the Heart* (University of California Press, 1996) may depend as much on how you vote as on what he wrote.

Of course, Tocqueville is not any sort of icon. How many of us could pick him out of a lineup? Tocqueville is a big name in America but not a brand name. His presence in modern life has remained almost entirely intellectual—an unusual fact in itself. Popular culture has never had any use for him. We don't see his face in advertisements or on T-shirts. Hollywood has never made a movie about him. In the 1990 public television documentary *The Civil War*, Ken Burns cast the British actor Jeremy Irons (of all people) to read Tocqueville's lines. A New York City restaurant named Tocqueville (try the venison) opened in 2000, appropriately aimed at middle-class patrons. Googling "tocqueville" pulls up 4.2 million hits in 2006, but www.tocqueville.com turns out to be an investment firm, while www.tocqueville.org takes you to C-Span. Searching for "tocqueville" and "twerp" gets you nowhere.

Even if Kurt Vonnegut was right that "there can never be a better book" about the promises and pitfalls of democracy in America, there are at least some *good* books to complement this one.

In hopes that this abridgement may pique rather than satisfy readers' curiosity, here are a very few suggestions. Joseph Epstein's brief biography, *Alexis de Tocqueville* (2006), is part of Harper-Collins' "Eminent Lives" series. Tocqueville's fellow traveler, Gustave de Beaumont, published the searing novel *Marie; or, Slavery in the United States* (Johns Hopkins University Press, 1998). Matthew Mancini's *Alexis de Tocqueville and American Intellectuals: From His Times to Ours* (Rowman & Littlefield, 2005) explains what all the ruckus is about. Harry Watson's *Liberty and Power: The Politics of Jacksonian America* (Hill & Wang, 1990) surveys that era clearly and concisely. Louis P. Masur's *1831: Year of Eclipse* (Hill & Wang, 2001) brings politics and culture to life during the turbulent year of

Tocqueville's visit. For a reality check 175 years later, try Bernard-Henri Lévy's *American Vertigo: Traveling America in the Footsteps of Tocqueville* (Random House, 2006).

But read Tocqueville first.

SCOTT A. SANDAGE
PITTSBURGH, PA.
2006

FOREWORD BY J. P. MAYER (1966 EDITION)

IT WAS IN 1957 when I decided to do a new edition of the *Democracy in America*. By 1960 the publishers had advanced the necessary funds for the translation, and my friend George Lawrence set to work. Lawrence had already proved his rare gift as a Tocqueville translator by having done my edition of Tocqueville's *Journey to America*. Once Lawrence had completed his gigantic task, I read his text, compared it with the original, and put many queries down on paper. Lawrence and I went over these queries together, and we hope we confront the reader with a faithful text.

Indeed the most authoritative statement for the need of a new translation comes from the author himself. On November 15, 1839, Tocqueville wrote to his translator, Henry Reeve, in London: "I am writing in a country and for a country where the cause for equality is from now on won—without the possibility of a return toward aristocracy. In this state of affairs I felt it my duty to stress particularly the bad tendencies which equality may bring about in order to prevent my contemporaries surrendering to them. . . . I therefore say often very severe truths on the French society of our days and on democratic societies in general, but I say these things

---

Jacob-Peter Mayer (1903–1992) was born in Frankenthal, Germany, and was active in the anti-Nazi movement before emigrating to Great Britain in 1936. In 1951, he became editor-in-chief of the official edition of Tocqueville's writings, *Oeuvres Complètes* (Paris: Gallimard, 1951–), producing some seventy volumes by 1980. The author or editor of many books on subjects as diverse as Tocqueville, Karl Marx, Max Weber, and British cinema, Mayer taught at the London School of Economics, Seattle University in the United States, and the University of Reading, England, where he established the Tocqueville Centre (now defunct). For an obituary, see the London *Daily Telegraph*, January 1, 1993, p. 19.

as friend and not as censor. . . . In the translation of the last book [Volume 1 of *Democracy in America*] you have . . . very lively colored what was contrary to democracy and rather appeased what could do wrong to aristocracy. I beg you earnestly to struggle against yourself on this point and to preserve my book its character, which is a veritable impartiality in the theoretical judgment of the two societies, the old and the new, and even the sincere wish to see the new one to establish itself." (Cf. *Oeuvres Complètes*, J. P. Mayer, ed., vol. 6, 1, pp. 47 f.)

I believe I have taken great pains, together with George Lawrence, to comply with the author's wish.

In other respects too, the present edition has novel features: I have verified quotations by Tocqueville and given precise references. Thus, for instance, we have inserted the original texts by Jefferson instead of as Reeve has done, printing them in a retranslated version from the French; etc.

Nearly all the books and documents to which Tocqueville refers have been consulted. Thus it will now be possible to study Tocqueville as an outstanding legal historian, a brilliant anthropologist, and a classic sociologist, fully equipped with the knowledge of his time.

Occasionally errors in Tocqueville's page references have been corrected. More serious mistakes, for instance wrong names or faulty references to texts, have been indicated to facilitate the use of his sources. Editor's notes have been indicated by brackets.

Our text is based on the second revised and corrected text of my 1961 French edition.

J. P. MAYER
JANUARY 1965

TOCQUEVILLE'S PREFACE
TO THE TWELFTH EDITION (1848)

HOWEVER SUDDEN AND MOMENTOUS be the events which have just taken place, the author of this book can claim that they have not taken him by surprise. This work was written fifteen years ago with a mind constantly preoccupied by the approaching irresistible and universal spread of democracy throughout the world. One finds on every page a warning that society is changing shape, that mankind lives under changing conditions, and new destinies are impending.

In the introduction it was stated that: "The gradual progress of equality is something fated. . . . Does anyone imagine that democracy, which has destroyed the feudal system and vanquished kings, will fall back before the middle classes and the rich?"

He who wrote these lines, which proved prophetic under a monarchy strengthened rather than shaken by the Revolution of July, 1830, need feel no diffidence now in again calling public attention to his work. The circumstances of the moment give this book a topical interest and practical utility which it did not have when it first appeared.

American institutions, which for France under the monarchy were simply a subject of curiosity, ought now to be studied by

---

This preface (which has been abridged) was written in 1848 for the next-to-last edition during Tocqueville's lifetime. It was reprinted in the thirteenth edition of 1850; this edition forms the basis of ours. The "sudden and momentous . . . events" to which Tocqueville's opening line refers were the revolutions of 1848, which began in France in February and followed in Germany, Italy, Poland, and the Hapsburg Empire.

republican France. It is not force alone, but rather good laws, which make a new government secure. After the battle comes the lawgiver. It is not a question now whether we are to have monarchy or republic in France; but whether it is to be an agitated or a tranquil republic, orderly or disorderly, pacific or warlike, liberal or oppressive, a republic which threatens the sacred rights of property and of the family, or one which honors them. It is a fearful problem concerning, not France alone, but the whole civilized world. If we can save ourselves, we shall at the same time save all the nations around us. If we fail, we shall bring them all down with us. According as we establish either democratic liberty or democratic tyranny, the fate of the world will be different. Indeed, one may say that it depends on us whether in the end republics will be established everywhere, or everywhere abolished.

Now this problem, newly posed for us, was solved in America sixty years ago. The principle of the sovereignty of the people has prevailed unchallenged there, put in practice in the most direct, unlimited, and absolute way. For sixty years that people has increased in population, territory, and wealth, and it has been not only the most prosperous but also the most stable in the world. Almost the whole of Europe has been convulsed by revolutions; America has not even suffered from riots. There the republic, so far from disturbing them, has preserved all rights. Private property is better guaranteed there than in any other land on earth. Anarchy is as unknown as despotism.

Where else can we find greater cause of hope or more valuable lessons? Let us not turn to America to copy her institutions slavishly, but in order that we may better understand what suits us; let us look there for instruction rather than models; let us adopt the principles rather than the details of her laws. The principles on which the constitutions of the American states rest, the principles of order, balance of powers, true liberty, and respect for law, are indispensable for all republics; and it is safe to forecast that where they are not found the republic will soon have ceased to exist.

1848

Volume One

CONTENTS OF VOLUME ONE

Tocqueville's Introduction   9

PART I

1. PHYSICAL CONFIGURATION OF NORTH AMERICA   19

2. CONCERNING THEIR POINT OF DEPARTURE
   AND ITS IMPORTANCE FOR THE FUTURE
   OF THE ANGLO-AMERICANS   24
   *Reasons for Some Peculiarities in the Laws
   and Customs of the Anglo-Americans*   37

3. SOCIAL STATE OF THE ANGLO-AMERICANS   38
   *The Striking Feature in the Social Condition
   of the Anglo-Americans Is That It Is
   Essentially Democratic*   38
   *Political Consequences of the Social State
   of the Anglo-Americans*   41

4. THE PRINCIPLE OF THE SOVEREIGNTY
   OF THE PEOPLE IN AMERICA   42

5. THE NEED TO STUDY WHAT HAPPENS IN THE
   STATES BEFORE DISCUSSING THE GOVERNMENT
   OF THE UNION   43
   The American System of Townships   44
   Spirit of the Township in New England   45
   Administration in New England   46

*General Ideas Concerning Administration
    in the United States*   48
Legislative Power of the State   49
The Executive Power of the State   50
*Political Effects of Administrative
    Decentralization in the United States*   51

6. JUDICIAL POWER IN THE UNITED STATES
    AND ITS EFFECT ON POLITICAL SOCIETY   55
    Other Powers Given to American Judges   58

7. POLITICAL JURISDICTION IN THE UNITED STATES   59

8. THE FEDERAL CONSTITUTION   61
    History of the Federal Constitution   61
    Summary of the Federal Constitution   63
    Prerogatives of the Federal Government   64
    Legislative Powers   65
    *Another Difference Between the Senate
        and the House of Representatives*   67
    The Executive Power   68
    *How the Position of the President
        of the United States Differs from
        That of a Constitutional King in France*   69
    Election of the President   70
    Mode of Election   72
    Crisis of the Election   75
    Concerning the Reelection of the President   76
    The Federal Courts   78
    *Means of Determining the Competence
        of the Federal Courts*   80
    *High Standing of the Supreme Court
        Among the Great Authorities in the State*   81
    *The Superiority of the Federal Constitution
        over That of the States*   83

*What Distinguishes the Federal Constitution
of the United States of America from
All Other Federal Constitutions* 85
*Advantages of the Federal System in General
and Its Special Usefulness in America* 87
*Why the Federal System Is Not Within the Reach
of All Nations and Why the Anglo-Americans
Have Been Able to Adopt It* 90

PART II

1. WHY IT CAN STRICTLY BE SAID THAT
THE PEOPLE GOVERN IN THE UNITED STATES 97

2. PARTIES IN THE UNITED STATES 98
Remains of the Aristocratic Party in the United States 101

3. FREEDOM OF THE PRESS IN THE UNITED STATES 102

4. POLITICAL ASSOCIATION IN THE UNITED STATES 106

5. GOVERNMENT BY DEMOCRACY IN AMERICA 109
Universal Suffrage 109
*The People's Choice and the Instincts
of American Democracy in Such Choices* 109
*Elements Which May Provide a Partial Corrective
to These Instincts of Democracy* 111
Public Officers Under the Rule of American Democracy 112
Administrative Instability in the United States 113
Public Expenses Under the Rule of American Democracy 114
*Corruption and Vices of the Rulers in a
Democracy and Consequent Effect on Public Morality* 117
The Efforts of Which Democracy Is Capable 118
American Democracy's Power of Self-Control 119
*How American Democracy Conducts the
External Affairs of the State* 121

6. THE REAL ADVANTAGES DERIVED BY
   AMERICAN SOCIETY FROM DEMOCRATIC GOVERNMENT   123
      *The General Tendency of Laws Under the Sway
         of American Democracy and the
         Instincts of Those Who Apply Them*   123
      Public Spirit in the United States   125
      The Idea of Rights in the United States   127
      Respect for Law in the United States   128
      *Activity Prevailing in All Parts
         of the Political Body in the United States;
         the Influence Thereby Exerted on Society*   129

7. THE OMNIPOTENCE OF THE MAJORITY
   IN THE UNITED STATES AND ITS EFFECTS   132
      Tyranny of the Majority   133
      *The Power Exercised by the Majority
         in America over Thought*   135
      *Effects of the Majority's Tyranny on
         American National Character;
         the Courtier Spirit in the United States*   137
      *The Greatest Danger to the American
         Republics Comes from the Omnipotence
         of the Majority*   138

8. WHAT TEMPERS THE TYRANNY
   OF THE MAJORITY IN THE UNITED STATES   139
      Absence of Administrative Centralization   139
      *The Temper of the American Legal Profession
         and How It Serves to Counterbalance Democracy* 140
      *The Jury in the United States Considered
         as a Political Institution*   142

9. THE MAIN CAUSES TENDING TO MAINTAIN
   A DEMOCRATIC REPUBLIC IN THE UNITED STATES   144
      *Accidental or Providential Causes Helping
         to Maintain a Democratic Republic
         in the United States*   144

Influence of the Laws upon the Maintenance
  of a Democratic Republic in the United States 149
Influence of Mores upon the Maintenance
  of a Democratic Republic
  in the United States 150
Religion Considered as a Political Institution
  and How It Powerfully Contributes to the
  Maintenance of a Democratic Republic
  Among the Americans 150
Indirect Influence of Religious Beliefs
  upon Political Society in the United States 152
The Main Causes That Make Religion
  Powerful in America 154
How the Enlightenment, Habits,
  and Practical Experience of the Americans
  Contribute to the Success of Democratic Institutions 156
The Laws Contribute More to the Maintenance
  of the Democratic Republic in the United States
  Than Do the Physical Circumstances of the Country,
  and Mores Do More Than the Laws 159
The Importance of the Foregoing in Relation to Europe 162

10. SOME CONSIDERATIONS CONCERNING THE
    PRESENT STATE AND PROBABLE FUTURE OF
    THE THREE RACES THAT INHABIT THE
    TERRITORY OF THE UNITED STATES 164
  The Present State and the Probable Future
    of the Indian Tribes Inhabiting
    the Territory of the Union 168
  Situation of the Black Race in the United States;
    Dangers Entailed for the Whites by Its Presence 180
  What Are the Chances That the American
    Union Will Last? What Dangers Threaten It? 195
  Concerning the Republican Institutions
    of the United States and Their Chances of Survival 211

*Some Considerations Concerning the Causes
    of the Commercial Greatness of the United States*   213

CONCLUSION   218

TOCQUEVILLE'S INTRODUCTION

No novelty in the United States struck me more vividly during my stay there than the equality of conditions. I soon realized that the influence of this fact extends far beyond political mores and laws, exercising dominion over civil society as much as over the government; it creates opinions, gives birth to feelings, suggests customs, and modifies whatever it does not create. All my observations constantly returned to this nodal point.

Later, when I came to consider our own side of the Atlantic, I thought I could detect something analogous. I saw an equality of conditions which, though it had not reached the extreme limits found in the United States, was daily drawing closer thereto; and that same democracy which prevailed over the societies of America seemed to be advancing rapidly toward power in Europe.

It was at that moment that I conceived the idea of this book.

A great democratic revolution is taking place in our midst; everybody sees it, but by no means everybody judges it in the same way. Some think it a new thing and, supposing it an accident, hope that they can still check it; others think it irresistible, because it seems to them the most continuous, ancient, and permanent tendency known to history.

And that is not something peculiar to France. Wherever one looks one finds the same revolution taking place throughout the Christian world. All men's efforts have aided it, both those who fought for democracy and those who were the declared enemies thereof; all have worked together, some against their will and some unconsciously, blind instruments in the hands of God.

Therefore the gradual progress of equality is something fated. Does anyone imagine that democracy, which has destroyed the feudal system and vanquished kings, will fall back before the middle classes and the rich? The movement is already too strong to be halted, but it is not yet so swift that we must despair of directing it; our fate is in our hands, but soon it may pass beyond control.

The first duty imposed on those who now direct society is to educate democracy; gradually to substitute understanding of statecraft for present inexperience and knowledge of its true interests for blind instincts; to adapt government to the needs of time and place; and to modify it as men and circumstances require.

A new political science is needed for a world itself quite new.

But it is just that to which we give least attention. Carried away by a rapid current, we obstinately keep our eyes fixed on the ruins still in sight on the bank, while the stream whirls us backward— facing toward the abyss.

As a result the democratic revolution has taken place in the body of society without those changes in laws, ideas, customs, and mores which might have mitigated its vices and brought out its natural good points.

When royal power supported by aristocracies governed the nations of Europe in peace, society, despite all its wretchedness, enjoyed several types of happiness which are difficult to appreciate or conceive today. On the one side were wealth, strength, and leisure combined with farfetched luxuries, refinements of taste, the pleasures of the mind, and the cultivation of the arts; on the other, work, coarseness, and ignorance. But among this coarse and ignorant crowd lively passions, generous feelings, deep beliefs, and untamed virtues were found.

The body social thus ordered could lay claim to stability, strength, and above all, glory.

But distinctions of rank began to get confused, and the barriers separating men to get lower. Great estates were broken up, power shared, education spread, and intellectual capacities became more equal. The social state became democratic, and the sway of democracy was finally peacefully established in institutions and in mores.

At that stage one can imagine a society in which all men, regarding the law as their common work, would love it and and submit to it without difficulty; the authority of the government would be respected as necessary, not as sacred. Each man having some rights and being sure of the enjoyment of those rights, there would be established between all classes a manly confidence and a sort of reciprocal courtesy, as far removed from pride as from servility.

Understanding its own interests, the people would appreciate that in order to enjoy the benefits of society one must shoulder its obligations. Free association of the citizens could then take the place of the individual authority of the nobles, and the state would be protected both from tyranny and from license.

I appreciate that in a democracy so constituted, one might find less glory than in an aristocracy, but there would be less wretchedness; pleasures would be less extreme, but well-being more general; the heights of knowledge might not be scaled, but ignorance would be less common; feelings would be less passionate, and manners gentler; there would be more vices and fewer crimes.

The nation as a body would be less brilliant, less glorious, and perhaps less strong, but the majority of the citizens would enjoy a more prosperous lot, and the people would be pacific not from despair of anything better but from knowing itself to be well-off.

Though all would not be good and useful in such a system of things, society would at least have appropriated all that it could of the good and useful; and men, by giving up forever the social advantages offered by aristocracy, would have taken from democracy all the good things that it can provide.

But in abandoning our ancestors' social state and throwing their institutions, ideas, and mores pell-mell behind us, what have we put in their place?

The prestige of the royal power has vanished but has not been replaced by the majesty of the law. The government alone has inherited all the prerogatives snatched from [aristocratic] families, corporations, and individuals; so the sometimes oppressive but often conservative strength of a small number of citizens has been succeeded by the weakness of all. The breakup of fortunes has diminished the distance between rich and poor, but while bringing them closer, it seems to have provided them with new reasons for hating each other, so that with mutual fear and envy they rebuff each other's claims to power.

Thus we have abandoned whatever good things the old order of society could provide but have not profited from what our present state can offer.

What is now taking place in the world of the mind is just as deplorable. It would seem that we have nowadays broken the natural link between opinions and tastes, acts and beliefs; that harmony which has been observed throughout history between the feelings and the ideas of men seems to have been destroyed.

There are still zealous Christians among us who draw spiritual nourishment from the truths of the other life and who no doubt will readily espouse the cause of human liberty as the source of all moral greatness. Christianity, which has declared all men equal in the sight of God, cannot hesitate to acknowledge all citizens equal before the law. But by a strange concatenation of events, religion for the moment has become entangled with those institutions which democracy overthrows, and so it is often brought to rebuff the equality which it loves and to abuse freedom as its adversary.

Partisans of freedom must know that one cannot establish the reign of liberty without that of mores, and mores cannot be firmly founded without beliefs. But they have seen religion in the ranks of their adversaries; some of them openly attack it, and the others do not dare to defend it.

Besides these, there are others whose object is to make men materialists, to find out what is useful without concern for justice, to have science quite without belief and prosperity without virtue. Such men are called champions of modern civilization, and they insolently put themselves at its head, usurping a place which has been abandoned to them, though they are utterly unworthy of it.

Have all ages been like ours? And have men always dwelt in a world in which nothing is connected? Where virtue is without genius, and genius without honor? Where love of order is confused with a tyrant's tastes, and the sacred cult of freedom is taken as scorn of law? Where conscience sheds but doubtful light on human actions? Where nothing any longer seems either forbidden or permitted, honest or dishonorable, true or false?

Am I to believe that the Creator made man in order to let him struggle endlessly through the intellectual squalor now surrounding us? I cannot believe that; God intends a calmer and more stable future for the peoples of Europe.

There is one country in the world in which this great social revolution seems almost to have reached its natural limits; it took place in a simple, easy fashion, or rather one might say that that country sees the results of the democratic revolution taking place among us, without experiencing the revolution itself.

The emigrants who colonized America at the beginning of the seventeenth century in some way separated the principle of democracy from all those other principles against which they contended when living in the heart of the old European societies, and transplanted that principle only on the shores of the New World. It could there grow in freedom and, progressing in conformity with mores, develop peacefully within the law.

It seems to me beyond doubt that sooner or later we, like the Americans, will attain almost complete equality of conditions. But I certainly do not draw from that the conclusion that we are necessarily destined one day to derive the same political consequences as the Americans from the similar social state. I am very far from believing that they have found the only form possible for democratic government; it is enough that the creative source of laws and mores is the same in the two countries, for each of us to have a profound interest in knowing what the other is doing.

Anyone who supposes that I intend to write a panegyric is strangely mistaken; nor have I aimed to advocate such a form of government in general, for I am one of those who think that there is hardly ever absolute right in any laws. I have not even claimed to judge whether the progress of the social revolution, which I consider irresistible, is profitable or prejudicial for mankind. I accept that revolution as an accomplished fact, or a fact that soon will be accomplished, and I selected of all the peoples experiencing it that nation in which it has come to the fullest and most peaceful completion, in order to see its natural consequences clearly, and if possible, to turn it to the profit of mankind. I admit that I saw in America more than America; it was the shape of democracy itself which I sought, its inclinations, character, prejudices, and passions; I wanted to understand it so as at least to know what we have to fear or hope therefrom.

Therefore, in the first part of this book I have endeavored to show the natural turn given to the laws by democracy when left in America to its own inclinations with hardly any restraint on its instincts, and to show its stamp on the government and its influence on affairs in general. I wanted to know what blessings and what ills it brings forth. I have inquired into the precautions taken by the Americans to direct it, and noticed those others which they have neglected, and I have aimed to point out the factors which enable it to govern society.

I had intended in a second part to describe the influence in America of equality of conditions and government by democracy upon civil society, customs, ideas, and mores, but my urge to carry out this plan has cooled off. Another author is soon to portray the main characteristics of the American people and, casting a thin veil over the seriousness of his purpose, give to truth charms I could not rival.[1]

I do not know if I have succeeded in making what I saw in America intelligible, but I am sure that I sincerely wished to do so and that I never, unless unconsciously, fitted the facts to opinions instead of subjecting opinions to the facts.

---

1. At the time when the first edition of this work was being published, M. Gustave de Beaumont, my traveling companion in America, was still working on his book *Marie; or, Slavery in the United States*, which has since been published. M. de Beaumont's main object was to draw emphatic attention to the condition of the Negroes in Anglo-American society. His book threw new and vivid light on the question of slavery, a vital question for the united republics. I may be mistaken, but I think M. de Beaumont's book, after arousing the vivid interest of those who sought emotions and descriptions therein, should have a more solid and permanent success with those readers who seek, above all, true appreciations and profound truths. [Cf. Gustave de Beaumont, *Marie; or, Slavery in the United States: A Novel of Jacksonian America*, translated by Barbara Chapman, with a new introduction by Gerard Fergerson, Johns Hopkins University Press, 1999.]

Wherever there were documents to establish facts, I have been at pains to refer to the original texts or the most authentic and reputable works. I have cited my authorities in the notes, so those who wish can check them. Where opinions, political customs, and mores were concerned, I have tried to consult the best-informed people. In important or doubtful cases I was not content with the testimony of one witness, but based my opinions on that of several.

I realize that despite the trouble taken, nothing will be easier than to criticize this book, if anyone thinks of doing so.

Those who look closely into the whole work will, I think, find one pregnant thought which binds all its parts together. But the diversity of subjects treated is very great, and whoever chooses can easily cite an isolated fact to contradict the facts I have assembled, or an isolated opinion against my opinions. I would therefore ask for my book to be read in the spirit in which it was written and would wish it to be judged by the general impression it leaves, just as I have formed my own judgments not for any one particular reason but in conformity with a mass of evidence.

To conclude, I will myself point out what many readers will consider the worst defect of this work. This book is not precisely suited to anybody's taste; in writing it I did not intend to serve or to combat any party; I have tried to see not differently but further than any party; while they are busy with tomorrow, I have wished to consider the whole future.

PART I

1

PHYSICAL CONFIGURATION
OF NORTH AMERICA

NORTH AMERICA HAS STRIKING geographical features which can be appreciated at first glance.

Land and water, mountains and valleys, seem to have been separated with systematic method, and the simple majesty of this design stands out amid the confusion and immense variety of the scene.

The continent is divided into two vast and almost equal regions.

One region is bounded by the North Pole and the great oceans to east and west, while to the south it stretches down in an irregular triangle to the Great Lakes of Canada.

The second starts where the other ends and covers the rest of the continent.

One region slopes gently toward the pole, the other toward the equator.

The second region is broken up more and is better suited as a permanent home for man. Two mountain chains run right across it; the Alleghenies parallel to the Atlantic, and the Rockies to the Pacific.

The area between these two mountain chains is 1,341,649 miles, or about six times that of France.

But the whole of this vast territory is a single valley sloping down from the smooth summits of the Alleghenies and stretching up to the peaks of the Rocky Mountains, with no obstacles in the way.

An immense river flows along the bottom of this valley, and all the waters falling on the mountains on every side drain into it.

Formerly the French called it the St. Louis River, in memory of their distant fatherland, and the Indians in their grandiloquent tongue named it the Father of Waters, the Mississippi.

Sometimes gently flowing along the clay bed which nature has carved out for it, and sometimes swollen by storms, the Mississippi waters some twenty-five hundred miles.

The valley watered by the Mississippi seems created for it alone; it dispenses good and evil at will like a local god. Near the river nature displays an inexhaustible fertility; the farther you go from its banks, the sparser the vegetation and the poorer becomes the soil. Nowhere have the great convulsions of the world left more evident traces than in the valley of the Mississippi. The whole countryside bears witness to the waters' work. Its sterility as well as its abundance is their work. Deep layers of fertile soil accumulated under the primeval ocean and had time to level out. On the right bank of the river there are huge plains as level as a rolled lawn. But nearer the mountains the land becomes more and more uneven and sterile; the soil is punctured in a thousand places by primitive rocks sticking out here and there like the bones of a skeleton when sinews and flesh have perished.

All things considered, the valley of the Mississippi is the most magnificent habitation ever prepared by God for man, and yet one may say that it is still only a vast wilderness.

On the eastern slopes of the Alleghenies, between the mountains and the Atlantic, there is a long strip of rock and sand which seems to have been left behind by the retreating ocean. This strip is only 48 leagues broad on the average,[1] 390 leagues long.[2] The soil in this part of the American continent can be cultivated only with difficulty.

That inhospital shore was the cradle of those English colonies which were one day to become the United States of America. The center of power still remains there, while in the land behind them are assembling, almost in secret, the real elements of the great people to whom the future of the continent doubtless belongs.

When the Europeans landed on the shores of the West Indies, and later of South America, they thought themselves transported

---

1. One hundred miles.
2. About nine hundred miles.

to the fabled lands of the poets. Here and there little scented islands float like baskets of flowers on the calm sea. Everything seen in these enchanted islands seems devised to meet man's needs or serve his pleasures.

North America seemed very different; everything there was grave and serious and solemn; one might say that it had been created to be the domain of the intelligence, as the other was that of the senses.

However, these vast wildernesses were not completely unvisited by man; for centuries some nomads had lived under the dark forests or on the meadows of the prairies. From the mouth of the St. Lawrence to the Mississippi Delta, from the Atlantic to the Pacific, the savages had some points of resemblance testifying to a common origin. But, apart from that they were different from all known races of men;[3] they were neither white like Europeans nor yellow like most Asiatics nor black like the Negroes; their skin was reddish, their hair long and glossy, their lips thin, and their cheekbones very high. The words of the various languages of the savage peoples of America were different, but they all had the same rules of grammar. The rules differed in several respects from those previously supposed to shape the formation of language among men.

These American languages seem to be the product of new combinations; those who invented them must have possessed an intellectual drive of which present-day Indians hardly seem capable.

The social state of these tribes was also different from anything known in the Old World. They would seem to have multiplied freely in their wilderness without contact with races more civilized than themselves. Hence they were untroubled by those muddled concepts of good and evil and by that deep corruption generally seen among once civilized peoples relapsed into barbarism. The Indian owed nothing to anybody but himself; his virtues, vices, and

---

3.   Since this was written, some resemblances have been observed between the North American Indians and the Tungus, Manchus, Mongols, Tartars, and other nomadic peoples of Asia. These tribes lived near the Bering Straits, which suggests the hypothesis that they may long ago have crossed that way to populate the empty continent of America. But research has not yet made the matter clear.

prejudices were all his own; his nature had matured in wild freedom.

In well-organized countries the coarseness of the common people is not due solely to ignorance and poverty, but is also affected by the fact that, being poor and ignorant, they are in daily contact with the wealthy and educated. The poor and weak feel themselves weighed down by their inferiority; seeing no prospect of regaining equality, they quite give up hope and allow themselves to fall below the proper dignity of mankind.

But there is no such vexatious contrast in savage life; the Indians, all poor and all ignorant, are also all equal and free.

When the Europeans first landed, the natives of North America were still unaware of the value of wealth and showed themselves indifferent to the prosperity acquired by civilized man. But nothing coarse was seen in them; on the contrary, there was in their manners a habitual reserve and a sort of aristocratic courtesy.

Gentle and hospitable in peace, in war merciless even beyond the known limits of human ferocity, the Indian would face starvation to succor the stranger who knocked on the door of his hut, but he would tear his prisoner's quivering limbs to pieces with his own hands. No famed republic of antiquity could record firmer courage, prouder spirit, or more obstinate love of freedom than lies concealed in the forests of the New World.[4] The Europeans

---

4.   We learn from President Jefferson (*Notes on the State of Virginia*) that among the Iroquois, when attacked by stronger forces, old men would scorn to fly or to survive the destruction of their country and braved death like the Romans when the Gauls sacked Rome.

Further on he tells us that there is no example of an Indian who, having fallen into the hands of his enemies, begged for his life; on the contrary, the prisoner would invite death at his captors' hands by all manner of insults and provocations. [The passages to which Tocqueville refers are to be found in Jefferson's *Notes on the State of Virginia*, Boston, 1832, p. 213: "that they are timorous and cowardly is a character with which there is little reason to charge them, when we recollect the manner in which the Iroquois met Mons, . . . who marched into their country, in which the old men, who scorned to fly or to survive the capture of their own, braved death, like the old Romans in the time of the Gauls. . . . But above all, the unshaken fortitude with which they bear the most excruciating tortures and death when taken prisoner ought to exempt them from that character."]

made but little impression when they landed; they were neither feared nor envied. What hold could they have on such men? The Indian knew how to live without wants, to suffer without complaint, and to die singing. In common, too, with all other members of the great human family, these savages believed in the existence of a better world, and under different names worshipped God, Creator of the universe. Their conceptions of the great intellectual truths were in general simple and philosophical.

Primitive as was the character of the people just described, there can be no doubt that another people, more civilized and in all respects more advanced, preceded them in these same regions.

A dim tradition, but one found among most of the Indians on the Atlantic coast, says that these tribes once lived to the west of the Mississippi. Along the banks of the Ohio and throughout the central plain, man-made tumuli are continually coming to light. It is said that if one excavates to the center of these tumuli, one almost always finds human bones, strange instruments, weapons, and utensils of all kinds either made of some metal or destined for some use unknown to the present inhabitants.

Present-day Indians can supply no information about this unknown people. When did they come there and what was their origin, history, and fate? No man can answer.

It is a strange thing that peoples should have so completely vanished from the earth, that even the memory of their name is lost; their languages are forgotten and their glory has vanished like a sound without an echo; but I doubt that there is any which has not left some tomb as a memorial of its passage. So, of all man's work, the most durable is that which best records his nothingness and his misery.

Although the huge territories just described were inhabited by many native tribes, one can fairly say that at the time of discovery they were no more than a wilderness. The Indians occupied but did not possess the land. It is by agriculture that man wins the soil, and the first inhabitants of North America lived by hunting. Their unconquerable prejudices, their indomitable passions, their vices, and perhaps still more their savage virtues delivered them to inevitable destruction. The ruin of these peoples began as soon as the Europeans landed on their shores; it has continued ever since and is coming to completion in our own day. Providence, when it placed them amid the riches of the New World, seems to have granted them a short lease only; they were there, in some sense, *only waiting*. Those coasts so well suited for trade and industry, those deep rivers, that inexhaustible valley of the Mississippi—in short, the whole continent—seemed the yet empty cradle of a great nation.

It was there that civilized man was destined to build society on new foundations, and for the first time applying theories till then unknown or deemed unworkable, to present the world with a spectacle for which past history had not prepared it.

2

CONCERNING THEIR POINT OF DEPARTURE AND ITS IMPORTANCE FOR THE FUTURE OF THE ANGLO-AMERICANS

WHEN A CHILD IS born, his first years pass unnoticed in the joys and activities of infancy. As he grows older and begins to become a man, then the doors of the world open and he comes into touch with his fellows. For the first time notice is taken of him, and people think they can see the germs of the virtues and vices of his maturity taking shape.

That, if I am not mistaken, is a great error.

Go back; look at the baby in his mother's arms. Only then will you understand the origin of the prejudices, habits, and passions which are to dominate his life. The whole man is there, if one may put it so, in the cradle.

Something analogous happens with nations. Peoples always bear some marks of their origin. Circumstances of birth and growth affect all the rest of their careers.

If we could go right back to the elements of societies and examine the very first records of their histories, I have no doubt that we should there find the first cause of their prejudices, habits, dominating passions, and all that comes to be called the national character.

America is the only country in which we can watch the natural quiet growth of society and where it is possible to be exact about the influence of the point of departure on the future of a state.

We seem now destined to see further into human history than could the generations before us; we are close enough to the time when the American societies were founded to know in detail the elements of which they were compounded, and far enough off to judge what these seeds have produced.

When, after careful study of the history of America, we turn with equal care to the political and social state there, we find ourselves deeply convinced of this truth, that there is not an opinion, custom, or law, nor, one might add, an event, which the point of departure will not easily explain. So this chapter provides the germ of all that is to follow and the key to almost the whole work.

The immigrants who came at different times to occupy what is now the United States were not alike in many respects; their aims were not the same, and they ruled themselves according to different principles.

But these men did have features in common, and they all found themselves in analogous circumstances.

Language is perhaps the strongest and most enduring link which unites men. All the immigrants spoke the same language and were children of the same people. Born in a country shaken for centuries by the struggles of parties, they had more acquaintance with notions of rights and principles of true liberty than most of the European nations at that time. At the time of the first immigrations, local government, that fertile germ of free institutions, had already taken deep root in English ways, and therewith the dogma of the sovereignty of the people had slipped into the very heart of the Tudor monarchy.

That was the time of religious quarrels shaking Christendom. England plunged vehemently forward in this new career. The English, who had always been staid and deliberate, became austere and argumentative. These intellectual battles greatly advanced education and a more profound culture.

Moreover, one observation, to which we shall come back later, applies not to the English only, but also to the French, Spaniards, and all Europeans who came in waves to the New World; all these new European colonies contained the germ of a complete democracy. There were two reasons for this; one may say, speaking generally, that when the immigrants left their motherlands they had no idea of any superiority of some over others. It is not the happy and the powerful who go into exile, and poverty with misfortune is the best-known guarantee of equality among men. Second, it was soon seen that the soil of America absolutely rejected a territorial aristocracy. It was obvious that to clear this untamed land nothing but the constant and committed labor of the landlord himself would serve. The ground, once cleared, was by no means fertile enough to make both a landlord and a tenant rich. So the land was naturally broken up into little lots which the owner himself cultivated.

Hence there was a strong family likeness between all the English colonies as they came to birth. All, from the beginning, seemed destined to let freedom grow, not the aristocratic freedom of their motherland, but a middle-class and democratic freedom of which the world's history had not previously provided a complete example.

But within this general picture there were two main branches of the great Anglo-American family which have, so far, grown up together without completely mingling—one in the South, and the other in the North.

Virginia was the first of English colonies, the immigrants arriving in 1607. At that time Europe was still peculiarly preoccupied with the notion that mines of gold and silver were the basis of the wealth of nations. It was therefore gold-seekers who were sent to

Virginia,[1] men without wealth or standards whose restless, turbulent temper endangered the infant colony and made its progress vacillating.[2] Craftsmen and farm laborers came later; they were quieter folk with better morals, but there was hardly any respect in which they rose above the level of the English lower classes. No noble thought or conception above gain presided over the foundation of the new settlements. The colony had hardly been established when slavery was introduced.[3] That was the basic fact destined to exert immense influence on the character, laws, and future of the whole South.

Slavery, as we shall show later, dishonors labor; it introduces idleness into society and therewith ignorance and pride, poverty and luxury. It enervates the powers of the mind and numbs human activity. Slavery, combined with the English character, explains the mores and social condition of the South.

In the North the English background was the same, but every nuance led the opposite way.

It was in the English colonies of the North, better known as the states of New England,[4] that the two or three main principles now forming the basic social theory of the United States were combined.

Their influence now extends beyond its limits over the whole

---

1.   The charter granted by the English Crown in 1609 contained, among other clauses, a provision that the colonists should pay a fifth of the output of gold and silver mines to the Crown. See Marshall's *Life of Washington*, vol. 1, pp. 18–66. [Tocqueville refers here to the French edition of Marshall's *Life of Washington*, 5 vols., Paris, 1807.]

2.   According to Stith's *History of Virginia*, a large proportion of the new colonists were unruly children of good family whose parents sent them off to escape from ignominy at home; for the rest there were dismissed servants, fraudulent bankrupts, debauchées, and others of that sort, people more apt to pillage and destroy than to consolidate the settlement. Seditious leaders easily enticed this band into every kind of extravagance and excess. [William Stith, *The History of the First Discovery and Settlement of Virginia Being an Essay Towards a General History of This Colony*, Williamsburg, 1747.]

3.   Slavery was first introduced [in] the year 1619 by a Dutch ship, which landed twenty Negroes on the banks of the James River.

4.   The states of New England are those states which lie east of the Hudson, and there are now six of them: Connecticut, Rhode Island, Massachusetts, Vermont, New Hampshire, and Maine.

American world. New England civilization has been like beacons on mountain peaks whose warmth is first felt close by but whose light shines to the farthest limits of the horizon.

The foundation of New England was something new in the world.

In almost all other colonies the first inhabitants have been men without wealth or education, driven from their native land by poverty or misconduct, or else greedy speculators and industrial entrepreneurs. Some colonies cannot claim even such an origin as this; San Domingo was founded by pirates, and in our day the English courts of justice are busy populating Australia.

But all the immigrants who settled New England belonged to the well-to-do classes at home. From the start, when they came together on American soil, they presented the unusual phenomenon of a society in which there were no great lords, no common people, and, one may almost say, no rich or poor. All, perhaps without a single exception, had received a fairly advanced education, brought with them wonderful elements of order and morality; they came with their wives and children to the wilds. But what most distinguished them from all others was the very aim of their enterprise. No necessity forced them to leave their country; they gave up a desirable social position and assured means of livelihood; nor was their object in going to the New World to better their position or accumulate wealth; they tore themselves away from home comforts in obedience to a purely intellectual craving; in facing the inevitable sufferings of exile they hoped for the triumph of *an idea*.

The immigrants, or as they so well named themselves, the Pilgrims, belonged to that English sect whose austere principles had led them to be called Puritans. Puritanism was not just a religious doctrine; in many respects it shared the most absolute democratic and republican theories. That was the element which had aroused its most dangerous adversaries. Persecuted by the home government, and with their strict principles offended by the everyday ways of the society in which they lived, the Puritans sought a land so barbarous and neglected by the world that there at last they might be able to live in their own way and pray to God in freedom.

The immigrants, including women and children, numbered about one hundred and fifty. Their object was to found a colony on the banks of the Hudson; but after long wandering over the ocean, they were finally forced to land on the arid coast of New England, on the spot where the town of Plymouth now stands. The rock on which the Pilgrims disembarked is still shown.[5]

It must not be imagined that the piety of the Puritans was merely speculative, taking no notice of the course of worldly affairs. Puritanism, as already remarked, was almost as much a political theory as a religious doctrine. No sooner had the immigrants landed on that inhospitable coast described by Nathaniel Morton than they made it their first care to organize themselves as a society. They immediately passed an act which stated:

"We whose names are underwritten [. . .] do by these presents solemnly and mutually, in the presence of God and one another, convenant and combine ourselves together into a civil body politic, for our better ordering and preservation, and furtherance of the ends aforesaid; and by virtue hereof, do enact, constitute, and frame such just and equal laws, ordinances, acts, constitutions, and officers, from time to time, as shall be thought most meet and convenient for the general good of the colony, unto which we promise all due submission and obedience."[6]

---

5.   This rock has become an object of veneration in the United States. I have seen fragments carefully preserved in several American cities. Does not that clearly prove that man's power and greatness resides entirely in his soul? A few poor souls trod for an instant on this rock, and it has become famous; it is prized by a great nation; fragments are venerated, and tiny pieces distributed far and wide. What has become of the doorsteps of a thousand palaces? Who cares about them?

6.   [Nathaniel Morton, *New England's Memorial*, Boston, 1826, p. 37 f.] The immigrants who founded the state of Rhode Island in 1638, those who settled at New Haven in 1637, the first inhabitants of Connecticut in 1639, and the founders of Providence in 1640 all began by publishing a social contract which was submitted for approval to every person concerned. Pitkin's *History*, pp. 42 and 47. [Timothy Pitkin, *A Political and Civil History of the United States of America from the Year 1763 to the Close of the Administration of President Washington, in March 1797: Including a Summary View of the Political and Civil State of the North American Colonies Prior to That Period*, 2 vols., New Haven, 1828.]

That happened in 1620. From that time onward immigration never ceased. The religious and political passions which ravaged the British Empire throughout the reign of Charles I drove fresh swarms of dissenters across to America every year. In England the nucleus of the Puritan movement continued to be in the middle classes, and it was from those classes that most of the emigrants sprang. The population of New England grew fast, and while in their homeland men were still divided by class hierarchies, the colony came to present the novel phenomenon of a society homogeneous in all its parts. Democracy more perfect than any of which antiquity had dared to dream sprang full-grown from the midst of the old feudal society.

The English government watched untroubled the departure of so many emigrants, glad to see the seeds of discord and of fresh revolutions dispersed afar. Indeed it did everything to encourage it and seemed to have no anxiety about the fate of those who sought refuge from its harsh laws on American soil. It seemed to consider New England as a land given over to dreamers, where innovators should be allowed to try out experiments in freedom.

It was at that time generally recognized that the lands of the New World belonged to that nation who first discovered them.

The means used by the British government to people these new domains were of various sorts; in some cases the king chose a governor to rule some part of the New World, administering the land in his name and under his direct orders;[7] that was the colonial system adopted in the rest of Europe. In others he granted ownership of some portion of the land to an individual or to a company.[8] In those cases all civil and political powers were concentrated in the hands of one man or a few individuals, who, subject to the supervision and regulation of the Crown, sold the land and ruled the inhabitants. Under the third system a number of immigrants were

---

7.   This was the case in the state of New York.
8.   Maryland, the Carolinas, Pennsylvania, and New Jersey were in this category. See Pitkin's *History*, vol. 1, pp. 11–31 [13–30. Tocqueville is not always exact in his page references].

given the right to form a political society under the patronage of the motherland and allowed to govern themselves in any way not contrary to her laws. This mode of colonization, so favorable to liberty, was put into practice only in New England.[9]

In 1628 a charter of that sort was granted by Charles I to the emigrants who were going to found the colony of Massachusetts.[10]

But generally charters were only granted to the New England colonies long after their existence had become an established fact. Plymouth, Providence, New Haven, and the states of Connecticut and Rhode Island were founded without the help and, in a sense, without the knowledge of the motherland. The new settlers, without denying the supremacy of the homeland, did not derive from thence the source of their powers, and it was only thirty or forty years afterward, under Charles II, that a royal charter legalized their existence.[11]

For this reason it is often difficult, when studying the earliest historical and legislative records of New England, to detect the link connecting the immigrants with the land of their forefathers. One continually finds them exercising rights of sovereignty; they

---

9.   See the work entitled *Historical Collections, Consisting of State Papers and Other Authentic Documents Intended as Materials for an History of the United States of America,* [Ebenezer Hazard, Philadelphia, 1792], which contains a great many valuable authentic documents concerning the early history of the colonies, including the various charters granted to them by the English Crown and the first acts of their governments. See also the analysis of all these charters by Mr. Story, judge of the Supreme Court of the United States, in the introduction to his *Commentary on the Constitution of the United States.* It emerges from all these documents that the principles of representative government and the external forms of political liberty were introduced into all the colonies almost as soon as they came into being. These principles were developed further in the North than in the South, but they existed everywhere.

10.   See Pitkin's *History,* vol. 1, p. 35. And see *The History of the Colony of Massachusetts,* by Hutchinson, vol. 1, p. 9. [Thomas Hutchinson, *The History of the Colony of Massachuset's-Bay: From the First Settlement Thereof in 1628, Until Its Incorporation with the Colony of Plimouth, Province of Main &c. by the Charter of King William and Queen Mary, in 1691.* London, 1765.]

11.   In shaping their criminal and civil laws and their procedures and courts of justice, the inhabitants of Massachusetts diverged from English usages; in 1650 the king's name no longer headed judicial orders. See Hutchinson, vol. 1, p. 452.

appointed magistrates, made peace and war, promulgated police
regulations, and enacted laws as if they were dependent on God
alone.

Nothing is more peculiar or more instructive than the legislation of this time; there, if anywhere, is the key to the social enigma
presented to the world by the United States now.

Among these records one may choose as particularly characteristic the code of laws enacted by the little state of Connecticut in
1650.[12]

The Connecticut lawgivers turned their attention first to the
criminal code and, in composing it, conceived the strange idea of
borrowing their provisions from the text of Holy Writ: "If any man
after legal conviction shall have or worship any other God but the
Lord God, he shall be put to death."

There follow ten or twelve provisions of the same sort taken
word for word from Deuteronomy, Exodus, or Leviticus.

Blasphemy, sorcery, adultery, and rape are punished by death;[13]
a son who outrages his parents is subject to the same penalty. Thus
the legislation of a rough, half-civilized people was transported
into the midst of an educated society with gentle mores; as a result
the death penalty has never been more frequently prescribed by
the laws or more seldom carried out.

The framers of these penal codes were especially concerned
with the maintenance of good behavior and sound mores, so they
constantly invaded the sphere of conscience, and there was hardly

---

12.   *Code of 1650*, p. 28. [Silas Andrus, *The Code of 1650; Being a Compilation of the
Earliest Laws and Orders of the General Court of Connecticut: also, the Constitution, or Civil
Compact, Entered Into and Adopted by the Towns of Windsor, Hartford, and Wethersfield in
1638–9. To Which Is Added Some Extracts from the Laws and Judicial Proceedings of New-
Haven Colony, Commonly Called Blue Laws*, Hartford, 1830.]

13.   The laws of Massachusetts also imposed the death penalty for adultery, and
Hutchinson (vol. 1, p. 441) says that several people were actually executed for that
crime; in this context he quotes a strange story of something which happened in
1663. A married woman had a love affair with a young man; her husband died and
she married him; several years passed; at length the public came to suspect the inti-
macy which had earlier existed between the spouses, and criminal proceedings were
brought against them; they were thrown into prison, and both were very near being
condemned to death.

a sin not subject to the magistrate's censure. The reader will have noticed the severity of the penalties for adultery and rape. Simple intercourse between unmarried persons was likewise harshly repressed. The judge had discretion to impose a fine or a whipping or to order the offenders to marry. If the records of the old courts of New Haven are to be trusted, prosecutions were not uncommon; under the date May 1, 1660, we find a sentence imposing a fine and reprimand on a girl accused of uttering some indiscreet words and letting herself be kissed. The code of 1650 is full of preventive regulations. Idleness and drunkenness are severely punished. Innkeepers may give each customer only a certain quantity of wine; simple lying, if it could do harm, is subject to a fine or a whipping.

In other places the lawgivers, completely forgetting the great principle of religious liberty which they themselves claimed in Europe, enforced attendance at divine service by threat of fines and went so far as to impose severe penalties, and often the death penalty, on Christians who chose to worship God with a ritual other than their own. Finally, sometimes the passion for regulation which possessed them led them to interfere in matters completely unworthy of such attention. Hence there is a clause in the same code forbidding the use of tobacco. We must not forget that these ridiculous and tyrannical laws were not imposed from outside—they were voted by the free agreement of all the interested parties themselves—and that their mores were even more austere and puritanical than their laws. In 1649 an association was solemnly formed in Boston to check the worldly luxury of long hair.

Alongside this criminal code so strongly marked by narrow sectarian spirit was a body of political laws, closely bound up with the penal law, which, though drafted two hundred years ago, still seems very far in advance of the spirit of freedom of our own age.

All the general principles on which modern constitutions rest are recognized by the laws of New England; the participation of the people in public affairs, the free voting of taxes, the responsibility of government officials, individual freedom, and trial by jury—all these things were established without question and with practical effect.

These pregnant principles were there applied and developed in a way that no European nation has yet dared to attempt.

In Connecticut the electoral body consisted, from the beginning, of all the citizens.[14] In that nascent community there prevailed an almost perfect equality of wealth and even greater intellectual equality.[15]

At that time in Connecticut all executive officials were elected, including the governor of the state.

Citizens over sixteen years of age were obliged to bear arms; they formed a militia which appointed its officers and was bound to be ready to march at any time.

In the laws of Connecticut and of all the other states of New England we see the birth and growth of that local independence which is still the mainspring and lifeblood of American freedom.

In most European nations political existence started in the higher ranks of society and has been gradually, but always incompletely, communicated to the various members of the body social.

Contrariwise, in America one may say that the local community was organized before the county, the county before the state, and the state before the Union.

In New England, local communities had taken complete and definite shape as early as 1650. Interests, passions, duties, and rights took shape around each individual locality, and there was a real, active political life which was completely democratic and republican. The colonies still recognized the mother country's su-

---

14.   [Tocqueville's phrase "all the citizens" must not be misread as all inhabitants; voting eligibility in most states required property ownership or other taxable status until 1830 and beyond, thereby denying suffrage not only to women, free Negroes, and Indians, but also to poor white men. Tocqueville explains the gradual elimination of "the voting qualification" and the advent of "universal suffrage," for white men, in chapter 4, and he returns to the issue in part 2, chapter 5.]

15.   In 1641 the general assembly of Rhode Island declared unanimously that the government of the state was a democracy and that power resided in the body of free men, who alone had the right to make the laws and provide for their enforcement. *Code of 1650*, p. 70. [Should refer to p. 12.]

premacy; legally the state was a monarchy, but each locality was already a lively republic.

The towns appointed their own magistrates of all sorts, assessed themselves, and imposed their own taxes. The New England towns adopted no representative institutions. As at Athens, matters of common concern were dealt with in the marketplace and in the general assembly of the citizens.

When one studies in detail the laws promulgated in this early period of the American republics, one is struck by their understanding of problems of government and by the advanced theories of the lawgivers.

But it is the provisions for public education which, from the very first, throw into clearest relief the originality of American civilization.

The code states: "It being one chief project of that old deluder, Satan, to keep men from the knowledge of the scriptures, as in former times, keeping them in an unknown tongue, . . . so that the true sense and meaning of the original might be clouded with false glosses of saint seeming deceivers; and that learning may not be buried in the grave of our forefathers, in church and commonwealth, the Lord assisting our endeavors . . . "[16] Provisions follow establishing schools in all townships, and obliging the inhabitants, under penalty of heavy fines, to maintain them. Municipal officials are bound to see that parents send their children to school, and can impose fines on those who refuse; if the parents remain recalcitrant, society can take over the charge of the children, depriving the parents of those natural rights which they abused. No doubt the reader has noticed the preamble to these regulations; in America it is religion which leads to enlightenment and the observance of divine laws which leads men to liberty.

With free rein given to its natural originality, human imagination there improvised unprecedented legislation. In that unconsidered democracy which had as yet produced neither generals, nor philosophers, nor great writers, a man could stand up in front

---

16.   Ibid., p. 90[f.].

of a free people and gain universal applause for this fine definition of freedom:

"Nor would I have you to mistake in the point of your own *liberty*. There is a *liberty* of corrupt nature, . . . inconsistent with *authority*, impatient of all restraint; by this *liberty*, *Sumus Omnes Deteriores*, 'tis the grand enemy of *truth* and *peace*, and all the *ordinances* of God are bent against it. But there is a civil, a moral, a federal *liberty*, which is the proper end and object of *authority*; it is a *liberty* for that only which is *just* and *good*; for this *liberty* you are to stand with the hazard of your very *lives*. This *liberty* is maintained in a way of *subjection* to *authority*; and the *authority* set over you will in all administrations for your good be quietly submitted unto, by all but such as have a disposition to *shake off the yoke*, and lose their true *liberty*, by their murmuring at the honour and power of *authority*."[17]

I have already said enough to put Anglo-American civilization in its true light. It is the product (and bear in mind this point of departure) of two perfectly distinct elements which elsewhere have often been at war with one another but which in America somehow formed a marvelous combination. I mean the *spirit of religion* and the *spirit of freedom*.

The founders of New England were both ardent sectarians and fanatical innovators. While held within the narrowest bounds by fixed religious beliefs, they were free from all political prejudices.

Hence two distinct but not contradictory tendencies plainly show their traces everywhere, in mores and in laws. Far from harming each other, these two apparently opposed tendencies work in harmony and seem to lend mutual support.

Religion regards civil liberty as a noble exercise of men's faculties, the world of politics being a sphere intended by the Creator

17.   Mather's *Magnalia Christi Americana*, vol. 2, p. 13. [Tocqueville's reference is faulty. The passage is to be found in the 1820 Hartford edition, which Tocqueville used, vol. 2, p. 116 f.] Winthrop is speaking; he had been accused of arbitrary behavior as a magistrate; when the speech of which the above forms part was finished, he was acquitted amid applause, and thereafter he was always reelected as governor of the state.

for the free play of intelligence. Religion, being free and powerful within its own sphere and content with the position reserved for it, realizes that its sway is all the better established because it relies only on its own powers and rules men's hearts without external support.

Freedom sees religion as the companion of its struggles and triumphs, the cradle of its infancy, and the divine source of its rights. Religion is considered as the guardian of mores, and mores are regarded as the guarantee of the laws and pledge for the maintenance of freedom itself.

Reasons for Some Peculiarities in the Laws and Customs of the Anglo-Americans

The reader should not draw exaggeratedly general and exclusive conclusions from what has been said before.

One often finds laws and customs in the United States which contrast with the rest of their surroundings. Such laws seem to have been drafted in a spirit opposed to the prevailing genius of American legislation, and such mores seem to run counter to the whole tone of society.

I will quote just one example to make my meaning clear.

The civil and criminal procedure of the Americans relies on two modes of action only, *committal* or *bail.* The first step in any lawsuit is to get bail from the defendant or to put him in prison; only after that is the validity or gravity of the charge discussed.

Clearly such a procedure is hard on the poor and favors the rich.

A poor man cannot always raise bail even in a civil case, and if he has to wait in prison for the hearing of the matter, his enforced idleness soon reduces him to destitution.

But if it is a civil suit, the rich man never has to go to prison, and, more important, if he has committed a crime, he can easily escape the proper punishment, for having given bail, he disappears. So, as far as he is concerned, the law actually imposes no penalty worse than a fine. What could be more aristocratic than such legislation?

Yet, in America, it is the poor who make the laws, and usually they reserve the greatest benefits of society for themselves.

One must look to England for the explanation of this phenomenon, for these laws are English. The Americans have not changed them at all, although they are repugnant to their laws in general, and to the bulk of their ideas.

One might put it this way. The surface of American society is covered with a layer of democratic paint, but from time to time one can see the old aristocratic colors breaking through.

3

SOCIAL STATE OF THE ANGLO-AMERICANS

THE SOCIAL STATE IS commonly the result of circumstances, sometimes of laws, but most often of a combination of the two. But once it has come into being, it may itself be considered as the prime cause of most of the laws, customs, and ideas which control the nation's behavior; it modifies even those things which it does not cause.

Therefore one must first study their social state if one wants to understand a people's laws and mores.

The Striking Feature in the Social Condition of the Anglo-Americans Is That It Is Essentially Democratic

There are many important things to be said about the social condition of the Anglo-Americans, but one feature dominates all the others.

The social state of the Americans is eminently democratic. It has been like that ever since the birth of the colonies but is even more so now.

I said in the last chapter that a high degree of equality prevailed among the immigrants who first settled on the coast of New England.

That was the case to the east of the Hudson. To the southwest of that river and right down to the Floridas things were different.

Great English landowners had come to settle in most of the states southwest of the Hudson. They brought with them aristocratic principles, including the English law of inheritance. In the South one man and his slaves could cultivate a wide extent of land. So there were rich landowners in that part of the country. That was the class which, in the South, put itself at the head of the rebellion; it provided the best leaders of the American Revolution.

At that time society was shaken to the core. The people, in whose name the war had been fought, became a power and wanted to act on their own; democratic instincts awoke; the English yoke had been broken, and a taste for every form of independence grew.

But it was the law of inheritance which caused the final advance of equality.

In nations where the law of inheritance is based on primogeniture, landed estates generally pass undivided from one generation to another. Hence family feeling finds a sort of physical expression in the land. The family represents the land, and the land the family, perpetuating its name, origin, glory, power, and virtue. It is an imperishable witness to the past and a precious earnest of the future.

When the law ordains equal shares, it breaks that intimate connection between family feeling and preservation of the land; the land no longer represents the family, for, as it is bound to be divided up at the end of one or two generations, it is clear that it must continually diminish and completely disappear in the end. The sons of a great landowner, if they are few, or if fortune favors them, may still hope to be no less rich than their parent, but they cannot expect to possess the same lands; their wealth is bound to be composed of different elements from his.

The English law concerning succession to property was abolished in almost all the states at the time of the revolution.

Now, hardly sixty years later, the families of the great landowners have almost mingled with the common mass. In the state of New York, where formerly there were many, only two still keep their heads above the waters which are ready to swallow them too. The last trace of hereditary ranks and distinctions has been destroyed; the law of inheritance has everywhere imposed its dead level.

It is not that in the United States there are no rich; indeed I know no other country where love of money has such a grip on men's hearts or where stronger scorn is expressed for the theory of permanent equality of property. But wealth circulates there with incredible rapidity, and experience shows that two successive generations seldom enjoy its favors.

This picture, which some may think overdrawn, would give only a very imperfect impression of what goes on in the new states of the West and Southwest.

At the end of the last century a few bold adventurers began to penetrate into the Mississippi Valley. It was like a new discovery of America; previously unheard of communities suddenly sprang up in the wilderness. States that had not even been names a few years before took their places in the American Union. It is in the West that one can see democracy in its most extreme form. In these states, the inhabitants have arrived only yesterday in the land where they dwell. They hardly know one another, and each man is ignorant of his nearest neighbor's history. So in that part of the American continent the population escapes the influence not only of great names and great wealth but also of the natural aristocracy of education and probity.

But it is not only fortunes that are equal in America; equality to some extent affects their mental endowments too.

I think there is no other country in the world where, proportionately to population, there are so few ignorant and so few learned individuals as in America.

Primary education is within reach of all; higher education is hardly available to anybody.

There are few rich men in America; hence almost all Americans have to take up some profession. Now, every profession requires an apprenticeship. Therefore the Americans can devote only the first years of life to general education; at fifteen they start on a career, so their education generally ends at the age when ours begins. If it is continued beyond that point, it aims only at some specialized and profitable objective.

A middling standard has been established in America for all human knowledge. All minds come near to it, some by raising and some by lowering their standards.

As a result one finds a vast multitude of people with roughly the same ideas about religion, history, science, political economy, legislation, and government.

Intellectual inequalities come directly from God, and man cannot prevent them existing always.

But it results from what we have just been explaining, that though mental endowments remain unequal as the Creator intended, the means of exercising them are equal.

So the social state of America is a very strange phenomenon. Men there are nearer equality in wealth and mental endowments, or, in other words, more nearly equally powerful, than in any other country in recorded history.

Political Consequences of the Social State of the Anglo-Americans

It is easy to deduce the political consequences of such a social state.

By no possibility could equality ultimately fail to penetrate into the sphere of politics as everywhere else. One cannot imagine that men should remain perpetually unequal in just one respect though equal in all others; within a certain time they are bound to become equal in all respects.

Now, I know of only two ways of making equality prevail in the political sphere; rights must be given either to every citizen or to nobody.

So, for a people who have reached the Anglo-Americans' social state, it is hard to see any middle course between the sovereignty of all and the absolute power of one man.

The Anglo-Americans who were the first to be faced with the above-mentioned alternatives were lucky enough to escape absolute power. Circumstances, origin, education, and above all mores allowed them to establish and maintain the sovereignty of the people.

4

THE PRINCIPLE OF THE SOVEREIGNTY OF THE PEOPLE IN AMERICA

ANY DISCUSSION OF THE political laws of the United States must always begin with the dogma of the sovereignty of the people.

"The will of the nation" is one of the phrases most generally abused by intriguers and despots of every age. But if there is one country in the world where one can hope to appreciate the true value of the dogma of the sovereignty of the people, study its application to the business of society, and judge both its dangers and its advantages, that country is America.

I have already said that from the beginning the principle of the sovereignty of the people was the creative principle of most of the English colonies in America.

But it was far from dominating the government of society then as it does now.

It was far from being the case that all public officials were elected and all citizens electors. Everywhere voting rights were restricted within certain limits and subject to some property qualification. That qualification was very low in the North but quite considerable in the South.

The American Revolution broke out. The dogma of the sovereignty of the people came out from the township and took possession of the government; every class enlisted in its cause; the war was fought and victory obtained in its name; it became the law of laws.

Once a people begins to interfere with the voting qualification, one can be sure that sooner or later it will abolish [restrictions on] it altogether. That is one of the most invariable rules of social behavior. The further the limit of voting rights is extended, the stronger is the need felt to spread them still wider; there is no halting place until universal suffrage has been attained.

In the United States in our day the principle of the sovereignty of the people has been adopted in practice in every way that imagination could suggest. It has been detached from all fictions in which it has elsewhere been carefully wrapped. The people reign over the American political world as God rules over the universe. It is the cause and the end of all things; everything rises out of it and is absorbed back into it.

5

THE NEED TO STUDY WHAT HAPPENS IN THE STATES BEFORE DISCUSSING THE GOVERNMENT OF THE UNION

THIS CHAPTER WILL EXAMINE the form of government established in America on the principle of the sovereignty of the people, its means of action, impediments, advantages, and dangers.

A preliminary difficulty must be faced. In a word, there are twenty-four little sovereign nations who together form the United States.

To study the Union before studying the state is to follow a path strewn with obstacles. The federal government was the last to take shape in the United States; the political principles on which it was based were spread throughout society before its time, existed independently of it, and only had to be modified to form the republic. So one must understand the state to gain the key to the rest.

The states which now compose the American Union all have institutions with the same external aspect. Political and administrative life is concentrated in three active centers, which could be compared to the various nervous centers that control the motions of the human body.

The township is the first in order, then the county, and last the state.

The American System of Townships

It is not by chance that I consider the township first.

The township is the only association so well rooted in nature that wherever men assemble it forms itself.

Communal society therefore exists among all peoples, whatever be their customs and their laws; man creates kingdoms and republics, but townships seem to spring directly from the hand of God. But though townships are coeval with humanity, local freedom is a rare and fragile thing.

Of all forms of liberty, that of a local community, which is so hard to establish, is the most prone to the encroachments of authority.

However, the strength of free peoples resides in the local community. Local institutions are to liberty what primary schools are to science; they put it within the people's reach; they teach people to appreciate its peaceful enjoyment and accustom them to make use of it. Without local institutions a nation may give itself a free government, but it has not got the spirit of liberty.

To help the reader understand the general principles on which the political organization of townships and counties in the United States depends, I thought it would be useful to take one particular state as an example and examine in detail what happens there, subsequently taking a quick look at the rest of the country.

I have chosen one of the states of New England [Massachusetts].

Spirit of the Township in New England

In America not only do municipal institutions exist, but there is also a municipal spirit which sustains and gives them life.

The New England township combines two advantages which, wherever they are found, keenly excite men's interest; they are independence and power.

It is important to appreciate that, in general, men's affections are drawn only in directions where power exists. Patriotism does not long prevail in a conquered country. The New Englander is attached to his township not so much because he was born there as because he sees the township as a free, strong corporation of which he is part and which is worth the trouble of trying to direct.

However, if you take power and independence from a municipality, you may have docile subjects but you will not have citizens.

With much care and skill power has been broken into fragments in the American township, so that the maximum possible number of people have some concern with public affairs. Apart from the voters, who from time to time are called on to act as the government, there are many and various officials who all, within their sphere, represent the powerful body in whose name they act. Thus a vast number of people make a good thing for themselves out of the power of the community and are interested in administration for selfish reasons.

The American system, which distributes local power among so many citizens, is also not afraid to multiply municipal duties. Americans rightly think that patriotism is a sort of religion strengthened by practical service.

Thus daily duties performed or rights exercised keep municipal life constantly alive. There is a continual gentle political activity which keeps society on the move without turmoil.

The New Englander is attached to his township because it is strong and independent; he has an interest in it because he shares in its management; he loves it because he has no reason to complain of his lot; he invests his ambition and his future in it; he learns to rule society; he gets to know those formalities without which freedom can advance only through revolutions, develops a taste for order, and in the end accumulates clear, practical ideas about the nature of his duties and the extent of his rights.

Administration in New England

There are two ways in which the power of authority in a nation may be diminished.

The first way is to weaken the very basis of power by depriving society of the right or the capacity to defend itself in certain circumstances. In Europe to weaken authority in this way is generally thought equivalent to establishing liberty.

But there is another way of diminishing the influence of authority without depriving society of some of its rights or paralyzing its efforts by dividing the use of its powers among several hands. Functions can be multiplied and each man given enough authority to carry out his particular duty. By sharing authority in this way its power becomes both less irresistible and less dangerous, but it is far from being destroyed.

The revolution in the United States was caused by a mature and thoughtful taste for freedom, not by some vague, undefined instinct for independence. No disorderly passions drove it on; on the contrary, it proceeded hand in hand with a love of order and legality.

No one in the United States has pretended that, in a free country, a man has the right to do everything; on the contrary, more varied social obligations have been imposed on him than elsewhere; no one thought to attack the very basis of social power or contest its rights; the object was only to divide up the right to exercise it. By this means it was hoped that authority would be made great, but officials small, so that the state could still be well regulated and remain free.

How, then, is the business of society conducted on a more or less uniform plan? How can obedience be imposed on the counties and their officials and on the townships and theirs?

In the states of New England the legislative power embraces more subjects than it does with us. In a sense the legislature penetrates to the very heart of the administration; the law descends into minute details; it prescribes both principles and the way in which they are to be applied; in this way the secondary authorities are tied down by a multitude of detailed obligations strictly defined.

Generally speaking, society has only two ways of making officials obey its laws.

It can entrust them with discretionary power to control all the others and dismiss them, if they disobey.

Or it can give the courts power to inflict judicial penalties on offenders.

One is not always free to choose either the one or the other of these methods.

The right to control an official assumes the right to dismiss him, if he does not follow the orders given and to promote him if he carries out all his duties zealously. Now, one can neither dismiss nor promote an elected official. It is the nature of elected offices to be irrevocable before the end of the [term]. In practice, the elected official has nothing to hope or fear except from the electors, when all public offices are elective. Therefore peoples who make use of elections to fill the secondary grades in their government are bound greatly to rely on judicial punishments as a weapon of administration.

If a public official in New England commits a *crime* in the exercise of his duty, the ordinary courts are *always* called on to try him. Should he commit one of those intangible offenses which human justice can neither define nor judge, he appears annually before a tribunal from which there is no appeal and which can suddenly reduce him to impotence; for with this [electoral] mandate, his power goes.

General Ideas Concerning Administration
in the United States

There are townships and municipal life in each state, but nowhere else in the Union do we find townships exactly similar to those of New England.

As one goes farther south, one finds a less active municipal life; the township has fewer officials, rights, and duties; the population does not exercise such a direct influence on affairs; the town meetings are less frequent and deal with fewer matters. For this reason the power of the elected official is comparatively greater and that of the voter less.

One begins to notice these differences in the state of New York; in Pennsylvania they are already much in evidence; but they become less striking as one goes farther to the northwest. Most of the immigrants who founded the northwestern states came from New England,[1] and they brought the administrative habits of their old home to the new. A township in Ohio is very like one in Massachusetts.[2]

We have seen that in Massachusetts the township is the main-spring of public administration. It is the center of men's interests and of their affections. But this ceases to be so as one travels down to those states in which good education is not universally spread and where, as a result, there are fewer potential administrators and less assurance that the township will be wisely governed. Hence, the farther one goes from New England, the more the county tends to take the place of the township in communal life.

---

1.   [In Tocqueville's day, "the northwestern states" meant Ohio, Indiana, and Illinois. These states (and later Michigan, Wisconsin, and part of Minnesota) were carved out of the Northwest Territory (demarcated by the Northwest Ordinance of 1787), which lay west of Pennsylvania, north of the Ohio River, and east of the Mississippi. As the Union expanded to the Pacific, this area eventually became known as "the old Northwest."]

2.   For details see *The Revised Statutes of the State of New York*, part 1, chapter 11, entitled "Of the Powers, Duties and Privileges of Towns," vol. 1, pp. 336–364 [Albany, 1829]. [See also] the *Digest of the Laws of Pennsylvania*, [John W. Purdon, Philadelphia, 1831], and in the *Acts of a General Nature of the State of Ohio*, the law of February 25, 1834, p. 412.

The county becomes the great administrative center and the intermediary between the government and the plain citizen.

County and township are not constituted everywhere in the same way, but one can say that the organization of township and county in the United States everywhere depends on the same idea, viz., that each man is the best judge of his own interest and the best able to satisfy his private needs. So township and county are responsible for their special interests. The state rules but does not administer.

But one can say that, in general, the striking feature of American public administration is its extraordinary decentralization.

Legislative Power of the State

The legislative power of the state is entrusted to two bodies; the first is generally called the Senate.

The Senate is generally a legislative body, but it sometimes becomes an administrative or judicial one.

It has judicial functions in that it judges political offenses.

Its membership is always small.

The other branch of the legislature, generally called the House of Representatives, has no share in administrative power, and its only judicial function is to prosecute public officers before the Senate.

The only difference between them is that generally the senators have a longer term of office than the representatives. The latter seldom remain in office for more than one year, but the former usually for two or three.

By extending the senators' term of office to several years, and by reelecting them *seriatim,* the law has been at pains to keep within the legislature a body of men accustomed to public affairs, who can exercise a useful influence on the newcomers.

In dividing the legislative body into two branches, the Americans had no intention to create one hereditary assembly and another elected one; the one an aristocratic body and the other a representative of democracy.

To divide the legislative power, thus slowing down the movement of the political assemblies, and to create an appeal tribunal for the revision of laws, such were the only advantages resulting from the Constitution of the United States with its two chambers.

Time and experience have convinced the Americans that although these are its only two advantages, the division of legislative powers is yet a necessity of the first order. Alone among all the united republics, Pennsylvania had at first tried to establish a single assembly. Franklin himself, carried away by the logical consequences of the dogma of the sovereignty of the people, had concurred in this measure. But it was soon necessary to change the law and establish two chambers. That was the final consecration of the principle of the division of legislative power; henceforth the need to share legislative activity between several bodies has been regarded as a demonstrated truth. This theory, hardly known to the republics of antiquity and misunderstood by several modern nations, has at last become an axiom of political science in our day.

The Executive Power of the State

The governor is the representative of the executive power of the state.

I have not chosen the word *representative* casually. The governor of the state does indeed represent the executive power, but he exercises only some of its rights.

That supreme officer, called the governor, is placed beside the legislature as a moderator and adviser. He is armed with a suspensive veto, which allows him to check its movements or at least to slow them down at will. He explains the country's needs to the legislative body and suggests the means he thinks advisable to provide for them.

All the military power of the state is in the governor's hands. He is the commander of the militia and head of the armed forces.

When the authority, due by general consent to the laws, is disregarded, the governor marches out at the head of the physical power of the state; he breaks down resistance and reestablishes accustomed order.

The governor is an elected officer. In general his term of office is carefully limited to one or two years; in this way he is always closely dependent on the majority who elected him.

Political Effects of Administrative Decentralization in the United States

Centralization is now a word constantly repeated but is one that, generally speaking, no one tries to define accurately.

There are, however, two very distinct types of centralization, which need to be well understood.

Certain interests, such as the enactment of general laws and the nation's relations with foreigners, are common to all parts of the nation.

There are other interests of special concern to certain parts of the nation, such, for instance, as local enterprises.

To concentrate all the former in the same place or under the same directing power is to establish what I call governmental centralization.

To concentrate control of the latter in the same way is to establish what I call administrative centralization.

We have seen that in the United States there was no administrative centralization. There is scarcely a trace of a hierarchy. But there is a high degree of governmental centralization in the United States. Not only is there but one legislative body in each state, but large district or county assemblies generally have been avoided, for fear that such assemblies might be tempted to step beyond their administrative functions and interfere with the working of the government. In America the legislature of each state is faced by no power capable of resisting it. Nothing can check its progress, neither privileges, nor personal influence, nor even the authority of reason, for it represents the majority, which claims to be the unique organ of reason. So its own will sets the sole limits to its action. Beside it and under its power is the representative of executive authority, who, with the aid of physical force, has the duty to compel the discontented to obedience.

Weakness is found only in certain details of government action.

The American republics have no permanent armed force with which to overawe minorities, but so far no minority has been reduced to an appeal to arms, and the necessity for an army has not yet been felt.

As the state has no administrative officers stationed at fixed points in its territory, to whom it can give a common impulse, it seldom tries to establish general police regulations. Yet the need for such regulations is acutely felt. Europeans often notice the lack. This apparent disorder prevailing on the surface convinces them, at first glance, that there is complete anarchy in society; it is only when they examine the background of things that they are undeceived.

The partisans of centralization in Europe maintain that the government administers localities better than they can themselves; that may be true when the central government is enlightened and the local authorities are not, when it is active and they lethargic, when it is accustomed to command and they to obey.

But I deny that that is so when, as in America, the people are enlightened, awake to their own interests, and accustomed to take thought for them.

On the contrary, I am persuaded that in that case the collective force of the citizens will always be better able to achieve social prosperity than the authority of the government. I also think that when the central administration claims completely to replace the free concurrence of those primarily concerned, it is deceiving itself, or trying to deceive you.

A central power, however enlightened and wise one imagines it to be, can never alone see to all the details of the life of a great nation. It cannot do so because such a task exceeds human strength. When it attempts unaided to create and operate so much complicated machinery, it must be satisfied with very imperfect results or exhaust itself in futile efforts.

I will not deny that in the United States one often regrets the absence of those uniform rules which constantly regulate our lives in France.

Granting, for the sake of argument, that the villages and counties of the United States would be more efficiently administered by a central authority from outside, remaining a stranger to them, than by officials chosen from their midst, I will, if you insist, admit that there would be more security in America and that social resources would be more wisely and judiciously employed, if the administration of the whole country were concentrated in one pair of hands. But the *political* advantages derived by the Americans from a system of decentralization would make me prefer that to the opposite system.

What good is it to me, after all, if there is an authority always busy to see to the tranquil enjoyment of my pleasures and going ahead to brush all dangers away from my path without giving me even the trouble to think about it, if that authority, which protects me from the smallest thorns on my journey, is also the absolute master of my liberty and of my life?

Look where you will, you will never find true power among men except in the free concurrence of their wills. Now, patriotism and religion are the only things in the world which will make the whole body of citizens go persistently forward toward the same goal.

No laws can bring back life to fading beliefs, but laws can make men care for the fate of their countries. It depends on the laws to awaken and direct that vague instinct of patriotism which never leaves the human heart, and by linking it to everyday thoughts, passions, and habits, to make it a conscious and durable sentiment.

What I most admire in America is not the *administrative* but the *political* effects of decentralization. In the United States the motherland's presence is felt everywhere. Each man takes pride in the nation; the successes it gains seem his own work, and he rejoices in the general prosperity from which he profits. He has much the same feeling for his country as one has for one's family, and a sort of selfishness makes him care for the state.

Often to a European a public official stands for force; to an American he stands for right. It is therefore fair to say that a man never obeys another man, but justice, or the law.

Moreover, he has conceived an opinion of himself which is often exaggerated but almost always salutary. He trusts fearlessly in his own powers, thinks of some enterprise, and it does not come into his head to appeal to public authority for its help. He publishes his plan, offers to carry it out, summons other individuals to aid his efforts, and personally struggles against all obstacles. No doubt he is often less successful than the state would have been in his place, but in the long run the sum of all private undertakings far surpasses anything the government might have done.

I could cite many facts in support of what I am saying, but I prefer to select one only, and that the one I know best.

In America the means available to the authorities for the discovery of crimes and arrest of criminals are few.

There is no administrative police force, and passports are unknown. The criminal police in the United States cannot be compared to that of France; the officers of the public prosecutor's office are few, and the examination of prisoners is rapid and oral. Nevertheless, I doubt whether in any other country crime so seldom escapes punishment.

The reason is that everyone thinks he has an interest in furnishing proofs of an offense and in arresting the guilty man.

During my stay in the United States I have seen the inhabitants of a county where a serious crime had been committed spontaneously forming committees with the object of catching the criminal and handing him over to the courts.

In Europe the criminal is a luckless man fighting to save his head from the authorities; in a sense the population are mere spectators of the struggle. In America he is an enemy of the human race and every human being is against him.

6

JUDICIAL POWER IN THE UNITED STATES AND ITS EFFECT ON POLITICAL SOCIETY

THE JUDICIAL ORGANIZATION OF the United States is the hardest thing there for a foreigner to understand. He finds judicial authority invoked in almost every political context, and from that he naturally concludes that the judge is one of the most important political powers in the United States. But when he then begins to examine the constitution of the courts, at first glance he sees nothing but judicial attributes and procedures. The judges seem to intervene in public affairs only by chance, but that chance recurs daily.

In all nations the judge's primary function is to act as arbitrator. An action must be brought before a judge can decide it. As long as a law leads to no dispute, the judges have no occasion to consider it. When a judge, in a given case, attacks a law relative to that case, he stretches the sphere of his influence but does not go beyond it, for he was, in a sense, bound to judge the law in order to decide the case. But if he pronounces upon a law without reference to a particular case, he steps right beyond his sphere and invades that of the legislature.

The second characteristic of judicial power is that it pronounces on particular cases and not on general principles. If a judge, in deciding a particular question, destroys a general principle, because all consequences deriving from that principle will be alike undermined, and so the principle becomes barren, he stays within the natural sphere of his authority. But when a judge directly attacks the general principle without having any particular case in view, he goes beyond the limit of his authority; he becomes something more important and perhaps more useful than a magistrate, but he no longer represents judicial power.

The third characteristic of judicial power is that it can act only when called upon, or in legal language, when it is seized of the matter. That characteristic is not so generally found as the other two. But despite the exceptions, I think one may consider it as essential. There is nothing naturally active about judicial power; to act, it must be set in motion. When a crime is denounced to it, it punishes the guilty party; when it is called on to redress an injustice, it redresses it; when an act requires interpretation, it interprets it; but it does not on its own prosecute criminals, seek out injustices, or investigate facts. In a sense judicial power would do violence to its passive nature if it should take the initiative and establish itself as censor of the laws.

The Americans have preserved these three distinctive characteristics of judicial power. An American judge can pronounce a decision only when there is litigation. He never concerns himself with anything except a particular case, and to act he must have cognizance of the matter.

So an American judge is exactly like the magistrates of other nations. Nevertheless, he is invested with immense political power.

The reason lies in this one fact: the Americans have given their judges the right to base their decisions on the *Constitution* rather than on the *laws*. In other words, they allow them not to apply laws which they consider unconstitutional.

I know that a similar right has sometimes been claimed by courts in other lands, but it has never been conceded.

In France the Constitution is, or is supposed to be, immutable. No authority can change anything in it; that is the accepted theory.

In England Parliament has the right to modify the Constitution. In England, therefore, the Constitution can change constantly, or rather it does not exist at all.

American political theories are simpler and more rational.

The American Constitution is not considered immutable, as in France; it cannot be changed by the ordinary authorities as in England. It is a thing apart; it represents the will of the whole people and binds the legislators as well as plain citizens, but it can be changed by the will of the people, in accordance with established forms.

So in America the Constitution can change, but so long as it exists, it is the fount of all authority. It is the primary law and cannot be modified by a mere law. Hence it is right that the courts should obey the Constitution rather than all the laws.

Therefore, if anyone invokes in an American court a law which the judge considers contrary to the Constitution, he can refuse to apply it. That is the only power peculiar to an American judge, but great political influence derives from it.

As soon as a judge refuses to apply a law in a case, it loses at once part of its moral force. Those who are harmed by it are notified of a means of escaping from its obligations; lawsuits multiply, and that law becomes ineffective. Then one of two things happens: either the people change the Constitution or the legislature repeals the law.

So, then, the Americans have given their courts immense political power; but by obliging them to attack the laws by judicial means, they have greatly lessened the dangers of that power [than] if the judges had been able to attack laws in a general and theoretical way.

I wonder if this way in which American courts behave is not both the best way of preserving public order and the best way of favoring liberty.

If a judge could only attack the lawmakers directly, there are occasions when he would be afraid to do so; on other occasions party spirit might drive him to do so continually.

But the American judge is dragged in spite of himself onto the political field. He only pronounces on the law because he has to judge a case, and he cannot refuse to decide the case. The political question he has to decide is linked to the litigants' interests, and to refuse to deal with it would be a denial of justice. It is by fulfilling the narrow duties imposed by his status as a judge that he also acts as a citizen.

Restricted within its limits, the power granted to American courts to pronounce on the constitutionality of laws is yet one of the most powerful barriers ever erected against the tyranny of political assemblies.

Other Powers Given to American Judges

It is so natural that I do not know if it is necessary to state that among a free people such as the Americans all citizens have the right to prosecute public officials before the ordinary judges and that all judges have the right to condemn public officials.

It does not seem to me that the energy of the American government has been weakened by making all officials responsible before the courts.

On the contrary, I think that by so doing the Americans have increased the respect due to executive officers, since the latter are much more careful to avoid criticism.

Nor did I observe that many political trials take place in the United States, and I can easily explain the reason. Whatever its nature, a lawsuit is always a difficult and expensive matter. It is easy to accuse a public man in the newspapers, but only serious reasons induce anybody to prosecute him in court. Therefore, one must have just cause of complaint before starting judicial proceedings against an official; but, with the fear of prosecution, officials hardly ever give ground for such complaint.

This does not depend on the republican form of government adopted by the Americans, for the same thing can be noted any day in England.

These two nations have not thought to assure their liberty by allowing the main agents of the executive to be brought to trial. They have rather thought that little everyday lawsuits within the scope of the least of the citizens were a better guarantee of liberty than those pompous procedures to which one never has recourse or which are used too late.

In the Middle Ages, it being very difficult to catch criminals, when the judges did seize a few they often inflicted terrible punishments on these unfortunates. But that did not lessen the number of the guilty. It has subsequently been found that by making justice both surer and milder, it has also been made more effective.

The Americans and English think that oppression and tyranny should be treated like theft, by making prosecution easier and the penalty lighter.

7

POLITICAL JURISDICTION
IN THE UNITED STATES

BY "POLITICAL JURISDICTION" I mean the decisions pronounced by a political body temporarily endowed with the right to judge.

In the United States, as in Europe, one of the two branches of the legislature has the right to prosecute and the other branch to judge. The House of Representatives denounces the offender, and the Senate punishes him.

In Europe the political courts can apply the provisions of the criminal law; in America, when the offender has had his public status taken away and been declared unworthy to hold any political position in future, their jurisdiction is at an end and that of the ordinary courts begins.

Suppose the president of the United States has committed high treason.

The House of Representatives impeaches him, and the Senate pronounces his dismissal. After that he appears before a jury, who alone can deprive him of life or liberty.

It is true that the Senate's decision is judicial in form; in pronouncing it the senators are bound to conform to the solemn formalities of procedure. It is also judicial in the motives on which it is based; the Senate is generally obliged to take an offense at common law as the basis of its decision. But it is administrative in its objective.

In establishing political tribunals, Europeans chiefly intended to *punish* the guilty, the Americans to *take away their power.*

But what makes American laws so formidable in this matter is, I dare assert, their very mildness.

In Europe, political tribunals are endowed with terrible attributes which they often do not know how to use, so it may happen that they do not punish, for fear of punishing too much. But in America no one shrinks back from a penalty which does not make humanity groan; to condemn a political enemy to death in order to take away his power is, in the eyes of all men, a horrible assassination; to declare one's adversary unworthy to possess that power and to take it away from him, while leaving him life and liberty, may seem the honest result of the struggle.

But that judgment, so easy to pronounce, is nonetheless the summit of misfortune for the general run of those to whom it applies. Great criminals would no doubt brave its vain rigors; ordinary men see it as a decree which destroys their status, stains their honor, and condemns them to a disgraceful leisure worse than death.

Hence American political jurisdiction has all the more influence on the conduct of society just because it seems less formidable. It has no direct effect on the governed, but does make the majority complete masters of those who govern.

In preventing political tribunals from pronouncing judicial penalties, the Americans seem to me to have provided against the more terrible consequences of legislative tyranny rather than against that tyranny itself. Everything considered, I wonder whether political jurisdiction as understood in the United States is not the most formidable weapon ever put into the majority's hands.

Once the American republics begin to degenerate, I think one will easily see that that is so; it will be enough to notice whether the number of political [prosecutions] increases.

8

THE FEDERAL CONSTITUTION

SO FAR I HAVE considered each state as forming a complete whole. But all these states which I have considered as independent are bound in certain cases to obey a superior authority, that of the Union. The time has now come to examine that portion of sovereignty which has been granted to the Union and to take a quick look at the federal Constitution.[1]

History of the Federal Constitution

The thirteen colonies which simultaneously shook off the English yoke at the end of the last century had, as I have already said, the same religion, language, and mores, and almost the same laws; they fought against a common enemy; they must therefore have had strong reasons for uniting closely with each other and becoming absorbed in one and the same nation.

But each of them, having always had a separate existence and a government within its control, had peculiar interests and revolted against its individual importance being merged in the greatness of the Union. Hence there were two opposite tendencies: one drove the Anglo-Americans to unite, while the other induced them to divide.

As long as the war with the mother country continued, necessity made the principle of union prevail. And though the laws by which

---

1. See the text of the federal Constitution. [The first edition of Tocqueville's *Democracy in America* reproduced the text of the Constitution; the last edition in Tocqueville's lifetime, on which our edition is based, dispensed with this.]

this union was constituted were defective, the link subsisted in spite of them.[2]

But as soon as peace was concluded, the defects of this legislation stood revealed: the state seemed to dissolve all at once. Each colony, become an independent republic, assumed an absolute sovereignty. The federal government, condemned to weakness and no longer sustained by the sense of public danger, could not even find resources sufficient to stand up to the Indian tribes or to pay the interest on the debts contracted during the War of Independence. On the verge of destruction, it officially declared itself powerless and appealed to the constituent power.[3]

The spectacle of a nation struggling energetically to obtain its independence is one which every century has seen. Moreover, the efforts made by the Americans to throw off the English yoke have been much exaggerated. With twenty-eight hundred miles of ocean between them and their enemies, aided by a powerful ally, the United States owed their victory much more to their position than to the valor of their armies or the patriotism of their citizens. Who would dare to compare the American war to those of the French Revolution, when France, without money, credit, or allies, threw a twentieth of her population in the face of her enemies, with one hand stifling the devouring flames within her and with the other brandishing the torch around her?

But that which is new in the history of societies is to see a great people, warned by its lawgivers that the wheels of government are stopping, turn its attention on itself without haste or fear and then finally submit to the remedy voluntarily, without its costing humanity a single tear or drop of blood.

---

2.   See the articles of the first confederation, formed in 1778 [but] not adopted by all the states until 1781.

See also the analysis of this Constitution in Nos. 15 to 22, inclusive, of *The Federalist* and that of Mr. Story in his *Commentaries on the Constitution of the United States*, pp. 85–115. [Tocqueville refers here to the abridged edition of Story's *Commentaries*, Boston, 1833.]

3.   Congress made this declaration on February 21, 1787. [Cf. Story, *Commentaries*, p. 107.]

The assembly responsible for drafting the second Constitution was not numerous,[4] and it included the men of greatest intelligence and noblest character ever to have appeared in the New World. George Washington presided over it.

After long and mature deliberation, this national commission finally offered for the people's acceptance that body of organic laws which is still in force in the Union now. All the states adopted it in turn.[5] The new federal government took up its duties in 1789, after an interregnum of two years. So the American Revolution ended exactly when ours began.

Summary of the Federal Constitution

The first difficulty which the Americans had to face was how to divide sovereignty so that the various states of the Union continued to govern themselves in everything to do with internal prosperity but so that the whole nation, represented by the Union, should still be a unit and should provide for all general needs. That was a complicated question and hard to resolve.

Therefore the attributes of the federal government were carefully defined, and it was declared that everything not contained within that definition returned to the jurisdiction of state governments. Hence state authority remained the rule and the federal government the exception.[6]

---

4.   It had only fifty-five members, including Washington, Madison, Hamilton, and the two Morrises [Robert Morris and Gouverneur Morris, of Pennsylvania].

5.   It was not the [state] legislators who adopted it. The people appointed deputies for this sole purpose. There were searching debates about the new Constitution in each of these assemblies.

6.   See amendments to the federal Constitution; *The Federalist,* No. 32, Story, p. 711; Kent's *Commentaries on American Law,* vol. 1, p. 364. [Tocqueville has used the first edition of James Kent's *Commentaries on American Law.*] Note, too, that every time the Constitution has not reserved for Congress the *exclusive* right to regulate certain matters, the states may do it before Congress sees fit to begin. Example: Congress has the right to make a general law about bankruptcy, but does not do so; each state drafts one of its own. Moreover, that point was established only after argument before the courts.

It was foreseen that in practice questions would arise about the exact limits of this exceptional authority and that it would be dangerous to leave the solution of these questions to the ordinary courts established in the different states by the states themselves. So they created a federal Supreme Court, a unique tribunal one of whose prerogatives was to maintain the division of powers appointed by the Constitution between these rival governments.[7]

Prerogatives of the Federal Government

To face foreigners with advantage, a nation needs a single government.

Therefore the Union was granted the exclusive right of making war and peace, concluding commercial treaties, levying armies, and equipping fleets.

The necessity for a national government was not so imperiously felt in the internal affairs of society.

Nevertheless, there are some general interests for which a general authority alone can usefully provide.

The right to regulate everything relating to the value of money was left to the Union; it was responsible for the postal service; it

---

7.   No. 45 of *The Federalist* explains the division of sovereignty between the Union and each state as follows: "The powers delegated by the proposed Constitution to the federal government are few and defined. Those which are to remain in the state governments are numerous and indefinite. The former will be exercised principally on external objects, as war, peace, negotiation, and foreign commerce, with which . . . the power of taxation will, for the most part, be connected. The powers reserved for the several states will extend to all the objects which, in the ordinary course of affairs, concern the lives, liberties, and properties of the people, and the internal order, improvement, and prosperity of the state." I shall often have occasion to quote *The Federalist* in this work. When the draft law, which has since become the Constitution of the United States, was still before the people and submitted for their adoption, three men, already famous and later to become even more celebrated—John Jay, Hamilton, and Madison—associated together with the object of pointing out to the nation the advantages of the plan submitted to it. With this intention they published in a journal a series of articles which together form a complete treatise. They gave their journal the name of *The Federalist*, and that name is used for the book. *The Federalist* is a fine book, and though it especially concerns America, it should be familiar to statesmen of all countries.

was given the right to open the main lines of communications uniting the different parts of the country.[8]

In general, the government of each state was considered free within its sphere; however, it might abuse that independence and by imprudent measures compromise the security of the whole Union; in these rare cases, defined in advance, the federal government was allowed to intervene in the internal affairs of the states. [9]

Finally, as the federal government had to have the means to fulfill the obligations imposed on it, it was given the unlimited right to levy taxes.

If one examines the division of powers settled by the federal Constitution, noting which portions of sovereignty have been reserved for the several states and what share has been assumed by the Union, it is easy to see that the federal lawgivers had formed very clear and just ideas concerning what I have previously called governmental centralization.

Legislative Powers

The federal legislative body of the Union was composed of a Senate and a House of Representatives.

I have made it plain earlier that when a federal constitution was desired, two opposing interests were brought face-to-face.

One party wanted to make the Union a league of independent states, a sort of congress where representatives of distinct peoples came to discuss certain matters of common interest.

The other party wished to unite all the inhabitants of the former colonies in a single people and to give them a government which, though its sphere would be limited, could act within that sphere as the one and only representative of the nation.

---

8.   It also has several other rights of the same sort, such as bankruptcy legislation and the granting of patents. It is easy to see what made it necessary for the Union as a whole to intervene in such matters.

9.   Even in this eventuality its intervention is indirect. The Union intervenes through the courts, as we shall see later.

One appreciates that the small states could not consent to the application of this doctrine without completely abdicating their existence as far as federal sovereignty was concerned; from being a coequal authority, they would become an insignificant fraction of a great people.

In these circumstances there occurred what almost always does happen when interests and theory are opposed: the rules of logic were bent. The lawgivers adopted a middle path which forcibly reconciled two theoretically irreconcilable systems.

The principle of state independence prevailed in the shaping of the Senate, the dogma of national sovereignty in the composition of the House of Representatives.

Each state was to send to Congress two senators and a number of representatives in proportion to its population.[10]

As a result of this arrangement the state of New York has now forty representatives in Congress and only two senators; the state of Delaware has two senators and only one representative. So in the Senate the state of Delaware is the equal of the state of the New York, whereas in the House of Representatives the latter has forty times as much influence. In this way it could happen that a minority of the nation dominating the Senate could completely paralyze the will of the majority represented in the other house, and that is contrary to the spirit of constitutional government.

All this clearly shows how rare and difficult it is rationally and logically to fit together all the machinery of legislation.

Within the same people in the long run time always generates different interests and consecrates different rights. When it comes to settling a general constitution, these interests and rights form so many natural obstacles preventing any political principle from being followed through to all its conclusions. It

---

10.   Every ten years Congress decides anew how many deputies each state should send to the House of Representatives. In 1789 the total was 65; in 1833 it was 240. (*American Almanac,* 1834, p. 100.) The Constitution provided that there should not be more than one representative for every thirty thousand, but no minimum was fixed. The population, for this purpose, was calculated as all free men and three-fifths of the number of slaves.

is therefore only at the birth of societies that lawmaking can be completely logical. When you see a people enjoying that advantage, do not hasten to conclude that it is wise; think rather that it is young.

Another Difference Between the Senate and the House of Representatives

There is a difference between the Senate and the other house not only in the principle of representation but also in the mode of election, length of the term of office, and diversity of prerogatives.

The House of Representatives is appointed by the people, the Senate by the legislatures of each state.

One results from direct election, the other from election in two stages.[11]

The representatives' term of office only lasts two years; that of the senators six.

The House of Representatives has only legislative functions; its only share in judicial power is the right to impeach public officials. The Senate shares in making the laws; it judges the political offenders brought before it by the House of Representatives; it is also the great executive council of the nation. Treaties concluded by the president must be ratified by the Senate; his appointments are not final till they have been approved by that body.

---

11.   [The Constitution stipulated that U.S. senators would be elected, in Tocqueville's words, "in two stages." Voters directly elected their state legislators, who in turn selected the state's U.S. senators. Tocqueville praises this procedure below, in the section of this chapter entitled, "The Superiority of the Federal Constitution over That of the States," and in an early section of chapter 5, "Elements Which May Provide a Partial Corrective to These Instincts of a Democracy." Americans did not elect U.S. senators by direct popular vote until 1913, when the Seventeenth Amendment took effect. The amendment stipulated that any voter deemed eligible to vote in a state's legislative elections was likewise qualified to vote in contests for the U.S. Senate.]

The Executive Power

The American lawgivers had a difficult task to fulfill; they wanted to create an executive power dependent on the majority that yet should be sufficiently strong to act freely on its own within its proper sphere.

The president is an elective magistrate. His honor, property, freedom, and life are a perpetual pledge to the people for the good use he will make of his power. Moreover, in exercising that power he is not completely independent; the Senate supervises him in his relations with foreign powers and in his appointments to offices so that he can neither corrupt nor be corrupted.

The president was appointed for four years and could be re-elected. With his future to consider, he should have the courage to work on the public interest and the means to do so.

The president was made the one and only representative of the executive power of the Union. Care was taken not to subordinate his will to that of a council, a dangerous expedient which both clogs government action and lessens the ruler's responsibility. The Senate has the right to annul certain of the president's acts, but it cannot force him to act or share executive power with them.

The power of the two houses to deprive a public official of his salary takes away some of his independence; with the making of laws at their command, there is always a danger that they will gradually encroach on that share of power which the Constitution intended the president to preserve.

This dependence of the executive power is one of the inherent vices of republican constitutions. The Americans could not eliminate that tendency which leads legislative assemblies to take over the government, but they did make it less irresistible.

The president's salary is fixed on his entry into office for the whole term thereof. Moreover, the president has a suspensive veto which allows him to check the passage of laws which might destroy that portion of independence which the Constitution entrusted to him. But a struggle between president and legislature is bound to be unequal, for the latter, if it sticks to its plans, is always able to overcome any resistance he can put up; but the suspensive veto at least forces it to go over the ground again; the matter must be reconsidered, and this time it requires a two-thirds majority to carry it. Moreover, the veto is a sort of appeal to the people. The executive power, which without that guarantee might be oppressed in secret, can then argue its case and make its reasons heard.

How the Position of the President of the United States Differs from That of a Constitutional King in France

To get a clear and precise idea of the position of the president in the United States, it is useful to compare him to a king in one of the constitutional monarchies of Europe.

Sovereignty in the United States is divided between the Union and the states, whereas with us it is unified and compact; that is the first and greatest difference which I see between a king of France and a president of the United States.

In France the king forms a real part of sovereignty, for the laws cannot exist if he refuses to sanction them; and he is also the executor of the laws.

The president is also the executor of the laws, but he has no real part in making them, for by refusing his assent he cannot prevent them existing. Thus he is not part of the sovereign power, but its agent only.

The French king not only is himself a part of the sovereign power but also has a hand in forming the legislature, which is the other part. He does this by nominating the members of one chamber and by terminating at will the mandate of the other. The president of the United States has no part in the composition of the legislative body, and he cannot dissolve it.

The president has no entry into Congress; his ministers also are excluded, and it is only by indirect means that he can insinuate his influence and advice into that great body.

Beside the legislature, the president is an inferior and dependent power.

The king of France is absolute master in the sphere of executive power.

The president of the United States is answerable for his acts. French law states that the person of the king is inviolable.

Nevertheless, over the one as over the other, there is a directing power, that of public opinion. In America it works through elections and decrees, in France by revolutions. So France and the United States, in spite of their different constitutions, have this point in common, that, in practice, public opinion is the dominant power. That principle is, by its nature, essentially republican. For this reason I think that France, with its king, has more resemblance to a republic than has the Union, with its president, to a monarchy.

Election of the President

The system of election, applied to the executive of a great people, presents dangers which experience and historians have sufficiently indicated.

I only wish to speak of them in reference to America.

There is reason for criticizing the elective system, when applied to the head of state, in that it offers so great an attraction to private ambition and so inflames passions in the pursuit of power that often legal means do not suffice them, and men appeal to force when they do not have right on their side.

Clearly, the greater the prerogatives of the executive power, the greater is this attraction. The more the ambitions of the candidates are excited, the more warmly is their cause espoused by a crowd of partisans who hope for a share of power when their man has triumphed.

For this reason the dangers of the elective system increase in direct proportion to the influence exercised by the executive power over affairs of state.

Therefore, before discussing the absolute goodness of the elective system, a preliminary question must be answered, namely, whether the geographical position, laws, habits, mores, and opinions of the nation into which one wishes to introduce it allow it to establish a weak and dependent executive power; for often to desire both that the head of state should be armed with great power and that he should be elected is, in my view, to express two contradictory wishes.

Hereditary monarchies have one great advantage: the private interest of a family is always intimately connected with the interest of the state, and therefore state interests are never for a moment left to look after themselves. I do not know whether business is better conducted in monarchies than elsewhere, but at least there is always someone who, well or ill, according to his capacity, does concern himself therewith.

Whereas in elective states, when an election draws near, the head of the executive power only thinks of the coming struggle; he has no future; he can undertake nothing new and only feebly pursues matters which, perhaps, another will bring to completion. "I am now so near the moment of retiring," wrote President Jefferson on January 21, 1809 (six weeks before the election), "that I take no part in affairs beyond the expression of an opinion. I think it fair that my successor should now originate those measures of which he will be charged with the execution and responsibility and that it is my duty to clothe them with the forms of authority."[12]

As for the nation, it has all eyes turned to one single point, it is only concerned to watch the birthpangs in progress.

In America the president exercises very substantial influence on affairs of state, but he does not conduct them; the preponderant power resides in the representatives of the nation as a whole. So the whole people would have to be changed, and not only the pres-

------

12. [*The Writings of Thomas Jefferson*, ed. P. L. Ford, vol. 9, New York, 1898, p. 243 f.]

ident, for the maxims of politics to be altered. Hence in America
the elective system, applied to the head of the executive power,
does not shake government stability to any very noticeable
extent.

The extent of the dangers of this mode of election, applied to
the head of the executive power, depends on the particular circumstances of the nation who elects him.

No matter what efforts are made to restrict its role and what position it legally occupies, in foreign affairs the influence of the executive is bound to be great; a negotiation cannot be initiated and
brought to a fruitful conclusion except by one man.

American policy toward the world at large is simple; one might
almost say that no one needs them, and they do not need anybody.
Their independence is never threatened.

With them therefore the role of the executive power is restrained
as much by circumstances as by the laws. The president can frequently change his views without the state perishing or suffering.

Whatever prerogatives are vested in the executive power, one
must always consider the time immediately before and during an
election as a period of national crisis.

The more embarrassed the internal position of a country, and
the greater its external perils, the more dangerous is that moment
of crisis for it. There are very few nations in Europe that would not
have reason to fear conquest or anarchy every time they provided
themselves with a new leader.

In America society is so constituted that it can carry on by itself
without help: there are never external dangers there. The election
of a president causes agitation, not ruin.

Mode of Election

As one studies the institutions of the United States and looks more
closely at the political and social state of that country, one discovers a wonderful harmony between fortune's favors and man's endeavors. America was a new country, but the people living there

had already a long experience of liberty elsewhere: two circumstances most favorable to internal order. Moreover, America stood in no fear of conquest. The lawgivers of America, profiting by these happy circumstances, found no difficulty in establishing a weak and dependent executive power; having shaped it in that way, they could without danger make it elective.

The problem was to find that mode of election which, while expressing the real will of the people, would least arouse their passions and leave them least in suspense. It was first of all agreed that a *simple* majority should decide the point. But in practice it seldom happens that one man can win a majority of the votes of a great nation at the first attempt. That is even more difficult in a republic of confederated states, where local influences are particularly well developed and strong.

To get around this second trouble, the following method was devised: the electoral powers of the nation were delegated to a body representing it.

This mode of election increased the chances of a majority, for the fewer the electors, the easier it is for them to come to an understanding. This method also made it more likely that their choice would be good.

But should the right of election be entrusted to the legislative body itself, the normal representatives of the nation, or should it rather be entrusted to an electoral college whose sole function would be the appointment of the president?

The Americans preferred the second alternative. They considered that the men sent to make the ordinary laws but incompletely represented the wishes of the people concerning the choice of their chief magistrate. Moreover, being elected for more than a year, they might represent a will which had already changed. They judged that if the legislature were responsible for choosing the executive, the members would be exposed to corrupting maneuvers and intrigues; whereas special electors would, like a jury, remain unrecognized in the crowd until the day when they had to act, and would then appear for one moment on the scene to pronounce their decision.

It was settled then that each state should nominate a certain number of electors,[13] who in turn would elect the president. As it had been noticed that assemblies responsible for choosing heads of government in countries with elective systems inevitably became centers of passion and of intrigue, that they sometimes took over powers not belonging to them, and that often their proceedings could drag on so long that they put the state in danger—for all these reasons it was settled that all the electors should vote on a fixed day, but without assembling together.[14]

The mode of election in two stages made a majority probable, but not assured, for the electors might differ among themselves just as much as their constituents might have done.

In that eventuality, a choice had to be made between one of three possible measures: either new electors had to be appointed, or those already nominated had to be consulted again, or finally the choice had to be handed over to a new authority.

The first two of these alternatives, apart from their uncertainty, entailed delays and would prolong a potentially dangerous excitement.

The third was therefore chosen, and it was arranged that the votes should be sent under seal to the president of the Senate; he was to break the seals on the appointed day in the presence of the two houses. If none of the candidates had obtained a majority, then the House of Representatives itself was to proceed immediately to elect a president; but this right of election was carefully limited. The representatives could choose only one of the three candidates who had received most votes.[15]

---

13.   Equal to the number of members it sent to Congress. There were 288 electors in the election of 1833.

14.   The electors from each state assemble, but they send in to the central government the list of individual votes, and not the result of a majority vote.

15.   In this context it was the majority of states, not the majority of members, which was decisive. As a result New York has no more influence in the matter than Rhode Island. Thus the citizens of the Union are first consulted as members of one united nation; when they cannot agree, the division into states is brought back into play, and each of the latter is given a separate and independent vote.

That is just one more of the oddities found in the federal Constitution, oddities which can only be explained by the clash of contrary interests.

It is therefore only a rare event, and one hard to foresee, that the election is entrusted to the normal representatives of the nation, and moreover, they can choose only a citizen who has already been designated by a strong minority of the special electors; that is a happy combination which reconciles respect for the will of the people with precautions demanded by the interest of the state. However, there may be no decided majority in the House of Representatives, and in that case the Constitution offers no remedy. Nevertheless, by fixing a limit of three possible candidates and by entrusting the choice to an enlightened body, it had smoothed out all those difficulties over which it could have some control;[16] the remaining difficulties were inherent in the elective system itself.

In the forty-four years during which the federal Constitution has been in force, the United States has twelve times chosen their president.

Ten elections were instantly decided by the simultaneous votes of the special electors scattered around the country.

The House of Representatives has only twice used the exceptional right given to it in case of a split: first in 1801 for the election of Mr. Jefferson, and for the second time in 1825, when Mr. Quincy Adams was appointed.

Crisis of the Election

The Americans are used to all sorts of elections. Experience has taught them what degree of agitation can be permitted and where they should stop. The vast extent of the territory over which the inhabitants spread makes collisions between the various parties less probable and less dangerous there than elsewhere. Up to the present the political circumstances of the nation at election time have presented no real danger.

Nevertheless, one may consider the time of the presidential election as a moment of national crisis.

---

16.   However, in 1801 Jefferson was not elected until the thirty-sixth ballot.

In the United States as elsewhere, parties feel the need to rally around one man in order more easily to make themselves understood by the crowd. Generally, therefore, they use the presidential candidate's name as a symbol; in him they personify their theories. Hence the parties have a great interest in winning the election, not so much in order to make their doctrines triumph by the president-elect's help, as to show, by his election, that their doctrines have gained a majority.

Long before the appointed day arrives, the election becomes the greatest, and one might say the only, affair occupying men's minds. At this time factions redouble their ardor; then every forced passion that imagination can create in a happy and peaceful country spreads excitement in broad daylight.

The president, for his part, is absorbed in the task of defending himself. He no longer rules in the interest of the state, but in that of his own reelection; he prostrates himself before the majority, and often, instead of resisting their passions as duty requires, he hastens to anticipate their caprices.

As the election draws near, intrigues grow more active and agitation is more lively and wider spread. The citizens divide up into several camps, each of which takes its name from its candidate. The whole nation gets into a feverish state, the election is the daily theme of comment in the newspapers and private conversation, the object of every action and the subject of every thought, and the sole interest for the moment.

It is true that as soon as fortune has pronounced, the ardor is dissipated, everything calms down, and the river which momentarily overflowed its banks falls back to its bed. But was it not astonishing that such a storm could have arisen?

Concerning the Reelection
of the President

Were the lawgivers of the United States right or wrong to allow the reelection of the president?

To refuse the head of the executive the chance of reelection seems, at first sight, contrary to reason. One knows what influence the talents or character of a single man exercise over the fate of a whole people, especially in times of difficulty or crisis. Laws forbidding the citizens from reelecting their first magistrate would deprive them of their best means of bringing prosperity to the state or of saving it. In that way one would reach this odd result that a man would be excluded from the government just at the moment when he had succeeded in proving his capacity to rule well.

No doubt those are powerful arguments, but can one not bring up even stronger ones against them?

Intrigue and corruption are natural vices of elective governments; but when the head of state can be reelected, these vices spread beyond bounds and compromise the very existence of the country. When a simple candidate forces himself forward by intrigue, his maneuvers can only take place within a restricted sphere. But when the head of state himself is in the lists, he can borrow all the power of the government for his private use.

It is impossible to observe the normal course of affairs in the United States without noticing that desire for reelection dominates the president's thoughts, that the whole policy of his administration is bent toward that aim, that his slightest actions are subordinate to that aim, and that, particularly as the moment of crisis draws nearer, his private interest takes the place of the general interest in his mind.

Therefore the principle of reelection makes the corrupting influence of elective governments wider spread and more dangerous. It tends to degrade the political morality of the nation and to substitute craft for patriotism.

The greatest merit of the lawgivers of America was to have seen this truth clearly and to have had the courage to act accordingly.

They agreed that, besides the people, there must be a certain number of authorities which, though not entirely independent of it, nevertheless could still struggle against its caprices and refuse to be the tools of its dangerous exigencies.

With this object, they concentrated the whole executive power of the nation in the hands of one man; they gave wide prerogatives to the president and armed him with the veto with which to resist the encroachments of the legislature.

But by introducing the principle of reelection they destroyed a part of their work. They gave the president much power, but took away from him the will to use it.

Had he not been reeligible, the people's favor would not have been so necessary to him that he must in everything bend to its will.

Reeligible (and this is especially true in our day, when political morality is growing lax and men of great character are vanishing from the scene), the president of the United States is only a docile instrument in the hands of the majority. He loves what it loves and hates what it hates; he sails ahead of its desires, anticipating its complaints and bending to its slightest wishes; the lawgivers wished him to guide it, but it is he who follows.

In this way, intending not to deprive the state of one man's talents, they have rendered those talents almost useless, and to preserve a resource against extraordinary eventualities, they have exposed the country to dangers every day.

The Federal Courts

I have dealt with the legislative and executive power of the Union. The judicial power remains to be considered.

Judicial institutions exercise a great influence on the fate of the Anglo-Americans; they have a very important place among their political institutions properly so called. From that point of view they particularly deserve our attention.

Governments in general have only two methods of overcoming the resistance of the governed: their own physical force and the moral force supplied to them by the decisions of courts.

A government for whom war was the only means of enforcing obedience to its laws would be on the verge of ruin.

The great object of justice is to substitute the idea of right for that of violence, to put intermediaries between the government and the use of its physical force.

The moral force in which tribunals are clothed makes the use of physical force infinitely rarer, for in most cases it takes its place; and when finally physical force is required, its power is doubled by this moral authority.

A federal government more than any other should desire this support of justice, for by its nature it is feeble and resistance can more easily be organized against it. If it had always and as its first move to use force, it would not be adequate to its task.

The Union therefore had a particular need for tribunals to make the citizens obey its laws and to repel the attacks that might be launched against it.

But what tribunals should it employ? Each state already had its own organized judicial authority. Should it turn to those courts? Or should it organize a federal judiciary? It is easy to show that the Union could not adapt the established state courts to its use.

When the federal Constitution was formed, there were already thirteen courts of justice in the United States, judging cases without appeal. Today there are twenty-four. How could a state carry on if its fundamental laws could be interpreted and applied in twenty-four different ways at the same time? Such a system would be equally contrary to reason and to the lessons of experience.

The American lawgivers therefore agreed to create a federal judicial authority to apply the laws of the Union and decide certain questions of general interest which were carefully defined in advance.

The whole judicial power of the Union was concentrated in a single tribunal called the Supreme Court of the United States, but in order to facilitate the dispatch of business, inferior courts were added to it which were empowered to decide cases of small importance without appeal and to act as courts of first instance in more serious disputes. The members of the Supreme Court were not elected by the people or by the legislature. The president of the

United States had to choose them after taking the advice of the Senate.

In order to render them independent of the other authorities, they were made irremovable, and it was decided that their salaries, once fixed, would be out of the control of the legislature.[17]

It is easy enough to proclaim the establishment of a federal judiciary in principle, but a mass of difficulties arose when it was a question of determining its prerogatives.

Means of Determining the Competence of the Federal Courts

In nations that form one and the same political society, when a question of competence arises between two courts of justice, it is generally brought before a third court, which serves as arbitrator.

But above a high court of a particular state and a high court of the United States it was impossible to establish any tribunal which would not belong to one or the other.

It was therefore necessary to give one of these courts the right to judge its own case and to accept or refuse competence in the matter disputed. One could not grant that privilege to the various courts of the states; that would have destroyed the sovereignty of the Union.

The intention in creating a federal tribunal was to deprive the

---

17.   The Union was divided into districts, each with a resident federal judge. The court over which he presided was called a district court. In addition, each judge of the Supreme Court had to tour a certain part of the territory of the republic annually in order to try the most important cases on the spot; the court over which he presided was called the circuit court. Finally, the most serious cases had to be brought, either directly or on appeal, before the Supreme Court. For this purpose all the circuit judges assembled annually to hold a solemn session. See the organic law of September 24, 1789, *Laws of the United States*, by Story, vol. 1, p. 3 [*The Public and General Statutes Passed by the Congress of the United States of America from 1789 to 1827 Inclusive*, published under the inspection of Joseph Story, 3 vols., Boston, 1827].

state courts of the right to decide, each in its own way, questions of national interest, and in that manner to form a uniform body of jurisprudence interpreting the laws of the Union.

The Supreme Court of the United States was therefore entrusted with the right to decide all questions of competence.

That was the most dangerous blow dealt against the sovereignty of the states. It was now restricted not only by the laws but also by the interpretation of the laws, by a known boundary and by another that was not known, by a fixed rule and by an arbitrary one. It is true that the Constitution had fixed precise limits to federal sovereignty, but each time that that sovereignty is in competition with that of the states, it is a federal tribunal that must decide.

However, the dangers with which this method of procedure seemed to threaten the sovereignty of the states were not in reality as great as they appeared to be.

We shall see later that in America real power resided in the provincial governments rather than in the federal government.

High Standing of the Supreme Court Among the Great Authorities in the State

When we come to consider the whole body of prerogatives granted to the Supreme Court, it soon becomes clear that a mightier judicial authority has never been constituted in any land.

The Supreme Court has been given higher standing than any known tribunal, both by the *nature* of its rights and by the *categories* subject to its jurisdiction.

In all the properly administered countries of Europe the government has always shown great repugnance to allowing the ordinary courts to deal with matters affecting itself. Naturally this repugnance is all the greater when the government is absolute. Contrariwise, as liberty increases, the prerogatives of the courts are continually enlarged; but no European nation has ever thought that all judicial questions, whatever their origin, could be left to judges of common law.

But that is just the theory which has been put in practice in America. The Supreme Court of the United States is the sole and unique tribunal of the nation.

It is responsible for the interpretation of laws and of treaties; questions to do with overseas trade or international law come within its exclusive competence. One might even say that its prerogatives are entirely political, although its constitution is purely judicial. Its sole object is to see that the laws of the Union are carried out; and the Union only controls relations between the government and the governed and between the nation and foreigners; relations between the citizens themselves are almost all regulated by state sovereignty.

To this first cause of its importance is added another even greater one. In the European nations only private persons come under the jurisdiction of the courts, but the Supreme Court of the United States may be said to summon sovereigns to its bar. When the court crier, mounting the steps of the tribunal, pronounces these few words: "The state of New York versus the state of Ohio," one feels that this is no ordinary court of justice. And when one considers that one of these parties represents a million men and the other two million, one is amazed at the responsibility weighing on the seven men whose decision will please or grieve so many of their fellow citizens.

The peace, prosperity, and very existence of the Union rest continually in the hands of these seven federal judges. Without them the Constitution would be a dead letter; it is to them that the executive appeals to resist the encroachments of the legislative body, the legislative to defend itself against the assaults of the executive, the Union to make the states obey it, the states to rebuff the exaggerated pretensions of the Union, public interest against private interest, conservative spirit against democratic instability. Their power is immense, but it is power springing from opinion. They are all-powerful so long as the people consent to obey the law; they can do nothing when they scorn it. Now, of all powers, that of opinion is the hardest to use, for it is impossible to say exactly where its limits come. Often it is as dangerous to lag behind as to outstrip it.

The federal judges therefore must not only be good citizens and men of education and integrity, qualities necessary for all magistrates, but must also be statesmen; they must know how to understand the spirit of the age, to confront those obstacles that can be overcome, and to steer out of the current when the tide threatens to carry them away, and with them the sovereignty of the Union and obedience to its laws.

The president may slip without the state suffering, for his duties are limited. Congress may slip without the Union perishing, for above Congress there is the electoral body which can change its spirit by changing its members.

But if ever the Supreme Court came to be composed of rash or corrupt men, the confederation would be threatened by anarchy or civil war.

The Superiority of the Federal Constitution over That of the States

The federal Constitution differs essentially from that of the states in its intended aims, but it is very similar in the means of attaining those aims. The government's objective is different, but the forms of government are the same. From this special point of view one can profitably compare them.

The great cause of the superiority of the federal Constitution lies in the actual character of the lawgivers.

At the time when it was drafted, the ruin of the confederation appeared imminent before all eyes. In that extremity the people chose, not perhaps the men it loved best, but those it held in highest esteem.

I have already noted above that the lawgivers of the Union were almost all remarkable for their enlightenment, and even more remarkable for their patriotism.

They had all grown up at a time of social crisis, when the spirit of liberty had been in constant conflict with a strong and dominating authority. When the struggle was over, and when, as is usual, the passions aroused in the crowd were still directed against dangers which had long ceased to exist, these men called a halt; they looked at their country more calmly and with greater penetration; they were aware that a final revolution had been accomplished and that henceforth the perils threatening the people could only spring from abuses of liberty. What they thought, they had the courage to say; because they felt in the bottom of their hearts a sincere and ardent love for that same liberty, they dared to speak about restraining it, because they were sure they did not want to destroy it.

Like the various state constitutions, the federal Constitution divided the legislature into two branches.

But in the states these two parts of the legislature were composed of the same elements elected in the same manner. As a result the passions and the whims of the majority came into the open with equal ease and found tools as ready and prompt to their hands in one house as in the other.

The federal Constitution also made the two houses depend on a popular vote, but it altered the conditions of eligibility and the manner of election; they intended that, even if one of the branches of the legislature did not represent interests different from the other, it should at least represent superior wisdom.

To be elected as a senator a man had to have reached mature years, and the assembly responsible for electing him was itself previously elected and not numerous.

Democracies are naturally inclined to concentrate all the power of society in the hands of the legislative body. That being the authority which springs most directly from the people, it establishes the despotism of the majority.

The lawgivers of the states frequently yielded to these democratic propensities; those of the Union have always courageously fought against them.

A few words are enough to summarize this chapter.

Two main dangers threaten the existence of democracies:

Complete subjection of the legislative power to the will of the electoral body.

Concentration of all the other powers of government in the hands of the legislative power.

The lawgivers of the states favored the growth of these dangers. The lawgivers of the Union did what they could to render them less formidable.

What Distinguishes the Federal Constitution of the United States of America from All Other Federal Constitutions

The United States has not provided the first and only example of a confederation. Without speaking of antiquity, modern Europe furnishes several examples. Switzerland, the German Empire, and the republic of the Netherlands have been, or still are, confederations.

Nevertheless, federal government in these various countries has always remained weak and impotent, whereas that of the Union conducts affairs with vigor and with ease.

This Constitution, which at first sight one is tempted to confuse with previous federal constitutions, in fact rests on an entirely new theory, a theory that should be hailed as one of the great discoveries of political science in our age.

In all confederations previous to that of 1789 in America, the peoples who allied themselves for a common purpose agreed to obey the injunctions of the federal government, but they kept the right to direct and supervise the execution of the union's laws in their territory.

The Americans who united in 1789 agreed not only that the federal government should dictate the laws but that it should itself see to their execution.

In both cases the right is the same, and only the application thereof different. But that one difference produces immense results.

In all confederations previous to that of contemporary America, one of two things has always happened: either the most powerful of the combined states assumed the prerogatives of the federal authority and dominated all the others in its name or the federal government has been left to its own resources, anarchy has reigned among the confederates, and the union has lost its power to act.[18]

In America the Union's subjects are not states but private citizens. When it wants to levy a tax, it does not turn to the government of Massachusetts, but to each inhabitant of Massachusetts. Former federal governments had to confront peoples, individuals of the Union. It does not borrow its power, but draws it from within. It has its own administrators, courts, officers of justice, and army.

No doubt the spirit, collective passions, and provincial prejudices of each state still tend to diminish federal authority and to create centers of resistance to its wishes; restricted in its sovereignty, it cannot be as strong as if it possessed complete sovereignty; but that is an evil inherent in the federative system.

In America each state has comparatively few opportunities or temptations to resist; if it does think of doing so, it cannot carry this out without openly violating the laws of the Union, interrupting the ordinary course of justice, and raising the standard of revolt; in a word, it would have directly to take up an extreme position, and men hesitate for a long time before doing that.

Clearly here we have not a federal government but an incomplete national government. Hence a form of government has been found which is neither precisely national nor federal; but things have halted there, and the new word to express this new thing does not yet exist.

It is because they have not understood this new type of confederation that all unions have come to civil war, subjection, or inertia. The peoples composing them have all lacked either

---

18. It has always been like this in the Swiss confederation. Switzerland would have ceased to exist centuries ago were it not for the jealousies of her neighbors.

enlightenment to see the remedies for their ills or courage to apply them.

The first American Union, too, suffered from the same defects.

But as soon as they felt the ill, the Americans firmly thought out the remedy. They amended their laws and saved their country.

Advantages of the Federal System in General and Its Special Usefulness in America

World history provides no example of a large nation long remaining a republic,[19] and so it has been said that such a thing is impracticable. What can be said with certainty is that the existence of a great republic will always be more exposed than that of a small one.

All passions fatal to a republic grow with the increase of its territory, but the virtues which should support it do not grow at the same rate.

The ambition of individuals grows with the power of the state; the strength of parties grows with the importance of the aim proposed; but love of country, which should combat these destructive passions, is no stronger in a vast republic than in a small one. One may also remark that human passions grow, not only with the greatness of the aim but also with the multitude of individuals feeling them at the same time. There is no one who does not find himself more moved in the midst of an excited crowd sharing his emotion than if he had experienced it alone. In a great republic political passions become irresistible because millions feel them in the same way at the same time.

It is therefore permissible to say in general terms that nothing is more inimical to human prosperity and freedom than great empires.

---

19.   I do not speak here of a confederation of small republics, but of a great consolidated republic.

However, great states have their peculiar advantages, which must be recognized.

In a large state, thought on all subjects is stimulated; ideas circulate more freely; the capitals are vast intellectual centers; that is why great nations contribute more and faster to the increase of knowledge and progress than small ones. One must add that important discoveries often require a concentration of national resources of which small nations are incapable.

Internal well-being is more complete and more widespread in little nations, so long as they remain at peace; but a state of war harms them more than the great ones. In the latter, distant frontiers sometimes allow the mass of the people to stay far from danger for centuries on end. For such a nation war is more a matter of discomfort than of ruin.

If there were only small nations and no large ones, humanity would most certainly be more free and happier; but there is no way of providing that there should not be large nations.

The latter bring into the world a new element of national prosperity, that is, force. What does comfort or freedom profit a nation if it is in danger of being conquered? What good are its industries and trade if another rules the seas and lays down the law in all markets? Small nations are often wretched not because they are small but because they are weak; the great ones prosper not because they are large but because they are strong. Therefore force is often for nations one of the primary conditions of happiness and even of existence.

The federal system was devised to combine the various advantages of large and small size for nations.

A glance at the United States of America will show all the advantages derived from adopting that system.

In large centralized nations the lawgiver is bound to give the laws a uniform character which does not fit the diversity of places and of mores; and from this, much trouble and unhappiness results.

That inconvenience does not exist in confederations: the congress regulates the main features of social behavior, and all the details are left to the provincial legislatures.

The confederation of all the American states does not suffer from those disadvantages usual to large conglomerations. The Union is a great republic in extent, but it can be likened to a small one because there are so few matters with which the government is concerned. Its acts are important but rare. As the Union's sovereignty is hampered and incomplete, its use is not dangerous to freedom. Moreover, it does not arouse that inordinate craving for power and renown which are so fatal to great republics. As there is no necessity for everything to end at one common center, one finds neither vast metropolises, nor immense wealth, nor extreme poverty, nor sudden revolutions. Political passions, instead of spreading like a sheet of fire instantaneously over the whole land, break up in conflict with individual passions of each state.

But things and ideas circulate freely throughout the Union as through one and the same people. Nothing restrains the soaring spirit of enterprise. Its government attracts men of talent and enlightenment. Within the frontiers of the Union profound peace reigns, as within a country subject to the same empire; outside it takes rank among the most powerful countries in the world; two thousand miles of coast are open to foreign trade; and, holding in its hands the keys to the New World, its flag is respected in the farthest seas.

The Union is free and happy like a small nation, glorious and strong like a great one.

Why the Federal System Is Not
Within the Reach of All Nations and
Why the Anglo-Americans Have Been
Able to Adopt It

I have shown what advantages the Americans derived from the federal system. It remains for me to make plain what allowed them
to adopt this system, for it is not given to all peoples to enjoy its
benefits.

The Constitution of the United States is like one of those beautiful creations of human diligence which give their inventors glory
and riches but remains sterile in other hands.

Contemporary Mexico has shown that.

The Mexicans, wishing to establish a federal system, took the
federal Constitution of their Anglo-American neighbors as a
model and copied it almost completely.[20] But when they borrowed
the letter of the law, they could not at the same time transfer the
spirit that gave it life. As a result, one sees them constantly entangled in the mechanism of their double government. The sovereignty of the states and that of the union, going beyond the
spheres assigned to them by the constitution, trespass continually
on each other's territory. In fact, at present Mexico is constantly
shifting from anarchy to military despotism and back from military
despotism to anarchy.

For a confederation to last for long, the diverse peoples forming
it must share a homogeneous civilization as well as common needs.
The difference between the Canton de Vaud and the Canton de
Uri is like that between the nineteenth and fifteenth centuries, as
Switzerland has never, in truth, had a federal government. The
union between its various cantons exists on the map only, as one
would clearly see if a central authority wanted to apply the same
laws throughout the territory.

In the United States one fact wonderfully smooths the existence of the federal government, namely, that the different

---

20.   See the Mexican Constitution of 1824.

states have not only more or less the same interests but also the same level of civilization, so it is almost always an easy matter for them to agree. I doubt whether there is any nation in Europe, however small, whose different parts are not less homogeneous than those of the United States with an area half the size of Europe.

From the state of Maine to that of Georgia is a distance of some thousand miles, but the difference in civilization between Maine and Georgia is less than that between Normandy and Brittany. Maine and Georgia, at the farthest ends of a vast land, have by nature better real opportunities of forming a confederation than Normandy and Brittany, separated only by a brook.

The geographical position of the country added further advantages to the American lawgivers beyond those derived from the mores and customs of the people. And the adoption and survival of the federal system is chiefly due to it.

War is the most important of all the events which can mark the life of a nation. In war a nation acts like a single individual toward foreign nations; it fights for its very existence.

For that reason all nations that have had to engage in great wars have been led, almost in spite of themselves, to increase the powers of the government. Those which have not succeeded in this have been conquered. A long war almost always faces nations with this sad choice: either defeat will lead them to destruction or victory will bring them to despotism.

Generally speaking, then, it is war which most obviously and dangerously reveals the weakness of a government, and I have shown that the inherent defect of federal governments is to be very weak.

Even in the federal Constitution of the United States, where the central government is invested with more real powers than in any other federal constitution, this evil is still strongly felt.

A single example will enable the reader to judge.

The Constitution gives Congress the right to call up the militia of the various states for active service when it is a question of suppressing a rebellion or repulsing an invasion; another article of the Constitution provides that in that case the president of the republic is the commander of the militia.

In the War of 1812 the president ordered the militias of the North to move toward the frontiers; Connecticut and Massachusetts, whose interests were harmed by the war, refused to send their contingents.

The Constitution, they maintained, authorized the federal government to make use of the militias in case of *rebellion* or *invasion*, but up to that moment there was neither. They added that the same Constitution which gave the Union the right to call up the militias left the states the right of appointing the officers; it followed, in their view, that no officer of the Union had the right to command the militias except the president in person. But this was a question of serving in an army commanded by someone other than he.

These absurd and noxious doctrines were supported not only by the governors and legislatures but also by the courts of these two states; and the federal government was constrained to look elsewhere for the troops it lacked.

How, then, does it come about that the American Union, protected though it be by the comparative perfection of its laws, does not dissolve in the midst of a great war? The reason is that it has no great wars to fear.

Placed in the middle of a huge continent with limitless room for the expansion of human endeavor, the Union is almost as isolated from the world as if it were surrounded on all sides by the ocean.

The great good fortune of the United States is not to have found a federal Constitution enabling them to conduct great wars, but to be so situated that there is nothing for them to fear.

No one can appreciate the advantages of a federal system more than I. I hold it to be one of the most powerful combinations favoring human prosperity and freedom. I envy the lot of the nations that have been allowed to adopt it. But yet I refuse to believe that, with equal force on either side, a confederated nation can long fight against a nation with centralized government power.

A nation that divided its sovereignty when faced by the great military monarchies of Europe would seem to me, by that single act, to be abdicating its power, and perhaps its existence and its name.

How wonderful is the position of the New World, where man has as yet no enemies but himself. To be happy and to be free, it is enough to will it to be so.

PART II

So far I have examined the institutions, reviewed the written laws, and described the present shape of political society in the United States.

But above all the institutions and forms there is a sovereign power, that of the people, which can abolish or change them as it pleases.

It remains for me to show how this power acts; what are its instincts and its passions; what secret springs urge on, retard, or direct its irresistible course; what are the effects of its almighty power; and what destiny is in store for it.

1

WHY IT CAN STRICTLY BE SAID
THAT THE PEOPLE GOVERN
IN THE UNITED STATES

IN AMERICA THE PEOPLE appoint both those who make the laws and those who execute them; the people from the jury which punishes breaches of the law; thus the people *directly* nominate their representatives and generally choose them *annually* so as to hold them more completely dependent. Though the form of government is representative, it is clear that the opinions, prejudices, interests, and even passions of the people can find no lasting obstacles preventing them from being manifest in the daily conduct of society.

In the United States, as in all countries where the people reign, the majority rules in the name of the people.

This majority is chiefly composed of peaceful citizens who by taste or interest sincerely desire the well-being of the country. They are surrounded by the constant agitation of parties seeking to draw them in and to enlist their support.

2

PARTIES IN THE UNITED STATES

I MUST FIRST DEFINE an important distinction between parties.

There are some countries so huge that the different populations inhabiting them, although united under the same sovereignty, do not, strictly speaking, form parties, but distinct nations; were civil war to break out, it would be a conflict between rival peoples rather than between factions.

But when there are differences between the citizens concerning matters of equal importance to all parts of the country, such for instance as the general principles of government, then what I really call parties take shape.

Parties are an evil inherent in free governments, but they do not always have the same character and the same instincts.

America has had great parties; now they no longer exist. This has been a great gain in happiness but not in morality.

When the War of Independence came to an end and a new government had to be established, the nation was divided between two opinions. Those opinions were as old as the world itself and are found under different forms in all free societies. One party wanted to restrict popular power and the other to extend it indefinitely.

With the Americans the struggle between these two opinions never took on the violent character that has often marked it elsewhere. In America the two parties agreed on the most essential points. Neither of the two had, to succeed, to destroy an ancient order or to overthrow the whole of a social structure. But immaterial interests of the first importance, such as love of equality and of independence, were affected. That was enough to rouse violent passions.

The party which wished to restrict popular power sought especially to have its ideas applied in the federal Constitution, from which it gained the name of Federal.

The other, which claimed to be the exclusive lover of liberty, called itself Republican.

America is the land of democracy. Consequently, the Federalists were always in a minority, but they included almost all the great men thrown up by the War of Independence, and their moral authority was far-reaching. Moreover, circumstances favored them. The ruin of the first confederation made the people afraid of falling into anarchy, and the Federalists profited from this passing tendency. For ten or twelve years they directed affairs and were able to apply some but not all of their principles, for the current running in the opposite direction became daily stronger and they could not fight against it.

In 1801 the Republicans finally got control of the government. Thomas Jefferson was elected president; he brought them the support of a famous name, great talents, and immense popularity.

Thenceforth the Republican, or Democratic, Party has gone on from strength to strength and taken possession of the whole of society.[1]

The Federalists, feeling themselves defeated, without resources, and isolated within the nation, divided up; some of them joined the victors; the others lowered their flag and changed their name. For many years now they have entirely ceased to exist as a party.

The period of Federalist power was, in my view, one of the luckiest circumstances attending the birth of the great American Union. The Federalists struggled against the irresistible tendency of their age and country. Whatever the virtues or defects of their theories, their rule at least gave the new republic time to settle down and the still-extant federal Constitution is a lasting memorial to their patriotism and wisdom.

Thus today there is no sign of great political parties in the United States. There are many parties threatening the future of

---

1.   [Tocqueville's allusion to "the Republican, or Democratic, Party" refers to the Jeffersonian party, known in its day as the Republican Party but "democratic" in its antifederalist stance. Historians have often referred to it as the "Jeffersonian Republican" or the "Democratic-Republican" party, to avoid confusion with the modern Republican Party, founded in 1856.]

the Union, but none which seem to attack the actual form of government and the general course of society. The parties that threaten the Union rely not on principles but on material interests. In so vast a land these interests make the provinces into rival nations rather than parties. Thus recently we have seen the North contending for tariffs and the South taking up arms for free trade, simply because the North is industrial and the South agricultural.

Lacking great parties, the United States is creeping with small ones and public opinion is broken up ad infinitum about questions of detail.[2] In the United States there is no religious hatred because religion is universally respected and no sect is predominant; there is no class hatred because the people is everything, and nobody dares to struggle against it; and finally, there is no public distress to exploit because the physical state of the country offers such an immense scope to industry that man has only to be left to himself to work marvels. Nevertheless, the ambitious are bound to create parties, for it is difficult to turn the man in power out simply for the reason that one would like to take his place. Hence all the skill of politicians consists in forming parties.

To a foreigner almost all the Americans' domestic quarrels seem at the first glance either incomprehensible or puerile.

But when one comes to study the secret instincts governing American factions, one finds that most of them are more or less connected with one of the two great parties which have divided mankind since free societies came into existence. One sees that some parties are working to restrict the use of public power and the others to extend it.

I am certainly not saying that American parties always have as their open or even their concealed aim to make aristocracy or democracy prevail in the country. I am saying that aristocratic or democratic passions can easily be found at the bottom of all par-

---

2.   [By 1832, notable American political parties included the Jacksonian Democrats, the radical "Loco Foco" Democrats, the National Republicans, the Whigs, and the Anti-Masonic Party, soon to be joined by myriad antislavery, anti-Catholic, anti-immigrant, and other reform parties.]

ties and that they are, as it were, the nerve and soul of the matter.

Remains of the Aristocratic
Party in the United States

When the Democratic Party gained preponderance it took exclusive control of affairs.[3] Since then it has not ceased to mold both mores and laws to its desires.

Nowadays the wealthy classes in the United States are almost entirely outside politics, and wealth, far from being an advantage, is a real cause of disfavor and an obstacle to gaining power.

The wealthy man submits to this state of affairs as to an irremediable evil; he is even careful to avoid showing that he is hurt by it; thus one may hear him boasting in public of the blessings of republican government and the advantages of democratic forms. For apart from hating one's enemies, what is more natural to man than flattering them?

For all this conventional enthusiasm and obsequious formality toward the dominant power, it is easy to see that the rich have a great distaste for their country's democratic institutions. The people are a power whom they fear and scorn. If some day the bad government of democracy were to lead to a political crisis or if ever monarchy appeared as a practical possibility in the United States, one would see the truth of what I am saying.

The two main weapons used by the parties to assure success are newspapers and associations.

---

3.   [The Democratic Party associated with its first presidential nominee, Andrew Jackson, who was elected in 1828 and reelected in 1832.]

3

FREEDOM OF THE PRESS
IN THE UNITED STATES

I ADMIT THAT I do not feel toward freedom of the press that complete love which one accords to things that are by nature supremely good. I love it more from considering the evils it prevents than on account of the good it does.

If someone showed me an intermediate position between complete independence and entire servitude of thought, perhaps I would adopt it; but who can discover any such position?

In a country where the dogma of the sovereignty of the people openly prevails, censorship is not only a danger but even more a great absurdity.

When each man is given a right to rule society, clearly one must recognize his capacity to choose between the different opinions debated among his contemporaries and to appreciate the various facts which may guide his judgment.

The sovereignty of the people and the freedom of the press are therefore two entirely correlative things, whereas censorship and universal suffrage contradict each other. Among the twelve million people living in the territory of the United States, there is not *one single man* who has dared to suggest restricting the freedom of the press.

The first newspaper I saw on arrival in America contained the following article, which I translate faithfully:

"In this whole affair the language used by Jackson (the president) was that of a heartless despot exclusively concerned with preserving his own power. Ambition is his crime, and that will be his punishment. Intrigue is his vocation, and intrigue will confound his plans and snatch his power from him. He governs by corruption, and his guilty maneuvers will turn to his shame and confusion. He has shown himself in the political arena as a gambler without shame or restraint. He has succeeded, but the hour of justice draws near . . ." (Vincenne's *Gazette*).[1]

At this moment perhaps there is no country in the world harboring fewer germs of revolution than America. But the press has much less power in the United States than with us. Nothing, however, is rarer than to see judicial proceedings taken against it. The reason is simple: the Americans, having accepted the dogma of the sovereignty of the people, apply it with perfect sincerity.

They also think that courts are powerless to check the press, and that as the subtlety of human language perpetually eludes judicial analysis, offenses of this nature somehow slip through the fingers of those who try to grasp them. Anyone who had the power would be absolute master of society itself and could get rid of the writers as well as their writings. So, where the press is concerned, there is not in reality any middle path between license and servitude. To cull the inestimable benefits assured by freedom of the press, it is necessary to put up with the inevitable evils springing therefrom.

That the newspapers in America have little power is due to many reasons, of which these are the chief:

The press, so skilled to inflame human passions, can yet not create them all on its own. American political life is active, varied, and even agitated, but it is seldom disturbed by deep passions; such passions are not often roused unless material interests are compromised, and in the United States such interests prosper. A glance at our papers and at theirs is enough to show the difference between the two nations in this respect. In France little space is given over to trade advertisements, and even news items are few; the vital part of the newspaper is devoted to political discussion. In America three-quarters of the

---

1.   [There was a Vincennes (Indiana) *Gazette* of this period, but we failed to trace the quotation. The Indiana state librarian doubts very much the correctness of Tocqueville's date.]

bulky newspaper put before you will be full of advertisements and the rest will usually contain political news or just anecdotes; only at long intervals and in some obscure corner will one find one of those burning arguments which for us are the readers' daily food.

The effective force of any power is increased in proportion to the centralization of its control. But there is no place in which the Americans have located the general control of thought, any more than that of affairs.

In the United States printers need no licenses, and newspapers no stamps or registration.

For these reasons it is a simple and easy matter to start a paper; a few subscribers are enough to cover expenses, so the number of periodical or semiperiodical productions in the United States surpasses all belief. The most enlightened Americans attribute the slightness of the power of the press to this incredible dispersion.

There is hardly a hamlet in America without its newspaper. Of course, with so many combatants, neither discipline nor unity of action is possible, and so each fights under his own flag. Therefore American papers cannot raise those powerful currents of opinion which sweep away or sweep over the most powerful dikes. There are other equally noteworthy effects of this division of the forces of the press; competition prevents any newspaper from hoping for large profits, and that discourages anybody with great business ability from bothering with such undertakings. Even if the papers were a source of wealth, as there is such an excessive number of them, there would not be enough talented journalists to edit them all. So generally American journalists have a low social status, their education is only sketchy, and their thoughts are often vulgarly expressed. The hallmark of the American journalist is a direct and coarse attack, without any subtleties, on the passions of his readers; he disregards principles to seize on people, following them into their private lives and laying bare their weaknesses and their vices.

That is a deplorable abuse of the powers of thought. Later I shall go into the question of the influence of newspapers on the taste and morality of the American people, but here I am concerned only with the world of politics.

However, the power of the American press is still immense. It makes political life circulate in every corner of that vast land. Its eyes are never shut, and it lays bare the secrets of politics, forcing public figures to appear before the tribunal of opinion. The press rallies interest around certain doctrines and gives shape to party slogans; through the press the parties, without actually meeting, listen and argue with one another. When many organs of the press do take the same line, their influence in the long run is almost irresistible.

Each individual American newspaper has little power, but after the people, the press is nonetheless the first of powers.

Once the American people have got an idea into their head, be it correct or unreasonable, nothing is harder than to get it out again.

The same can be noticed in England, which for a century has been the European country with the greatest freedom of thought and with the most invincible prejudices.

I think this is due to that very fact that one would have thought bound to prevent it, namely, the freedom of the press. People enjoying that freedom become attached to their opinions as much from pride as from conviction. They love them because they think them correct, but also because they have chosen them; and they stick to them, not only as something true but also as something of their very own.

4

POLITICAL ASSOCIATION
IN THE UNITED STATES

BETTER USE HAS BEEN made of association and this powerful instrument of action has been applied to more varied aims in America than anywhere else in the world.

The inhabitant of the United States learns from birth that he must rely on himself to combat the ills and trials of life; he is restless and defiant in his outlook toward the authority of society and appeals to its power only when he cannot do without it.

The right of association being recognized, citizens can use it in different ways. An association simply consists in the public and formal support of specific doctrines by a certain number of individuals, who have undertaken to cooperate in a stated way in order to make these doctrines prevail. Thus the right of association can almost be identified with freedom to write, but already associations are more powerful than the press. When some opinion is represented by an association, it must take clearer and more precise shape. It counts its supporters and involves them in its cause; these supporters get to know one another, and numbers increase zeal. An association unites the energies of divergent minds and vigorously directs them toward a clearly indicated goal.

Freedom of assembly marks the second stage in the use made of the right of association. When a political association is allowed to form centers of action at certain important places in the country, its activity becomes greater and its influence more widespread. There men meet, active measures are planned, and opinions are expressed with that strength and warmth which the written word can never attain.

But the final stage is the use of association in the sphere of politics.

It must be admitted that unlimited freedom of association in the political sphere has not yet produced in America the fatal results that one might anticipate from it elsewhere. The right of association is of English origin and always existed in America. Use of this right is now an accepted part of customs and of mores.

In our own day freedom of association has become a necessary guarantee against the tyranny of the majority. In the United States, once a party has become predominant, all public power passes into its hands; its close supporters occupy all offices and have control of all organized forces. The most distinguished men of the opposite party, unable to cross the barrier keeping them from power, must be able to establish themselves outside it; the minority must use the whole of its moral authority to oppose the physical power oppressing it. Thus the one danger has to be balanced against a more formidable one.

The omnipotence of the majority seems to me such a danger to the American republics that the dangerous expedient used to curb it is actually something good.

One must not shut one's eyes to the fact that unlimited freedom of association for political ends is, of all forms of liberty, the last that a nation can sustain. While it may not actually lead it into anarchy, it does constantly bring it to the verge thereof. But this form of freedom, howsoever dangerous, does provide guarantees in one direction; in countries where associations are free, secret societies are unknown. There are factions in America, but no conspirators.

In America the citizens who form the minority associate in the first place to show their numbers and to lessen the moral authority of the majority, and secondly, by stimulating competition, to discover the arguments most likely to make an impression on the majority, for they always hope to draw the majority over to their side and then to exercise power in its name.

Political associations in the United States are therefore peaceful in their objects and legal in the means used; and when they say that they only wish to prevail legally, in general they are telling the truth.

There are several reasons for this difference between the Americans and ourselves. In Europe there are parties differing so much from the majority that they can never hope to win its support, and yet these parties believe themselves strong enough to struggle against it on their own. When such a party forms an association it intends not to convince but to fight.

So the exercise of the right of association becomes dangerous when great parties see no possibility of becoming the majority. In a country like the United States, where differences of view are only matters of nuance, the right of association can remain, so to say, without limits.

But perhaps universal suffrage is the most powerful of all the elements tending to moderate the violence of political associations in the United States. In a country with universal suffrage the majority is never in doubt, because associations know, and everyone knows, that they do not represent the majority. The very fact of their existence proves this, for if they did represent the majority, they themselves would change the law instead of demanding reforms.

Almost all associations in Europe believe or claim that they represent the wishes of the majority. This greatly increases their strength and wonderfully serves to legitimize their acts. For what is more excusable than violence to bring about the triumph of the oppressed cause of right?

Thus in the immense complication of human laws it sometimes comes about that extreme freedom corrects the abuse of freedom, and extreme democracy forestalls the dangers of democracy.

In Europe associations regard themselves in a way as the legislature and executive council of the nation which cannot raise its own voice; starting from this conception, they act and they command. In America, where everyone sees that they represent only a minority in the nation, they talk and petition.

5

GOVERNMENT BY DEMOCRACY IN AMERICA

Universal Suffrage

I have previously mentioned that all the states of the Union have adopted universal suffrage;[1] consequently it functions among communities at very different stages on the social ladder. I have had the chance to see its effects in diverse places and among men who by race, language, religion, or mores are almost total strangers one to another, in Louisiana as well as New England and in Georgia as well as Canada. I noted that in America universal suffrage was far from producing all the blessings or ills expected from it in Europe and that, generally speaking, its effects are other than is supposed.

The People's Choice and the Instincts of American Democracy in Such Choices

In Europe many people either believe without saying or say without believing that one of the great advantages of universal suffrage is to summon men worthy of public confidence to the direction of affairs. The people, men say, do not know how themselves to rule but always sincerely desire the good of the state, and their instinct unfailingly tells them who are most capable of wielding power.

For my part, I am bound to say that what I saw in America gives me no cause to think that so. When I arrived in the United States I

---

1.   [Tocqueville here refers to white manhood suffrage, but in fact only 10 of 24 states had abolished all voting restrictions for white men by 1830. As of 1860, 7 of 33 states still imposed tax or property qualifications on white male voters.]

discovered with astonishment that good qualities were common among the governed but rare among the rulers. In our day it is a constant fact that the most outstanding Americans are seldom summoned to public office, and it is clear that during the last fifty years the race of American statesmen has strangely shrunk.

One can point to several reasons for this phenomenon.

Whatever one does, it is impossible to raise the standard of enlightenment in a nation above a certain level.

It is therefore as difficult to conceive a society in which all men are very enlightened as one in which all are rich. I freely admit that the mass of the citizens very sincerely desires the country's good; I would go further and say that the lower classes of society generally confuse their personal interests with this desire less than the upper classes do; but what they always lack to some extent is skill to judge the means to attain this end. Consider the prolonged study involved in forming an exact notion of the character of a single man. Where the greatest geniuses go astray, are the masses to succeed? The people are bound always to make hasty judgments. That is why charlatans of every sort so well understand the secret of pleasing them, whereas for the most part their real friends fail in this.

One must not blind oneself to the fact that democratic institutions most successfully develop envy in the human heart. This is not because they provide the means for everybody to rise to the level of everybody else but because these means are constantly proving inadequate in the hands of those using them. Democratic institutions awaken the passion for equality without ever being able to satisfy it entirely. This complete equality is always slipping through the people's finger at the moment when they think to grasp it. They are excited by the chance and irritated by the uncertainty of success; the excitement is followed by weariness and then by bitterness at any superiority, however legitimate.

While the natural instincts of democracy lead the people to keep men of distinction from power, an equally strong instinct diverts the latter from a political career, in which it would be difficult to remain completely themselves or to make any progress without cheapening themselves.

I take it as proved that those who consider universal suffrage as a guarantee of excellent choices suffer under a complete delusion. Universal suffrage has other advantages, but not that one.

Elements Which May Provide a Partial Corrective to These Instincts of Democracy

I have said above that the statesmen of modern America seem greatly inferior to those at the head of affairs fifty years ago. Circumstances, as well as laws, were responsible for that. When America was engaged in the most just of struggles, that of a people escaping from another people's yoke and creating a new nation, the spirits of all rose to the height of their goal. Outstanding men anticipated the people's call, and the people welcomed them with open arms and put them at their head. But such events are rare, and one must judge by the ordinary aspect of things.

When one enters the House of Representatives at Washington, one is struck by the vulgar demeanor of that great assembly. One can often look in vain for a single famous man. Almost all the members are obscure people, mostly village lawyers, tradesmen, or even men of the lowest classes. In a country where education is almost universal, it is said that the people's representatives do not always know how to write correctly.

A couple of paces away is the entrance to the Senate, which contains a large proportion of the famous men of America. There is scarcely a man to be seen there without some recent claim to fame. They are eloquent advocates, distinguished generals, wise magistrates, and noted statesmen. Every word uttered in this assembly would add luster to the greatest parliamentary debates in Europe.

What is the reason for this bizarre contrast? Why are the elite of the nation in one room and not in the other? Why does the former assembly attract such vulgar elements, whereas the latter has a monopoly of talents and enlightenment? I can see only one fact to explain it: the election which produces the House of Representatives is direct, whereas the Senate is subject to election in two stages. All citizens together appoint the legislature of each state, and then the federal Constitution turns each of these legislatures into electoral bodies that return the members of the Senate. The senators therefore do represent the result, albeit the indirect result, of universal suffrage, for the legislature which appoints the senators essentially depends on the totality of citizens; it is generally annually elected by them, and they can always control its choice by giving it new members. But it is enough that the popular will has passed through this elected assembly for it to have become in some sense refined and to come out clothed in nobler and more beautiful shape.

It is easy to see a time coming when the American republics will be bound to make more frequent use of election in two stages, unless they are to be miserably lost among the shoals of democracy.

Public Officers Under the Rule
of American Democracy

American public officials blend with the mass of citizens; they have neither palaces nor ceremonial clothes. This external simplicity is not due to some peculiar twist in the American character but derives from the fundamental principles of their society.

In democratic eyes government is not a blessing but a necessary evil. Officials must be given certain powers, but the external pomps of power are by no means essential to the conduct of business; the sight of them would offend the public uselessly.

The officials themselves are perfectly aware that they have won power only on condition that their manners keep them on a level with everybody else.

I can imagine no one more straightforward in his manners, accessible to all, attentive to requests, and civil in his answers than an American public official.

I like this natural demeanor of democratic authority, which goes more with the office than with the official and more with the man than with external symbols of power, for there is something admirably virile therein.

I believe that in such an age as ours the importance attached to uniforms has been much exaggerated. I have not noticed American officials in the exercise of their duties treated with less respect or regard because they rely on merit alone. The public pays for all services of whatever sort performed in its interest; hence any man has the chance as well as the right to perform them.

Although in democratic states all citizens can hold office, not all are disposed to seek it.

There is, properly speaking, no public career in a nation where the principle of election is universally applied. There is an element of chance about who is chosen, and no one can be sure of remaining in office. This is particularly the case where elections are annual. Consequently in calm times public office offers little attraction to ambition. In the United States it is men of moderate pretensions who engage in the twists and turns of politics. Men of vaulting ambition generally avoid power to pursue wealth; the frequent result is that men undertake to direct the fortunes of the state only when they doubt their capacity to manage their private affairs.

These causes, quite as much as the ill choices of democracy, are responsible for the large number of vulgar men holding public positions. Should men of parts compete for their votes, I am sure that the American people would choose them, but it is certain that they do not so compete.

Administrative Instability in the United States

After one brief moment of power, officials are lost again amid the ever-changing crowd, and as a result, the proceedings of American society often leave fewer traces than do events in a private family. There is a sense in which public administration is oral and traditional. Nothing is written, or if it is, the slightest gust of wind carries it off, to vanish without recall.

Newspapers are the only historical records in the United States. If one number is missing, it is as if the link of time was broken: present and past cannot be joined together again. I have no doubt that in fifty years' time it will be harder to collect authentic documents about the details of social life in modern America than about French medieval administration.

Administrative instability has begun to become a habit; I might almost say that by now everyone has developed a taste for it. Nobody bothers about what was done before his time. No method is adopted; no archives are formed; no documents are brought together, even when it would be easy to do so.² When by chance someone has them, he is casual about preserving them. Among my papers I have original documents given to me by public officials to answer some of my questions. American society seems to live from day to day, like an army on active service. Nevertheless, the art of administration is certainly a science, and all sciences, to make progress, need to link the discoveries of succeeding generations. It is very difficult for American administrators to learn anything from each other. Thus the lights that guide them are widespread throughout society, and not any particular administrative techniques. So democracy, pressed to its ultimate limits, harms the progress of the art of government.

Moreover, this does not apply only to the science of administration. Democratic government, founded on such a simple and natural idea, nevertheless always assumes the existence of a very civilized and knowledgeable society. At first glance it might be supposed to belong to the earliest ages of the world, but looking closer, one soon discovers that it could only have come last.

Public Expenses Under the Rule
of American Democracy

Is democratic government economical? First we must know with what we are comparing it.

The question could easily be answered if we wanted to compare a democratic republic with an absolute monarchy. One would find public expenses in the former considerably greater than in the latter. But that is so of all free states compared with those not free.

---

2.   [Until the establishment in 1934 of the National Archives and Records Administration, each federal department maintained its own files more or less haphazardly. For a hundred years after Tocqueville's observation, no central repository or preservation policy governed federal records.]

At present I am concerned to make comparisons between free peoples and to discover what effect democracy there has on state finances.

Countries where lawmaking falls exclusively to the lot of the poor cannot hope for much economy in public expenditure;[3] expenses will always be considerable, either because taxes cannot touch those who vote for them or because they are assessed in a way to prevent that. In other words, a democratic government is the only one in which those who vote for a tax can escape the obligation to pay it.

Someone may stop me and say: "Who has ever thought of entrusting lawmaking to the poor alone?" Who? Those who introduced universal suffrage. Is it the majority or the minority who make the law? The majority certainly, and if I show that the poor always compose the majority, have I not reason to add that in countries where all are called to vote, the poor alone make the law?

Now, it is certain that up to the present in all countries of the world those without property or those whose property was so modest that they could not live comfortably without working have always formed the largest number. So universal suffrage really does hand the government over to the poor.

There are other causes too that may increase the total budget in democracies.

Those in charge of affairs of state under an aristocracy are naturally free of all wants; content with their lot, it is especially power and glory that they ask of society. An aristocracy thinks more about preservation than about improvement.

But the people, when sovereign, feeling discontented, seek everywhere for something better.

The thirst for improvement is especially bent on those types of improvement that require expenditure, for it is a question of bettering the lot of the poor, who cannot help themselves.

---

3. It will be understood that the word *poor* here and in the rest of this chapter has a relative and not an absolute meaning. The poor of America, compared to those of Europe, might often seem rich; nevertheless, they can rightly be called poor when compared to their richer fellow citizens.

There is also in democratic societies a prevailing feverish excitement over innovations of all sorts, and innovations are almost always expensive.

Moreover, when the people begin to reflect on their position, they notice a mass of hitherto unfelt wants, which cannot be satisfied without recourse to the resources of the state. For that reason public expenditure increases with civilization, and as enlightenment spreads, taxes rise.

Democracy is excessively parsimonious only toward its principal agents; officials of secondary rank are better paid than elsewhere, but high officials are much less well paid.

The same cause is responsible for these contradictory effects; in both cases the people fix the salaries of public officials, and the scale of remuneration is determined by a comparison with their own wants. Living in great comfort themselves, it seems natural to them that their servants should share therein. But when it comes to fixing the salaries of high officials of the state, such a rule gives no guidance, and things are decided at random.

A poor man has no distinct idea of the needs which the upper classes of society may feel. What seems a moderate sum to a rich man strikes the man accustomed to be satisfied with necessities as prodigious, and he supposes that a state governor with his six thousand francs must feel himself lucky and the object of envy.

The parsimony of democracy toward its chief functionaries has caused it to be credited with very economical inclinations, which it does not possess.

It is true that democracy hardly provides its rulers with a decent living, but it spends huge sums to succor the needs or facilitate the pleasures of the people.[4] That is a better use of taxes, not an economy.

---

4.   See *inter alia* in American budgets what maintenance of the needy and free education cost.

In 1831 the state of New York spent $245,433 on the care of paupers. And the sum devoted to public education is estimated to rise to at least $1,080,698. (Williams' *New York Annual Register*, 1832, pp. 205, 243.)

The state of New York had only 1,900,000 inhabitants in 1830, which is less than twice the population of the Department du Nord.

In general, democracy gives little to the rulers and much to the ruled. The opposite occurs in aristocracies, where the state's money especially benefits the class in control of affairs.

Corruption and Vices of the Rulers in a Democracy and Consequent Effect on Public Morality

Aristocracy and democracy mutually reproach each other for making corruption easy: a distinction must be made.

In aristocratic governments those who get to the head of affairs are rich men desiring power only. The statesmen in democracies are poor, with their fortunes to make.

As a result, the rulers in aristocratic states are little open to corruption and have only a very moderate taste for money, whereas the opposite occurs in democracies.

But in aristocracies those who wish to get to the head of affairs have great wealth at their disposal, and as the number of those by whose assistance they may rise is comparatively small, the government is in a sense up for auction. In democracies those who intrigue for power are hardly ever rich, and the number of those who help to give it to them is very great. Perhaps there are just as many men for sale in democracies, but there are hardly any buyers; besides, one would have to buy too many men at the same time to attain one's end.

I have never heard it said in the United States that a man used his wealth to bribe the governed, but I have often heard the integrity of public officials put in doubt. More often still, I have heard their success attributed to base intrigues or culpable maneuvers.

The people never penetrate the obscure labyrinth of the spirit of a court. But stealing from the public purse or selling the favors of the state for money—those are matters any wretch can understand and hope to emulate in turn.

In democracies private citizens see men rising from their ranks and attaining wealth and power in a few years; that spectacle excites their envy; they wonder how he who was their equal yesterday, has today won the right to command them. To attribute his rise to his talents or virtues is inconvenient, for it means admitting that they are less virtuous or capable than he. They therefore regard some of his vices as the main cause, and often they are correct. In this way there comes about an odious mingling of the conceptions of baseness and power, of unworthiness and success, and of profit and dishonor.

The Efforts of Which Democracy Is Capable

No great democratic republic has yet existed. It would be an insult to republics to use that name for the oligarchy which ruled France in 1793. Only the United States presents this new phenomenon.

Now, in the half century since the Union took shape, its existence has only once been threatened, during the War of Independence.

Since that time the United States has not had a single serious war to sustain.

To judge what sacrifices democracies are capable of imposing on themselves, we must await a time when the American nation will be forced to put half its income into the hands of the government, as England has done, or is bound to throw a twentieth of its population onto the battlefield, as has been done by France.

In America conscription is unknown; men are induced to enlist for pay. Compulsory recruitment is so alien to the habits of the people of the United States that I doubt whether anyone would ever dare to bring in such a law. In France conscription is certainly the heaviest of all state impositions, but without conscription, how could we sustain a great continental war?

Democracy seems to me much better suited to directing a peaceful society, or if necessary, to making some sudden and violent effort rather than to braving the great storms that beset a nation's existence. Enthusiasm leads men to face dangers and privations, but only reflection will induce them to continue to brave them over a long period.

The people not only see less clearly than the upper classes what can be hoped or feared for the future, but they also suffer the ills of the present in quite another way. The noble who risks his life has equal chances of glory and of danger. In handing over to the state the greater part of his income, he temporarily deprives himself of some of the pleasures of wealth; but there is no glamour in the poor man's death, and that tax which is merely irksome to the rich often threatens his livelihood.

This relative weakness of democratic republics in time of crisis is perhaps the greatest obstacle preventing the foundation of such a republic in Europe.

I think that in the long run government by democracy should increase the real strength of society, but it cannot immediately assemble forces as great as those at the disposal of an aristocratic government or an absolute monarchy. If for a century a democratic country were to remain under a republican government, one can believe that at the end of that time it would be richer, more populated, and more prosperous than neighboring despotic states; but during that century it would often have run the risk of being conquered by them.

American Democracy's Power of Self-control

Democracy's difficulty in conquering the passions and silencing momentary requirements in the interest of the future can be observed in the United States in the most trivial things.

The people, surrounded by flatterers, find it hard to master themselves. Whenever anyone tries to persuade them to accept privation, even for an aim that they approve, they always begin by refusing. The Americans rightly boast of their obedience to law, made by the people and for the people who everywhere else have the greatest interest in violating it. It is therefore fair to suppose that an irksome law of which the majority did not see the immediate utility either would not be passed or would not be obeyed.

There is no American legislation against fraudulent bankruptcies. Is that because there are no bankrupts? No, on the contrary, it is because there are many. The majority fear being prosecuted as a bankrupt more than being ruined by other bankrupts, and so the public conscience has a sort of guilty tolerance for an offense which everyone individually condemns.

In the new states of the Southwest the citizens almost always take justice into their own hands, and murders are frequent occurrences. That is because the people's habits are too rough and because enlightenment is not sufficiently widespread in that wilderness for people to see the advantage of giving strength to the law; duels are still preferred to lawsuits there.

Someone once told me in Philadelphia that almost all crimes in America are due to the abuse of strong drink, which, being sold cheaply, the lowest classes could consume at will. "How comes it," I asked, "that you do not put a duty on brandy?" "Our legislators have often thought about it," he answered, "but that is a difficult undertaking. There is fear of a revolt, and those who voted for such a law could be certain not to be reelected." "So," I replied, "with you, drunkards are in a majority and temperance is unpopular."

When one points out matters such as these to statesmen, the only answer they give is: "Let time do its work; a sense of the evil will enlighten the people and show them what they need." A democracy may be more likely to be deceived than a king or a body of nobles, but it also has a better chance of retrieving the truth, because generally there are no interests opposed to the majority and ready to fight against reason. But a democracy cannot get at the truth without experience, and many nations may perish for lack of the time to discover their mistakes.

Therefore the great privilege enjoyed by the Americans is not only to be more enlightened than other nations but also to have the chance to make mistakes that can be retrieved.

How American Democracy Conducts
the External Affairs of the State

We have noted that the federal Constitution put the permanent control of the nation's foreign interests in the hands of the president and the Senate,[5] which to some extent frees the Union's general policy from direct and daily popular control. One should not therefore assert without qualification that American democracy controls the state's external affairs.

Two men have set a direction for American policy which is still followed today; the first is Washington and the second Jefferson.

Washington, in that admirable letter addressed to his fellow citizens which was that great man's political testament, says:

"The great rule of conduct for us, in regard to foreign nations, is, in extending our commercial relations, to have with them as little *political* connection as possible. So far as we have already formed engagements, let them be fulfilled with perfect good faith. Here let us stop. . . .

"Why, by interweaving our destiny with that of any part of Europe, entangle our peace and prosperity in the toils of European ambition, rivalship, interest, humor, or caprice?

"It is our true policy to steer clear of permanent alliances with any portion of the foreign world; . . .

"Taking care always to keep ourselves, by suitable establishments, in a respectable defensive posture, we may safely trust to temporary alliances for extraordinary emergencies."[6]

Washington's political conduct was always guided by these maxims. He succeeded in keeping his country at peace while all the rest of the world was at war, and he established it as a fundamental doctrine that the true interest of the Americans was never to take part in the internal quarrels of Europe.

---

5.   The Constitution (Article 2, section 2, subsection 2) states that the president "shall have power, by and with the advice and consent of the Senate, to make treaties. . . ." The reader should not forget that senators are elected for a term of six years by the legislatures of each state and they are the result of election by two stages.

6.   [Marshall, *The Life of George Washington*, London, 1807, vol. 5, pp. 776 ff.]

Jefferson went still further and introduced another maxim into American politics: "that the Americans should never ask for privileges from foreign nations, in order not to be obliged to grant any in return."

These two principles, whose evident truth makes them easily grasped by the multitudes, have greatly simplified the foreign policy of the United States.

As the Union does not meddle in the affairs of Europe, it has, so to say, no external interests at stake, for as yet it has no powerful neighbors in America. Expectancy is the keynote of American foreign policy; it consists much more in abstaining than in doing.

It is therefore hard as yet to know what talents American democracy might develop in conducting foreign affairs. Both friends and enemies should suspend judgment on that point.

For my part, I have no hesitation in saying that in foreign affairs, democratic governments do appear decidedly inferior to others.

Foreign policy does not require the use of any of the good qualities peculiar to democracy but does demand the cultivation of almost all those which it lacks. Democracy favors the growth of the state's internal resources but finds it difficult to coordinate the details of a great undertaking and carry it through in spite of obstacles. It has little capacity for combining measures in secret and waiting patiently for the result. Such qualities are more likely to belong to a single man or to an aristocracy. But these are just the qualities which, in the long run, prevail.

The tendency to obey its feelings rather than its calculations and to abandon a long-matured plan to satisfy a momentary passion was well seen in America at the time when the French Revolution broke out. The simplest lights of reason were enough to make the Americans see that they had no interest in joining the bloodshed in Europe, from which the United States could suffer no damage.

Nevertheless, the people's sympathies for France declared themselves with such violence that nothing less than the inflexible character of Washington and the immense popularity he enjoyed sufficed to prevent them from declaring war on England. More-over, the austere arguments used by that great man to combat the ill-considered passions of his fellow citizens came near to depriv-ing him of the only reward he ever claimed, the love of his coun-try. The majority pronounced against his policy; now the whole nation approves it.

6

THE REAL ADVANTAGES DERIVED BY AMERICAN SOCIETY FROM DEMOCRATIC GOVERNMENT

THE POLITICAL CONSTITUTION OF the United States seems to me to be one of the forms that democracy can give to its government, but I do not think that American institutions are the only ones, or the best, that a democratic nation might adopt.

So in pointing out the blessings which the Americans derive from democratic government, I am far from claiming or from thinking that such advantages can only be obtained by the same laws.

The General Tendency of Laws Under the Sway of American Democracy and the Instincts of Those Who Apply Them

The vices and weaknesses of democratic government are easy to see but its good qualities are revealed only in the long run.

The laws of American democracy are often defective or incom-plete; they sometimes violate acquired rights or sanction danger-ous ones; even if they were good, their frequent changes would be a great evil. All this is seen at first glance.

How, then, do the American republics maintain themselves and prosper?

In general, the laws of a democracy tend toward the good of the greatest number, for they spring from the majority of all the citizens, which may be mistaken but cannot have an interest contrary to its own, although it often unintentionally works against itself.

Suppose a society so organized that it can tolerate the passing effect of bad laws and await the *general tendency* of its laws, and you will appreciate that democratic government, for all its faults, is best suited to make society prosper.

That is just what does happen in the United States; I here repeat what I have described elsewhere: the great privilege of the Americans is to be able to make retrievable mistakes.

Notice first that in a democratic state, though the rulers be less honest or less capable, the governed are constantly occupied with their affairs and jealous of their rights, preventing their representatives from deviating from their interests.

Note also that although a democratic magistrate may use his power worse than another, he generally holds it for a shorter time.

But there is a more general and satisfactory reason than any of these.

I have said that it was important for the rulers not to have interests different from those of the mass of the ruled. I do not say that they should have interests similar to those of all the governed, for I don't suppose that such a thing has ever happened.

No one has yet found a political structure that equally favors the growth and prosperity of all the classes composing society. When the rich alone rule, the interests of the poor are always in danger; and when the poor make the law, the interests of the rich run great risks. What, then, is the advantage of democracy? The real advantage of democracy is not, as some have said, to favor the prosperity of all, but only to serve the well-being of the greatest number.

In the United States those who direct public affairs are often inferior in capacity and morality to those whom an aristocracy might bring to power; but their interest is mingled with that of the majority of their fellow citizens. Hence they may often prove untrustworthy and make great mistakes, but they will never systematically follow a tendency hostile to the majority; they will never turn the government into something exclusive and dangerous.

The bad administration of one magistrate under a democracy is, moreover, an isolated fact that has an influence only during the short period of his tenure of office. Corruption and incapacity are not common interests capable of linking men in any permanent fashion.

Quite the contrary, the ambition and intrigues of the one will help to unmask the other. Generally speaking, in a democracy the vices of a magistrate are altogether personal.

In the United States, where public officials have no class interest to promote, the general and continuous course of the government is beneficial, although the rulers are often inept and sometimes contemptible.

There is therefore at the bottom of democratic institutions some hidden tendency which often makes men promote the general prosperity, in spite of their vices and their mistakes, whereas in aristocratic institutions there is sometimes a secret bias which, in spite of talents and virtues, leads men to contribute to the afflictions of their fellows. In this way it may come about that under aristocratic governments public men do evil without intending it, and in democracies they bring about good results of which they have never thought.

Public Spirit in the United States

There is a patriotism which mainly springs from the feeling that ties a man's heart to the place where he was born. This instinctive love is mingled with a taste for old habits, respect for ancestors, and memories of the past; those who feel it love their country as one loves one's father's house. It is itself a sort of religion; it does not reason, but believes, feels, and acts. Some nations have personified their country and see the monarch as standing for it. Hence they have transferred some of the feelings of patriotism to him, and they boast of his triumphs and are proud of his power.

There is also another sort of patriotism more rational than that; less generous, perhaps less ardent, but more creative and more lasting, it is engendered by enlightenment, grows by the aid of laws and the exercise of rights, and in the end mingles with personal interest. A man understands the influence which his country's well-being has on his own; he knows the law allows him to contribute to the production of this well-being, and he takes an interest in his country's prosperity, first as a thing useful to him and then as something he has created.

But sometimes there comes a time in the life of nations when old beliefs are shaken, and the prestige of memories has vanished, but when nonetheless enlightenment has remained incomplete and political rights are ill-assured. Then men see their country only by a doubtful light; their patriotism is not centered on the soil, which in their eyes is just inanimate earth, nor on the customs of their ancestors, which they regard as a yoke, nor on religion, which they doubt, nor on the laws, which they do not make, nor on the lawgiver, whom they fear and scorn.

What can be done in such a condition? In our day it seems to me that civic spirit is inseparable from the exercise of political rights.

How is it that in the United States, where the inhabitants arrived but yesterday in the land they occupy, where they meet for the first time without knowing each other, where, to say it in one word, the instinct of country can hardly exist—how does it come about that each man is as interested in the affairs of his township and of the whole state as he is in his own affairs? It is because each man in his sphere takes an active part in the government of society.

The common man in the United States sees the public fortune as his own, and he works for the good of the state, not only from duty or from pride, but, I dare almost say, from greed.

The American, taking part in everything that is done in his country, feels a duty to defend anything criticized there, for it is not only his country that is being attacked, but himself.

Nothing is more annoying than this irritable patriotism of the Americans. A foreigner will gladly agree to praise much in their country, but he would like to be allowed to criticize something, and that he is absolutely refused.

So America is the land of freedom where, in order not to offend anybody, the foreigner may speak freely neither about public undertakings nor about private ones—indeed, about nothing that one comes across, except perhaps the climate and the soil, but yet one meets Americans ready to defend both of these, as if they had a share in forming them.

In our day we must make up our minds and dare to choose between the patriotism of all and the government of the few, for one cannot combine the social strength and activity given by the first with the guarantees of tranquility sometimes provided by the second.

The Idea of Rights in the United States

Next to virtue as a general idea, nothing, I think, is so beautiful as that of rights, and indeed the two ideas are mingled. The idea of rights is nothing but the conception of virtue applied to the world of politics.

By means of the idea of rights men have defined the nature of license and of tyranny. Guided by its light, we can each of us be independent without arrogance and obedient without servility. When a man submits to force, that surrender debases him; but when he accepts the recognized right of a fellow mortal to give him orders, in a sense he rises above the giver of the commands. No man can be great without virtue, nor any nation great without respect for rights.

Why is it that in America, the land par excellence of democracy, no one makes that outcry against property in general that often echoes through Europe? Is there any need to explain? It is because there are no proletarians in America. Everyone, having some possession to defend, recognizes the right to property in principle.

It is the same in the world of politics.

Democratic government makes the idea of political rights pene-trate right down to the least of citizens, just as the division of prop-erty puts the general idea of property rights within reach of all. That, in my view, is one of its greatest merits.

I am not asserting it to be an easy matter to teach all men to make use of political rights; I only say that when that can happen, the results are important.

However, I do not wish to press the example of America too far.

In America the people were invested with political rights at a time when it was difficult for them to make ill use of them, be-cause the citizens were few and their mores simple. As they have grown, the Americans have not appreciably increased the powers of democracy; rather they have extended its domain.

The moment when political rights are granted to a people who have been deprived of them is a time of crisis, a crisis which is often necessary but always dangerous.

A child may kill when he does not understand the value of life; he carries off other people's property before he knows that his own may be snatched from him. The man of the people, at the moment when political rights are granted to him, is much in the same position with respect to those rights as is a child faced by the whole of nature.

Nothing is harder than freedom's apprenticeship. The same is not true of despotism. Despotism often presents itself as the de-fender of the oppressed and founder of order. Peoples are lulled to sleep by the temporary prosperity it engenders, and when they do wake up, they are wretched. But liberty is generally born in stormy weather, growing with difficulty amid civil discords, and only when it is already old does one see the blessings it has brought.

Respect for Law in the United States

It is not always feasible to call on the whole people, either directly or indirectly, to take its part in lawmaking, but no one can deny that when that can be done the law derives great authority there-from. This popular origin, though often damaging to the wisdom and quality of legislation, gives it peculiar strength.

In the United States, except for slaves, servants, and paupers fed by the township, no one is without a vote and, hence, an indirect share in lawmaking.

Therefore, however annoying a law may be, the American will submit to it, not only as the work of the majority but also as his own doing; he regards it as a contract to which he is one of the parties.

So in the United States there is no numerous and perpetually turbulent crowd regarding the law as a natural enemy to fear and to suspect. On the contrary, one is bound to notice that all classes show great confidence in their country's legislation, feeling a sort of paternal love for it.

I am wrong in saying all classes. As in America, the European ladder of power has been turned upside down; where the poor man rules, the rich have always some fear that he may abuse his power against them.

This state of mind among the wealthy may produce a silent discontent, but it creates no violent trouble for society, for among civilized nations it is generally only those with nothing to lose who revolt. Moreover, in America the people obey the law not only because it is their work but also because they can change it if by any chance it does injure them; they submit to it primarily as a self-imposed evil, and secondly as a passing one.

Activity Prevailing in All Parts of the Political Body in the United States; the Influence Thereby Exerted on Society

It is not impossible to conceive the immense freedom enjoyed by the Americans, and one can also form an idea of their extreme equality, but the political activity prevailing in the United States is something one could never understand unless one had seen it.

No sooner do you set foot on American soil than you find yourself in a sort of tumult; a confused clamor rises on every side, and a thousand voices are heard at once. All around you everything is on the move: here the people of a district are assembled to discuss the possibility of building a church; there they are busy choosing a representative; further on, the delegates of a district are hurrying to town to consult about some local improvements; elsewhere it's the village farmers who have left their furrows to discuss the plan for a road or a school. One group of citizens assembles for the sole object of announcing that they disapprove of the government's course, while others unite to proclaim that the men in office are the fathers of their country. And here is yet another gathering which regards drunkenness as the main source of ills in the state and has come to enter into a solemn undertaking to give an example of temperance.[1]

The great political agitation which bestirs American legislatures continually, and which alone is noticed from outside, is only an episode and a sort of extension of the universal agitation, which begins in the lowest ranks of the people and thence spreads successively through all classes of citizens. No one could work harder to be happy.

It is hard to explain the place filled by political concerns in the life of an American; even the women often go to public meetings and forget household cares while they listen to political speeches. For them clubs to some extent take the place of theaters. An American does not know how to converse, but he argues; if an American should be reduced to occupying himself with his own affairs alone, at that moment half his existence would be snatched from him; he would feel it as a vast void in his life and would become incredibly unhappy.

That constantly renewed agitation introduced by democratic government into political life passes, then, into civil society. Perhaps, taking everything into consideration, that is the greatest advantage of democratic government, and I praise it much more on account of what it causes to be done than for what it does.

---

1.   Temperance societies are associations whose members undertake to abstain from strong drink. At the time of my visit temperance societies already counted more than 270,000 members, and consequently, in the state of Pennsylvania alone the consumption of strong liquors had fallen by 500,000 gallons a year.

It is incontestable that the people often manage public affairs very badly, but their concern therewith is bound to extend their mental horizon and shake them out of the rut of ordinary routine. I have no doubt that democratic institutions, combined with the physical nature of the land, are the indirect reason, and not, as is often claimed, the direct one, for the prodigious industrial expansion seen in the United States. It is not the laws' creation, but the people have learned to achieve it by making the laws.

Democracy does not provide a people with the most skillful of governments, but it does that which the most skillful government often cannot do: it spreads throughout the body social a restless activity, superabundant force, and energy never found elsewhere, which, however little favored by circumstance, can do wonders. Those are its true advantages.

What do you expect from society and its government? We must be clear about that.

Do you wish to raise mankind to an elevated and generous view of the things of this world? Do you want to inspire men with a certain scorn of material goods?

Are you concerned with refining mores, elevating manners, and causing the arts to blossom? Do you set out to organize a nation so that it will have a powerful influence over all others? Do you expect it to leave a great mark on history?

If in your view that should be the main object of society, do not support democratic government; it surely will not lead to that goal.

But if you think it profitable to turn man's intellectual and moral activity toward the necessities of physical life and use them to produce well-being, if in place of a brilliant society you are content to live in one that is prosperous, and finally, if in your view the main object of government is not to achieve the greatest strength or glory for the nation as a whole but to provide for every individual therein the utmost well-being, protecting him as far as possible from all afflictions, then it is good to make conditions equal and to establish a democratic government.

7

THE OMNIPOTENCE OF THE MAJORITY
IN THE UNITED STATES AND ITS EFFECTS

THE ABSOLUTE SOVEREIGNTY OF the will of the majority is the essence of democratic government, for in democracies there is nothing outside the majority capable of resisting it.

Most American state constitutions have sought further artificially to increase this natural strength of the majority.[1]

Several particular circumstances also tend to make the power of the majority not only predominant but irresistible.

The moral authority of the majority is partly based on the notion that there is more enlightenment and wisdom in a numerous assembly than in a single man, and the number of the legislators is more important than how they are chosen. It is the theory of equality applied to brains.

Under the old monarchy the French took it as a maxim that the king could do no wrong, and when he did do wrong, they thought the fault lay with his advisers. This made obedience much easier. One could grumble against the law without ceasing to love and respect the lawgiver. The Americans take the same view of the majority.

The moral authority of the majority is also founded on the principle that the interest of the greatest number should be preferred to that of those who are fewer. But as men equal among themselves came to people the United States, there is as yet no natural or permanent antagonism between the interests of the various in-

---

1. In examining the federal Constitution we have seen that the lawgivers of the Union strove in the opposite direction. The result of their efforts has been to make the federal government more independent in its sphere than are the states in theirs. But the federal government is hardly concerned with anything except foreign affairs; it is the state governments which really control American society.

habitants, and all the parties are ready to recognize the rights of the majority because they all hope one day to profit themselves by them.

Hence the majority in the United States has immense actual power and a power of opinion which is almost as great. When once its mind is made up on any question, no obstacles can retard, much less halt, its progress and give it time to hear the wails of those it crushes as it passes.

The consequences of this state of affairs are fate-laden and dangerous for the future.

Tyranny of the Majority

I regard it as an impious and detestable maxim that in matters of government the majority of a people has the right to do everything, and nevertheless I place the origin of all powers in the will of the majority. Am I in contradiction with myself?

There is one law which has been made, or at least adopted, not by the majority of this or that people, but by the majority of all men. That law is justice.

Justice therefore forms the boundary to each people's right.

Consequently, when I refuse to obey an unjust law, I by no means deny the majority's right to give orders; I only appeal from the sovereignty of the people to the sovereignty of the human race.

Some say that in matters which only concern itself, a nation cannot go completely beyond the bounds of justice and reason, and that there is therefore no need to fear giving total power to the majority representing it. But that is the language of a slave.

What is a majority, in its collective capacity, if not an individual with opinions, and usually with interests, contrary to those of another individual, called the minority? Now, if you admit that a man vested with omnipotence can abuse it against his adversaries, why not admit the same concerning a majority? For my part, I will never grant to several that power to do everything which I refuse to a single man.

Omnipotence in itself seems a bad and dangerous thing. Its exercise is beyond man's strength. Only God can be omnipotent without danger, because His wisdom and justice are always equal to His power. So there is no power on earth in itself so worthy or sacred that I would wish to let it act without control and dominate without obstacles. So when I see the right and capacity to do all given to any authority whatsoever, whether it be called people or king, democracy or aristocracy, and whether the scene of action is a monarchy or a republic, I say: the germ of tyranny is there, and I will go look for other laws under which to live.

My greatest complaint against democratic government as organized in the United States is not, as many Europeans make out, its weakness, but rather its irresistible strength. What I find most repulsive in America is not the extreme freedom reigning there but the shortage of guarantees against tyranny.

When a man or a party suffers an injustice in the United States, to whom can he turn? To public opinion? That is what forms the majority. To the legislative body? It represents the majority and obeys it blindly. To the executive power? It is appointed by the majority and serves as its passive instrument. To the police? They are nothing but the majority under arms. A jury? The jury is the majority vested with the right to pronounce judgment; even the judges in certain states are elected by the majority. So, however iniquitous or unreasonable the measure which hurts you, you must submit.[2]

---

2.   At Baltimore during the War of 1812 there was a striking example of the despotism of the majority. At that time the war was very popular at Baltimore. A newspaper which came out in strong opposition to it aroused indignation. The people assembled, broke the presses, and attacked the house of the editors. An attempt was made to summon the militia, but it did not respond. Finally, to save the lives of those threatened by the fury of the public, they were taken to prison like criminals. During the night the people assembled again; the prison was broken open; one of the journalists was killed on the spot and the others left for dead; the guilty were brought before a jury and acquitted.

I once said to a Pennsylvanian: "Please explain to me why in a state founded by Quakers and renowned for its tolerance, freed Negroes are not allowed to use their rights as citizens? They pay taxes; is it not right that they should vote?"

"Do not insult us," he replied, "by supposing that our legislators would commit an act of such gross injustice and intolerance."

I am not asserting that at the present time in America there are frequent acts of tyranny. I do say that one can find no guarantee against it there and that the reasons for the government's gentleness must be sought in circumstances and in mores rather than in the laws.

The Power Exercised by the Majority in America over Thought

It is when one comes to look into the use made of thought in the United States that one most clearly sees how far the power of the majority goes beyond all powers known to us in Europe.

Thought is an invisible power and one almost impossible to lay hands on, which makes sport of all tyrannies. In our day the most absolute sovereigns in Europe cannot prevent certain thoughts hostile to their power from silently circulating in their states and even in their own courts.

It is not like that in America; while the majority is in doubt, one talks; but when it has irrevocably pronounced, everyone is silent, and friends and enemies alike seem to make for its bandwagon. The reason is simple: no monarch is so absolute that he can control all the forces of society and overcome all resistance, as a majority invested with the right to make the laws and to execute them, can do.

"So, with you, Negroes do have the right to vote?"

"Certainly."

"Then how was it that at the electoral college this morning I did not see a single one of them in the meeting?"

"That is not the fault of the law," said the American. "It is true that Negroes have the right to be present at elections, but they voluntarily abstain from appearing."

"That is extraordinarily modest of them."

"Oh! It is not that they are reluctant to go there, but they are afraid they may be maltreated. With us it sometimes happens that the law lacks force when the majority does not support it. Now, the majority is filled with the strongest prejudices against Negroes, and the magistrates do not feel strong enough to guarantee the rights granted to them by the lawmakers."

"What! The majority, privileged to make the law, wishes also to have the privilege of disobeying the law?"

Moreover, a king's power is physical only, controlling actions but not influencing desires, whereas the majority is invested with both physical and moral authority, which acts as much upon the will as upon behavior and at the same moment prevents both the act and the desire to do it.

I know no country in which, speaking generally, there is less independence of mind and true freedom of discussion than in America.

In America the majority has enclosed thought within a formidable fence. A writer is free inside that area, but woe to the man who goes beyond it. Not that he stands in fear of an *auto-da-fé,*[3] but he must face all kinds of unpleasantness and everyday persecution. A career in politics is closed to him, for he has offended the only power that holds the keys. Those who condemn him express their views loudly, while those who think as he does, but without his courage, retreat into silence as if ashamed of having told the truth.

Princes made violence a physical thing, but our contemporary democratic republics have turned it into something as intellectual as the human will it is intended to constrain. Under the absolute government of a single man, despotism, to reach the soul, clumsily struck at the body, and the soul, escaping from such blows, rose gloriously above it; but in democratic republics that is not at all how tyranny behaves; it leaves the body alone and goes straight for the soul. The master no longer says: "Think like me or you die." He does say: "You are free not to think as I do; you can keep your life and property and all; but from this day you are a stranger among us. . . . When you approach your fellows, they will shun you as an impure being, and even those who believe in your innocence will abandon you too, lest they in turn be shunned. Go in peace. I have given you your life, but it is a life worse than death."

In the proudest nations of the Old World, works were published which faithfully portrayed the vices and absurdities of contemporaries; Molière criticized the court in plays acted before the court-

---

3.   [A public execution, by burning at the stake.]

iers. But the power which dominates in the United States does not understand being mocked like that. The least reproach offends it, and the slightest sting of truth turns it fierce; and one must praise everything, from the turn of its phrases to its most robust virtues. No writer, no matter how famous, can escape from this obligation to sprinkle incense over his fellow citizens. Hence the majority lives in a state of perpetual self-adoration; only strangers or experience may be able to bring certain truths to the Americans' attention.

We need seek no other reason for the absence of great writers in America so far; literary genius cannot exist without freedom of the spirit, and there is no freedom of the spirit in America.

Effects of the Majority's Tyranny on American National Character; the Courtier Spirit in the United States

The influence of what I have been talking about is as yet only weakly felt in political society, but its ill effects on the national character are already apparent. I think that the rareness now of outstanding men on the political scene is due to the ever-increasing despotism of the American majority.

When the revolution broke out, a crowd of them appeared; at that time public opinion gave direction to men's wills but did not tyrannize over them. The famous men of that time, while they freely took part in the intellectual movement of the age, had a greatness all their own; their renown brought honor to the nation, not vice versa.

Today, among the thrusting crowd of American political aspirants, very few show that virile candor and manly independence of thought which often marked the Americans of an earlier generation and which, wherever found, is the most salient feature in men of great character. At first glance one might suppose that all American minds had been fashioned after the same model, so exactly do they follow the same paths. A foreigner does, it is true, sometimes meet Americans who are not strict slaves of slogans; such men may even go as far as to point out the defects which are changing the national character and to suggest means by which this tendency could be corrected, but no one, except yourself, listens to them, and when they go down into the marketplace they use quite different language.

If these lines ever come to be read in America, I am sure of two things; first, that all readers will raise their voices to condemn me; secondly, that in the depths of their conscience many will hold me innocent.

The Greatest Danger to the American Republics Comes from the Omnipotence of the Majority

Governments ordinarily break down either through impotence or through tyranny. In the first case power slips from their grasp, whereas in the second it is taken from them.

The government of the American republics seems to me as centralized and more energetic than the absolute monarchies of Europe. So I do not think that it will collapse from weakness.[4]

If ever freedom is lost in America, that will be due to the omnipotence of the majority driving the minorities to desperation and forcing them to appeal to physical force.

President James Madison has given expression to just these thoughts. (*The Federalist*, No. 51.) [Everyman edition, pp. 266 f.]

"It is of great importance in a republic not only to guard the society against the oppression of its rulers, but to guard one part of the society against the injustice of the other part. . . . In a society under the forms of which the stronger faction can readily unite and oppress the weaker, anarchy may as truly be said to reign as in a state of nature, where the weaker individual is not secured against the violence of the stronger. . . ."

Jefferson also said: "The executive, in our government is not the sole, it is scarcely the principal, object of my jealousy. The tyranny of the legislature is the most formidable dread at present and will

---

4.   Here, and throughout this chapter, I am speaking not of the federal government but of the governments of each state, where a despotic majority is in control.

be for many years. That of the executive will come in its turn, but it will be at a remote period."[5]

I prefer to quote Jefferson rather than anybody else on this topic, regarding him as the most powerful apostle of democracy there has ever been.

8

WHAT TEMPERS THE TYRANNY OF THE MAJORITY IN THE UNITED STATES

Absence of Administrative Centralization

In all the American republics the central government is only occupied with a small number of matters important enough to attract its attention. It does not regulate society's secondary concerns and evidently has no thought or desire to do so. The majority, though increasingly absolute, has not enlarged the prerogatives of the central authority; the majority has only made the central government omnipotent within its own sphere. Thus despotism, though very oppressive on one point, cannot cover all.

Besides, however far the national majority may be carried away by its passions for its projects, it cannot make all the citizens everywhere bow to its will in the same way and at the same time. Municipal bodies and county administrations are like so many hidden reefs retarding the flood of the popular will. If the law were oppressive, liberty would still find some shelter in the way the law is executed, for the majority would not know how to enter into the

---

5. Letter from Jefferson to Madison, March 15, 1789. [Cf. *The Writings of Thomas Jefferson,* Washington, 1905, vol. 7, p. 312.]

details and, if I dare call them so, the puerilities of administrative tyranny. Indeed, it is not entirely conscious of its own power. It is only aware of its natural strength, ignorant of how art might increase its scope.

The Temper of the American Legal Profession and How It Serves to Counterbalance Democracy

Visiting Americans and studying their laws, one discovers that the prestige accorded to lawyers and their influence in the government are now the strongest barriers against the faults of democracy.

In America there are neither nobles nor men of letters, and the people distrust the wealthy. Therefore the lawyers form the political upper class and the most intellectual section of society. Consequently they stand only to lose from any innovation; this adds a conservative interest to their natural taste for order.

If you ask me where the American aristocracy is found, I have no hesitation in answering that it is not among the rich, who have no common link uniting them. It is at the bar or the bench. The legal profession forms the most powerful and, today, the only counterbalance to democracy in that country.

It is easy to discover how well adapted the legal spirit is, both by its qualities and even by its defects, to neutralize the vices inherent in popular government.

When the American people let themselves get intoxicated by their passions or carried away by their ideas, the lawyers apply an almost invisible brake which slows them down and halts them. Their aristocratic inclinations are secretly opposed to the instincts of democracy, their superstitious respect for all that is old to its love of novelty, their narrow views to its grandiose designs, their taste for formalities to its scorn of regulations, and their habit of advancing slowly to its impetuosity.

The courts are the most obvious organs through which the legal body influences democracy.

The judge is a lawyer who, apart from the taste for order and for rules imparted by his legal studies, is given a liking for stability by the permanence of his own tenure of office. His knowledge of the law in itself has assured him already high social standing among his equals, and his political power as a judge puts him in a rank apart with all the instincts of the privileged classes.

An American judge, armed with the right to declare laws unconstitutional, is constantly intervening in political affairs. He cannot compel the people to make laws, but at least he can constrain them to be faithful to their own laws and remain in harmony with themselves.

Besides, no one should imagine that in the United States a legalistic spirit is confined strictly to the precincts of the courts; it extends far beyond them.

Lawyers, forming the only enlightened class not distrusted by the people, are naturally called on to fill most public functions. The legislatures are full of them, and they head administrations; in this way they greatly influence both the shaping of the law and its execution.

There is hardly a political question in the United States which does not sooner or later turn into a judicial one. Consequently the language of everyday party-political controversy has to be borrowed from legal phraseology and conceptions. As most public men are or have been lawyers, they apply their legal habits and turn of mind to the conduct of affairs. Juries make all classes familiar with this. So legal language is pretty well adopted into common speech; the spirit of the law, born within schools and courts, spreads little by little beyond them; it infiltrates through society right down to the lowest ranks, till finally the whole people have contracted some of the ways and tastes of a magistrate.

In the United States the lawyers constitute a power which is little dreaded and hardly noticed; it has no banner of its own; it adapts itself to the exigencies of the moment and to every movement of the body social; but it enwraps the whole of society, penetrating each component class and constantly working in secret upon its unconscious patient, till in the end it has molded it to its desire.

The Jury in the United States Considered
as a Political Institution

My subject having led me to discuss the administration of justice in the United States, I shall not leave it without speaking of the jury.

To regard the jury simply as a judicial institution would be taking a very narrow view, for great though its influence is on the outcome of lawsuits, its influence on the fate of society itself is much greater still. The jury is above all a political institution.

By a "jury" I mean a certain number of citizens selected by chance and temporarily invested with the right to judge.

To use a jury to suppress crimes seems to me to introduce an eminently republican element into the government, for the following reasons:

The jury may be an aristocratic or a democratic institution, according to the class from which the jurors are selected; but there is always a republican character in it, inasmuch as it puts the real control of affairs into the hands of the ruled, puts the people themselves or at least one class of citizen on the judge's bench. Therefore the jury as an institution really puts control of society into the hands of the people.

When juries are reserved to criminal cases, the people only see them in action at long intervals and in a particular context; they do not form the habit of using them in the ordinary business of life and look on them as just a means, and not the only means, of obtaining justice.

But juries used in civil cases are constantly attracting attention; they then impinge on all interests and everyone serves on them; in that way the system infiltrates into the business of life, thought follows the pattern of its procedures, and it is hardly too much to say that the idea of justice becomes identified with it.

Juries, especially civil juries, instill some of the habits of the judicial mind into every citizen, and just those habits are the very best way of preparing people to be free.

Juries teach men equity in practice. Each man, when judging his neighbor, thinks that he may be judged himself. That is especially true of juries in civil suits; hardly anyone is afraid that he will have to face a criminal trial, but anybody may have a lawsuit.

Juries teach each individual not to shirk responsibility for his own acts, and without that manly characteristic no political virtue is possible.

Juries invest each citizen with a sort of magisterial office; they make all men feel that they have duties toward society and that they take a share in its government. By making men pay attention to things other than their own affairs, they combat that individual selfishness which is like rust in society.

Juries are wonderfully effective in shaping a nation's judgment and increasing its natural lights. That, in my view, is its greatest advantage. It should be regarded as a free school which is always open and in which each juror learns his rights, comes into daily contact with the best-educated and most-enlightened members of the upper classes, and is given practical lessons in the law, lessons which the advocate's efforts, the judge's advice, and also the very passions of the litigants bring within his mental grasp. I think that the main reason for the practical intelligence and the political good sense of the Americans is their long experience with juries in civil cases.

I do not know whether a jury is useful to the litigants, but I am sure it is very good for those who have to decide the case. I regard it as one of the most effective means of popular education at society's disposal.

The foregoing applies to all nations, but what follows especially concerns the Americans and democratic peoples in general.

I have said above that in democracies the lawyers, and the judges in particular, are the only aristocratic body that can check the people's movements. This aristocracy has no physical power but exercises its influence over men's minds. It follows that civil juries are the main source of its power.

Above all, it is the jury in civil cases that enables the American bench to make what I have called the legal spirit penetrate right down into the lowest ranks of society.

The jury is both the most effective way of establishing the people's rule and the most efficient way of teaching them how to rule.

9

THE MAIN CAUSES TENDING
TO MAINTAIN A DEMOCRATIC REPUBLIC
IN THE UNITED STATES

THE UNITED STATES GOES on being a democratic republic, and the main object of this book is to make clear the reasons for this phenomenon.

I have come to the conclusion that all the causes tending to maintain a democratic republic in the United States fall into three categories:

The first is the peculiar and accidental situation in which Providence has placed the Americans. Their laws are the second. Their habits and mores are the third.

Accidental or Providential Causes Helping
to Maintain a Democratic Republic in the United States

I have said before that I regarded the origin of the Americans, what I have called their point of departure, as the first and most effective of all the elements leading to their present prosperity. The chances of birth favored the Americans; their fathers of old brought over that equality of conditions and of mental endowments from which a democratic republic was one day to arise. But that is not all; with a republican social state they bequeathed to their descendants the habits, ideas, and mores best fitted to make a republic flourish. When I consider all that has resulted from this first fact, I think I can see the whole destiny of America contained in the first Puritan who landed on those shores.

Among the lucky circumstances that favored a democratic republic in the United States, the most important was the choice of the land itself in which the Americans live. Their fathers gave them a love of equality and liberty, but it was God who, by handing a limitless continent over to them, gave them the means of long remaining equal and free.

General prosperity favors stability in all governments, but particularly in a democratic one. When the people rule, they must be happy, if they are not to overthrow the state. With them wretchedness has the same effect as ambition has on kings. Now, the physical causes, which can lead to prosperity are more numerous in America than in any other country at any other time in history.

In the United States not legislation alone is democratic, for Nature herself seems to work for the people.

Where, among all that man can remember, can we find anything like what is taking place before our eyes in North America?

The famous societies of antiquity were all founded in the midst of enemy peoples who had to be conquered in order to take their place. Modern nations have found in some parts of South America vast lands inhabited by peoples less enlightened than themselves, but those peoples had already taken possession of the soil and were cultivating it. The newcomers, to found their states, had to destroy or enslave numerous populations, and civilization blushes at their triumphs.

But North America was only inhabited by wandering tribes who had not thought of exploiting the natural wealth of the soil. One could still properly call North America an empty continent, a deserted land waiting for inhabitants.

Everything about the Americans, from their social condition to their laws, is extraordinary; but the most extraordinary thing of all is the land that supports them.

When North America was discovered, it was as if God had held it in reserve and it had only just arisen above the waters of the flood.

There, as on the first days of creation, there are rivers whose founts never run dry and limitless fields never yet turned by the plowshare. In this condition it offers itself not to the isolated, ignorant, and barbarous man of the first ages, but to man who has already mastered the most important secrets of nature, united to his fellows, and taught by the experience of fifty centuries.

Now, at the time of writing, thirteen million civilized Europeans are quietly spreading over these fertile wildernesses whose exact resources and extent they themselves do not yet know. Three or four thousand soldiers drive the wandering native tribes before them; behind the armed men woodcutters advance, penetrating the forests, scaring off the wild beasts, exploring the course of rivers, and preparing the triumphal progress of civilization across the wilderness.

It is generally supposed that the wildernesses of America are peopled by European immigrants arriving annually on the shores of the New World; that is a great mistake. The European arriving in the United States comes without friends and often without resources; in order to live he is obliged to hire out his services, and he seldom goes beyond the great industrial zone stretching along the ocean. One cannot clear the wilderness without either capital or credit. So the European quits his hovel to go and dwell on the transatlantic coast, while the American who was born there moves off in turn into the central solitudes of America.

This double movement of immigration never halts; it starts from the depths of Europe, continues across the great ocean, and then goes on through the solitudes of the New World. Millions of men are all marching together toward the same point on the horizon; their languages, religions, and mores are different, but they have one common aim. They have been told that fortune is to be found somewhere toward the west, and they hasten to seek it.

It is hard to give an impression of the avidity with which the American throws himself on the vast prey offered him by fortune. To pursue it he fearlessly braves the arrows of the Indian and the diseases of the wilderness; he faces the silence of the forest and is not afraid of wild beasts. A passion stronger than love of life goads him on. An almost limitless continent stretches before him, and he seems in such a hurry that one might think him afraid of finding no room left.

I have spoken about emigration from the older states, but what should one say about that from the new? Ohio was only founded fifty years ago, most of its inhabitants were not born there, its capital is not thirty years old, and an immense stretch of unclaimed wilderness still covers its territory; nevertheless, the population of Ohio has already started to move west; most of those who come down to the fertile prairies of Illinois were inhabitants of Ohio. These men had left their first fatherland to better themselves; they leave the second to do better still. To start with, emigration was a necessity for them; now it is a sort of gamble, and they enjoy the sensations as much as the profit.

Sometimes man advances so quickly that the wilderness closes in again behind him. The forest has only bent beneath his feet and springs up again when he has passed. Traveling through the new states of the West, one often finds abandoned houses in the middle of the forest, ruined cabins in the remotest solitude, and, to one's astonishment, attempts at clearings, bearing witness alike to the power and the fickleness of man.

In Europe we habitually regard a restless spirit, immoderate desire for wealth, and an extreme love of independence as great social dangers. But precisely those things assure a long and peaceful future for the American republics. Without such restless passions the population would be concentrated around a few places and would soon experience, as we do, needs which are hard to satisfy. What a happy land the New World is, where man's vices are almost as useful to society as his virtues!

This exercises a great influence over the way human actions are judged in the two hemispheres. What we call love of gain is praiseworthy industry to the Americans, and they see something of a cowardly spirit in what we consider moderation of desires.

In France we regard simple tastes, quiet mores, family feeling, and love of one's birthplace as great guarantees for the tranquility and happiness of the state. But in America nothing seems more prejudicial to society than virtues of that sort. The French of Canada, who loyally preserve the tradition of their ancient mores, are already finding it difficult to live on their land, and this small nation which has only just come to birth will soon be a prey to all the afflictions of old nations. The most enlightened, patriotic, and humane men in Canada make extraordinary efforts to render people dissatisfied with the simple happiness that still contents them.

In America, new wants are not to be feared, for there all wants can easily be satisfied; there is no need to dread the growth of excessive passions, for there is healthy food easily available to feed them all; men there cannot have too much freedom, for they are hardly ever tempted to make ill use thereof.

The present-day American republics are like companies of merchants formed to exploit the empty lands of the New World, and prosperous commerce is their occupation.

Americans carry a trader's habits over into the business of politics. They like order, without which affairs do not prosper, and they set an especial value on regularity of mores, which are the foundation of a sound business. They prefer good sense, which creates fortunes, to genius which often dissipates them. Their minds, accustomed to definite calculations, are frightened by general ideas; and they hold practice in greater honor than theory.

One must go to America to understand the power of material prosperity over political behavior, and even over opinions too, though those should be subject to reason alone. It is the foreigners who best illustrate this. Occasionally in the United States I met Europeans who had been forced to leave their country on account of their political opinions. The conversation of all of them astonished me, but one most of all. As I was passing through one of the remotest parts of Pennsylvania, I was overtaken by night and asked for hospitality at the house of a rich planter. He was French. He welcomed me to his fireside, and we began to talk with the freedom suitable to people meeting in the depths of the forest two thousand leagues from their native land. I was aware that my host had been a great leveler and an ardent demagogue forty years before, for his name had left a mark on history.

It was therefore strange and astonishing to hear him talk like an economist—I almost said a landowner—about the rights of property; he spoke of the necessary hierarchy that wealth establishes among men, of obedience to law, of the influence of good mores in republics, and of the support to order and freedom afforded by religious ideas; and it even happened that he inadvertently quoted the authority of Jesus Christ in support of one of his political opinions.

I listened and marveled at the feebleness of human reason. A thing is true or false; but how can one find out amid the uncertainties of knowledge and the diverse lessons of experience? A new fact may come and remove all my doubts. I was poor, and now, look, I am rich; if only prosperity, while affecting my conduct, would leave my judgment free! In fact, my opinions do change with my fortune, and lucky circumstances prompt that decisive argument I could not find before.

Prosperity's influence operates even more freely over Americans than over foreigners. The American has always seen order and prosperity marching in step; it never strikes him that they could be separate; consequently he has nothing to forget and has no need to unlearn, as Europeans must, the lessons of his early education.

Influence of the Laws upon the Maintenance of a Democratic Republic in the United States

The main object of this book has been to make American laws known. If my whole book has not achieved this, much less will this chapter do so.

I do not therefore want to go back over old ground, and a few lines of recapitulation will be enough.

Three factors seem to contribute more than all others to the maintenance of a democratic republic in the New World.

The first is the federal form adopted by the Americans, which allows the Union to enjoy the power of a great republic and the security of a small one.

The second are communal institutions which moderate the despotism of the majority and give the people both a taste for freedom and the skill to be free.

The third is the way the judicial power is organized. I have shown how the courts correct the aberrations of democracy and how, though they can never stop the movements of the majority, they do succeed in checking and directing them.

Influence of Mores upon the Maintenance of a Democratic Republic in the United States

I here mean the term *mores* (*moeurs*) to have its original Latin meaning; I mean it to apply not only to *moeurs* in the strict sense, which might be called the habits of the heart, but also to the different notions possessed by men, the various opinions current among them, and the sum of ideas that shape mental habits.[1]

So I use the word to cover the whole moral and intellectual state of a people. It is not my aim to describe American mores; just now I am only looking for the elements in them which help to support political institutions.

Religion Considered as a Political Institution and How It Powerfully Contributes to the Maintenance of a Democratic Republic Among the Americans

Most of English America was peopled by men who, having shaken off the pope's authority, acknowledged no other religious supremacy; they therefore brought to the New World a Christianity which I can only describe as democratic and republican. From the start

---

1. [The word *moeurs* signified a central theme for Tocqueville, but beyond his famous reference to "habits of the heart," he used the word in myriad senses that are difficult to convey. The modern term *mores* suggests this range, but it should be read in context. *Moeurs* has sometimes been translated as *customs* or *manners*, but according to historians, "Tocqueville himself tried to render the meaning more precise than when it appeared in common French usage, where it might mean, depending on context," anything "from loosely defined habits to an absolute moral code which distinguish a nation or a cultural group." Lynn L. Marshall and Seymour Drescher, "American Historians and Tocqueville's *Democracy*," *Journal of American History* 55 (December 1968): pp. 512–532, esp. 524 n. 33.]

politics and religion agreed, and they have not since ceased to do so.

About fifty years ago Ireland began to pour a Catholic population into the United States. Also American Catholicism made converts. There are now in the United States more than a million Christians professing the truths of the Roman Church.

These Catholics are very loyal in the practice of their worship and full of zeal and ardor for their beliefs. Nevertheless, they form the most republican and democratic of all classes in the United States. At first glance this is astonishing, but reflection easily indicates the hidden causes therefore.

Most of the Catholics are poor, and unless all citizens govern, they will never attain to the government themselves. The Catholics are in a minority, and it is important for them that all rights should be respected so that they can be sure to enjoy their own in freedom. For these two reasons they are led, perhaps in spite of themselves, toward political doctrines which, maybe, they would adopt with less zeal were they rich and predominant.

The Catholic clergy in the United States has made no effort to strive against this political tendency but rather seeks to justify it. American Catholic priests have divided the world of the mind into two parts; in one are revealed dogmas to which they submit without discussion; political truth finds its place in the other half, which they think God has left to man's free investigation. Thus American Catholics are both the most obedient of the faithful and the most independent citizens.

Therefore one can say that there is not a single religious doctrine in the United States hostile to democratic and republican institutions. All the clergy there speak the same language; opinions are in harmony with the laws, and there is, so to say, only one mental current.

Indirect Influence of Religious Beliefs
upon Political Society in the United States

Among the Anglo-Americans there are some who profess Christian dogmas because they believe them and others who do so because they are afraid to look as though they did not believe. So Christianity reigns without obstacles, by universal consent; consequently, as I have said elsewhere, everything in the moral field is certain and fixed, although the world of politics seems given over to argument and experiment.

Nature and circumstances have made the inhabitant of the United States a bold man, as is sufficiently attested by the enterprising spirit with which he seeks his fortune. If the spirit of the Americans were free of all impediment, one would soon find among them the boldest innovators and the most implacable logicians in the world. But American revolutionaries are obliged ostensibly to profess a certain respect for Christian morality and equity, and that does not allow them easily to break the laws when those are opposed to the executions of their designs; nor would they find it easy to surmount the scruples of their partisans even if they were able to get over their own.

Thus, while the law allows the American people to do everything, there are things which religion prevents them from imagining and forbids them to dare.

Religion, which never intervenes directly in the government of American society, should therefore be considered as the first of their political institutions, for although it did not give them the taste for liberty, it singularly facilitates their use thereof.

The inhabitants of the United States themselves consider religious beliefs from this angle. I do not know if all Americans have faith in their religion—for who can read the secrets of the heart?—but I am sure that they think it necessary to the maintenance of republican institutions. That is not the view of one class or party among the citizens, but of the whole nation; it is found in all ranks.

While I was in America, a witness called at the county court of Chester (state of New York) declared that he did not believe in the existence of God and the immortality of the soul. The judge refused to allow him to be sworn in, on the ground that the witness had destroyed beforehand all possible confidence in his testimony. Newspapers reported the fact without comment.[2]

For the Americans the ideas of Christianity and liberty are so completely mingled that it is almost impossible to get them to conceive of the one without the other; it is not a question with them of sterile beliefs bequeathed by the past and vegetating rather than living in the depths of the soul.

I have known Americans to form associations to send priests out into the new states of the West and establish schools and churches there; they fear that religion might be lost in the depths of the forest and that the people growing up there might be less fitted for freedom than those from whom they sprang. I have met rich New Englanders who left their native land in order to establish the fundamentals of Christianity and of liberty by the banks of the Missouri or on the prairies of Illinois. You will be mistaken if you think that such men are guided only by thoughts of the future life; you will be surprised to hear them so often speaking of the goods of this world and to meet a politician where you expected to find a priest. "There is a solidarity between all the American republics," they will tell you; "if the republics of the West were to fall into anarchy or to be mastered by a despot, the republican institutions now flourishing on the Atlantic coast would be in great danger; we therefore have an interest in seeing that the new states are religious so that they may allow us to remain free."

That is what the Americans think, but our pedants find it an obvious mistake; constantly they prove to me that all is fine in Amer-

---

2.   This is how the New York *Spectator* of August 23, 1831, reported the matter: "The court of common pleas of Chester county (New York) a few days since, rejected a witness who declared his disbelief in the existence of God. The presiding judge remarked that he was not before aware that there was a man living who did not believe in the existence of God; that this belief constituted the sanction of all testimony in a court of justice; and that he knew of no cause in a Christian country, where a witness had been permitted to testify without such belief."

ica except just that religious spirit which I admire. Such men
sincerely wish to prepare mankind for liberty, but in attacking religious beliefs they obey their passions, not their interests. Despotism may be able to do without faith, but freedom cannot. Religion
is much more needed in the republic they advocate than in the
monarchy they attack, and in democratic republics most of all.
How could society escape destruction if, when political ties are relaxed, moral ties are not tightened? And what can be done with a
people master of itself, if it is not subject to God?

The Main Causes That Make
Religion Powerful in America

Eighteenth-century philosophers had a very simple explanation
for the gradual weakening of beliefs. Religious zeal, they said, was
bound to die down as enlightenment and freedom spread. The
facts do not fit this theory at all.

There are sections of the population in Europe where unbelief
goes hand in hand with brutishness and ignorance, whereas in
America the most free and enlightened people in the world zealously perform all the external duties of religion.

The religious atmosphere of the country was the first thing that
struck me on arrival in the United States. The longer I stayed in
the country, the more conscious I became of the important political consequences resulting from this novel situation.

In France I had seen the spirits of religion and of freedom
almost always marching in opposite directions. In America I found
them intimately linked together in joint reign over the same land.

My longing to understand the reason for this phenomenon increased daily.

To find this out, I questioned the faithful of all communions; I
particularly sought the society of clergymen, who are the deposi-
taries of the various creeds and have a personal interest in their
survival. As a practicing Catholic I was particularly close to the
Catholic priests; all thought that the main reason for the quiet
sway of religion over their country was the complete separation of

church and state. Throughout my stay in America I met nobody, lay or cleric, who did not agree about that.

This led me to examine more closely than before the position of American priests in political society. I was surprised to discover that they held no public appointments. There was not a single one in the administration, and I found that they were not even represented in the assemblies.

In several states the law, and in all the rest public opinion, excludes them from a career in politics.[3]

When I finally came to inquire into the attitudes of the clergy themselves, I found that most of them seemed voluntarily to steer clear of power and to take a sort of professional pride in claiming that it was no concern of theirs.

These facts convinced me that I had been told the truth. I then wondered how it could come about that by diminishing the apparent power of religion one increased its real strength.

There have been religions intimately linked to earthly governments, dominating men's souls both by terror and by faith; but when a religion makes such an alliance, I am not afraid to say that it makes the same mistake as any man might; it sacrifices the future for the present, and by gaining a power to which it has no claim, it risks its legitimate authority.

When a religion comes to uniting itself with a government, it must adopt maxims which apply only to certain nations. By allying itself with any political power, religion increases its strength over some but forfeits the hope of reigning over all.

Hence any alliance with any political power whatsoever is bound to be burdensome for religion. It does not need their support in order to live, and in serving them it may die.

---

3.   See the [1821] constitution of New York, Article 7, paragraph 4: "And whereas the ministers of the gospel are, by their profession, dedicated to the service of God and the cure of souls and ought not to be diverted from the great duties of their functions, therefore, no minister of the gospel or priest of any denomination whatever . . . be eligible to or capable of holding any civil or military office or place within this state." [Tocqueville also cites similar articles in the constitutions of North Carolina, Virginia, South Carolina, Kentucky, Tennessee, and Louisiana.]

When a nation adopts a democratic social state and communities show republican inclinations, it becomes increasingly dangerous for religion to ally itself with authority. For the time is coming when power will pass from hand to hand, political theories follow one another, and men, laws, and even constitutions vanish or alter daily, and that not for a limited time but continually.

If the Americans, who change the head of state every four years, elect new legislators every two years, and replace provincial administrators every year, and if the Americans, who have handed over the world of politics to the experiments of innovators, had not placed religion beyond their reach, what could it hold on to in the ebb and flow of human opinions? Amid the struggle of parties, where would the respect due to it be? What would become of its immortality when everything around it was perishing?

The American clergy were the first to perceive this truth and to act in conformity with it. They saw that they would have to give up religious influence if they wanted to acquire political power.

In America religion is perhaps less powerful than it has been at certain times and among certain peoples, but its influence is more lasting. It restricts itself to its own resources, of which no one can deprive it; it functions in one sphere only, but it pervades it and dominates there without effort.

How the Enlightenment, Habits, and Practical Experience of the Americans Contribute to the Success of Democratic Institutions

So far America has had only a very small number of noteworthy writers, no great historians, and not a single poet. The inhabitants have a sort of prejudice against anything really worthy of the name of literature, and there are towns of the third rank in Europe which yearly publish more literary works than all the twenty-four states of the Union put together.

The spirit of the Americans is averse to general ideas and does not seek theoretical discoveries. New laws are continually made in the United States, but there have not yet been great writers there inquiring into the general principles of the laws.

The same is true for the mechanical arts.

America is an industrial society but does not cultivate the science of industry. There are good workmen but few inventors. Fulton long hawked his genius in foreign lands before he was given a chance to devote it to his own.

Anyone trying to find out how enlightened the Anglo-Americans are is liable to see the same phenomenon from two different angles. If his attention is concentrated on the learned, he will be astonished how few they are; but if he counts the uneducated, he will think the Americans the most enlightened people in the world.

The whole population falls between these two extremes, as I have noted elsewhere.

In New England every citizen is instructed in the elements of human knowledge; he is also taught the doctrine of his religion; he must know the history of his country and the main features of its Constitution. In Connecticut and Massachusetts you will very seldom find a man whose knowledge of all these things is only superficial, and anybody completely unaware of them is quite an oddity.

But the farther one goes to the west or the south, the less public education is found. In the states bordering the Gulf of Mexico one may find, as with us, a certain number of individuals uninstructed in the rudiments of human knowledge, but one would search in vain through the United States for a single district sunk in complete ignorance. There is a simple reason for this: the peoples of Europe started from darkness and barbarism to advance toward civilization and enlightenment. Their progress has been unequal: some have run ahead, while others have done no more than walk; there are some who have halted and are still sleeping by the roadside.

Nothing like that happened in the United States.

The Anglo-Americans were completely civilized when they arrived. It is the children of these same Americans who yearly move forward into the wilderness, bringing their knowledge and a re-

spect for learning. Education has made them realize the usefulness of enlightenment and put them in a position to pass this
enlightenment on to their children. So in the United States, society had no infancy, being born adult.

The Americans never use the word *peasant* because the idea is
unknown; the ignorance of primitive times, rural simplicity, and
rustic villages has not been preserved with them.

At the extreme border, where society and wilderness meet, there
is a population of bold adventurers who, to escape the poverty
threatening them in their fathers' homes, have dared to plunge
into the solitudes of America. As soon as the pioneer reaches his
place of refuge, he hastily fells a few trees and builds a log cabin in
the forest. Nothing could look more wretched than these isolated
dwellings. The traveler approaching one toward evening sees the
hearth fire flicker through the chinks in the walls. Who would not
suppose that this poor hut sheltered some rude and ignorant folk?
But one should not assume any connection between the pioneer
and the place that shelters him. All his surroundings are primitive
and wild, but he is the product of eighteen centuries of labor and
experience. He wears the clothes and talks the language of a town;
he is aware of the past, curious about the future, and ready to
argue about the present; he is a very civilized man prepared for a
time to face life in the forest, plunging into the wildernesses of the
New World with his Bible, ax, and newspapers.

It is hard to imagine quite how incredibly quickly ideas circulate
in these empty spaces.[4]

I do not believe that there is so much intellectual activity in the
most enlightened and populous districts of France.

---

4.   I traveled through part of the frontier districts of the United States in a sort of
open cart called the mail coach. We went at a great pace day and night along roads
that had only just been cleared through immense forests of green trees; when the
darkness became impenetrable, our driver set fire to branches of larch, by whose
light we continued our way. From time to time we came to a hut in the forest; that was
the post office. The mail dropped an enormous bundle of letters at the door of this
isolated dwelling, and we went galloping on again, leaving each inhabitant of the
neighborhood to come and fetch his share of that treasure.

It cannot be doubted that in the United States the instruction of the people powerfully contributes to support the democratic republic.

But I would not exaggerate this advantage and am very far from thinking, as many people in Europe do think, that to teach men to read and write is enough to make them good citizens immediately.

True enlightenment is in the main born of experience, and having lived much among the people in the United States, I cannot say how much I admire their experience and their good sense.

Do not lead an American on to talk about Europe; he will usually stick to those general ideas which, in all countries, are such a comfort to the ignorant. But ask him about his own country and his thought and his language will become plain, clear, and precise. He will tell you what his rights are and what means he can use to exercise them. The citizen of the United States has not obtained his practical knowledge and his positive notions from books; his literary education has prepared him to receive them but has not furnished them.

It is by taking a share in legislation that the American learns to know the law; it is by governing that he becomes educated about the formalities of government. The great work of society is daily performed before his eyes, and so to say, under his hands.

The Laws Contribute More to the Maintenance of the Democratic Republic in the United States Than Do the Physical Circumstances of the Country, and Mores Do More Than the Laws

I have said that the maintenance of democratic institutions in the United States must be attributed to circumstances, laws, and mores.[5]

Most Europeans are aware of the first of these three causes only and give it an undue importance.

---

5. I would remind the reader of the general sense in which I use the word *mores*: to cover the sum of the moral and intellectual dispositions of men in society.

It is true that the Anglo-Americans brought equality of conditions with them to the New World.

But that fact was by no means peculiar to the United States; almost all the colonies in America were founded by men who either started as equals among themselves or became so by living there. There is not a single place in the New World where the Europeans were able to create an aristocracy.

Nevertheless, democratic institutions prosper in the United States alone.

The American Union has no enemies to fight, but geography gave the Spaniards of South America equal isolation, and that isolation has not prevented them from maintaining great armies. They have made war on one another when there were no foreigners to fight. It is only the Anglo-American democracy which has so far been able to maintain itself in peace.

The territory of the Union offers unlimited scope to human activity; but where in the world can one find more fertile wildernesses, greater rivers, and more untouched and inexhaustible riches than in South America? Nevertheless, South America cannot maintain a democracy. Even if they could not enjoy the same happiness as the United States, they ought at least to be the envy of Europe. Yet there are no nations on earth more miserable than those of South America.

Thus physical causes not only fail to produce analogous results in South and in North America, but in the former land they cannot even bring the population up to the European level, though in Europe geography is unfavorable.

Therefore physical causes do not influence the destiny of nations as much as is supposed.

Other nations in America have the same opportunities for prosperity as the Anglo-Americans, but not their laws or mores, and these nations are wretched. So the laws and mores of the Anglo-Americans are the particular and predominant causes, which I have been seeking, of their greatness.

A great part of the success of democratic government must be attributed to these good American laws, but while they have more influence on American social happiness than the nature of the country, I still have reasons for thinking that mores are even more important.

Almost everyone living within the Union is sprung from the same stock. They all speak the same language, pray to God in the same fashion, are subject to the same material conditions, and obey the same laws.

From what, then, do the obvious differences between them spring?

Why, in the East of the Union, is republican government strong and orderly, proceeding with mature deliberation?

On the other hand, in the West, why is the conduct of public affairs so disorderly, passionate, and, one might almost say, feverish?

I am no longer comparing the Americans to foreign nations, but contrasting some Anglo-Americans with others and trying to find out why they are not alike. All arguments derived from the nature of the country and differences of laws are here irrelevant. There must be some other reason, and where can it be found if not in mores?

It is in the East that the Anglo-Americans have had the longest experience of democratic government and have formed the habits and ideas most favorable to its maintenance. Their customs, opinions, and behavior have been gradually penetrated by democracy, and this shows in every detail of social life, as much as in the laws. It is in the East that both literary and practical education have been carried furthest, and it is there that religion and freedom are most closely linked. What name can one give to all these habits, opinions, usages, and beliefs except the one I have chosen, namely, mores?

But in the West some of these advantages are still lacking. Many Americans of the western states were born in the forest, and they mix the ideas and customs of savage life with the civilization of their fathers. Passions are more violent with them, religious morality has less authority, and their convictions are less decided. There men have no control over each other, for they hardly know each other. So, to some extent, the Westerners display the inexperience and disorderly habits of a nation coming to birth.

It is their mores, then, that make the Americans of the United States, alone among Americans, capable of maintaining the rule of democracy. The importance of mores is a universal truth to which study and experience continually bring us back. It occupies the central position in my thoughts.

I have only one more word to add on this subject.

If in the course of this book I have not succeeded in making the reader feel the importance I attach to the practical experience of the Americans, to their habits, opinions, and, in a word, their mores, in maintaining their laws, I have failed in the main object of my work.

The Importance of the Foregoing in Relation to Europe

It is easy to see why I have devoted such time to the foregoing investigations. The question I raise is of interest not to the United States only, but to the whole world; not to one nation, but to all mankind.

If peoples with a democratic social state could not remain free when they live in the wilderness, one would have to despair of the future of the human race, for men are progressing rapidly toward democracy, and the wildernesses are filling up.

If it were true that laws and mores were not enough to maintain democratic institutions, what refuge would remain open to the nations if not the despotism of one man?

I know that there are many worthy persons nowadays who are not afraid of this alternative and who, tired of liberty, would like finally to rest far from its storms.

I find those very blind who think to rediscover the monarchy of Henry IV or Louis XIV. For my part, when I consider the state already reached by several European nations and that toward which all are tending, I am led to believe that there will soon be no room except for either democratic freedom or the tyranny of the caesars.

Is not this worth thinking about? If men must, in fact, come to choose between all being free or all slaves, all having equal rights or all being deprived of them, if the rulers of societies are reduced to either gradually raising the crowd up to their own level or letting all citizens fall below the level of humanity, would not that be enough to overcome many doubts?

Should we not, then, consider the gradual development of democratic institutions and mores not as the best but as the only means to remain free? And, without loving democratic government, would one not be disposed to adopt it as the readiest and most honorable remedy against the present ills of society?

It is hard to make the people take a share in government; it is even harder to provide them with the experience and to inspire them with the feelings they need to govern well.

The will of a democracy is changeable, its agents rough, its laws imperfect. I grant that. But if it is true that there will soon be nothing intermediate between the sway of democracy and the yoke of a single man, should we not rather steer toward the former than voluntarily submit to the latter? And if we must finally reach a state of complete equality, is it not better to let ourselves be leveled down by freedom rather than by a despot?

Those who, having read this book, should imagine that I am urging all nations with a democratic social state to imitate the laws and mores of the Anglo-Americans would be making a great mistake; they must have paid more attention to the form than to the substance of my thought.

My aim has been to show, by the American example, that laws and more especially mores can allow a democratic people to remain free. But I am very far from thinking that we should follow the example of American democracy, for I am well aware of the influence of the nature of a country and of antecedent events on political constitutions. I should regard it as a great misfortune for mankind if liberty were bound always and everywhere to have the same features.

But I do think that if we do not succeed in gradually introducing democratic institutions among us, and if we despair of imparting to all citizens those ideas and sentiments which first prepare them for freedom and then allow them to enjoy it, there will be no

independence left for anybody; neither for the middle classes nor
for the nobility, neither for the poor nor for the rich, but only an
equal tyranny for all. If the peaceful dominion of the majority is
not established among us in good time, we shall sooner or later
fall under the *unlimited* authority of a single man.

10

SOME CONSIDERATIONS CONCERNING THE PRESENT STATE AND PROBABLE FUTURE OF THE THREE RACES THAT INHABIT THE TERRITORY OF THE UNITED STATES

I HAVE NOW FINISHED the main task that I set myself and have, to
the best of my ability, described the laws and mores of American
democracy. I could stop here, but perhaps the reader would feel
that I had not satisfied his expectations.

There are other things in America besides an immense and
complete democracy, and the inhabitants of the New World may
be considered from more than one point of view.

In the course of this work I have been led to mention the Indians and the Negroes, but I have never had the time to stop and describe the position of these two races within the democratic nation
I was bent on depicting.

These topics are like tangents to my subject, being American,
but not democratic, and my main business has been to describe
democracy. So at first I had to leave them on one side, but now at
the end I must return to them.

It is obvious that there are three naturally distinct, one might
almost say hostile, races. Education, law, origin, and external features too have raised almost insurmountable barriers between

them; chance has brought them together on the same soil, but they have mixed without combining, and each follows a separate destiny.

Among these widely different people, the first that attracts attention, and the first in enlightenment, power, and happiness, is the white man, the European, man par excellence; below him come the Negro and the Indian.

These two unlucky races have neither birth, physique, language, nor mores in common; only their misfortunes are alike. Both occupy an equally inferior position in the land where they dwell; both suffer the effects of tyranny, and, though their afflictions are different, they have the same people to blame for them.

Seeing what happens in the world, might one not say that the European is to men of other races what man is to the animals? He makes them serve his convenience, and when he cannot bend them to his will he destroys them.

In one blow oppression has deprived the descendants of the Africans of almost all the privileges of humanity. The United States Negro has lost even the memory of his homeland; he no longer understands the language his fathers spoke; he has abjured their religion and forgotten their mores. Ceasing to belong to Africa, he has acquired no right to the blessings of Europe; he is left in suspense between two societies and isolated between two peoples, sold by one and repudiated by the other; in the whole world there is nothing but his master's hearth to provide him with some semblance of a homeland.

The Negro has no family; for him a woman is no more than the passing companion of his pleasures, and from their birth his sons are his equals.

Plunged in this abyss of wretchedness, the Negro hardly notices his ill fortune; he was reduced to slavery by violence, and the habit of servitude has given him the thoughts and ambitions of a slave; he admires his tyrants even more than he hates them and finds his joy and pride in a servile imitation of his oppressors.

His intelligence is degraded to the level of his soul.

The Negro is a slave from birth. What am I saying? He is often sold in his mother's belly and begins, so to say, to be a slave before he is born.

Devoid both of wants and of pleasures, useless to himself, his first notions of existence teach him that he is the property of another who has an interest in preserving his life; he sees that care for his own fate has not devolved on him; the very use of thought seems to him an unprofitable gift of Providence.

If he becomes free, he often feels independence as a heavier burden than slavery itself, for his life has taught him to submit to everything, except to the dictates of reason; and when reason becomes his only guide, he cannot hear its voice. A thousand new wants assail him, and he lacks the knowledge and the energy needed to resist them. Desires are masters against whom one must fight, and he has learned nothing but to submit and obey. So he has reached this climax of affliction in which slavery brutalizes him and freedom leads him to destruction.

Oppression has weighed as heavily upon the Indian tribes, but with different effects.

Before the white man's arrival in the New World, the inhabitants of North America lived tranquilly in the forests.

In its dealings with the North American Indians, the European tyranny weakened their feeling for their country, dispersed their families, obscured their traditions, and broke their chain of memories; it also changed their customs and increased their desires beyond reason, making them more disorderly and less civilized than they had been before. At the same time, the moral and physical condition of these peoples has constantly deteriorated, and in becoming more wretched, they have also become more barbarous. Nevertheless, the Europeans have not been able to change the character of the Indians entirely, and although they can destroy them, they have not been able to establish order or to subdue them.

The Negro has reached the ultimate limits of slavery, whereas the Indian lives on the extreme edge of freedom. The effect of slavery on the former is not more fatal than that of independence on the latter.

The Negro makes a thousand fruitless efforts to insinuate himself into a society that repulses him; he adapts himself to his oppressors' tastes, adopting their opinions and hoping by imitation to join their community. From birth he has been told that his race is naturally inferior to the white man and almost believing that, he holds himself in contempt. He sees a trace of slavery in his every feature, and if he could he would gladly repudiate himself entirely.

In contrast, the pretended nobility of his origin fills the whole imagination of the Indian. He lives and dies amid these proud dreams. Far from wishing to adapt his mores to ours, he regards barbarism as the distinctive emblem of his race, and in repulsing civilization he is perhaps less moved by hatred against it than by fear of resembling the Europeans.

The Negro would like to mingle with the European and cannot. The Indian might to some extent succeed in that, but he scorns to attempt it. The servility of the former delivers him over into slavery; the pride of the latter leads him to death.

I remember that, passing through the forests that still cover the state of Alabama, I came one day to the log cabin of a pioneer. I did not wish to enter the American's dwelling, but went to rest a little beside a spring not far off in the forest. While I was there, an Indian woman came up (we were in the neighborhood of the Creek territory); she was holding by the hand a little girl of five or six who was of the white race and who, I supposed, must be the pioneer's daughter. A Negro woman followed her. There was a sort of barbarous luxury in the Indian woman's dress; metal rings hung from her nostrils and ears; there were little glass beads in the hair that fell freely over her shoulders, and I saw that she was not married, for she was still wearing the bead necklace which it is the custom of virgins to lay down on the nuptial couch; the Negro was dressed in European clothes almost in shreds.

All three came and sat down by the edge of the spring, and the young savage, taking the child in her arms, lavished upon her such fond caresses as mothers give; the Negro, too, sought, by a thousand innocent wiles, to attract the little Creole's attention. The latter showed by her slightest movements a sense of superiority which contrasted strangely with her weakness and her age, as if she received the attentions of her companions with a sort of condescension.

Crouched down in front of her mistress, anticipating her every desire, the Negro woman seemed equally divided between almost maternal affection and servile fear, whereas even in the effusions of her tenderness, the savage woman looked free, proud, and almost fierce.

I had come close and was contemplating the sight in silence; no doubt my curiosity annoyed the Indian woman, for she got up abruptly, pushed the child away from her, almost roughly, and giving me an angry look, plunged into the forest.

I had often seen people of the three races inhabiting North America brought together in the same place; I had already noted very many different signs of white predominance, but there was something particularly touching in the scene I have just described; here a bond of affection united oppressors and oppressed, and nature bringing them close together made the immense gap formed by prejudices and by laws yet more striking.

The Present State and the Probable Future of the Indian Tribes Inhabiting the Territory of the Union

All the Indian tribes who once inhabited the territory of New England—the Narragansetts, the Mohicans, the Pequots—now live only in men's memories; the Lenapes, who received Penn one hundred and fifty years ago on the banks of the Delaware, have now vanished. I have met the last of the Iroquois; they were begging. All of the nations I have just named once reached to the shores of the ocean; now one must go more than a hundred leagues inland to meet an Indian. These savages have not just drawn back, they have been destroyed.[1]

---

1.   In the thirteen original states there are only 6,373 Indians left. (See *Legislative Documents*, 20th Congress, [Second Session], No. 117, p. 20 [?].)

It is easy to show how this destruction came about.

When the Indians alone dwelt in the wilderness from which now they are driven, their needs were few. They made their weapons themselves, the water of the rivers was their only drink, and the animals they hunted provided them with food and clothes.

The Europeans introduced firearms, iron, and brandy among the indigenous population of North America; they taught it to substitute our cloth for the barbaric clothes which had previously satisfied Indian simplicity. In return for these goods, which they did not know how to make, the savages could offer nothing but the rich furs still abounding in their forests. From that time forward hunting had to provide not only for their own needs but also for the frivolous passions of Europe. They no longer hunted for forest animals simply for food, but in order to obtain the only things they could barter with us.[2]

While the needs of the natives were thus increasing, their resources were constantly diminishing.

As soon as a European settlement forms in the neighborhood of territory occupied by the Indians the wild game takes fright.[3]

---

2.   Mr. [William] Clark and Mr. [Lewis] Cass, in their *Report to Congress* [Second Session, House of Representatives, No. 117], February 4, 1829, p. 23 f., said that:

"The time is already far away from us when the Indians could produce the objects necessary for their nourishment and clothing without resorting to the industry of civilized men. Beyond the Mississippi, in a country where one still finds immense herds of buffalo, live Indian tribes which follow these wild animals in their migrations; the Indians of whom we are speaking still find the means of living in conforming to all the customs of their fathers; but the buffalo are constantly retreating. Now, only with guns or traps can one reach wild animals of a smaller species, such as the bear, the deer, the beaver, the muskrat, which particularly supply the Indian with what is necessary for the maintenance of life, . . . and so there are many of them who die of hunger each winter." [Tocqueville paraphrases. Pennsylvania congressman William Clark (1774–1851) is not to be confused with "Captain" William Clark (1770–1838) of the Lewis and Clark Expedition.]

3.   "Five years ago," says Volney in his *Tableau des États-Unis*, p. 370, going from Vincennes to Kaskaskia, territory now included in the state of Illinois, but then completely wild (1797), "one could not cross the prairies without seeing herds of four or five hundred buffalo; but now there are none. They have swum across the Mississippi, disturbed by the hunters, but even more by the bells of the American cattle." [C.-F. Volney, *Tableau du Climat et du Sol des États-Unis d'Amérique*, Paris, 1822, p. 370.]

Thousands of savages wandering in the forest without fixed dwelling did not disturb it; but as soon as the continuous noise of European labor is heard in the vicinity, it begins to flee and retreat toward the west, where some instinct teaches it that it will still find limitless wildernesses. In their report to Congress of February 4, 1829, Messrs. Clark and Cass say: "The herds of bison are constantly retreating; several years ago they were approaching the foot of the Alleghenies; in a few years it will perhaps be difficult to see any of them in the immense plains that stretch the length of the Rocky Mountains." I have been assured that this effect of the approach of the white men is often felt at two hundred leagues distance from their frontier. So their influence is exerted over tribes whose names they hardly know and who suffer the ills of usurpation long before they see the authors of their distress.

Hardy adventurers soon penetrate into the Indian country; they go fifteen or twenty leagues beyond the white man's extreme frontier, and there build a dwelling for a civilized man in the midst of barbarism. It is easy for them to do so: a hunting people's boundaries are ill-defined. Moreover, the land is the common property of the tribe and does not exactly belong to anybody in particular; therefore no one has an individual interest in defending any part of it.

Instinctive love of country holds them to the soil where they were born,[4] but there is nothing but affliction and death there. At last they come to a decision; they depart, and following the tracks of elk, buffalo, and beaver, leave to these wild animals the choice of their new homeland. So, strictly speaking, it is not the Europeans who chase the natives of America away, but famine.

It is impossible to imagine the terrible afflictions involved in these forced migrations. The Indians leaving their ancestral

---

4.   On page 15 of their *Report to Congress* Messrs. Clark and Cass say that the Indians are attached to their country by the same feelings of affection as we are to ours; and moreover, they attach to the idea of alienating the land which the Great Spirit granted to their ancestors certain superstitious ideas which greatly influence the tribes who have still ceded nothing, or only a small portion of their territory, to the Europeans. "We will not sell the spot which contains the bones of our fathers"—that is the first answer they always make to anybody proposing to buy their land.

fields are already worn down and exhausted. The country in which they intend to live is already occupied by tribes and who regard newcomers jealously. There is famine behind them, war in front, and misery everywhere. Their homeland has already been lost, and soon they will have no people; families hardly remain together; the common name is lost, the language forgotten, and traces of their origin vanish. The nation has ceased to exist. With my own eyes I have seen some of the miseries just described; I have witnessed afflictions beyond my powers to portray.

At the end of the year 1831 I was on the left bank of the Mississippi, at the place the Europeans called Memphis. While I was there a numerous band of Choctaws (or Chactas as they are called by the French of Louisiana) arrived; these savages were leaving their country and seeking to pass over to the right bank of the Mississippi, where they hoped to find an asylum promised to them by the American government. It was then the depths of winter, and that year the cold was exceptionally severe; the snow was hard on the ground, and huge masses of ice drifted on the river. The Indians brought their families with them; there were among them the wounded, the sick, newborn babies, and the old men on the point of death. They had neither tents nor wagons, but only some provisions and weapons. I saw them embark to cross the great river, and the sight will never fade from my memory. Neither sob nor complaint rose from that silent assembly. Their afflictions were of long standing, and they felt them to be irremediable. All the Indians had already got into the boat that was to carry them across; their dogs were still on the bank; as soon as the animals finally realized that they were being left behind forever, they all together raised a terrible howl and plunged into the icy waters of the Mississippi to swim after their masters.

Nowadays the dispossession of the Indians is accomplished in a regular and, so to say, quite legal manner.

When the European population begins to approach the wilderness occupied by a savage nation, the United States government usually sends a solemn embassy to them; the white men assemble the

Indians in a great plain, and after they have eaten and drunk with them, they say: "What have you to do in the land of your fathers? Soon you will have to dig up their bones in order to live. In what way is the country you dwell in better than another? Are there not forests and marshes and prairies elsewhere, and can you live nowhere but under your own sun? Beyond these mountains that you see on the horizon, there are vast countries where wild beasts are still found in abundance; sell your lands to us and go and live happily in those lands." That speech finished, they spread before the Indians firearms, woolen clothes, kegs of brandy, glass necklaces, pewter bracelets, earrings, and mirrors.[5] If, after the sight of all these riches, they still hesitate, it is hinted that they cannot refuse to consent to what is asked of them and that soon the government itself will be powerless to guarantee their rights. What can they do? Half convinced, half constrained, the Indians go off to dwell in new wildernesses, where the white men will not let them remain in peace for ten years. In this way the Americans cheaply acquire whole provinces which the richest sovereigns in Europe could not afford to buy.[6]

---

5.   See *Legislative Documents*, 20th Congress, No. 117 [p. 15 f.; Tocqueville summarizes], for an account of what happens in these circumstances. This curious record is found in the already cited *Report to Congress* of Messrs. Clark and Lewis Cass of February 4, 1829. Mr. Cass is now secretary of war. "When the Indians arrive in the place where the treaty is to take place, they are poor and almost naked. There they see and examine a large number of objects which are precious to them, which the American merchants have been careful to bring along. The women and children who wish to have their needs provided for . . . torment the men with a thousand importunate demands and employ all their influence . . . to cause the sale of land to take place. The improvidence of the Indians is habitual. . . . To provide for his immediate needs and gratify his present desires is the irresistible passion of the savage; . . . he easily forgets the past and is not concerned with the future. It would be useless to ask the Indians to cede part of their territory if one were not in a position to satisfy their needs on the spot."

6.   On May 19, 1830, Mr. Edward Everett asserted before the House of Representatives that the Americans had already acquired by *treaty* 230,000,000 acres east and west of the Mississippi.

In 1808 the Osages ceded 48,000,000 acres for a rent of $1,000.

In 1818 the Quapaws ceded 20,000,000 acres for $4,000; a territory of 1,000,000 acres was reserved for them to hunt in. A solemn oath had been given to respect this, but it was not long before that too was invaded.

On February 24, 1830, Mr. Bell, in his report to Congress of the Committee on Indian Affairs, said: "The Indians are paid for their unimproved lands as much as the

The ills I have just described are great, and I must add that they seem to me irremediable. I think that the Indian race is doomed to perish, and I cannot prevent myself from thinking that on the day when the Europeans shall be established on the coasts of the Pacific Ocean, it will cease to exist.[7]

Whatever the vices and prejudices preventing the North American Indians from becoming cultivators and civilized, necessity sometimes drives them to it.

Several considerable nations in the South, among others the Cherokees and the Creeks,[8] have found themselves practically surrounded all at once by Europeans who landed on the Atlantic coast and came simultaneously down the Ohio and up the Mississippi. These Indians were not chased from place to place, as were the Northern tribes, but had been gradually pressed within too narrow limits. The Indians, thus faced with the choice of civiliza-

---

privilege of hunting and taking games upon them is supposed to be worth. . . . To pay an Indian tribe what their ancient hunting grounds are worth to them, after the game is fled or destroyed, . . . has been found more convenient, and . . . more agreeable to the forms of Justice, as well as more merciful, than to assert the possession of them by the sword. Thus, the practice of buying Indian titles is but the substitute which humanity and expediency have imposed, in place of the sword in arriving at the actual enjoyment of property claimed by the right of discovery, and sanctioned by the natural superiority allowed to the claims of civilized communities over those of savage tribes." (*Legislative Documents*, 21st Congress, [First Session], No. 227, p. 6 [f.].)

7.   Furthermore, this opinion is shared by almost all American statesmen.

Mr. Cass told Congress that "if one judges the future by the past, one can predict a progressive diminution in the number of Indians, and one can expect the final extinction of their race. In order that this event should not take place, it would be necessary that our frontiers cease to extend, and the savages settle beyond them, or that a complete change operate in our relations with them, which would be unreasonable to expect."

8.   These nations are now contained within the states of Georgia, Tennessee, Alabama, and Mississippi.

In the South there were formerly four great nations (remnants of which still exist): the Choctaws, Chickasaws, Creeks, and Cherokees.

In 1830 the remnants of these four nations still numbered about 75,000 individuals. It is calculated that there are now about 313,130 Indians in the territory occupied or claimed by the Anglo-Americans. (See *Legislative Documents*, 20th Congress, [Second Session], No. 117, pp. 90–105.)

tion or death, became cultivators, and not entirely giving up their habits and mores, sacrificed only as much of them as was absolutely necessary to survival.

The Cherokees went further; they created a written language and established a fairly stable form of government, and since everything goes forward at an impetuous rate in the New World, they had a newspaper before they all had clothes.[9]

The success of the Cherokees proves that the Indians have the capacity to become civilized, but it by no means proves that they will succeed in this.

If the Indian tribes now dwelling in the middle of the continent could summon up energy enough to try to civilize themselves, perhaps they would succeed. Having become superior to the barbarous nations surrounding them, when the Europeans finally appeared on their borders, they would be in a position, if not to maintain their independence, at least to assert their right to the soil and to incorporate themselves with the conquerors. But the Indians' misfortune has been to come into contact with the most civilized nation in the world and I would add, the greediest, at a time when they are themselves half barbarians, having enlightenment and oppression brought to them together.

Living in freedom in the forest, the North American Indian was wretched but felt himself inferior to no man; as soon as he wants to penetrate the social hierarchy of the white men, he can only occupy the lowest rank therein, for he comes as a poor and ignorant man into a society where knowledge and wealth prevail. Having led an adventurous life, full of afflictions and dangers but also full of proud emotions, he must submit to a monotonous, obscure, and degraded existence.[10]

---

9. I have brought back to France one or two copies of this singular publication.

10. There is something in the adventurous life of a hunting people which seizes the heart of man and carries him away in spite of reason and experience. Anyone who has read [John] Tanner's *Mémoires* must be convinced of this. [*A Narrative of the Captivity and Thirty Years' Residence Among the Indians in the Interior of North America*, New York, 1830.]

The truth of this sad description can be judged by what is happening to the Creeks and Cherokees, to whom I have already alluded.

In the little that they have done, these Indians have assuredly displayed as much natural genius as the European peoples in their greatest undertakings; but nations, like men, need time to learn, whatever their intelligence or endeavors.

While these savages were laboring to civilize themselves, the Europeans continued to surround them on all sides and to hem them in more and more. Today the two races have finally met and come into contact. The Indian is already superior to his savage father but still very inferior to his white neighbor. With their resources and their knowledge, the Europeans have made no delay in appropriating most of the advantages the natives derived from possession of the soil; they have settled among them, having taken over the land or bought it cheaply, and have ruined the Indians by a competition which the latter were in no sort of position to face. Isolated within their own country, the Indians have come to form a

---

Tanner was a European who was carried off by the Indians at the age of six, and stayed for thirty years in the forests with them. Nothing can be more terrible than the afflictions he describes. He tells us of tribes without a chief, families without a nation, isolated men, the wrecks of powerful tribes, wandering at random through the ice and snow and desolate solitudes of Canada. Hunger and cold are their companions, and every day seems likely to be their last. Among such men mores have lost their sway, and traditions are powerless. Men become more and more barbarous. Tanner shares all these afflictions; he knows his European origin; it is not force that keeps him away from the white men; on the contrary, he goes every year to trade with them, enters their houses, and sees their comfort; he knows that any day that he wished to go back to civilized life he could easily do so, and he stays for thirty years in the wilderness. When he does in the end return to civilized society, he confesses that the existence whose afflictions he has described has secret charms which he cannot define; he returned to it again and again after he had left it, and only with a thousand regrets could tear himself away from so many afflictions. And when he was finally settled among the white men, several of his children refused to share his tranquility and comfort.

I myself met Tanner at the lower end of Lake Superior. He struck me as much more like a savage than a civilized man.

little colony of unwelcome foreigners in the midst of a numerous and dominating people.[11]

In one of his messages to Congress Washington said: "We are more enlightened and more powerful than the Indian nations; it behooves our honor to treat them with kindness and even generosity."

The noble and virtuous policy has not been followed.

Although the Cherokees and Creeks were established on the land where they now live before the arrival of the Europeans and although the Americans have often treated with them as with foreign nations, the states in which they are found have not been willing to recognize them as independent peoples.

If one studies the tyrannous measures adopted by the legislators of the southern states, the conduct of their governors, and the decrees of their courts, one is readily convinced that the complete expulsion of the Indians is the final objective to which all their simultaneous endeavors are directed. The Americans in this part of the Union look jealously at the lands occupied by the natives;[12] and before civilization has firmly attached them to the soil, they want to reduce them to despair and force them to go away.

---

11. See *Legislative Documents,* 21st Congress, [First Session], No. 89, for the excesses of all sorts committed by the white population in Indian territory. Sometimes the Anglo-Americans establish themselves on part of the territory, as if land were lacking elsewhere, and troops sent by Congress have to drive them out; at other times they [the whites] carry off their [the Indians'] cattle, burn their houses, cut down the natives' crops, and do them personal violence.

All these documents prove that the natives are daily the victims of abuse of force. The Union maintains an agent among the Indians with the duty of representing them; the agent with the Cherokees almost always expresses himself in terms favorable to the savages; on page 12 [of his report] he says that the intrusion of the whites into Cherokee territory "would encourage and occasion a great number of white families to rush into, and settle on, the lands, . . . to the great annoyance, distress, and ruin of the poor, helpless, and inoffensive Cherokees who inhabit them." Further on he remarks that the state of Georgia, wishing to restrict the boundaries of the Cherokees, proceeded to demarcate the frontier; the federal agent points out that the demarcation was carried out by the whites alone and consequently had no validity.

12. The inhabitants of Georgia, who find the proximity of the Indians such an inconvenience, inhabit a territory which does not at present contain more than 7 inhabitants to the square mile. In France the corresponding figure is 162.

Oppressed by the individual states, the Creeks and Cherokees appealed to the central government, and it readily resolves to let a few already half-destroyed savage tribes perish rather than put the American Union in danger.

Unable to protect the Indians, the federal government wished at least to mitigate their fate; to that end it undertook to move them elsewhere at its expense.

The government of the Union wished to transport the remnants of the native populations in the South to the part of this territory nearest Mexico, and at a great distance from the American settlements.

At the end of 1831 we were assured that ten thousand Indians had already gone down to the banks of the Arkansas; more were arriving daily. Some gladly consent to leave the abode of tyranny; the better educated refuse to leave their growing crops and new dwellings, for they think that if the process of civilization is once interrupted, it will never be resumed in still-savage country, where nothing is prepared for the subsistence of an agricultural people. Moreover, the Indians readily perceive all that is provisional about the settlement proposed for them. Who can guarantee that they will be able to remain in peace in their new asylum? The United States pledges itself to maintain them there, but the territory they now occupy was formerly secured to them by the most solemn oaths.[13] Now, the American government does not, it is true, take their land from them, but it allows encroachments on it. No doubt within a few years that same white population which is now pressing around them will again be on their tracks in the solitudes of Arkansas; then they will suffer again from the same ills without the

---

13.   This clause is found in the treaty of 1790 with the Creeks: "The United States solemnly guarantees to the Creek nation all the land it owns in the territory of the Union."

The treaty concluded in July [2nd], 1791, with the Cherokees includes the following: "The United States solemnly guarantees to the Cherokee nation all their lands not hereby ceded [Article 7]. If any citizen of the United States or other person, not being an Indian, shall settle on any of the Cherokees' lands, such person shall forfeit the protection of the United States, and the Cherokees may punish him or not, as they please (Article 8). [Cf. *Indian Treaties and Laws and Regulations Relating to Indian Affairs*, Washington, 1826, p. 117.]

same remedies; and because sooner or later there will be no land left for them, their only refuge will be the grave.

There is less of cupidity and violence in the Union's policy toward the Indians than in that of the individual states, but in both cases the governments are equally lacking in good faith.

The states, in extending what they are pleased to call the benefit of their laws over the Indians, calculate that the latter will sooner depart than submit; and the central government, when it promises these unlucky people a permanent asylum in the West, is well aware of its inability to guarantee this.[14]

In their petition to Congress[15] the Cherokees declare: "By the will of our heavenly Father, who rules the universe, the race of red men of America has become small; the white race has become large and renowned.

"When your ancestors arrived on our shores, the red man was strong, and although he was ignorant and savage, he allowed them to rest their numb feet on dry land. Our fathers and yours gave one another their hands as a sign of friendship and lived in peace.

"Everything the white man asked for to satisfy his needs, the Indian hastened to grant to him. Then the Indian was master, and the white man was supplicant. Today the scene has changed. . . .

"Here, we are the last of our race; must we also die?

"From time immemorial, our common Father, who is in heaven, has given our ancestors the land we occupy; our ancestors have

---

14.   That does not prevent it from expressing its promises in the most formal terms. See the letter of March 23, 1829, from the president to the Creeks (*Proceedings of the Indian Board in the City of New York*, p. 5): "Beyond the great river Mississippi, where a part of your nation has gone, your father has provided a country large enough for all of you, but he advises you to remove to it. There your white brothers will not trouble you; they will have no claim to the land, and you can live upon it, you and all your children, as long as the grass grows or the water runs, in peace and plenty. It will be yours for ever."

The secretary of war, in a letter of April 18, 1829, to the Cherokees, declares that they must not hope to retain the land they now occupy, but he gives them the same positive assurance when they shall have crossed to the other side of the Mississippi (*Ibid.*, p. 6)—as if he would then have the power now lacking to keep his promise!

15.   November 19, 1829.

transmitted it to us as their heritage. We have preserved it with respect, for it contains their ashes. Have we ever ceded or lost this heritage? Permit us to ask you humbly what better right a nation can have to a country than the right of inheritance and immemorial possession? We know that the state of Georgia and the president of the United States claim today that we have lost this right. But this seems to us to be a gratuitous allegation. At what time have we lost it? What crime have we committed which could deprive us of our homeland? Are we being reproached for having fought under the flags of the king of Great Britain in the War of Independence? If this is the crime in question, why, in the first treaty following this war, did you not declare that we had lost the ownership of our lands? Why did you not insert an article thus conceived: 'The United States wishes to grant peace to the Cherokees but to punish them for having taken part in the war; it is declared that they shall no longer be considered farmers of the soil and that they shall be subjected to departing when their neighboring states demand that they shall do so'? That was the moment to speak thus; but no one thought of it then, and our fathers never consented to a treaty whose result was to deprive them of their most sacred rights and to rob them of their country." [Tocqueville slightly summarizes; for the full text see 21st Congress, First Session, House of Representatives, No. 311, p. 7 f.]

Such is the language of the Indians; what they say is true; what they foresee seems to me inevitable.

The Spaniards let their dogs loose on the Indians as if they were wild beasts; they pillaged the New World like a city taken by storm, without discrimination or mercy.

On the other hand, the conduct of the United States toward the natives was inspired by the most chaste affection for legal formalities. They did not allow lands to be occupied unless they had been properly acquired by contract; and if by chance an Indian nation cannot live on its territory, they take them by the hand in brotherly fashion and lead them away to die far from the land of their fathers.

The Spaniards, by unparalleled atrocities which brand them with indelible shame, did not succeed in exterminating the Indian

Democracy in America

race and could not even prevent them from sharing their rights; the United States Americans have attained both these results with wonderful ease, quietly, legally, and philanthropically, without spilling blood and without violating a single one of the great principles of morality in the eyes of the world.[16] It is impossible to destroy men with more respect to the laws of humanity.

Situation of the Black Race in the United States; Dangers Entailed for the Whites by Its Presence[17]

The Indians die as they have lived, in isolation; but the fate of the Negroes is in a sense linked with that of the Europeans. The two races are bound one to the other; it is equally difficult for them to separate or unite.

The most formidable evil threatening the future of the United States is the presence of the blacks on their soil. From whatever angle one sets out to inquire into the present or future dangers facing the United States, one is almost always brought up against this fact.

Generally speaking, it requires great efforts for men to create lasting ills; but there is one evil which has percolated furtively into

---

16.   See *inter alia* the report of February 24, 1830, written by Mr. Bell on behalf of the Committee of Indian Affairs, in which on page 5 it is established by very logical arguments and most learnedly proved that: "The fundamental principle, that the Indians had no rights by virtue of their ancient possession either of soil or sovereignty, has never been abandoned either expressly or by implication."

Reading this report, written, moreover, by an able man, one is astonished at the facility and ease with which, from the very first words, the author disposes of arguments founded on natural right and reason, which he calls abstract and theoretical principles. The more I think about it, the more I feel that the only difference between civilized and uncivilized man with regard to justice is this: the former contests the justice of rights, the latter simply violates them.

17.   Before dealing with this matter, I would call the reader's attention to a book already mentioned, and soon to be published, by my traveling companion, M. Gustave de Beaumont, the main object of which is to make known in France the position of the Negroes among the white population of the United States. M. de Beaumont has plumbed the depths of a question which I need only touch upon.

the world: at first it was hardly noticed among the usual abuses of power; it began with an individual whose name history does not record and spread with the society that accepted it; that evil was slavery.

In antiquity the slave was of the same race as his master and was often his superior in education and enlightenment.[18] Only freedom kept them apart; freedom once granted, they mingled easily for the freedman was so completely like the man born free that it was soon impossible to distinguish between them.

In antiquity the most difficult thing was to change the law; in the modern world the hard thing is to alter mores, and our difficulty begins where theirs ended.

This is because in the modern world the insubstantial and ephemeral fact of servitude is most fatally combined with the physical and permanent fact of difference in race. Memories of slavery disgrace the race, and race perpetuates memories of slavery. You can make the Negro free, but you cannot prevent him facing the European as a stranger.

That is not all; this man born in degradation, this stranger brought by slavery into our midst, is hardly recognized as sharing the common features of humanity. His face appears to us hideous, his intelligence limited, and his tastes low; we almost take him for some being intermediate between beast and man.[19]

When they have abolished slavery, the moderns still have to eradicate three much more intangible and tenacious prejudices: the prejudice of the master, the prejudice of race, and the prejudice of the white.

So, those who hope that the Europeans will one day mingle with the Negroes seem to me to be harboring a delusion. I plainly see that in some parts of the country the legal barrier between the two

---

18.   It is known that several of the most celebrated authors of antiquity were or had been slaves: Aesop and Terence are among them. Slaves were not always captured from barbarian nations; war subjected very civilized men to servitude.

19.   To induce the whites to abandon the opinion they have conceived of the intellectual and moral inferiority of their former slaves, the Negroes must change, but they cannot change so long as this opinion persists.

races is tending to come down, but not that of mores: I see that slavery is in retreat, but the prejudice from which it arose is immovable.

Race prejudice seems stronger in those states that have abolished slavery than in those where it still exists, and nowhere is it more intolerant than in those states where slavery was never known.

It is true that in the North of the Union the law allows legal marriages between Negroes and whites, but public opinion would regard a white man married to a Negro woman as disgraced, and it would be very difficult to quote an example of such an event.

In almost all the states where slavery has been abolished, the Negroes have been given electoral rights, but they would come forward to vote at the risk of their lives. When oppressed, they can bring an action at law, but they will find only white men among their judges. It is true that the laws make them eligible as jurors, but prejudice wards them off. The Negro's son is excluded from the school to which the European's child goes. In the theaters he cannot for good money buy the right to sit by his former master's side; in the hospitals he lies apart. He is allowed to worship the same God as the white man but must not pray at the same altars. He has his own clergy and churches. The gates of heaven are not closed against him, but his inequality stops only just short of the boundaries of the other world. When the Negro is no more, his bones are cast aside, and some difference in condition is found even in the equality of death.

In the South, where slavery still exists, less trouble is taken to keep the Negro apart: they sometimes share the labors and the pleasures of the white men; people are prepared to mix with them to some extent; legislation is more harsh against them, but customs are more tolerant and gentle.

In the South the master has no fear of lifting the slave up to his level, for he knows that when he wants to he can always throw him down into the dust. In the North the white man no longer clearly sees the barrier that separates him from the degraded race, and he keeps the Negro at a distance all the more carefully because he fears lest one day they be confounded together.

Thus it is that in the United States the prejudice rejecting the Negroes seems to increase in proportion to their emancipation, and inequality cuts deep into mores as it is effaced from the laws.

But if the relative position of the two races inhabiting the United States is as I have described it, why is it that the Americans have abolished slavery in the North of the Union, and why have they kept it in the South and aggravated its rigors?

The answer is easy. In the United States people abolish slavery for the sake not of the Negroes but of the white men.

When a century had passed since the foundation of the colonies, an extraordinary fact began to strike the attention of everybody. The population of those provinces that had practically no slaves increased in numbers, wealth, and well-being more rapidly than those that had slaves.

The inhabitants of the former had to cultivate the ground themselves or hire another's services; in the latter they had laborers whom they did not need to pay. With labor and expense on the one side and leisure and economy on the other, nonetheless the advantage lay with the former.

This result seemed all the harder to explain since the immigrants all belonged to the same European stock, with the same habits, civilization, and laws.

As time went on, the Anglo-Americans left the Atlantic coast and plunged daily farther into the solitudes of the West. The farther they went, the clearer it became that slavery, so cruel to the slave, was fatal to the master.

But the banks of the Ohio provided the final demonstration of this truth.

The stream that the Indians had named the Ohio, or Beautiful River par excellence, waters one of the most magnificent valleys in which man has ever lived. On both banks of the Ohio stretched soil offering the cultivator inexhaustible treasures; on both banks the air is equally healthy and the climate temperate; they both form the frontier of a vast state: that on the Ohio on the left bank is called Kentucky; the other takes its name from the river itself.

There is only one difference between the two states: Kentucky allows slaves, but Ohio refuses to have them.

So the traveler who lets the current carry him down the Ohio till it joins the Mississippi sails, so to say, between freedom and slavery; and he has only to glance around him to see instantly which is best for mankind.

On the left bank of the river the population is sparse; from time to time one sees a troop of slaves loitering through half-deserted fields; the primeval forest is constantly reappearing; one might say that society had gone to sleep; it is nature that seems active and alive, whereas man is idle.

But on the right bank a confused hum proclaims from afar that men are busily at work; fine crops cover the fields; elegant dwellings testify to the taste and industry of the workers; on all sides there is evidence of comfort; man appears rich and contented; he works.[20]

The state of Kentucky was founded in 1775 and that of Ohio as much as twelve years later; twelve years in America counts for as much as half a century in Europe. Now the population of Ohio is more than 250,000 greater than that of Kentucky.[21]

On the left bank of the Ohio work is connected with the idea of slavery, but on the right with well-being and progress; on the one side it is degrading, but on the other honorable. In Kentucky, of course, the masters make the slaves work without any obligation to pay them, but they get little return from their work, whereas money paid to free workers comes back with interest from the sale of what they produce.

The free laborer is paid, but he works faster than the slave, and the speed with which work is done is a matter of great economic importance. The white man sells his assistance, but it is bought

---

20.   It is not only man as an individual who is active in Ohio; the state itself undertakes immense enterprises; the state of Ohio has constructed between Lake Erie and the Ohio a canal which connects the Mississippi Valley with the river of the North. Thanks to this canal, European merchandise arriving at New York can go by water to New Orleans, across more than five hundred leagues of the continent.

21.   The exact figures from the 1830 census are Kentucky, 688,844; Ohio, 937,679. [Cf. *Fifth Census or Enumeration of the Inhabitants of the United States, 1830,* Washington, 1832, pp. 117, 143.]

only when needed; the black can claim no money for his services, but he must be fed the whole time; he must be supported in old age as well as in the vigor of his years, in his useless childhood as well as in his productive youth, and in sickness as well as in health. So in both cases it is only by paying that one can get service; the free worker receives wages, the slave receives an upbringing, food, medicine, and clothes; the master spends his money little by little in small sums to support the slave; he scarcely notices it. The workman's wages are paid all at once and seem only to enrich the man who receives them; but in fact the slave has cost more than the free man, and his labor is less productive.[22]

The influence of slavery extends even further, penetrating the master's soul and giving a particular turn to his ideas and tastes.

On both banks of the Ohio live people with characters by nature enterprising and energetic, but these common characteristics are turned to different use on one side and the other.

The white man on the right bank, forced to live by his own endeavors, has made material well-being the main object of his existence; as he lives in a country offering inexhaustible resources to his industry and continual inducements to activity, his eagerness to possess things goes beyond the ordinary limits of human cupidity; tormented by a longing for wealth, he boldly follows every path to fortune that is open to him; he is equally prepared to turn into a sailor, pioneer, artisan, or cultivator; there is something wonderful in his resourcefulness and a sort of heroism in his greed for gain.

The American on the left bank scorns not only work itself but also enterprises in which work is necessary to success; living in idle ease, he

22. Apart from these reasons which, wherever there are plenty of free laborers, make their work more productive and economical than that of slaves, there is another reason peculiar to the United States: there is as yet only one place in the whole Union where sugar cane has been successfully cultivated, and that is on the banks of the Mississippi near its mouth on the Gulf of Mexico. In Louisiana sugar is a very profitable crop; nowhere else does labor earn so high a return; and since there is always some relation between production expenses and produce, the price of slaves is very high in Louisiana. As Louisiana is one of the states, slaves can be transported there from all parts of the Union; therefore the price paid for a slave in New Orleans raises their cost in all other markets, giving a great advantage to free laborers.

has the tastes of idle men; money has lost some of its value in his eyes; he is less interested in wealth than in excitement and pleasure and expends in that direction the energy which his neighbor puts to other use; he is passionately fond of hunting and war; he enjoys all the most strenuous forms of bodily exercise; he is accustomed to the use of weapons and from childhood has been ready to risk his life in single combat. Slavery therefore not only prevents the white men from making their fortunes but even diverts them from wishing to do so.

. The constant operation of these opposite influences throughout two centuries in the English North American colonies has in the end brought about a vast difference in the commercial capabilities of Southerners and Northerners. Today the North alone has ships, manufactures, railways, and canals.

Slavery, first introduced in the South, spread to the North, but now it is in retreat. Freedom, starting from the North, is spreading without interruption toward the South. Of all the great states Pennsylvania is now the extreme limit of slavery toward the North, but even within those limits the system is shaken; Maryland, immediately to the south of Pennsylvania, is just on the point of abolishing it, and in Virginia, which comes next to Maryland, its profitability and dangers are under discussion.[23]

In many states of the West the Negro race never made its appearance, and in all the northern states it is disappearing. So the great question of its future concerns a limited area, which makes it less frightening but not easier to solve.

The farther south one goes, the less profitable it becomes to abolish slavery. There are several physical reasons for this which need to be explained.

---

23.   There is a particular reason tending to detach these two last-mentioned states from slavery's cause.

Formerly the wealth of this part of the Union was derived mainly from growing tobacco. Slaves are especially well suited to working on that crop; it happens that for a good many years now the price of tobacco has been falling, whereas the cost of slaves remains the same. So the balance between cost of production and value of the crop has changed. And the inhabitants of Maryland and Virginia are more disposed than they would have been thirty years ago to give up the use of slaves in the tobacco fields or to give up both slavery and the cultivation of tobacco.

The first is the climate: certainly the closer they get to the tropics, the harder Europeans find it to work; many Americans maintain that below a certain latitude it is fatal for them, whereas Negroes can work there without danger;[24] but I do not think that this idea, with its welcome support for the Southerner's laziness, is based on experience. The south of the Union is not hotter than the south of Spain or of Italy.[25] Why cannot the European do the same work there? And if slavery has been abolished in Italy and Spain without the masters perishing, why should not the same happen in the Union? I do not think that nature has forbidden the Europeans of Georgia and the Floridas themselves, on pain of death, to draw their sustenance from the soil; but they would certainly be doing more troublesome work for less return than the New Englanders. Therefore, in the South free labor loses some of its superiority over the slaves and there is less advantage in abolishing slavery.

All European plants grow in the North of the Union, but the South has its own specialities.

Tobacco, cotton, and sugar cane grow in the South only and are there the main sources of the country's wealth. If they abolished slavery, the Southerners would be faced with one of these two alternatives: either they must change their system of cultivation, in which case they would find themselves in competition with the more active and experienced Northerners, or they must grow the same crops without slaves, in competition with other countries farther south that still keep theirs.[26]

---

24.   This is true where rice is cultivated. Paddy fields are unhealthy the world over, and especially so under a burning tropical sun. Europeans would find it very troublesome to cultivate the ground in that part of the New World if they were obstinately determined to grow rice. But could one not manage without paddy fields?

25.   These states are nearer to the equator than Spain or Italy is, but the American continent is very much cooler than Europe.

26.   [In 1831, slavery still existed in the Caribbean and in South America. Emancipation had occurred in the Federal Republic of Central America in 1824, in Mexico in 1829 and in Bolivia in 1831, but the institution continued in British colonies until 1838, in Uruguay until 1842, in French and Danish colonies until 1848, in Ecuador until 1851, in Peru and Venezuela until 1854, and in Dutch colonies until 1863. The Thirteenth Amendment to the U.S. Constitution ended slavery in 1865. Emancipation came later only in Puerto Rico (1873), Cuba (1886), and Brazil (1888).]

Therefore the South has particular reasons for preserving slavery, which the North has not.

But there is yet another motive more powerful than all the rest. The South could, at a pinch, abolish slavery, but how could it dispose of the blacks? The North rids itself of slavery and of the slaves in one move. In the South there is no hope of attaining this double result at the same time.

In proving that servitude is more natural and more advantageous in the South than in the North, I have given sufficient indication that the number of slaves should be much greater there. Africans were brought to the South first, and ever since then the largest numbers have been imported there. The farther south one goes, the stronger is the prejudice glorifying idleness. In the states nearest the tropics, not one white man works. So of course the Negroes are more numerous in the South than in the North. As mentioned before, this difference becomes daily greater, for as slavery is abolished at one end of the Union, the Negroes crowd into the other. So the black population grows not only by natural increase but also on account of forced emigration from the North. Much the same type of reason makes the African race increase there as makes the European population grow in the North at such a rate.

In the state of Maine there is one Negro to every three hundred of the population; in Massachusetts, one in a hundred; in the state of New York, two in a hundred; in Pennsylvania, three; in Maryland, thirty-four; in Virginia, forty-two; and finally in South Carolina, fifty-five.[27] Those were the comparative figures for the year

---

27. An American book, Carey's *Letters on the Colonization Society,* published in 1833, states that "in South Carolina, for forty years, the black race has grown faster than the white race. Taking together the population of the five states of the South which first had slaves, Maryland, Virginia, North Carolina, South Carolina, and Georgia, we discover from 1790 to 1830 the whites increased in a ratio of 80 to 100 in these states, and the blacks in a ratio of 112 to 100." [Tocqueville summarizes Carey. Cf. M. Carey, *Letters on the Colonization Society and on Its Probable Results,* Philadelphia, April 15, 1833, p. 12 f.]

In the United States in 1830 the two races were distributed as follows: states in which slavery was abolished, 6,565,434 whites, 120,520 Negroes; states in which slavery still exists, 3,960,814 whites, 2,208,102 Negroes.

1830. But the proportions are continually changing, getting less in the North and higher in the South.

It is clear that the most southern states of the Union could not abolish slavery, as has been done in the northern states, without running very great risks which did not face the latter.

So by abolishing slavery the Southerners could not succeed, as their brothers in the North have done, in advancing the Negroes gradually toward freedom; and they would be left alone to keep them in check. In the course of a few years one would have a large free Negro population among an approximately equal white population.

Those same abuses of power which now maintain slavery would then become the sources of the greatest dangers facing the southern whites. Nowadays only descendants of Europeans own the land and are absolute masters of the whole labor force; they alone are rich, educated, and armed. The black man has none of these advantages, but being a slave, he can manage without them. When he has become free and responsible for his own fate, can he be deprived of all these things and not die? What gave the white man his strength in times of slavery would expose him to a thousand dangers once slavery is abolished.

As long as the Negro is kept as a slave, he can be held in a condition not far removed from that of a beast; once free, he cannot be prevented from learning enough to see the extent of his ills and to catch a glimpse of the remedy. There is, moreover, a curious principle of relative justice very deeply rooted in the human heart. Men are much more struck by inequalities within the same class than by inequalities between classes. Slavery is understood, but how can one allow several million citizens to live under a burden of eternal infamy and hereditary wretchedness? The free Negro population in the North feels these ills and resents these injustices, but it is weak and in decline; in the South it would be numerous and strong.

Once one admits that whites and emancipated Negroes face each other like two foreign peoples on the same soil, it can easily be understood that there are only two possibilities for the future:

the Negroes and the whites must either mingle completely or they must part.

I have already expressed my conviction concerning the first possibility.[28] I do not think that the white and black races will ever be brought anywhere to live on a footing of equality.

But I think that the matter will be still harder in the United States than anywhere else. It can happen that a man will rise above prejudices of religion, country, and race, and if that man is a king, he can bring about astonishing transformations in society; but it is not possible for a whole people to rise, as it were, above itself.

Some despot subjecting the Americans and their former slaves beneath the same yoke might perhaps force the races to mingle; while American democracy remains at the head of affairs, no one would dare attempt any such thing, and it is possible to foresee that the freer the whites in America are, the more they will seek to isolate themselves.

The real link between the European and the Indian was the half-breed; in the same way, it is the mulatto who forms the bridge between black and white; everywhere where there are a great number of mulattoes, the fusion of the two races is not impossible.

There are parts of the United States where European and Negro blood are so crossed that one cannot find a man who is either completely white or completely black; but of all Europeans, the English have least mingled their blood with that of Negroes. There are more mulattoes in the South of the Union than in the North, but infinitely fewer than in any other European colony; they have no strength by themselves, and in racial disputes they generally make common cause with the whites.

---

28.   This opinion is moreover supported by authorities much more weighty than I. For instance, in Jefferson's *Memoirs* one reads: "Nothing is more certainly written in the book of fate than that these people are to be free; nor is it less certain that the two races, equally free, cannot live in the same government. Nature, habit, opinion, have drawn indelible lines of distinction between them." (See *Extracts from Jefferson's Memoirs*, by M. Conseil.) [See also *The Writings of Thomas Jefferson*, Washington, 1853, vol. 1, p. 49.]

This pride of origin, which is natural to the English, is most re-markably increased in the American by the personal pride derived from democratic liberty. The white man in the United States is proud of his race and proud of himself.

Furthermore, if whites and Negroes do not mingle in the North of the Union, how should they do so in the South?

If I absolutely had to make some guess about the future, I should say that in the probable course of things the abolition of slavery in the South would increase the repugnance felt by the white population toward the Negroes. I base this opinion on anal-ogy with what I have previously noticed in the North. White North-erners shun Negroes with all the greater care, the more legislation has abolished any legal distinction between them; why should it not be the same in the South? In the North the white man afraid of mingling with the black is frightened by an imaginary danger. In the South, where the danger would be real, I do not think the fear would be less.

Negroes are increasing faster than the whites, and if one agrees that it is impossible to foresee when blacks and whites will mingle and derive the same benefits from society, must one conclude that sooner or later in the southern states whites and blacks must come to blows?

What would be the final result of such a struggle?

If the whites of North America remain united, it is difficult to believe that the Negroes will escape the destruction threatening them; the sword or misery will bring them down. But the black populations have a chance of salvation if the struggle between the two races comes at a time when the American confederation has been dissolved. Once the federal link has been broken, the South-erners would be wrong to count on lasting support from their brothers in the North. The latter know that the danger can never reach them; if no positive duty compelled them to march to the help of the South, one may anticipate that racial sympathy would be powerless.

Whenever the struggle should come, the southern whites would enter the arena with an immense superiority in education and resources, but the blacks would have on their side numbers and the energy of despair. Those are great resources once a man has arms in his hands.

The more or less distant but inevitable danger of a conflict between the blacks and whites of the South is a nightmare constantly haunting the American imagination. The Northerners make it a common topic of conversation, though they have nothing directly to fear from it.

In the southern states there is silence; one does not speak of the future before strangers; one avoids discussing it with one's friends; each man, so to say, hides it from himself. There is something more frightening about the silence of the South than about the North's noisy fears.

Fearing the dangers which I have just described, some American citizens combined in a society with the object of transporting to the Guinea coast at their expense such free Negroes as wished to escape the tyranny weighing down upon them.[29]

In 1820 this society succeeded in founding a settlement, which it called Liberia, in Africa on the seventh degree of latitude north. The latest information is that 2,500 Negroes have already gathered there. Transported to their old country, the blacks have introduced American institutions there. Liberia has a representative system, Negro juries, Negro magistrates, and Negro clergy; there are churches and newspapers there, and by a singular reversal of fortune, whites are forbidden to settle within its walls.

This is certainly a strange caprice of fortune! Two centuries have passed since Europe first began to snatch Negroes from their families and country to transport them to the North Atlantic coast. Now the European is again busy carrying the descendants of these same Negroes across the Atlantic to settle them on that very soil from which his fathers had seized them. Barbarians have in servi-

---

29.   This society took the name of the Society for the Colonization of the Blacks. [The Society for the Colonization of Free People of Color of America, its official name, was better known as the American Colonization Society.]

tude acquired the enlightenment of civilization and learned through slavery the art of being free.

In twelve years the Colonization Society has transported 2,500 Negroes to Africa. Within the same space of time about 700,000 were born in the United States.

Were the colony of Liberia in a position to receive thousands of new inhabitants every year and if there were Negroes ready to be sent there with advantage, if the Union took the place of the society and annually devoted its wealth and its ships to sending the Negroes to Africa, it would still not be possible to counterbalance the natural increase of the black population;[30] being unable each year to carry away as many as were born, it would not even be able to halt the growth of this constantly increasing internal malady.[31]

The Negro race will never leave the American continent, to which the passions and vices of Europe brought it; it will not disappear from the New World except by ceasing to exist. The inhabitants of the United States may postpone the misfortunes they dread, but they cannot now remove their cause.

In the North there was every advantage in freeing the slaves without having anything to fear from the free Negroes. They were too few ever to claim their rights. But it is not the same in the South.

For the masters in the North slavery was a commercial and industrial question; in the South it is a question of life and death.

God protect me from trying, as certain American writers do try, to justify the principle of Negro slavery; I am only saying that all

---

30. There are many other difficulties besides in such an undertaking. If, in order to send the American Negroes to Africa, the Union started buying them from their masters, the price of Negroes, growing in proportion to their rarity, would soon reach enormous sums, and it is unbelievable that the northern states would agree to such an expense from which they would reap no benefit. If the Union seized the southern slaves by force or bought them at a low price fixed by itself, it would come up against insurmountable resistance from the states of that part of the Union. In both cases the matter would become impossible.

31. In the United States in 1830 there were 2,010,327 slaves and 319,439 emancipated blacks; in all, 2,329,766 Negroes, which is a little more than one-fifth of the total population of the United States at that time.

those who formerly accepted this terrible principle are not now equally free to get rid of it.

I confess that in considering the South I see only two alternatives for the white people living there: to free the Negroes and to mingle with them or to remain isolated from them and keep them as long as possible in slavery. Any intermediate measures seem to me likely to terminate, and that shortly, in the most horrible of civil wars, and perhaps in the extermination of one or other of the two races.

Present-day legislation concerning slaves in the southern states is of unprecedented atrocity, which by itself indicates some profound disturbance in humanity's laws. To judge the desperate position of the two races living there, it is enough to read the legislation of the southern states.

Not that the Americans living in that part of the Union have actually increased the hardships of slavery; on the contrary, they have bettered the physical condition of the slaves. The ancients only knew of fetters and death as means to maintain slavery; the Americans of the South of the Union have found guarantees of a more intellectual nature. They have, if I may put it in this way, spiritualized despotism and violence. In antiquity men sought to prevent the slave from breaking his bonds; nowadays the attempt is made to stop him wishing to do so.

The ancients bound the slave's body but left his spirit free and allowed him to educate himself. The Americans of the South, who do not think that at any time the Negroes can mingle with them, have forbidden teaching them to read or write under severe penalties. Not wishing to raise them to their own level, they keep them as close to the beasts as possible. In most cases the Americans of the South have deprived the masters of the right to emancipate.[32]

If it is impossible to foresee a time when the Americans of the South will mix their blood with that of the Negroes, can they, without exposing themselves to peril, allow the latter to attain freedom? And if, to save their own race, they are bound to keep the

---

32.   Emancipation is not actually forbidden, but it is subjected to formalities which make it difficult.

other race in chains, should one not pardon them for using the most effective means to that end?

What is happening in the South of the Union seems to me both the most horrible and the most natural consequence of slavery. When I see the order of nature overthrown and hear the cry of humanity complaining in vain against the laws, I confess that my indignation is not directed against the men of our own day who are the authors of these outrages; all my hatred is concentrated against those who, after a thousand years of equality, introduced slavery into the world again.

Whatever efforts the Americans of the South make to maintain slavery, they will not forever succeed. Slavery is limited to one point on the globe and attacked by Christianity as unjust and by political economy as fatal; slavery, amid the democratic liberty and enlightenment of our age, is not an institution that can last. Either the slave or the master will put an end to it. In either case great misfortunes are to be anticipated.

If freedom is refused to the Negroes in the South, in the end they will seize it themselves; if it is granted to them, they will not be slow to abuse it.

What Are the Chances That the American Union Will Last? What Dangers Threaten It?

The maintenance of the existing conditions in the various component states partly depends on the existence of the Union. So we must first examine the probable fate of the Union.

We have seen that the government of the Union is invested with authority to act in the name of the whole nation when it has to act as a single and undivided power. It represents it in relations with foreigners, and it directs the common forces against the common enemy. In a word, it is concerned with those questions I have called exclusively national.

In this division of the rights of sovereignty, at first the Union's share appears larger than that of the states, but a deeper examination shows that in fact it is less.

The Union secures the independence and greatness of the nation, matters which do not affect private persons directly. The state preserves liberty, regulates rights, guarantees property, and makes the life and whole future of each citizen safe.

The federal government stands at a great distance from its subjects; the provincial government is within reach of all. One has only to raise his voice to be heard by it. The central government is supported by the zeal of a few outstanding men who aspire to direct it; the provincial government is supported by the interest of men of the second rank who only hope for power in their own state; and it is men of that sort who, being close to the people, have the most influence over them.

Americans therefore have much more to expect and to fear from the state than from the Union and, in view of the natural inclinations of the human heart, are bound to feel a more lively attachment to the former than to the latter.

The Union is a vast body and somewhat vague as the object of patriotism. But the state has precise shape and circumscribed boundaries; it represents things which are dear to those living there. It is identified with the soil, with the right of property, the family, memories of the past, activities of the present, and dreams for the future. Patriotism, which is most often nothing but an extension of individual egoism, therefore remains attached to the state and has not yet, so to say, been passed on to the Union.

The federal government, in spite of the efforts of its founders, is, as I have said before, one of such naturally feeble sort that it requires, more than any other, the free support of the governed in order to survive.

It is easy to see that its object is to facilitate the desire of the states to remain united; but in forming the federal government it was not anticipated that the states, or several among them, would cease to wish to be united. If today the sovereignty of the Union was to come into conflict with one of the states, one can readily foresee that it would succumb; I even doubt whether such a struggle would ever be seriously undertaken. Each time that determined resistance has been offered to the federal government, it has yielded. Experience has proven that up till now, when a state has been obstinately determined on anything and demanded it resolutely, it has never failed to get it; and when it has flatly refused to act, it has been allowed to refuse.

If the government of the Union had a force of its own, the physical nature of the country would make it very hard to use.[33]

The United States covers an immense territory with long distances separating its parts, and the population is scattered over a country still half wilderness. If the Union attempted to enforce by arms the allegiance of the confederated states, it would be in very much the same position as that of England in the War of Independence.

Moreover, the confederation was formed by the free will of the states; these, by uniting, did not lose their nationality or become fused in one single nation. If today one of those same states wished to withdraw its name from the contract, it would be hard to prove that it could not do so. In resisting it the federal government would have no obvious source of support either in strength or in right.

In America the present Union is useful to all the states but is not essential to any of them. Several states could break the federal bond without compromising the fate of the others, although their sum of happiness would be less. As neither the existence nor the prosperity of any state is entirely bound up with the present confederation, none of them would be prepared to make very great sacrifices to preserve it.

I therefore think it certain that if some part of the Union wished to separate from the rest, not only would it be able to do so, but there would be no one to prevent this. The present Union will only last so long as all the states composing it continue to wish to remain a part thereof.

---

33. The present state of peace enjoyed by the Union gives it no pretext for having a permanent army. Without a permanent army, a government has nothing prepared in advance to take advantage of a favorable opportunity, overcome resistance, and take over sovereign power by surprise.

Among all the reasons that tend to render the existing Union useful to the Americans, two main ones are particularly obvious to any observer.

Although, in a sense, the Americans are alone on their continent, trade makes neighbors of all the nations of the world with whom they have commerce. In spite of their apparent isolation, the Americans need to be strong, and they can only be strong if they all remain united.

Therefore the Americans have an immense interest in remaining united.

On the other hand, it is almost impossible to discover what sort of material interest any part of the Union would at present have in separating from the rest; different parts of the Union have different interests, but I cannot discover any interests in which they are opposed to one another.

The states of the South are almost exclusively agricultural; those of the North specialize more in trade and manufacture; those of the West go in both for manufacture and for agriculture. Tobacco, rice, cotton, and sugar are grown in the South; in the North and the West there is corn and wheat. These are varied sources of wealth, but to draw the benefit from them there is one common method equally advantageous to all, and that is union.

The North, which conveys the wealth of the Anglo-Americans to all parts of the world and brings back the world's wealth to the Union, is the most natural intermediary, both between the South and West of the Union and between the whole Union and the rest of the world; therefore the North wishes the South and West to be united and prosperous so that they can supply its manufactures with raw materials and its ships with freight.

On their side the South and West have an even more direct interest in the preservation of the Union and the prosperity of the North. Southern crops are, for the most part, exported overseas; therefore the South and West need the commercial resources of the North. They are bound to wish the Union to have a strong fleet to protect them efficiently.

Apart from this commercial interest, the South and the West see great political advantage in their union with the North. The South has a large slave population, which is a menace now and will be a greater menace in the future. All the states of the West are in a single valley, entirely isolated from the traditions of Europe and the civilization of the Old World.

So the Southerners must wish to preserve the Union so that they should not face the blacks alone, and the Westerners must desire it so that they should not be shut up within central America without free communication with the outside world.

Consequently there is a close link between the material interests of all parts of the Union.

I would say the same about opinions and feelings, which may be called man's immaterial interests.

What keeps a great number of citizens under the same government is much less a reasoned desire to remain united than the instinctive and, in a sense, involuntary accord which springs from like feelings and similar opinions.

Anyone taking the matter up from that angle, who studies what happens in the United States, will readily discover that the inhabitants, though divided under twenty-four distinct sovereign authorities, nevertheless constitute a single nation.

Although there are many sects among the Anglo-Americans, they all look at religion from the same point of view.

They do not always agree about the best means of governing well, and they have varied views about some of the forms of government expedient to adopt, but they agree about the general principles which should rule human societies. From Maine to the Floridas, from Missouri to the Atlantic Ocean, it is believed that all legitimate powers have their origin in the people. Men have the same ideas concerning freedom and equality; they profess the same opinions about the press, the right of association, juries, and the responsibilities of agents of authority.

If we turn from political and religious ideas to philosophical and moral opinions controlling the daily actions of life and the general lines of behavior, we find the same agreement.

The Anglo-Americans regard universal reason as the source of moral authority,[34] just as the universality of the citizens is the source of political power. Most of them think that knowledge of his own interest properly understood is enough to lead a man to what is just and honest. They believe that each man at birth receives the faculty to rule himself and that nobody has the right to force his fellow man to be happy. All have a lively faith in human perfectibility; they see humanity as a changing picture in which nothing either is or ought to be fixed forever; and they admit that what seems good to them today may be replaced tomorrow by something better that is still hidden.

I do not assert that all these opinions are correct, but they are American.

While the Americans are thus united together by common ideas, they are separated from everybody else by one sentiment, namely, pride.

For fifty years the inhabitants of the United States have been repeatedly and constantly told that they are the only religious, enlightened, and free people. They see that democratic institutions flourish among them, whereas they come to grief in the rest of the world; consequently they have an immensely high opinion of themselves and are not far from believing that they form a species apart from the rest of the human race.

Hence the dangers threatening the American Union spring no more from diversity of opinions than from diversity of interests. They must be sought in the variety of American characteristics and passions.

Almost all the dwellers in the immense territory of the United States have sprung from the same stock, but over the years the climate and, more especially, slavery have introduced marked differences of character between the English in the southern states and the English in the northern ones.

It is generally believed among us that slavery gives one part of the Union some interests opposed to those of the other part. I have

---

34.   It is hardly necessary to explain that when I say "the Anglo-Americans" I am speaking of the great majority of them. There are always some isolated individuals outside that majority.

not noticed that this was so. In the South slavery has not created interests opposed to those of the North, but it has modified the character of the Southerners and given them different customs.

The Northerner has knowledge as well as experience; nevertheless, he does not value knowledge as a pleasure, but only as a means, and he is only greedy to seize on its useful applications.

The Southerner is more spontaneous, witty, open, generous, intellectual, and brilliant.

The Northerner is more active, has more common sense, and is better informed and more skillful.

The former has the tastes, prejudices, weaknesses, and grandeur of every aristocracy.

The latter has the good and bad qualities characteristic of the middle classes.

If two men belonging to the same society have the same interests and, to some extent, the same opinions, but their characters, education, and style of civilization are different, it is highly probable that the two will not be harmonious. The same observation applies to a society of nations.

Slavery therefore does not attack the American confederation directly, through interests, but indirectly, through mores.

Thirteen states adhered to the federal pact of 1790, but there are now twenty-four in the confederation. The population, which was nearly four million in 1790, has quadrupled in forty years; in 1830 it was nearly thirteen million.[35]

Such changes cannot take place without danger.

At present the interests of the different parts of the Union are not opposed to one another, but who can foresee the various changes of the near future in a country where new towns spring up every day and new nations every five years?

Since the time of the English settlements the population has been doubling about every twenty-two years; I see no reason why this rate of increase should be halted during the next hundred years. I think that before that time has run out, the land now occu-

---

35.   Census of 1790, 3,929,328; census of 1830, 12,856,163.

pied or claimed by the United States will have a population of over one hundred million and be divided into forty states.[36]

I would like to believe in human perfectibility, but until men have changed their nature and been completely transformed, I shall refuse to believe in the duration of a government which is called upon to hold together forty different nations covering an area half that of Europe,[37] to avoid all rivalry, ambition, and struggles between them, and to unite all their independent wills in the accomplishment of common designs.

But the greatest risk which growth makes the Union run arises from the continual shift of its internal forces.

All the states of the Union are simultaneously growing rich, but they cannot all grow and prosper at the same rate.

Trade and industry are bound to flourish more in the North than in the South.[38] It is natural that both population and wealth should pile up there more quickly.

---

36.   If the population of the United States continues to double every twenty-two years, as it has done for the last two hundred years, by 1852 it would be twenty-four million; by 1874, forty-eight; and by 1896, ninety-six. [The U.S. Census of 1850 reported 23.1 million inhabitants; by 1900, the total population had reached 76.2 million.]

37.   The area of the United States is 295,000 square leagues, and that of Europe, according to Malte-Brun, vol. 6, p. 4, is 500,000. [*Précis de la géographie universelle au description de toutes les parties du monde*, Malte-Brun, vol. 6, Paris, 1826. The whole work is in eight volumes: Paris, 1810–1829.]

38.   A glance at the following statistics is enough to show the difference between commercial activity in South and North:

In 1829 the total tonnage of ocean-going and coastal shipping belonging to the four great states of the South—Virginia, the two Carolinas, and Georgia—was only 5,234 tons.

In the same year that of Massachusetts alone amounted to 17,322 tons (See *Legislature Documents*, 21st Congress, Second Session, No. 140, p. 244), three times as much shipping as those four states put together.

However, Massachusetts has an area of only 959 square leagues (7,335 square miles) and 610,014 inhabitants, whereas the area and population of the four states of which I am speaking are 27,204 square leagues (210,000 square miles) and 3,047,767 inhabitants. Thus Massachusetts forms only one-thirtieth of the area of the four states, and its population is only one-fifth. (See Darby's *View of the United States*.) [William Darby, *View of the United States, Historical, Geographical and Statistical*, Philadelphia, 1828; Tocqueville used this edition.]

The disproportionately rapid growth of some states threatens the independence of the others. If New York, with its two million inhabitants and forty representatives, tried to lay down the law in Congress, perhaps it might succeed. But even if the most powerful states did not seek to oppress the lesser ones, the danger would still be there, for it lies as much in the possibility of such action as in any actual act.

The weak seldom have confidence in the justice and reasonableness of the strong. States which are growing comparatively slowly therefore look with jealous distrust on fortune's favorites. That is the reason for the deep uneasiness and vague restlessness which one notices in one part of the Union, in contrast to the well-being and confidence prevailing in the other. I think there are no other reasons for the hostile attitude of the South.

Of all Americans the Southerners are those who ought to be most attached to the Union, for it is they who would suffer most if left to themselves; nevertheless, they alone threaten to break the federal bond. Why is that so? The answer is easy: the South, which provided the Union with four presidents,[39] which now knows that federal power is slipping from it, which yearly sees its number of representatives in Congress falling and that of the North and West rising—the South, whose men are ardent and irascible, is getting angry and restless. It turns its melancholy gaze inward and back to the past, perpetually fancying that it may be suffering oppression. Noticing that a law of the Union is not obviously favorable to itself, it cries out against this abuse of power, and when no one listens to its ardent remonstrances, it grows indignant and threatens to leave an association whose burdens it bears without share of the profits.

Hence the greatest danger threatening the United States springs from its very prosperity, for in some of the confederate states it brings that intoxication which goes with sudden access of fortune, and in others it brings the envy, distrust, and regrets which most often follow where it is lost.

---

39. Washington, Jefferson, Madison, and Monroe.

The Americans rejoice at this extraordinary change, but I think they should regard it with sorrow and fear. Whatever they do, the Americans of the United States will become one of the greatest nations in the world; their offshoots will cover almost the whole of North America; the continent in which they dwell is their domain and will not slip from them. Why need they hurry, then, to take possession of it today? Wealth, power, and glory cannot fail to be theirs one day, but they rush at this immense fortune as if they had only one moment in which to seize it.

I think I have proved that the existence of the present confederation entirely depends on the agreement of all the confederates in wishing to remain united, and starting from that premise, I have investigated the various causes that might lead the different states to wish to separate. But there are two ways in which the Union might perish: one of the united states might wish to withdraw from the contract and use force to break the common bond; most of the observations I have made so far concern that possibility; but the federal government might progressively lose its power owing to a simultaneous tendency on the part of all the united republics to reclaim the use of their independence. The central power, deprived of all its prerogatives in turn and reduced to impotence by a tacit agreement, would become incompetent to fulfill its purpose, and the second Union, like the first, would die of a sort of senile debility.

So, having investigated all that strains Anglo-American unity, it is also important to see, if the Union subsists, whether the sphere of government action will expand or retract and whether it is becoming more energetic or weaker.

When one examines what is happening in the United States closely, one soon discovers two contrary tendencies; they are like two currents flowing in the same bed in opposite directions.

In the forty-five years of the Union's existence time has mellowed a mass of provincial prejudices which at first strove against its authority. The patriotism attaching each American to his state has become less exclusive. By getting to know each other better, the various parts of the Union have drawn closer. The [postal system], that great link between minds, now penetrates into the heart of the wilderness,[40] and steamships provide daily connections between all points on the coast. Trade flows up and down the rivers of the interior with unexampled rapidity.[41] To these facilities may be added the desires, restless mind, and the love of wealth which constantly drive the American from his home and put him in contact with many of his fellow citizens. He travels through his country in all directions and visits all its various populations. There is no French province where the inhabitants know each other as well as do the thirteen million men spread over the extent of the United States.

In step with the progress of American industry, all the commercial links uniting the confederated states are tightened, and the Union, which at first was the child of their imagination, is now a part of their habits. The march of time has dissipated alarms that tormented the imagination of the men of 1789. Federal authority has not become oppressive; it has not destroyed the independence of the states; it has not led toward monarchy; and the small states have not fallen into dependence on the great ones. The confederation has continuously grown in population, wealth, and power.

Therefore I am convinced that the natural obstacles to the continuance of the American Union are not so great as they were in 1789 and that fewer men are hostile to the Union now than then.

Nevertheless, a careful study of the history of the United States over the last forty-five years readily convinces one that federal power is decreasing.

The reasons for this phenomenon are not hard to indicate.

When the Constitution of 1789 was promulgated, everything was falling to pieces in anarchy; the Union which followed on this

---

40. In 1832 the district of Michigan, with no more than 31,639 inhabitants and hardly more than clearings in the wilderness, constructed 940 miles of post road. There were already 1,938 miles of post road through the almost entirely wild territory of Arkansas. See the *Report of the Postmaster General,* November 30, 1833. The carriage of newspapers alone brought in $254,796 annually.

41. In the ten years from 1821 to 1831, 271 steamships have been launched on the rivers watering the Mississippi Valley alone.

In 1829 there were only 256 steamships in the United States. See *Legislative Documents,* No. 140, p. 274.

disorder aroused both fear and hate, but because it answered a deeply felt need, it had ardent supporters.

As the federal government consolidated its power, America again took her due place among the nations, peace returned to her frontiers, and confidence in public credit was restored; a settled state of affairs followed the confusion, and each man's industry could find its natural outlet and develop in freedom.

The consequent prosperity itself made men forget the cause that had produced it. As soon as a strong government did not seem necessary, people began to think it troublesome. There was a general desire to remain united, but in each particular case the tendency was to reclaim independence. It was ever increasingly easy to subscribe to the principle of federation and to apply it less and less; in this way the peace and order brought about by the federal government led to its own decline.

As soon as this tendency in public opinion began to be obvious, the party hacks, for whom the people's passions are meat and drink, began to exploit it to their own advantage.

From then onward, every time the federal government has gone into the ring against those of the states it has almost invariably been obliged to retreat. When it has been a question of interpreting the terms of the Constitution, that interpretation has generally been against the Union and in favor of the states.

The Constitution entrusted the federal government to carry out or to encourage those great internal improvements such as canals that added to the prosperity of the whole Union.

The states became frightened at the thought of some authority other than themselves thus disposing of a portion of their territory. They were afraid that by that means the central power would acquire formidable patronage within their sphere and would come to exercise an influence which they wanted to keep for their agents alone.

Therefore the Democratic Party, which has always opposed any extension of federal power, raised its voice; Congress was accused of usurpation; the head of state, of ambition. Intimidated by this outcry, the central government in the end admitted its mistake and confined its activity precisely within the prescribed sphere.

It is enough to travel through the United States in order to appreciate the advantages derived from [its] bank. These advantages are of several kinds, but there is one that especially strikes the foreigner: the Bank of the United States' notes are accepted for the same value upon the border of the wilderness as at Philadelphia, which is the seat of its operations.[42]

The Bank of the United States is, nevertheless, the object of great animosity.

The bank forms the great monetary link of the Union, just as Congress is the great legislative link, and the same passions which tend to make the states independent of the central power tend toward the destruction of the bank.

The provincial banks are impatient at this salutary control. The newspapers that they have brought up, and the president, whose interest makes him their mouthpiece, therefore attack the bank with the greatest vehemence. According to them, the directors of the bank constitute a permanent aristocratic body whose influence is bound to make itself felt on the government and will sooner or later change the principles of equality on which American society rests.

The bank's battle against its enemies is only one incident in the great American fight between the provinces and the central power, but the Union has never shown so much weakness as in the famous tariff affair.[43]

The French revolutionary wars and the War of 1812, by preventing free communication between America and Europe, brought into being manufacturing establishments in the North of the Union. When peace allowed European products to reach the New World again, the Americans felt that they should establish a cus-

---

42.   The present Bank of the United States was created in 1816, with a capital of $35,000,000; its privilege expires in 1836. Last year Congress passed a law to renew it, but the president refused his sanction. The struggle is now on and is conducted by both sides with extreme violence; it is easy to predict the approaching collapse of the bank.

43.   The main source for the details of this affair is *Legislative Documents*, 22nd Congress, Second Session, No. 30.

toms system both to protect their nascent industry and to pay all the debts contracted in the war. The southern states, who have no manufactures to encourage, being exclusively agricultural, were quick to complain.

In the year 1820, in a petition to Congress, South Carolina declared that the tariff law was *unconstitutional, oppressive, and unjust.* Later on, Georgia, Virginia, North Carolina, Alabama, and Mississippi all made energetic complaints. Far from taking these murmurs into account, Congress in the years 1824 and 1828 raised the customs levels higher.

A famous doctrine was then proclaimed in the South, which took the name of nullification.

The nullifiers of the South claimed that the Americans when they united did not intend to fuse themselves into one people, but only to form a league of independent peoples; from which it follows that each state, having preserved its complete sovereignty, has the right to interpret the laws of Congress and to suspend those which seem opposed to the Constitution or to justice.

The doctrine of nullification is summed up in a statement made in 1833 before the United States Senate by Mr. [John C.] Calhoun, the leader of the southern nullifiers, who said: "The Constitution is a contract in which the states appear as sovereigns. Now, every time there is a contract between parties having no common arbitrator, each of them retains the right to judge the extent of its obligation by itself."

It is clear that such a doctrine would in principle destroy the federal bond and actually bring back that anarchy from which the Constitution of 1789 delivered the Americans.

When South Carolina saw that Congress was deaf to its complaints, in 1832 the people[44] appointed a convention [that] on November 24 published an ordinance that nullified the federal tariff law, forbade raising the duties imposed by it, and forbade

---

44.   That is to say, a majority of the people, for the opposition party, called Union Party, always claimed a very strong and active minority in its favor. Carolina must have had about 47,000 voters; 30,000 were in favor of nullification and 17,000 against it.

recognition of any appeal that might be made to the federal courts.[45] This decree was not to come into force until the following February.

Meanwhile, South Carolina armed its militia and prepared for war.

What did Congress do? Congress, which had been deaf to the complaints of its suppliant subjects, listened to them when they had arms in their hands. A law was passed by which the tariff duties were to be reduced by stages over ten years.[46] Thus Congress completely abandoned the principle of the tariff. At the same time, it passed another law investing the president with extraordinary power to use force to overcome a resistance no longer to be feared.

South Carolina did not even [allow] the Union this feeble appearance of victory; the same convention that nullified the tariff law assembled again and accepted the offered concession, but at the same time it declared its intention to persevere in the doctrine of nullification and nullified the law giving the president extraor-

---

45.   This decree was preceded by a report from the committee appointed to draft it; this report contains an explanation of the motive and object of the law: "We believe that the redeeming spirit of our system is STATE SOVEREIGNTY . . . that when the rights reserved to the several states are deliberately invaded, it is their right and their duty to 'interpose for the purpose of arresting the progress of the evil of usurpation, and to maintain, within their respective limits, the authorities and privileges belonging to them as independent sovereignties.' (Virginia Resolutions of '98.) If the several states do not possess this right, it is vain that they claim to be sovereign. They are at once reduced to the degrading condition of humble dependents on the will of the Federal Government. South Carolina claims to be a Sovereign State. She recognizes no tribunal upon earth as above her authority. It is true, she has entered into a solemn compact of union with other Sovereign States—but she claims, and will exercise, the right to determine the extent of her obligations. . . . And when that compact is violated by her co-states, or by the Government which they have created, she asserts her unquestionable right '*to judge of the infractions,* as well as of the *mode* and *measure of redress.*' (Kentucky Resolutions of '98.)" [*State Papers on Nullification: Including the Public Acts of the Convention of the People of South Carolina, Assembled at Columbia, November 19, 1832, and March 11, 1833; the Proclamation of the President of the United States, and the Proceedings of the Several State Legislatures Which Have Acted on the Subject,* Boston, 1834, p. 326 f.]

46.   Law of March 2, 1833.

dinary powers, though it was quite certain that they would not be used.

Almost all these events took place during General Jackson's presidency. One hears it said that General Jackson is prone by nature and habit to the use of force, covetous of power, and a despot by inclination.

General Jackson is supposed to wish to establish a dictatorship in the United States, bringing a militaristic spirit to the fore and extending central-government powers in a way dangerous to provincial liberties. But far from wishing to extend federal power, the present president belongs to the party which wishes to limit that power to the clear and precise terms of the Constitution and never to allow it to be interpreted in a way favorable to the Union's government.

Whenever there is some dispute between the Union and a state government, the president is almost always the first to express doubts about his rights; when it is a case of interpreting the extent of federal power, in a sense he takes sides against himself. Not that he is by nature either weak or hostile to the Union. After bowing before the majority to gain its favor, General Jackson rises again; he tramples his personal enemies underfoot wherever he finds them, with an ease impossible to any previous president; sometimes he even treats the national representatives with a sort of disdain that is almost insulting; he refuses to sanction laws of Congress and often fails to answer that important body. He is a favorite who is sometimes rude to his master. Hence General Jackson's power is constantly increasing, but that of the president grows less. The federal government is strong in his hands; it will pass to his successor enfeebled.

The Americans want their Union, but one reduced to a shadow; they want it strong in some cases and weak in all others. At present I can see nothing to stop this general tendency of opinion; the causes which have brought it about still operate in the same way. So it will continue, and barring some extraordinary circumstance, one can foresee that the government of the Union will go on getting weaker.

Nevertheless, I think that the day is still far off when the federal power, unable to protect itself or to keep the country at peace, will, in a sense, extinguish itself of its own accord. The Union is a part of American mores and is desired; its results are obvious and its benefits visible. When men come to notice that the weakness of the federal government hazards the Union's existence a change of opinion, an internal crisis, or a war could all at once restore the vigor it needs.

The point I want to make is simply this: many think that there is a trend of American public opinion favoring centralization of power in the hands of the president and of Congress. I hold that a contrary tendency can be distinctly observed. What will the final result of this tendency be, and what events may halt, slow down, or accelerate the movement I have described? That is hidden in the future, and I cannot pretend to be able to lift the veil.

Concerning the Republican Institutions of the United States and Their Chances of Survival

The dismemberment of the Union, bringing with it war between the states, might in the long run compromise the fate of republican institutions.

Nevertheless, the future of the republic should not be confused with that of the Union. The Union principally exists in the law that created it. A revolution or a change in public opinion could shatter it forever. The republic has deeper roots.

What is meant by *republic* in the United States is the slow and quiet action of society upon itself. It is an orderly state really founded on the enlightened will of the people. It is a conciliatory government under which resolutions have time to ripen, being discussed with deliberation and executed only when mature.

In the United States republicans value mores, respect beliefs, and recognize rights. They hold the view that a nation must be moral, religious, and moderate all the more because it is free. In the United States *republic* means the tranquil reign of the majority.

The majority, when it has had time to examine itself and to prove its standing, is the common source of every power. But even then the majority is not all-powerful. Humanity, justice, and reason stand above it in the moral order; and in the world of politics, acquired rights take precedence over it. The majority recognizes these limits, and if it does break through them, that is because, like any man, it has its passions and, like him, may do evil [despite] knowing what is good.

In the United States the dogma of the sovereignty of the people is not an isolated doctrine, bearing no relation to the people's habits and prevailing ideas; on the contrary, one should see it as the last link in a chain of opinions which binds around the whole Anglo-American world. Providence has given each individual the amount of reason necessary for him to look after himself in matters of his own exclusive concern. That is the great maxim on which civil and political society in the United States rests.

Hence the republic penetrates, if I may put it so, into the ideas, the opinions, and all the habits of the Americans at the same time that it becomes established in their laws; and in order to change their laws, they would in a sense have to change the whole of themselves. For most people in the United States religion, too, is republican. Each man is allowed to choose freely the path that will lead him to heaven, just as the law recognizes each citizen's right to choose his own government.

If republican principles are to perish in the United States, they will do so only after long social travail, frequently interrupted and as often resumed; they will have many apparent revivals and will vanish beyond recall only when an entirely new people has taken the place of the one there now. There is no reason to foresee such a revolution, and no symptom indicates its approach.

I repeat what I have said before, that the present tendency of American society seems to me to be toward ever-increasing democracy.

But I do not deny that at some future date the Americans may restrict the sphere of political rights, taking some of them away in order to entrust them to a single man; but I do not believe that they will ever entrust exclusive control of them to one particular class of citizen, or in other words, that they will establish an aristocracy.

An aristocratic body is composed of a certain number of citizens who, without being elevated very far above the mass of the citizens, are nevertheless permanently stationed above them—a body with which the people are in daily contact but with which they can never mingle.

An aristocracy cannot last unless it is founded on an accepted principle of inequality, legalized in advance, and introduced into the family as well as into the rest of society—all things so violently repugnant to natural equity that only constraint will make men submit to them.

There have been cases of societies which, as a result of events before they took shape, have, so to say, been born aristocratic and which each succeeding century then led closer to democracy. That is what happened to the Romans and to the barbarians who followed after them. But a nation which, starting from a basis of civilization and democracy, should gradually establish inequality of condition, until it arrived at inviolable privileges and exclusive castes, would be a novelty in the world.

There is no indication that America is destined to provide the first example of such a spectacle.

Some Considerations Concerning the Causes of the Commercial Greatness of the United States

No other nation in the world possesses vaster, deeper, or more secure ports for commerce than the Americans.

At all times the Anglo-Americans have shown a decided taste for the sea. Independence, by breaking their commercial links with England, gave a new and powerful stimulus to their maritime genius. Since that time the number of the Union's ships has grown at almost as quick a rate as the number of its inhabitants. Today it is the Americans themselves who carry to their shores nine-tenths of the products of Europe.[47] It is the Americans too who carry three-quarters of the exports of the New World to European consumers.[48]

American ships fill the docks of Le Havre and Liverpool, while the number of English and French vessels in New York harbor is comparatively small.[49]

I think it is no good looking for physical advantages as the reason for this superiority; it depends on purely intellectual and moral qualities.

The European navigator is prudent about venturing out to sea; he only does so when the weather is suitable; if any unexpected accident happens, he returns to port; at night he furls some of his sails; and when the whitening billows indicate the approach of land, he checks his course and takes an observation of the sun.

The American, neglecting such precautions, braves these dangers; he sets sail while the storm is still rumbling; by night as well as by day he spreads full sails to the wind; he repairs storm damage as he goes; and when at last he draws near the end of his voyage, he flies toward the coast as if he could already see the port.

---

47.   The total value of imports for the year ending September 30, 1832, was $101,129,266. The imports made on foreign ships accounted for a sum of only $10,731,039, about one-tenth of the total.

48.   The total value of exports during the same year was $87,176,945; the value exported on foreign vessels was $21,036,183, or about one-quarter of the total. (Williams's *Register*, 1833, p. 398.) [*The New-York Annual Register for the Year of Our Lord 1833*, by Edwin Williams, New York, 1833.]

49.   During the years 1829, 1830, and 1831 ships drawing a total of 3,307,719 tons entered the Union's ports. Foreign shipping amounted to only 544,571 tons out of this total. So they were in a proportion of about 16 to 100. (*National Calendar*, 1833, p. 305.) [*The National Calendar and Annals of the United States for 1833*, vol. 11, Washington, 1833.]

During the years 1820, 1826, and 1831 the total tonnage of English vessels entering the ports of London, Liverpool, and Hull was 443,800. In the same years in these ports the total of foreign shipping was 159,431 tons. So the proportion between the two is about 36 to 100. (*Companion to the Almanac*, 1834, p. 169.) [*The Companion to the Almanac, or, Yearbook of General Information for 1834*, in *The British Almanac of the Society for the Diffusion of Useful Knowledge for the Year 1834*, London, 1834.]

In the year 1832 the proportion of foreign to English ships entering the ports of Great Britain was 29 to 100.

The American is often shipwrecked, but no other sailor crosses the sea as fast as he. Doing what others do but in less time, he can do it at less expense.

I cannot express my thoughts better than by saying that the Americans put something heroic into their way of trading.

It will always be very difficult for a European merchant to imitate his American competitor in this. In acting in the way just described, the American is not just working by calculation but is rather obeying an impulse of his nature.

The inhabitant of the United States experiences all the desires to which a high civilization can give rise, but, unlike the European, he does not find himself part of a society expertly organized to satisfy them; consequently he often has to provide for himself the various things that education and habit have made necessary for him. In America it sometimes happens that one and the same man will till his fields, build his house, make his tools, cobble his shoes, and with his own hands weave the coarse cloth that covers him. This is bad for improving craftsmanship but greatly serves to develop the worker's intelligence. An extreme division of labor, more than anything else whatsoever, tends to turn men into machines and to deprive the things made of any trace of soul. In such a country as America, where specialists are very rare, it is impossible to insist on a long apprenticeship before a man enters a profession. Consequently an American finds it very easy to change his trade, suiting his occupation to the needs of the moment. One comes across those who have been in turn lawyers, farmers, merchants, ministers of the Gospel, and doctors. Though the American may be less skilled than a European in each particular craft, there is hardly any skill to which he is a complete stranger. His capacities are more general and the sphere of his intelligence wider, and he can easily rid himself of any influence foreign habits might have over his mind, for he knows that his country is like no other and that his situation is something new in the world.

The American lives in a land of wonders; everything around him is in constant movement, and every movement seems an advance. Consequently, in his mind the idea of newness is closely

linked with that of improvement. Nowhere does he see any limit
placed by nature to human endeavor; in his eyes something which
does not exist is just something that has not been tried yet. For an
American the whole of life is treated like a game of chance, a time
of revolution, or the day of a battle.

These same causes working simultaneously on every individual finally give an irresistible impulse to the national character. Choose
any American at random, and he should be a man of burning desires, enterprising, adventurous, and, above all, an innovator. The
same bent affects all he does; it plays a part in his politics, his religious doctrines, his theories of social economy, and his domestic occupations; he carries it with him into the depths of the backwoods
as well as into the city's business. This same spirit applied to maritime commerce makes the American cross the sea faster and sell his
goods cheaper than any other trader in the whole world.

As long as American sailors keep these intellectual advantages
and the practical superiority derived from them, they will not only
continue to provide for the needs of producers and consumers in
their own country, but they will increasingly tend to become, like
the English, the commercial agents of other nations.

The Americans of the United States already have great moral influence over all the peoples of the New World. Enlightenment
comes from them. All the nations inhabiting the same continent
are already accustomed to consider them as the most enlightened,
the most powerful, and the richest member of the great American
family. Consequently all eyes are turned toward the United States,
and as far as they can, they imitate the peoples dwelling there.
They are continually deriving political doctrines from the United
States and borrowing their laws.

England is now the natural commercial center for all neighboring nations; the American Union is destined to fill the same role
in the other hemisphere. So every nation that comes to birth or
grows up in the New World does so, in a sense, for the benefit of
the Anglo-Americans.

Should the Union be dissolved, whatever may happen, the trading states will remain united. Even if the South of the Union did

become independent of the North, it still could not manage without it. I have said that the South is not a land of commerce, and there is nothing at present to indicate that it will become so. Therefore for a long while ahead the Americans of the southern states will be obliged to rely on foreigners to export their produce and to bring them the things they need. Of all possible intermediaries, their northern neighbors are most certainly those able to serve them most cheaply. So they will serve them, for low cost is the supreme law of trade. There is no sovereign will or national prejudice that can fight for long against cheapness.

Reason suggests and experience proves that there is no lasting commercial greatness unless it can, at need, combine with military power.

That truth is as well understood in the United States as anywhere else. Already the Americans can enforce respect for their flag; soon they will be able to make it feared.

I am convinced that dismemberment of the Union, far from reducing American naval strength, would have a strong tendency to increase it. At present the trading states are linked to others that do not trade and that therefore are often reluctant to increase a maritime power from which they benefit only indirectly.

But if all the trading states of the Union were combined in one coherent nation, then for them trade would become a national interest of the first importance; they would then be disposed to make great sacrifices to protect their ships, and there would be nothing to stop their following their inclinations in this respect.

I think that nations, like men, in their youth almost always give indications of the main features of their destiny. Seeing how energetically the Anglo-Americans trade, their natural advantages, and their success, I cannot help believing that one day they will become the leading naval power on the globe. They are born to rule the seas, as the Romans were to conquer the world.

CONCLUSION

Up to now, in discussing the future destiny of the United States, I have tried to divide my subject into various parts so as to study each of them more carefully.

It is time to take a general look at the whole from a single point of view. What I am going to say will be less detailed but more certain. Each object will stand out less distinctly, but the general lines will be clearer.

The territory now occupied or owned by the United States of America forms about one-twentieth of the habitable globe.

But wide though these bounds are, it would be a mistake to suppose that the Anglo-American race will always remain within them; it is already spreading far beyond them.

There was a time when we too might have created a great French nation in the wilds of America and might have shared the destinies of the New World with the English. There was a time when France possessed in North America a territory almost as vast as the whole of Europe.

But a combination of circumstances too long to enumerate deprived us of the magnificent heritage. The 400,000 French inhabitants of Lower Canada now constitute the remnants of an ancient people lost in the flood of a new nation. The foreign population around them is constantly increasing and spreading out on all sides, dominating their cities and corrupting their language. That population is identical with that of the United States. I am right, therefore, to say that the English race does not stop at the boundaries of the Union but advances far beyond toward the northwest.

To the northwest there is nothing but a few Russian settlements of no importance, but to the southwest Mexico presents a barrier to the Anglo-Americans.

In truth, therefore, there are only two rival races sharing the New World today: the Spaniards and the English.

The boundaries between these two races have been fixed by a treaty. But however favorable that treaty may have been to the Anglo-Americans, I have no doubt that they will soon infringe it.

Vast provinces extending beyond the frontiers of the Union toward Mexico are still empty of inhabitants. The people of the United States will penetrate into these solitary regions even sooner than those who have a right to occupy them. They will appropriate the soil and establish a society, so that when the legitimate owner finally arrives, he will find the wilderness cultivated and strangers quietly settled in his heritage.

The lands of the New World belong to the first man to occupy them, and dominion is the prize in that race.

I have previously referred to what is happening in the province of Texas. Daily, little by little, the inhabitants of the United States are infiltrating into Texas, acquiring land there, and, though submitting to the country's laws, establishing there the empire of their language and mores. The province of Texas is still under Mexican rule, but soon there will, so to say, be no more Mexicans there.

The same sort of thing happens in every place where the Anglo-Americans come into contact with populations of a different origin.

It is no good pretending that the English race has not established an immense preponderance over all the other Europeans in the New World. It is far superior to them in civilization, industry, and power. As long as there lie before it only empty lands or ones thinly inhabited, and it does not encounter crowded populations through which it is impossible to force a passage, the English race will go on spreading constantly. It will not halt at lines drawn in treaties, but will flow over such imaginary bounds in all directions.

So, then, it must not be thought possible to halt the impetus of the English race in the New World. The dismemberment of the Union, bringing war into the continent, or the abolition of the republic, bringing tyranny, might slow expansion down, but cannot prevent the people ultimately fulfilling their inevitable destiny. Whatever the future may hold in store, it cannot deprive the Americans of their climate, their inland seas, their great rivers, or the fertility of their soil. Bad laws, revolutions, and anarchy cannot destroy their taste for well-being or that spirit of enterprise which seems the characteristic feature of their race.

Thus, in all the uncertainty of the future, one event at least is sure. At a period which we may call near, for we are speaking of the life of nations, the Anglo-Americans alone will cover the whole of the immense area between the polar ice and the tropics, extending from the Atlantic to the Pacific coast.

Therefore, the time must come when there will be in North America 150 million people all equal one to the other,[1] belonging to the same family, having the same point of departure, the same civilization, language, religion, habits, and mores, and among whom thought will circulate in similar forms and with like nuances. All else is doubtful, but that is sure. And this is something entirely new in the world, something, moreover, the significance of which the imagination cannot grasp.

There are now two great nations in the world which, starting from different points, seem to be advancing toward the same goal: the Russians and the Anglo-Americans.

Both have grown in obscurity, and while the world's attention was occupied elsewhere, they have suddenly taken their place among the leading nations, making the world take note of their birth and of their greatness almost at the same instant.

All other peoples seem to have nearly reached their natural limits and to need nothing but to preserve them; but these two are

---

1.   This figure assumes a population density like that of Europe, namely, 410 people to the square league.

growing.[2] All the others have halted or advanced only through great exertions; they alone march easily and quickly forward along a path whose end no eye can yet see.

The American fights against natural obstacles; the Russian is at grips with men. The former combats the wilderness and barbarism; the latter, civilization with all its arms. America's conquests are made with the plowshare, Russia's with the sword.

To attain their aims, the former relies on personal interest and gives free scope to the unguided strength and common sense of individuals.

The latter in a sense concentrates the whole power of society in one man.

One has freedom as the principal means of action; the other has servitude.

Their point of departure is different and their paths diverse; nevertheless, each seems called by some secret design of Providence one day to hold in its hands the destinies of half the world.

---

2.   The population of Russia, proportionately speaking, is increasing more rapidly than that of any other nation in the Old World.

Volume Two

Volume Two

CONTENTS OF VOLUME TWO

Tocqueville's Preface to Volume Two   231

PART I

Influence of Democracy on the Intellectual Movements in
the United States

1. CONCERNING THE PHILOSOPHICAL APPROACH
   OF THE AMERICANS   235

2. CONCERNING THE PRINCIPAL SOURCE
   OF BELIEFS AMONG DEMOCRATIC PEOPLES   237

3. WHY THE AMERICANS SHOW MORE APTITUDE AND TASTE
   FOR GENERAL IDEAS THAN THEIR ENGLISH
   FOREFATHERS   240

4. HOW RELIGION IN THE UNITED STATES MAKES
   USE OF DEMOCRATIC INSTINCTS   241

5. HOW EQUALITY SUGGESTS TO THE AMERICANS THE IDEA
   OF THE INDEFINITE PERFECTIBILITY OF MAN   245

6. WHY THE EXAMPLE OF THE AMERICANS DOES
   NOT PROVE THAT A DEMOCRATIC PEOPLE CAN HAVE
   NO APTITUDE OR TASTE FOR SCIENCE, LITERATURE,
   OR THE ARTS   246

7. WHY THE AMERICANS ARE MORE CONCERNED
   WITH THE APPLICATIONS THAN WITH
   THE THEORY OF SCIENCE   250

8. IN WHAT SPIRIT THE AMERICANS CULTIVATE THE ARTS   253

9. WHY THE AMERICANS ERECT SOME PETTY
   MONUMENTS AND OTHERS THAT ARE VERY GRAND   256

10. LITERARY CHARACTERISTICS OF
    DEMOCRATIC CENTURIES   257

11. THE INDUSTRY OF LITERATURE   260

12. HOW AMERICAN DEMOCRACY HAS MODIFIED
    THE ENGLISH LANGUAGE   260

13. ON SOME SOURCES OF POETIC INSPIRATION
    IN DEMOCRACIES   264

14. WHY AMERICAN WRITERS AND SPEAKERS
    ARE OFTEN BOMBASTIC   268

15. SOME OBSERVATIONS ON THE THEATER
    AMONG DEMOCRATIC PEOPLES   269

16. SOME CHARACTERISTICS PECULIAR TO
    HISTORIANS IN DEMOCRATIC CENTURIES   270

17. OF PARLIAMENTARY ELOQUENCE IN
    THE UNITED STATES   273

PART II

The Influence of Democracy
on the Sentiments of the Americans

1. WHY DEMOCRATIC NATIONS SHOW A MORE ARDENT AND
   ENDURING LOVE FOR EQUALITY THAN FOR LIBERTY   279

2. OF INDIVIDUALISM IN DEMOCRACIES   281

3. HOW INDIVIDUALISM IS MORE PRONOUNCED
   AT THE END OF A DEMOCRATIC REVOLUTION
   THAN AT ANY OTHER TIME   283

4. HOW THE AMERICANS COMBAT THE EFFECTS
   OF INDIVIDUALISM BY FREE INSTITUTIONS   284

5. ON THE USE WHICH THE AMERICANS MAKE
   OF ASSOCIATIONS IN CIVIL LIFE   286

6. ON THE CONNECTION BETWEEN ASSOCIATIONS
   AND NEWSPAPERS   289

7. RELATIONSHIPS BETWEEN CIVIL
   AND POLITICAL ASSOCIATIONS   290

8. HOW THE AMERICANS COMBAT INDIVIDUALISM
   BY THE DOCTRINE OF SELF-INTEREST
   PROPERLY UNDERSTOOD   293

9. HOW THE AMERICANS APPLY THE DOCTRINE
   OF SELF-INTEREST PROPERLY UNDERSTOOD
   TO RELIGION   295

10. THE TASTE FOR PHYSICAL COMFORT IN AMERICA   297

11. PARTICULAR EFFECTS OF THE LOVE OF PHYSICAL
    PLEASURES IN DEMOCRATIC TIMES   299

12. WHY SOME AMERICANS DISPLAY ENTHUSIASTIC
    FORMS OF SPIRITUALITY   300

13. WHY THE AMERICANS ARE OFTEN SO RESTLESS
    IN THE MIDST OF THEIR PROSPERITY   302

14. HOW IN AMERICA THE TASTE FOR PHYSICAL
    PLEASURES IS COMBINED WITH LOVE OF FREEDOM
    AND ATTENTION TO PUBLIC AFFAIRS   305

15. HOW RELIGIOUS BELIEFS AT TIMES TURN
    THE THOUGHTS OF AMERICANS TOWARD
    SPIRITUAL THINGS   307

16. HOW EXCESSIVE LOVE OF PROSPERITY
    CAN DO HARM TO IT   310

17. WHY IN AGES OF EQUALITY AND SKEPTICISM
    IT IS IMPORTANT TO SET DISTANT GOALS
    FOR HUMAN ENDEAVOR   311

18. WHY AMERICANS CONSIDER ALL HONEST CALLINGS
    HONORABLE   312

19. WHAT GIVES ALMOST ALL AMERICANS
    A PREFERENCE FOR INDUSTRIAL CALLINGS   314

20. HOW AN ARISTOCRACY MAY BE CREATED BY INDUSTRY   316

PART III

Influence of Democracy on Mores Properly So Called

1. HOW MORES BECOME MORE GENTLE
    AS SOCIAL CONDITIONS BECOME MORE EQUAL   323

2. HOW DEMOCRACY LEADS TO EASE AND SIMPLICITY
    IN THE ORDINARY RELATIONS BETWEEN AMERICANS   325

3. WHY THE AMERICANS ARE SO HARD TO
    OFFEND IN THEIR OWN COUNTRY AND SO
    EASILY OFFENDED IN OURS   326

4. CONSEQUENCES DERIVING FROM THE
    THREE PRECEDING CHAPTERS   329

5. HOW DEMOCRACY MODIFIES THE RELATIONS
    BETWEEN MASTER AND SERVANT   330

6. INFLUENCE OF DEMOCRACY ON WAGES   333

7. INFLUENCE OF DEMOCRACY ON THE FAMILY   335

8. EDUCATION OF GIRLS IN THE UNITED STATES   338

9. THE YOUNG WOMAN AS A WIFE   340

10. HOW EQUALITY HELPS TO MAINTAIN
    GOOD MORALS IN AMERICA   342

11. HOW THE AMERICAN VIEWS
THE EQUALITY OF THE SEXES 344

12. HOW EQUALITY NATURALLY DIVIDES
THE AMERICANS INTO A MULTITUDE
OF SMALL PRIVATE CIRCLES 348

13. SOME REFLECTIONS ON AMERICAN MANNERS 350

14. ON THE GRAVITY OF THE AMERICANS
AND WHY IT OFTEN DOES NOT PREVENT
THEIR DOING ILL-CONSIDERED THINGS 351

15. WHY AMERICAN NATIONAL PRIDE HAS
A MORE RESTLESS AND QUARRELSOME
CHARACTER THAN THAT OF THE ENGLISH 354

16. HOW THE ASPECT OF SOCIETY IN THE UNITED
STATES IS AT ONCE AGITATED AND MONOTONOUS 355

17. CONCERNING HONOR IN THE UNITED STATES
AND DEMOCRATIC SOCIETIES 357

18. WHY THERE ARE SO MANY MEN OF AMBITION
IN THE UNITED STATES BUT SO FEW LOFTY
AMBITIONS 361

19. CONCERNING PLACE-HUNTING IN SOME
DEMOCRATIC COUNTRIES 365

20. WHY GREAT REVOLUTIONS WILL BECOME RARE 367

21. WHY DEMOCRATIC PEOPLES NATURALLY
WANT PEACE BUT DEMOCRATIC ARMIES WAR 373

22. SOME CONSIDERATIONS CONCERNING
WAR IN DEMOCRATIC SOCIETIES 376

PART IV

On the Influence of Democratic Ideas and Feelings on Political Society

1. EQUALITY NATURALLY GIVES MEN THE TASTE
   FOR FREE INSTITUTIONS   381

2. WHY THE IDEAS OF DEMOCRATIC PEOPLES
   ABOUT GOVERNMENT NATURALLY FAVOR
   THE CONCENTRATION OF POLITICAL POWER   382

3. HOW BOTH THE FEELINGS AND THE
   THOUGHTS OF DEMOCRATIC NATIONS ARE IN
   ACCORD IN CONCENTRATING POLITICAL POWER   384

4. CONCERNING CERTAIN PECULIAR AND
   ACCIDENTAL CAUSES WHICH EITHER LEAD A
   DEMOCRATIC PEOPLE TO COMPLETE THE
   CENTRALIZATION OF GOVERNMENT OR DIVERT
   THEM FROM IT   386

5. WHAT SORT OF DESPOTISM DEMOCRATIC
   NATIONS HAVE TO FEAR   390

6. CONTINUATION OF THE PRECEDING CHAPTERS   394

7. GENERAL SURVEY OF THE SUBJECT   399

TOCQUEVILLE'S PREFACE TO VOLUME TWO

THE DEMOCRATIC SOCIAL ORDER in America springs naturally from some of their laws and conceptions of public morality.

Moreover, a great many points of view that were unknown in old Europe have come into their world as the offspring of this social order. Changes in civil society have been as great as those in the world of politics.

The book about American democracy which I published five years ago dealt with the latter. This book is concerned with the former. The two volumes are complementary and should be read as a single book.

I must at once warn the reader against a mistake through which I might be seriously misunderstood.

Noticing how many different effects I hold due to equality, he might suppose that I consider equality the sole cause of everything that is happening now. That would be a very narrow view to attribute to me.

There are nowadays a great number of opinions, feelings, and instincts due to circumstances unrelated, even antipathetic, to equality. Thus, I could easily show that ways of thinking and feeling are profoundly influenced by the nature of the country, the origin of the colonists, the religion of the founding fathers, the enlightenment they acquired, and their former habits, all things unconnected with democracy. In like manner a great deal of what is happening in Europe can be explained by various factors, different from those operative in America but equally untouched by the fact of equality.

I know that all these different elements are powerful, but this book does not deal with them. I have not undertaken to account for all our inclinations and all our ideas, but only wish to demonstrate how equality has modified both.

As I am firmly convinced that the democratic revolution occurring before our eyes is irresistible and that it would be neither desirable nor wise to try to combat it, it may seem surprising that this book expresses severe criticisms of the democratic societies created by this revolution.

My answer is simply that, being no enemy of democracy, I want to treat it with sincerity.

Enemies never tell men the truth, and it is seldom that their friends do so. That is why I have done so.

Many people are ready to advertise the benefits which democracy promises to mankind, but few point out the distant perils it threatens. So my attention has been directed principally against these dangers, and I have not played the coward and kept silent.

I hope that the impartiality for which my first book was credited will be found again in this work.

The ground I wish to cover is vast. It includes the greater part of the feelings and ideas which are responsible for the changed state of the world. Such a subject is certainly beyond my strength, and I am far from satisfied with my own achievement.

But if I have not succeeded, I hope I shall be credited with pursuing the undertaking in a spirit which could make me worthy of success.

PART I

Influence of Democracy
on the Intellectual Movements
in the United States

1

CONCERNING THE PHILOSOPHICAL
APPROACH OF THE AMERICANS

LESS ATTENTION, I SUPPOSE, is paid to philosophy in the United States than in any other country of the civilized world. The Americans have no school of philosophy peculiar to themselves, and they pay very little attention to the European schools. Indeed they hardly know their names. Nevertheless, though they have not taken the trouble to define the rules, the people of the United States have a philosophical method shared by all.

To escape from imposed systems, the yoke of habit, family maxims, class prejudices, and to a certain extent national prejudices; to treat tradition as valuable for information only and to accept existing facts as no more than a sketch to show how things could be done better; to seek by and in themselves for the only reason for things, and looking through forms to the basis of things—such are the principal characteristics of what I would call the American philosophical method.

To select the chief among these various features, which includes almost all the others within itself, I should say that in most mental operations each American relies on individual effort and judgment.

So, of all countries in the world, America is the one in which the precepts of Descartes are least studied and best followed. No one should be surprised at that.

When it comes to the influence of one man's mind over another's, that is very restricted in a country where citizens have become more or less similar, see each other at close quarters, and since they do not recognize any incontestable superiority in their fellows, are continually brought back to their own judgment as the test of truth. There is a general distaste for accepting any man's word as proof of anything.

So each man is narrowly shut up in himself, and from that basis makes the pretension to judge the world.

This American way of relying on themselves alone leads to the conclusion that everything in the world can be explained and that nothing passes beyond the limits of intelligence.

So the Americans have needed no books to teach them philosophic method, having found it in themselves.

This same method has only become established and popular in Europe as conditions of life have become more equal and men more like one another.

The sixteenth-century reformers subjected some of the dogmas of ancient faith to individual reason, but they still refused to allow all others to be discussed. In the seventeenth century Bacon, in natural science, and Descartes, in philosophy, abolished accepted formulas, destroyed the dominion of tradition, and upset the authority of masters.

The eighteenth-century philosopher turned this same principle into a general rule and undertook to submit the object of all his beliefs to each man's individual examination. Luther, Descartes, and Voltaire all used the same method.

It was discovered at a time when men were beginning to grow more equal. It could not be generally followed except when conditions had become more or less similar and people like each other.

It follows that the eighteenth-century philosophic method is not just French, but democratic. The reason the French turned the world upside down is not simply that they changed their ancient beliefs. They were the first to generalize a philosophic method by which all ancient things could be attacked and the way opened for everything new.

If I am asked why nowadays that method is more often and more strictly applied by the French than by the Americans, though liberty is of longer date among the latter, I reply that that is partly due to two circumstances that must first be understood.

It was religion that gave birth to the English colonies in America. One must never forget that. In the United States religion is mingled with all the national customs and all those feelings which the word *fatherland* evokes. This puts strict limits on individual analysis and many of the most important subjects about which men can have opinions.

The other circumstance is this:

The state of society and the Constitution in America are democratic, but there has been no democratic revolution. They were pretty well as they now are when they first arrived in the land. That is a very important point.

Every revolution must shake ancient beliefs, sap authority, and cloud shared ideas. So any revolution, to a greater or lesser extent, throws men back on themselves and opens to each man's view an almost limitless empty space. Consequently each man undertakes to be sufficient to himself and glories in the fact that his beliefs about everything are peculiar to himself.

Thus the independence of mind which equality supposes to exist is never so great as at the moment when equality begins to be established. One must make a careful distinction between that intellectual liberty which can result from equality and the anarchy brought by revolution. Each of these two elements must be considered separately if we are not to exaggerate hopes and fears for the future.

2

CONCERNING THE PRINCIPAL SOURCE OF BELIEFS AMONG DEMOCRATIC PEOPLES

DOGMATIC BELIEFS ARE MORE or less numerous at different periods. But it can never happen that there are no beliefs which men take on trust without discussion. If each man undertook to make up his mind about everything, it is unlikely that people would ever agree on any common belief.

However, without ideas in common, no common action would be possible. So for society to exist and, even more, for society to prosper, it is essential that the minds of the citizens be rallied and held together by some leading ideas; and that could never happen unless each was ready to accept some beliefs ready made.

If man had to prove for himself all the truths of which he makes use every day, he would wear himself out and make no progress. Since life is too short and human faculties are too limited, man has to accept a whole heap of facts and opinions which cleverer men than he have discovered and which the crowd accepts. On that foundation he then builds the house of his own thoughts. Among all the things about which men have opinions, some beliefs must be accepted without discussion so that it is possible to go deeply into a few selected ones for examination.

It is true that any man accepting any opinion on trust from another puts his mind in bondage. But it is a salutary bondage, which allows him to make good use of freedom.

Thus men who live in times of equality find it hard to place the intellectual authority to which they submit, beyond and outside humanity. One can anticipate that democratic peoples will not easily believe in divine missions, that they will be quick to laugh at new prophets, and that they will wish to find the chief arbiter of their beliefs within, and not beyond, the limits of their kind.

The nearer men are to a common level of uniformity, the less are they inclined to believe blindly in any man or any class. But they are readier to trust the mass, and public opinion becomes more and more mistress of the world.

Not only is public opinion the only guide left to aid private judgment, but its power is infinitely greater in democracies than elsewhere. For they think that, all having the same means of knowledge, truth will be found on the side of the majority.

The citizen of a democracy compares himself with all his fellows and is overwhelmed by a sense of his insignificance and weakness. The same equality which makes him independent of each separate citizen leaves him isolated and defenseless in the face of the majority.

So in democracies public opinion has a strange power of which aristocratic nations can form no conception. It uses no persuasion, but by some mighty pressure of the mind of all upon the intelligence of each it imposes its ideas and makes them penetrate men's very souls.

The majority in the United States takes over the business of supplying the individual with ready-made opinions and so relieves him of the necessity of forming his own. So there are many theories of philosophy, morality, and politics which everyone adopts unexamined on the faith of public opinion. And if one looks very closely into the matter, one finds that religion is strong less as a revealed doctrine than as part of common opinion.

I know that American political laws give the majority the right to rule society, and this political omnipotence augments the power which public opinion would have had without it over each citizen, but it is not the foundation thereof. One must look to equality itself for the source of that influence. In times of equality, no matter what political laws men devise for themselves, it is safe to foresee that trust in common opinion will become a sort of religion, with the majority as its prophet.

If democratic peoples substituted the absolute power of a majority for all the various powers that used to impede individual thought, the evil itself would only have changed its form. Men would by no means have found the way to live in independence; they would only have succeeded in giving slavery a new face. There is matter for deep reflection there. I cannot say this too often for all those who see freedom of the mind as something sacred and who hate despotism. For myself, if I feel the hand of power heavy on my brow, I am no better inclined to pass my head under the yoke because a million men hold it for me.

3

WHY THE AMERICANS SHOW MORE APTITUDE AND TASTE FOR GENERAL IDEAS THAN THEIR ENGLISH FOREFATHERS

GENERAL IDEAS HAVE THIS excellent quality, that they permit human minds to pass judgment quickly on a great number of things; but the conceptions they convey are always incomplete, and what is gained in extent is always lost in exactitude.

The Americans use general ideas much more than the English and have a greater relish for them. This seems very strange at first sight, considering that the two nations have a common origin, that for centuries they have lived under the same laws, and that there is still a continual give and take of ideas and moral standards between them.

Men living in times of equality have much curiosity and little leisure. Life is so practical, complicated, agitated, and active that they have little time for thinking. So democratic man likes generalizations because they save him the trouble of studying particular cases. They contain, if I may put it so, a lot in a small space and give a great return quickly. So when, after a cursory and casual glance, they think they can see a common link between certain things without looking into the matter further, and disregarding the details in which these various things may be like or unlike, they are in a hurry to class them all under the same formula so as to go on to something else.

One of the characteristics of democratic times is that all men have a taste for easy successes and immediate pleasures. This is true of intellectual pursuits as well. Most men who live in times of equality are full of lively yet indolent ambition. They want great success at once, but without great efforts. These contrary instincts lead them straight to looking for generalizations, by which they flatter themselves that they can paint vast canvases cheaply and attract public attention without trouble.

I do not know that they are wrong in thinking so. For their readers are just as afraid of profundity as they are themselves and generally look only for facile pleasures and effortless instruction in the works of the mind.

4

HOW RELIGION IN THE UNITED STATES MAKES USE OF DEMOCRATIC INSTINCTS

AN EARLIER CHAPTER HAS shown that men cannot do without dogmatic beliefs, and even that it is most desirable that they should have them. I would add here that religious dogmas seem to me the most desirable of all. That can clearly be deduced, even if one only considers the interests of this world.

There is hardly any human action, however private it may be, which does not result from some very general conception men have of God. It is of immense importance to have fixed ideas about God, their souls, and their duties toward their Creator and their fellows, for doubt about these would leave all their actions to chance and condemn them, more or less, to anarchy and impotence.

That is the most important question about which all of us need fixed ideas, and unfortunately it is the subject which is most difficult for each of us, left to his own unaided reason. General ideas

---

[Originally chapter 5. Tocqueville's chapter 4, "Why the Americans Have Never Been as Eager as the French for General Ideas About Political Affairs," has been omitted.]

respecting God and human nature are therefore the ideas above all others which ought to be withdrawn from private judgment.

The chief object and one of the principal advantages of religion is to provide answers to primordial questions; these answers must be clear, precise, intelligible to the crowd, and very durable.

When there is no authority in religion or in politics, men are soon frightened by the limitless independence with which they are faced. For my part, I doubt whether man can support complete religious independence and entire political liberty at the same time. If he has no faith, he must obey; and if he is free, he must believe.

The great usefulness of religions is even more apparent among egalitarian peoples than elsewhere. One must admit that equality, while it brings great benefits to mankind, tends to isolate men from each other so that each thinks only of himself. It lays the soul open to an inordinate love of material pleasure.

Every religion places the object of man's desires beyond worldly goods and lifts the soul above the realm of the senses. Every religion also imposes on each man some obligations toward mankind, and so draws him away, from time to time, from thinking about himself.

Thus religious peoples are naturally strong just at the point where democratic peoples are weak. And that shows how important it is for people to keep their religion when they become equal.

I have pointed out how in times of enlightenment and democracy the human spirit is loath to accept dogmatic beliefs and has no need for them except in the matter of religion. At such times above all, religions should be most careful to confine themselves to their proper sphere, for if they extend beyond spiritual matters they run the risk of not being believed at all.

Muhammad brought down from heaven and put into the Koran not religious doctrines only, but political maxims, criminal and civil laws, and scientific theories. The Gospels, on the other hand, deal only with the general relations between man and God and between man and man. Beyond that, they teach nothing and do not oblige people to believe anything. That alone, among a thousand reasons, is enough to show that Islam will not be able to hold its power long in ages of enlightenment and democracy, while Christianity is destined to reign in such ages, as in all others.

Another truth seems very clear to me, that religions should pay less attention to external practices in democratic times than in any others.

In speaking of the philosophical method of the Americans I have made clear that in a time of equality nothing is more repugnant than the idea of submitting to formalities. Men living at such times are impatient of figures of speech; symbols appear to them as childish artifices used to hide or dress up truths which could more naturally be shown to them naked and in broad daylight. Ceremonies leave them cold, and their natural tendency is to attach but secondary importance to the details of worship.

In democratic ages those who regulate the external forms of worship should pay special attention to these propensities in order not to run counter to them unnecessarily.

I believe firmly in the need for external ceremonies. They fix the human spirit in contemplation of abstract truths and help it to grasp them firmly and believe ardently in them. I do not imagine that it is possible to maintain a religion without external observances. Nevertheless, I think that in the coming centuries that they should be limited to such as are absolutely necessary to perpetuate dogma itself, which is the essence of religions,[1] whereas ritual is only the form. A religion which became more inflexible and more burdened with petty observances at a time when people were becoming more equal would soon find itself reduced to a band of fanatic zealots in the midst of a skeptical multitude.

A passion for well-being is, as we shall see, the most lively of all the emotions aroused by equality, and it is the most striking and unalterable characteristic of democratic ages.

---

1. In all religions there are ceremonies which are inherent in the very substance of belief, and one must take care not to change anything in them. That is especially seen in the Catholic religion, where form and substance are so closely united that they are one.

It may be that, should any religion attempt to destroy this mother of all desires, it would itself be destroyed thereby. If it attempted to wean men entirely from thinking of the good things of this world in order to concentrate on the next, sooner or later men's souls would slip through its fingers to plunge headlong into the delights of purely material and immediate satisfactions.

The main business of religions is to purify and restrain that excessive taste for well-being which men acquire in times of equality, but it would be a mistake to attempt to conquer it entirely. They will never succeed in preventing men from loving wealth, but they may be able to induce them to use only honest means to enrich themselves.

Religion in America is a world apart in which the clergyman is supreme, but one which he is careful never to leave; within its limits he guides men's minds, while outside he leaves men to themselves, to the freedom and instability natural to the times they live in.

While [clergymen] do no productive work, they take an interest in industry and praise its achievements; while they are ever pointing to the other world as the great object of hopes and fears, they do not forbid the honest pursuit of prosperity in this. Far from trying to show that these two worlds are opposed to each other, they seek to discover the points of connection and alliance.

All the clergy of America are aware of the intellectual domination of the majority, and they treat it with respect. They never struggle against it unless necessary. They keep aloof from party squabbles, but they freely adopt the general views of their country and let themselves go with the tide of feeling which carries everything around them along with it. They try to improve their contemporaries but do not quit fellowship with them. Public opinion is therefore never hostile to them but rather supports and protects them. Faith thus derives its authority partly from its inherent strength and partly from the borrowed support of public opinion.

Thus, by respecting all democratic instincts which are not against it and making use of many favorable ones, religion succeeds in struggling successfully with that spirit of individual independence which is its most dangerous enemy.

5

HOW EQUALITY SUGGESTS TO THE AMERICANS THE IDEA OF THE INDEFINITE PERFECTIBILITY OF MAN

EQUALITY PUTS MANY IDEAS into the human mind which would not have come there without it, and it changes almost all the ideas that were there before. I take the concept of human perfectibility as an example, for that is a great philosophical theory, whose effects can be seen at every moment in the conduct of affairs.

Though man resembles the animals in many respects, he improves himself, and they do not. Mankind could not fail to discover this difference from the beginning. So the idea of perfectibility is as old as the world; equality had no share in its birth but has given it a new character.

When citizens are classified by rank, profession, or birth, and when all are obliged to follow the career before them, no one attempts to fight against an inevitable fate. It is not that aristocratic peoples deny man's capacity to improve himself, but they do not think it unlimited. They think in terms of amelioration, not change; they imagine that societies of the future will be better but not really different; and as nothing around them is on the move, they gladly assume that everything is in its right place.

But when castes disappear and men are jumbled together, when old conceptions vanish and new ones take their place, then the human mind imagines an indefinite capacity for improvement. His setbacks teach him that no one has discovered absolute good;

[Originally chapter 8. Tocqueville's chapter 6, "Concerning the Progress of Roman Catholicism in the United States," and chapter 7, "What Causes Democratic Nations to Incline Toward Pantheism," have been omitted.]

his successes inspire him to seek it without slackening. Thus, searching always, falling, picking himself up again, often disappointed, never discouraged, he is ever striving toward that immense grandeur glimpsed indistinctly at the end of the long track humanity must follow.

I once met an American sailor and asked him why his country's ships are made so that they will not last long. He answered offhand that the art of navigation was making such quick progress that even the best of boats would be almost useless if it lasted more than a few years.

I recognized in these casual words of an uneducated man about a particular subject the general and systematic conception by which a great people conducts all its affairs.

Aristocratic nations are by their nature too much inclined to restrict the scope of human perfectibility; democratic nations sometimes stretch it beyond reason.

6

WHY THE EXAMPLE OF THE AMERICANS DOES NOT PROVE THAT A DEMOCRATIC PEOPLE CAN HAVE NO APTITUDE OR TASTE FOR SCIENCE, LITERATURE, OR THE ARTS

IT MUST BE ADMITTED that few civilized nations of our time have made less progress than the United States in the higher sciences or had so few great artists, poets, or writers.

Some Europeans, struck by this fact, have considered it the inevitable result of equality and have supposed that if democratic soci-

[Originally chapter 9.]

ety were ever to prevail over the earth, the human mind would gradually fall back into darkness.

Those who argue in this way unintentionally confuse what is democratic with what is only American.

The religion professed by the first immigrants was austere and almost harsh in its principles, and therefore unfavorable to the fine arts and the pleasures of literature. In America everyone finds opportunities unknown anywhere else for making or increasing his fortune. A breathless cupidity perpetually distracts the mind of man from the pleasures of the imagination and the labors of the intellect and urges it on to nothing but the pursuit of wealth.

However, I am convinced that if the Americans had been alone in the world, they would not have been slow to discover that progress cannot long be made in the application of the sciences without studying the theory of them. But just at the time when the Americans were naturally inclined to require nothing of science but useful arts and ways of making life comfortable, the learned men of Europe were undertaking the search for the basic principles of truth, and at the same time improving everything that can minister to the pleasures or satisfy the wants of men.

The people of the United States were particularly closely linked to one of the leading nations in the cultural life of the Old World, and so could gather the treasures of the mind without working to produce them themselves.

I do not think the intervening ocean really separates America from Europe. Thus the Americans are in an exceptional situation, and it is unlikely that any other democratic people will be similarly placed. Their strictly Puritan origin; their exclusively commercial habits; the accessibility of Europe, which allows them to neglect these things without relapsing into barbarism—a thousand special causes fix the mind of the American on purely practical objects. His desires, needs, education, and circumstances all draw the American's mind earthward. Only religion from time to time makes him turn a transient and distracted glance toward heaven.

We should therefore give up looking at all democratic peoples through American spectacles and try at last to see them as they actually are.

Enlightened men living in a democracy readily discover that nothing can confine them, hold them, or force them to be content with their present lot.

They all therefore conceive the idea of bettering themselves. Being free, they all attempt it, but all do not succeed in the same way. The law, it is true, no longer grants privileges, but nature does so. Natural inequality will soon make itself felt, and wealth will pass spontaneously into the hands of the most capable.

Free democratic societies will then always include a number of people who are rich or comfortably off. There will not be the same close ties between these rich people as there was between the members of the old aristocracy; their temperaments will be different and they will hardly ever be assured of such complete leisure. But they will be infinitely more numerous than any aristocracy could be. These persons will not be strictly tied to the drudgery of practical life, and they will be able, in different degrees of course, to devote themselves to the labors and pleasures of the mind.

Not only will the number of those who can take an interest in things of the mind be greater, but the taste for intellectual enjoyment will descend step by step even to those who in aristocratic societies have neither time nor ability to enjoy them.

When there is no more hereditary wealth, class privilege, or prerogatives of birth, and when every man derives his strength from himself alone, it becomes clear that the chief source of disparity between the fortunes of men lies in the mind. Whatever tends to invigorate, expand, or adorn the mind rises instantly to a high value.

Even the crowd can now plainly see the utility of knowledge, and those who have no taste for its charms set store by its results and make some effort to acquire it.

In times of freedom and enlightened democracy there is nothing to separate men or to keep them in their place. They rise or fall extraordinarily quickly. Men of different classes are continually meeting. Every day they mix and exchange ideas, imitating and emulating one another. So the people get many ideas and desires which they never would have if distinctions of rank had been fixed and society static.

Therefore no one easily allows himself to be confined to the mere material cares of life, and the humblest artisan occasionally casts an eager, furtive glance at the higher regions of the mind. The circle of readers continually increases and finally includes all the citizens.

As soon as the crowd begins to take an interest in the labors of the mind it finds out that to excel in some of them is a powerful aid to the acquisition of fame, power, or wealth. Restless ambition born of equality turns to this as to all other directions. The number of those studying science, literature, and the arts becomes immense. Everyone tries to blaze a trail for himself and attract public attention. Much the same happens as in the political life of the United States; what is done is often imperfect, but the attempts are innumerable; and though each individual achievement is generally very small, the total effect is always very great.

So it is not true that men living in democratic times are naturally indifferent to science, literature, and the arts; only it must be acknowledged that they cultivate them in their own fashion and bring their own peculiar qualities and defects to the task.

7

WHY THE AMERICANS ARE MORE CONCERNED WITH THE APPLICATIONS THAN WITH THE THEORY OF SCIENCE

SEVERAL OBSERVATIONS MADE EARLIER about the philosophical method of the Americans are applicable here.

Equality stimulates each man to want to judge everything for himself and gives him a taste for the tangible and real and a contempt for tradition and formalities. These general tendencies are especially to the fore in the context of this chapter.

Those in democracies who study sciences like to stick to the facts and study them for themselves. As they have little deference for the mere name of any fellow, they are never inclined to take a master's word on trust, but tend to look for the weak side of his argument. Scientific traditions have little hold over them, and they will not accept big words as sterling coin. They penetrate, as far as they can, into the main parts of the subject that interests them, and they like to expound in popular language. Scientific pursuits thus follow a freer and safer course but a less lofty one.

In America the purely practical side of science is cultivated admirably. About the theoretical side, immediately necessary to application, the Americans always display a clear, free, original, and creative turn of mind. But hardly anyone devotes himself to the essentially theoretical and abstract side of human knowledge. In this the Americans carry to excess a trend which can, I think, be noticed, though in a less degree, among all democratic nations.

Everyone is on the move, some in quest of power, others of gain. In the midst of this universal tumult, this incessant conflict of

---

[Originally chapter 10.]

jarring interests, this endless chase for wealth, where is one to find the calm for the profound researches of the intellect?

Not only is meditation difficult for men in democracies, but habits of thought useful in action are not always helpful to thought. The man of action often has to make do with approximations, for he would never accomplish his purpose if he wanted to make every detail perfect. He must always be acting on ideas which he has not had time to plumb deeply, for the seasonableness of an idea is more often useful to him than its strict accuracy. Moreover, by and large it is less risky to rely on some false principles than to waste time establishing the truth of them all. It is not long and learned demonstrations which keep the world going. A quick glance at a particular fact, the chance of the moment, and skill to grasp it—such things decide all its affairs.

In democratic centuries when almost everyone is engaged in active life, the darting speed of a quick, superficial mind is at a premium, while slow, deep thought is undervalued.

If Pascal had had nothing in view beyond great gain, or the love of fame alone, I cannot conceive that he would have been able to rally all the powers of his mind to discover the most hidden secrets of the Creator. When I see him tearing his soul free from the cares of this life so as to stake the whole of it on this quest, so that he died of old age before he was forty, I understand that no ordinary cause was at work in such an extraordinary effort.

The future will show whether such rare, creative passions come to birth and grow as easily in democracies as in aristocratic communities. For myself, I confess that I can hardly believe it.

In aristocratic societies vast ideas are generally entertained of the dignity, the power, and the greatness of man. Such opinions influence those who cultivate the sciences, as they do all others. Men of learning are consequently impelled toward theory and even contempt for practice. "Archimedes," Plutarch tells us, "was of such a lofty spirit that he never condescended to write any treatise on the way to make all these engines of war. As he held this science of inventing and putting together machines, and all arts, generally speaking, which tended to any useful end in practice, to be vile,

low, and mercenary, he spent his talents and his studious hours in
writing only of those things whose beauty and subtlety had in them
no admixture of necessity."[1] That is the aristocratic view of science.

It cannot be the same in democracies.

Most of the people in these nations think about nothing but
changing their lot and bettering it. Every new way of getting wealth
more quickly, every machine which lessens work, every means of
diminishing the costs of production, every invention which makes
pleasures easier or greater, seems the most magnificent accomplishment of the human mind. It is chiefly from this line of approach that democratic peoples come to study sciences and to
value them. In aristocratic ages the chief function of science is to
give pleasure to the mind, but in democratic ages to the body.

I certainly do not mean to imply that the democratic nations of
our time will witness the extinction of the transcendent lights of
the mind, or even that they will not light new flames. While so
many things are being tried out, with new experiments every day,
it is almost impossible that very general laws should not frequently
be brought to light.

Besides that, democracy may not lead men to study science for
its own sake, but it does immensely increase the number who do
study it. Nor is it credible that among so great a multitude a speculative genius should not from time to time arise inspired by the
love of truth alone. Such a one will surely penetrate the deepest
mysteries of nature, whatever be the spirit of his time and place.
All that I mean to say is this: permanent inequality leads men to
confine themselves to the search for abstract truths, while the institutions of democratic society tend to make them look only for the
practical applications of science.

If those who direct the affairs of nations can understand these
new tendencies, they will see that, granted enlightenment and liberty, people living in a democratic age are quite certain to bring

1. [Cf. *Life of Marcellus*, Plutarch's *Lives*, Bohn's Edition, vol. 2, p. 47, London
1887. Tocqueville seems to quote rather freely.]

the industrial side of science to perfection anyhow. Henceforth the whole energy of organized society should be directed to the support of higher studies and the fostering of a passion for pure science. Nowadays the need is to keep men interested in theory. They will look after the practical side of things for themselves.

Because Roman civilization perished through barbarian invasions, we are perhaps too much inclined to think that that is the only way a civilization can die.

If the lights that guide us ever go out, they will fade little by little, as if of their own accord. Confining ourselves to practice, we may lose sight of basic principles, and when these have been forgotten, we may apply the methods derived from them badly; we might be left without the capacity to invent new methods, and only able to make clumsy use of wise procedures no longer understood.

We therefore should not console ourselves by thinking that the barbarians are still a long way off. Some peoples may let the torch be snatched from their hands, but others stamp it out themselves.

8

IN WHAT SPIRIT THE AMERICANS CULTIVATE THE ARTS

IT WOULD BE A waste of my readers' time and of my own to explain how the general standard of wealth and the universal desire for comfort encourage a taste for the useful more than the love of beauty. Democratic peoples with these characteristics cultivate those arts which help to make life comfortable rather than those

---

[Originally chapter 11.]

which adorn it. They habitually put use before beauty, and they want beauty itself to be useful.

But I want to carry the argument further, and having made this first point, to sketch several other characteristics.

The immobility natural to aristocratic peoples tends to form all those who practice the same craft into a distinct class, always composed of the same families, among whom a sense of corporate pride soon develop[s]. Hence each craftsman belonging to this industrial class has not only his fortune to make but also his professional standing to preserve. Corporate interests count for more than either his own self-interest or the purchaser's needs. So in aristocratic ages the emphasis is on doing things as well as possible, not as quickly or as cheaply as one can.

In contrast, when every profession is open to all, with a crowd of folk forever taking it up and dropping it again, the craftsmen don't know or care about one another and indeed hardly ever meet, being so many. The social link between them is broken, and each tries to make as much money as easily as possible.

This affects the whole way a people looks at the arts.

Craftsmen in aristocratic societies work for a strictly limited number of customers who are very hard to please. Perfect workmanship gives the best hope of profit.

The situation is very different when privileges have been abolished and classes intermingled and when men are continually rising and falling. [The latter] still have tastes acquired in their time of prosperity without the means to indulge them, and they are on the lookout for some roundabout way of doing so. There are, too, in any democracy men whose fortunes are on the increase but whose desires increase much more quickly than their wealth. They are always on the lookout for shortcuts to these anticipated delights. These two elements, whose desires outrun their means, will gladly put up with an imperfect substitute rather than do without the object of their desire altogether.

The craftsman in aristocracies charged very high prices to a few. He now sees that he can get rich quicker by selling cheaply to all.

There are only two ways of making a product cheaper.

The first is to find better, quicker, more skillful ways of making it. The second is to make a great number of objects which are more or less the same but not so good. In a democracy every workman applies his wits to both these points. In this way democracy, apart from diverting attention to the useful arts, induces workmen to make shoddy things very quickly and consumers to put up with them.

Craftsmen in democratic ages do not seek only to bring the useful things they make within the reach of every citizen, but also try to give each object a look of brilliance unconnected with its true worth.

In the confusion of classes each man wants to appear as something he is not. Such feelings are not born of democracy, for they are all too natural to the heart of man, but it is democracy which applies them to material products. The hypocrisy of virtue is of every age, but the hypocrisy of luxury is peculiar to democratic centuries.

Unable any longer to conceive greatness, they try for elegance and prettiness. Appearance counts for more than reality.

Aristocracies produce a few great pictures, democracies a multitude of little ones. The one makes statues of bronze, the other of plaster.

When I first arrived in New York by that part of the Atlantic known as the East River, I was surprised to notice along the shore a number of little white marble palaces, some of them in classical architectural style. The next day, when I looked more closely at one that had struck me most, I found that it was built of whitewashed brick and that the columns were of painted wood. All the buildings I had admired the day before were the same.

The social conditions and institutions of democracy impart peculiar tendencies to all the imitative arts. The soul is often left out of the picture which portrays the body only; movement and sensation take the place of feeling and thought; finally realism takes the place of the ideal.

9

WHY THE AMERICANS ERECT
SOME PETTY MONUMENTS AND OTHERS
THAT ARE VERY GRAND

NOWHERE ELSE DO THE citizens seem smaller than in a democratic nation, and nowhere else does the nation itself seem greater, so that it is easily conceived as a vast picture. Hence people living cramped lives in tiny houses often conceive their public monuments on a gigantic scale.

When the Americans planned to build a capital, they marked out a vast extent of land for a huge city; that city, even today, has hardly more inhabitants than Pontoise, but according to them it should one day hold a population of a million. They have already rooted up trees for ten miles around, lest they should get in the way of the future citizens of this imagined capital. They have erected a magnificent palace for Congress in the center of the city and given it the pompous name of the Capitol.

The several states of the Union are daily planning and carrying out prodigious enterprises which would astonish the engineers of the great nations of Europe.

Thus democracy not only encourages the making of a lot of trivial things but also inspires the erection of a few very large monuments. However, there is nothing at all between these two extremes. A few enormous buildings can therefore tell us nothing about the social conditions and institutions of the people who put them up.

I may add, though this goes beyond my subject, that they tell us nothing about their greatness, civilization, and real prosperity.

[Originally chapter 12.]

10

LITERARY CHARACTERISTICS
OF DEMOCRATIC CENTURIES

WHEN ONE VISITS A bookshop in the United States and notes the American books crowding the shelves, one is struck by the great number of them, but the number of authors one has heard of seems, on the contrary, very small.

First of all there are a multitude of elementary treatises intended to teach the rudiments of human knowledge. Most of these books were written in Europe; the Americans reprint them, adapting them for their use. Next come an almost innumerable quantity of religious books, Bibles, sermons, pious stories, controversial tracts, and reports of charitable societies. Then there comes the long catalog of political pamphlets, for in America the parties do not publish books to refute each other, but pamphlets which circulate at an incredible rate, last a day, and die.

Among this host of dim productions appear the more remarkable works of only a small number of authors who are known in Europe or deserve to be known there.

Although America now pays perhaps less attention to literature than any other civilized country, there is nevertheless a large number of people who take an interest in things of the mind, and if they do not give their lives to such studies, at least entertain their leisure with them. But it is England which supplies them with most of the books they need. Almost all important English books are republished in the United States. The literary inspiration of Great Britain darts its beams into the depths of the forests of the New World. There is hardly a pioneer's hut which does not contain a

---

[Originally chapter 13.]

few odd volumes of Shakespeare. I remember reading the feudal drama of *Henry V* for the first time in a log cabin.

American citizens seem so convinced that books are not published for their benefit that before deciding on the merits of one of their own writers they usually wait till the English have had a chance to sample his work.

So the Americans have not yet, properly speaking, got any literature. Only the journalists strike me as truly American. They certainly are not great writers, but they speak their country's language and they make themselves heard. If the Americans, with the same social condition and laws, had had a different origin and been transplanted into a different country, I do not doubt that they would have had a literature. As things are, I am sure that they will have one in the end. But it will have a character peculiarly its own. No one can guess that character beforehand.

Imagine a democracy prepared by old tradition and present culture to enjoy the pleasures of the mind. Classes there are intermingled and confused; knowledge as well as power is divided and scattered.

Here, then, is a motley multitude with intellectual wants to be supplied. They are not guided by the same lights and are changing every moment with changing place of residence, feelings, and fortune. It is from this heterogeneous, stirring crowd that authors spring, and from it they must win profit and renown.

In these circumstances one will not expect to find many of those strict conventions accepted by writers and readers in aristocracies. Even if a few conventions are accepted by one generation, it does not follow that the next will observe them too, for in a democracy each generation is a new people. Most of those who have some acquaintance with good writing go into politics or adopt some profession which leaves only short, stolen hours for passing relaxation needed from the serious business of life. Such men will never have a deep understanding of literature. With but short time to spend on books, they want it all to be profitable. They like books which are easily got and quickly read, self-explanatory and immediately enjoyable; above all, they like things unexpected and new. Accustomed to the monotonous struggle of practical life, what they want is vivid, lively emotions, sudden revelations, brilliant truths or errors to plunge them into the middle of the subject.

Need I say any more? Who does not guess what is coming before I say it?

By and large the literature of a democracy will never exhibit the order, regularity, skill, and art characteristic of aristocratic literature; formal qualities will be neglected or actually despised. The style will often be strange, incorrect, overburdened, and loose, and almost always strong and bold. Writers will be more anxious to work quickly than to perfect details. Short works will be commoner than long books, wit than erudition, imagination than depth. There will be a rude and untutored vigor of thought with great variety and singular fecundity. Authors will strive to astonish more than to please, and to stir passions rather than to charm taste.

No doubt there will occasionally be writers who want to follow a different path, and if their merit is great, in spite of their faults and also in spite of their good qualities, they will find readers. But these exceptions will be rare.

I should say more than I mean if I asserted that a nation's literature is always subordinated to its social state and political constitution. I know that, apart from these, there are other causes that give literature certain characteristics, but those do seem the most important to me.

There are always numerous connections between the social and political condition of a people and the inspiration of its writers. He who knows the one is never completely ignorant of the other.

11

THE INDUSTRY OF LITERATURE

DEMOCRACY NOT ONLY GIVES the industrial classes a taste for letters but also brings an industrial spirit into literature.

In aristocracies readers are few and fastidious; in democracies they are immensely more numerous and easier to please. In consequence, a writer may hope to gain moderate renown and great wealth cheaply. The ever-growing crowd of readers always wanting something new ensures the sale of books that nobody esteems highly. A democratic public often treats its authors much as kings usually behave toward their courtiers: it enriches and despises them.

Democratic literature is always crawling with writers who look upon letters simply as a trade, and for each of the few great writers you can count thousands of idea-mongers.

12

HOW AMERICAN DEMOCRACY
HAS MODIFIED THE ENGLISH LANGUAGE

THE READER WHO HAS followed my argument about literature in general will easily understand the sort of influence brought to

---

[Originally chapter 14.]

[Originally chapter 16. Tocqueville's chapter 15, "Why the Study of Greek and Latin Literature Is Peculiarly Useful in Democratic Societies," has been omitted.]

bear on language itself, language which is the chief tool of thought, by democratic society and its institutions.

American authors may fairly be said to live more in England than in America, for they are continually studying English writers and invariably take them as models. But the general population is not like that, being much more immediately affected by the conditions peculiar to the United States. So we must take note of the spoken, not the written, language if we want to understand how the speech of an aristocracy is modified when it becomes the language of a democracy.

Educated Englishmen, better able to appreciate these fine nuances than I, have often told me that the language of well-educated Americans is decidedly different from that spoken by the same class in Great Britain.

Their complaint is not only that the Americans have introduced a lot of new words (the difference between the two countries and the distance between them would have been enough to account for that), but that these new words are generally taken from the jargon of parties, the mechanical arts, or trade. They also say that the Americans have given new meanings to old English words. Finally, they maintain that the Americans often mix their styles in an odd way.

But the continual restlessness of a democracy leads to endless change of language as of all else. In the general stir of intellectual competition a great many new ideas take shape; old ideas get lost or take new forms. So some words must go out of currency, while others come in.

Moreover, democracies like movement for its own sake. That applies to language as well as politics. Even when there is no need to change words, they do so because they want to.

The genius of democracies is seen not only in the great number of new words introduced but even more in the new ideas they express. The majority lays down the law about language as about all else. Now, the majority is more interested in business than study, in trade and politics than in philosophic speculation or fine writing. It is easy to tell where democratic nations will find their new words and how they will shape them.

Citizens living in democratic countries are hardly aware of the languages spoken in Rome and Athens, and they will not be at pains to go back to the classics for the word they need. Democratic peoples willingly borrow from living languages rather than from dead ones, for there is continual communication between them, and peoples of different nations gladly copy one another as they daily grow more like one another.

But democracies chiefly use their own languages when making innovations. Occasionally they pick up forgotten words and put them back into use, or they borrow a technical term and put it into general currency with a figurative meaning. Many phrases originally limited to the trade slang of a craft or group have thus become part of the language.

However, the most common innovation is to give an unwonted meaning to an expression already in use. That method is simple, quick, and easy. But it involves great dangers for the language. In thus giving double meanings to one word, democratic peoples often make both the old and the new signification ambiguous. Then, since there is no accepted judge, no permanent court to decide the meaning of a word, the phrase is left to wander free, leaving the reader to guess which is intended.

This is an annoying feature of democracy. I would rather have the language decked out with Chinese, Tartar, or Huron words than let the meaning of French words become doubtful. You cannot have a good language without clear terms.

But when men are no longer held to a fixed social position, when they continually see one another and talk together, when castes are destroyed and classes change and merge, all of the words of a language get mixed up too. This social revolution affects style as much as language.

Not only does everyone use the same words, but they get into the habit of using them without discrimination. The rules of style are almost destroyed. Hardly any expressions seem, by their nature, vulgar, and hardly any seem refined. Individuals from different strata have brought along, to whatever station they may have risen, the expressions they were accustomed to use; the origin of words is as much forgotten as that of men, and language is in as much confusion as society.

I will not pass on from this subject without pointing out one last trait that is perhaps more characteristic of democratic languages than all the others.

I have noted before that democracies have a taste, and often a passion, for general ideas; that is because of their peculiar qualities, good and bad. A continual use of generic terms and abstract words and a particular way of using them, broaden the scope of thought and allow the mind to include much in few words.

A democratic writer will speak of "actualities," thereby including everything taking place before his eyes in one word, and he will use "eventualities" to cover all that can happen in the universe after the moment at which he is speaking.

Democratic writers are forever using abstract words of this sort, and using them in a more and more abstract sense.

They go further, and to make speech run quicker, personify these abstractions and make them act like real men. They will say, "The force of things wills that capacities govern."

I can best illustrate my meaning by my own example.

I have often used the word *equality* in an absolute sense, and several times have even personified it, so that I have found myself saying that equality did certain things or abstained from others. Frenchmen in the reign of Louis XIV would never have spoken in that way; it would never have entered the head of any of them to use the word *equality* without applying it to some particular thing, and they would have preferred not to use the word at all rather than turn it into a living being.

This abundance of abstract terms in the language of democracy, used without reference to any particular facts, both widens the scope of thought and clouds it. They make expression quicker but conceptions less clear.

Besides, I wonder if vagueness may not have a secret charm for talkers and writers too in these lands.

As these people are often left to depend on the unaided powers of their own minds, they are almost always harassed by doubts. Be-

sides this, in a continually changing situation they are never
obliged to stick firmly to any view once held.

Democratic citizens, then, will often have vacillating thoughts,
and so language must be loose enough to leave them play. As they
never know whether what they say today will fit the facts of tomorrow, they have a natural taste for abstract terms. An abstract word
is like a box with a false bottom; you may put in it what ideas you
please and take them out again unobserved.

The languages of all peoples have a base of generic and abstract
terms, and I do not make out that they are only found among democracies. I only assert that the tendency of men in times of equality is to increase the number of words of this type, to use them with
the most abstract possible meaning, and to use them on every con-
ceivable occasion, whether needed or not.

13

ON SOME SOURCES OF POETIC
INSPIRATION IN DEMOCRACIES

FOR ME POETRY IS the search for and representation of the ideal.

The poet is one who, by omitting parts of what is there, adding
some imaginary touches, and putting together things actual but not
found together, ennobles nature. It is not the poet's function to portray reality but to beautify it and offer the mind some loftier image.

I want to find out whether among the activities, feelings, and
ideas of democracies there are any which lead to a conception of
the ideal and may for that reason be considered natural sources of
poetry.

[Originally chapter 17.]

It must first be acknowledged that the taste for ideal beauty and the pleasure derived from it are never as lively or as widespread in democracies as in aristocracies.

In aristocratic societies it can happen that the needs of the body see to themselves, while the soul is burdened with abundance of leisure. Even the lower classes often have a taste for poetry, the spirit rising beyond and above its surroundings.

But in democracies the love of physical pleasures, the hope to better one's lot, competition, and the lure of success all goad men to activity in their chosen careers and the soul's chief effort goes in that direction. Imagination is not dead, but its chief function is to conceive what may be useful and to portray what is actual.

Aristocracy naturally leads the mind back to the past and fixes it in the contemplation thereof. But democracy engenders a sort of instinctive distaste for what is old. Having deprived poetry of the past, equality also takes away part of the present. Where all are insignificant and very much alike, each man, as he looks at himself, sees all his fellows at the same time. So poets in democracies can never take a particular man as the subject of their poetry, for something of medium size, seen clearly from every angle, never has the making of the ideal.

Thus the spread of equality over the earth dries up the old springs of poetry.

We must try to show how other springs are revealed.

When skepticism had depopulated heaven, and equality had cut each man to a smaller size, the poets, wondering what to substitute for the great themes lost with the aristocracy, first turned their eyes to inanimate nature. Gods and heroes gone, they began by painting rivers and mountains.

This gave rise in the eighteenth century to what is known, par excellence, as descriptive poetry. Some have thought that this is the true poetry of democracy. But I think it only a transitional phenomenon.

In the long run I am sure that democracy turns man's imagination away from externals to concentrate it on himself alone.

Democratic peoples may amuse themselves momentarily by look-ing at nature, but it is about themselves that they are really excited. Here, and here alone, are the true springs of poetry among them.

Democratic peoples do not bother at all about the past, but they gladly start dreaming about the future, and in that direction their imagination spreads and grows beyond measure.

Here, then, are wide vistas open to poetic inspiration that give the chance of painting distant scenes. Democracy shuts the past to poetry but opens the future.

None of the single, nearly equal, roughly similar citizens of a de-mocracy will do as a subject for poetry, but the nation itself calls for poetic treatment. The very likeness of individuals, which rules them out as subjects for poetry on their own, helps the poet to group them in imagination and make a coherent picture of the nation as a whole. Democracies see themselves more vividly than do other nations, an aspect wonderfully suited to painters of the ideal.

I gladly agree that there are no American poets, but I could not admit that Americans have no poetic ideas.

Europeans think a lot about the wild, open spaces of America, but the Americans themselves hardly give them a thought. One may almost say, they do not see the marvelous forests surrounding them until they begin to fall beneath the ax. The American people see themselves marching through wildernesses, drying up marshes, diverting rivers, peopling the wilds, and subduing nature. Not just occasionally, it is something which plays a real part in the least, as in the most important, actions of every man, and it is always flit-ting before his mind.

There is nothing more petty, insipid, crowded with paltry interests—in one word, antipoetic—than the daily life of an Amer-ican. But among the thoughts that direct his life there is always one full of poetry.

In ages of democracy men are always on the move from place to place, peoples of different countries mix, see, hear, and borrow from one another. So it is not only the members of a single nation that come to resemble each other; the nations themselves are assimilated, and one can form the picture of one vast democracy in which a nation counts as a single citizen. Thus for the first time all mankind can be seen together in broad daylight.

The existence of the entire human race, its vicissitudes and its future, thus becomes a fertile theme for poetry.

Incidents in the life of a man or people have made fine subjects for poetry in aristocratic ages, but none of their poets has ever attempted to include the destiny of the whole human race in the scope of his work. That is a task which poets writing in democratic ages may be able to undertake.

Just when every man, raising his eyes above his country, begins at last to see mankind at large, God shows himself more clearly to human perception in full majesty. God's intervention in human affairs appears in a new and brighter light.

This too may be a rich source for the poetry about to blossom in democratic times.

There is no need to traverse earth and sky to find a wondrous object full of contrasts of infinite greatness and littleness, of deep gloom and amazing brightness, capable at the same time of arousing piety, wonder, scorn, and terror. I have only to contemplate myself; man comes from nothing, passes through time, and disappears forever in the bosom of God. He is seen but for a moment wandering on the verge of two abysses, and then is lost.

If man were wholly ignorant of himself he would have no poetry in him. If he saw himself clearly, his imagination would remain idle. But the nature of man is sufficiently revealed for him to know something of himself and sufficiently veiled to leave much in impenetrable darkness, a darkness in which he gropes, forever in vain, trying to understand himself.

Among a democratic people poetry will not feed on legends or memories of old days nor coldly personify virtues and vices better seen in their natural state. All these resources fail, but man remains, and the poet needs no more. Human destiny, man himself, not with his passions, his doubts, his unexpected good fortune, and his incomprehensible miseries, will for these peoples be the chief and almost the sole subject of poetry.

The writers of our time who have so wonderfully portrayed Childe Harold, René, and Jocelyn[1] have not sought to record the actions of an individual, but by exaggeration to illuminate certain dark corners of the human heart.

Such are the poems of democracy.

Equality, then, does not destroy all the subjects of poetry. It makes them fewer but more vast.

14

WHY AMERICAN WRITERS AND SPEAKERS ARE OFTEN BOMBASTIC

I HAVE OFTEN NOTICED that the Americans, whose language when talking business is clear and dry, and of such extreme simplicity as often to be vulgar, easily turn bombastic when they attempt a poetic style. They are then pompous, from beginning to end of a speech, and one would have supposed, that they could never say anything simply.

The English fall into the same mistake, but less often.

The reason is easily pointed out.

Each citizen of a democracy generally spends his time considering the interests of a very insignificant person, namely, himself. When he is drawn out, he expects to have some prodigious subject put before him. That is the only consideration which would induce him for one moment to tear himself away from the complicated little cares and joy of his life.

---

1.   [Lord Byron, George Gordon Byron; François-René, vicomte de Chateaubriand; and Alphonse de Lamartine, respectively.]

[Originally chapter 18.]

This appears to explain why democratic citizens, whose concerns are in general so paltry, call on their poets for such vast conceptions and descriptions out of proportion.

Writers, for their part, almost always pander to this propensity; they inflate their imaginations so that they achieve gigantism, missing real grandeur. Writer and public join in corrupting each other.

15

SOME OBSERVATIONS ON THE THEATER AMONG DEMOCRATIC PEOPLES

OF ALL FORMS OF literature it is generally the drama that is first affected by the social and political revolution upsetting an aristocratic order, and its influence is always conspicuous there. If you want advance knowledge of the literature of a people which is turning toward democracy, pay attention to the theater.

Democratic audiences like to see the same medley of conditions, feelings, and opinions that occur in life. The drama becomes more striking, more vulgar, and more true.

When democratic audiences rule the stage they introduce as much license in the manner of treating subjects as in the choice of them.

As love of the drama is, of all literary tastes, that most natural to democratic peoples, the number of authors, spectators, and plays is constantly on the increase. Such a multitude, composed of such varied elements and scattered so widely over the land, cannot acknowledge the same rules or submit to the same laws.

[Originally chapter 19.]

No agreement is possible among judges so numerous, who never know when they may meet again and who all like to judge for themselves. All literary rules and conventions are shaken by the impact of democracy, but in the drama they are entirely abolished, leaving only the caprice of each author and each audience.

A democratic audience listens in the theater but does not read plays. Most of the spectators are not looking for pleasures of the mind, but for lively emotions of the heart. They want to see a play, not to discover a fine work of literature, and provided the author writes his native tongue well enough to be understood, and his characters excite curiosity and arouse sympathy, the audience is satisfied with perpetual novelty, unexpectedness, and speed.

16

SOME CHARACTERISTICS PECULIAR TO HISTORIANS IN DEMOCRATIC CENTURIES

HISTORIANS WHO WRITE IN aristocratic ages generally attribute everything that happens to the will and character of particular men. Historians who live in democratic ages show contrary tendencies. Most of them attribute hardly any influence over the destinies of mankind to individuals, or over the fate of a people to the citizens. But they make great general causes responsible for the smallest particular events.

I am firmly convinced that even in democratic nations the genius, vices, or virtues of individuals delay or hasten the destiny

[Originally chapter 20.]

of a people. But in periods of equality, causes of this nature are more various, better hidden, more complex, less powerful, and hence less easy to sort out and trace.

The historian is soon tired of such a labor. Lost in a labyrinth, unable clearly to see or to explain individual influences, he ends by denying that they exist. He prefers to talk about the nature of races, the physical character of the country, or the spirit of civilization. That shortens his labors and satisfies the reader better at less cost.

M. de la Fayette says somewhere in his memoirs that an exaggerated belief in general causes is wonderfully consoling for mediocre public men. It is the same for mediocre historians. A few mighty reasons extricate them from the most difficult part of their task, and while indulging their incapacity or laziness gives them a reputation for profundity.

For my part, I think that in all ages some of the happenings in this world are due to very general causes and others depend on very particular influences. These two kinds of causes are always in operation; only their proportion varies. General causes explain more, and particular influences less, in democratic than in aristocratic ages.

Therefore historians who describe the happenings in democratic societies are right in attaching much importance to general causes and in spending most of their time discovering them. They would, however, be wrong to deny entirely the importance of the actions of individuals just because that is hard to find and trace out.

Historians who live in democratic ages are not only prone to attribute each happening to a great cause but also are led to link facts together to make a system.

In aristocratic ages, as the attention of historians is constantly drawn to individuals, the connection of events escapes them, or rather they do not believe in such a connection. It seems to them that the thread of history is being constantly broken as a man crosses its path.

But the historian of democratic epochs, seeing the actors less and the events more, can easily string facts together in a methodical order.

Ancient literature, so rich in fine historical writing, has not left us one great historical system, whereas even the poorest of modern literatures is swarming with them. Apparently classical historians made too little use of general theories, whereas our own are always on the verge of using them too much.

Those who write in democratic ages have another tendency that is more dangerous.

Once the trace of the influence of individuals has been lost, we are often left with the sight of the world moving without anyone moving it. Even supposing that it is on earth that we must find the general law controlling the particular wills of all individuals, that does not serve to preserve human freedom. A cause so vast that it acts at the same time on millions of men, and so strong that it bends them all in the same direction, may easily seem irresistible.

Thus historians in democratic times not only refuse to admit that some citizens influence the destiny of a people, but also take away from the peoples themselves the faculty of modifying their own lot and make them depend either on an inflexible providence or on a kind of blind fatality.

Not content to show how events have occurred, they pride themselves on proving that they could not have happened differently. They see a nation which has reached a certain point in its history, and they assert that it was bound to have followed the path that led it there. That is easier than demonstrating how it might have taken a better road.

I would add that such a doctrine is particularly dangerous at the present moment. Our contemporaries are all too much inclined to doubts about free will, since each of them feels himself confined on every side by his own weakness. But they will freely admit the strength and independence of men united in a body social. It is important not to let this idea grow dim, for we need to raise men's souls, not to complete their prostration.

17

OF PARLIAMENTARY ELOQUENCE
IN THE UNITED STATES

AMONG ARISTOCRATIC PEOPLES THE members of political assemblies are also aristocrats. Each of them possesses on his own account a high and secure rank. In America a deputy is generally a nobody apart from his position in the assembly. He is therefore perpetually stung by the need to acquire importance there, and he has a petulant longing to air his ideas in and out of season.

In a democratic country such as the United States a deputy hardly ever has a lasting hold over the minds of his constituents. However small an electoral body may be, it is constantly changing shape with the fluctuations of democracy. It must therefore be courted unceasingly. He is never sure of them, and if they forsake him, he is left without resource.

So it is natural that democratic representatives think more about their constituents than about their party, while those of aristocracies think more of party than of constituents.

But what needs to be said to please constituents is not always the same as what needs to be done to help forward the political view they profess to support.

It is often to the general interest of a party that a deputy should never talk about great matters which he does not well understand, that he should speak little about the small matters that might interfere with great ones, and finally, that he should keep quiet. Silence is the most useful service an indifferent speaker can render to the common good.

But this is not at all how his constituents see the matter.

[Originally chapter 21.]

The population of a neighborhood choose a citizen to take part in the government because they have a vast opinion of his merit. Since men always look bigger when surrounded by small objects, the slighter the supply of talents among his constituents, the greater will be their admiration of him. The less it is reasonable to expect from him, the more they do expect. However incapable he may be, they expect exertions appropriate to their belief in him.

The electors see their representative as the natural protector of local interests in the legislature; indeed, they take it for granted that their chosen deputy is an orator, that if he can he will speak often, both of all the great affairs of state and of all their petty grievances. On these terms they promise to vote for him again.

This drives to despair those honest mediocrities who, knowing their limitations, would never willingly have stepped forward. There is hardly a congressman prepared to go home until he has at least one speech printed and sent to his constituents, and he won't let anybody interrupt his harangue until he has made all his useful suggestions about the twenty-four states of the Union, and especially the district he represents. So his audience has to listen to great general truths which he often does not understand himself and makes a muddle of exposing, and very minute particulars which he has not much chance of verifying or explaining. Consequently the debates of that great assembly are frequently vague and perplexed, seeming to be dragged, rather than to march, to the intended goal.

Lucky circumstances and good laws might combine to provide a democratic legislature with much more remarkable men than those sent by the Americans to Congress. But nothing will ever stop the mediocrities who do get there from complacently airing all their views.

Americans themselves seem to see the matter like that, and they bear witness not by refraining from dull speeches but by summoning their courage to listen to them. They are resigned to them, as to an evil that they know by experience cannot be cured.

We have seen the petty side of democratic political debates; let us now consider their imposing aspects.

For 150 years the proceedings of the English Parliament have never caused much stir outside that land, even in the countries nearest to that great theater of British liberty. But Europe was stirred by the first debates that took place in the little colonial assemblies of America at the time of the revolution.

This was due not only to particular and accidental circumstances but also to general and lasting reasons.

There is nothing more wonderful or more impressive than a great orator discussing great affairs in a democratic assembly. As precedents have little force, and there are no more privileges inherent in certain bodies or certain men, the argument must be carried back to general propositions derived from the nature of humanity. For this reason the political discussions of a democracy, no matter how small, have a general character which often attracts the interest of the human race. All men are interested because they treat of man, who is everywhere the same.

PART II

The Influence of Democracy
on the Sentiments of the Americans

PART II

The Influence of Columbus
on the Americas

1

WHY DEMOCRATIC NATIONS SHOW
A MORE ARDENT AND ENDURING LOVE
FOR EQUALITY THAN FOR LIBERTY

THE FIRST AND LIVELIEST of the passions inspired by equality is, I need not say, love of that equality itself.

Everybody has noticed that in our age, and especially in France, this passion for equality is daily acquiring a greater hold over the human heart. It has been said a hundred times that our contemporaries love equality much more ardently than liberty. But I do not think that anyone has yet adequately explained the reason.

It is possible to imagine an extreme point at which freedom and equality would meet and blend; men will be perfectly free because they are entirely equal, and they will be perfectly equal because they are entirely free. Democratic peoples are tending toward that ideal.

That is the completest possible form for equality on this earth. But men's taste for freedom and their taste for equality are in fact distinct, and, I have no hesitation in adding, among democracies they are two unequal elements.

Freedom is found at different times and in different forms, and one finds it elsewhere than in democracies. It cannot therefore be taken as the distinctive characteristic of democratic ages.

The predominating fact peculiar to those ages is equality of conditions, and the chief passion at such times is the love of this same equality. That is enough to explain why they prefer it to all the rest, but apart from that reason there are several others which at all times lead men to prefer equality to liberty.

If a people could ever succeed in destroying or even diminishing the equality prevailing in its body social, it could only do so by long and laborious efforts. They would have to modify their social condition, repeal their laws, supersede their opinions, change their habits, and alter their mores. But political liberty is easily lost; neglect to hold it fast, and it is gone.

Men therefore hold on to equality not only because it is precious to them; they are also attached to it because they think it will last forever.

Nobody is so superficial as not to realize that political liberty can, if carried to excess, endanger the peace, property, and lives of individuals. Men cannot enjoy political liberty without some sacrifice, and they have never won it without great effort. But equality offers its pleasures free.

Democratic peoples always like equality, but there are times when their passion for it turns to delirium. This happens when the old social hierarchy finally collapses after a severe internal struggle and the barriers of rank are thrown down. At such times men pounce on equality as their booty and cling to it as a precious treasure they fear to have snatched away. They want equality in freedom, and if they cannot have that, they still want equality in slavery. They will put up with poverty, servitude, and barbarism, but they will not endure aristocracy.

This is true at all times, but especially in our own. All men and all powers who try to stand up against this irresistible passion will be overthrown and destroyed by it. In our day freedom cannot be established without it, and despotism itself cannot reign without its support.

2

OF INDIVIDUALISM IN DEMOCRACIES

I HAVE SHOWN HOW, in ages of equality, every man finds his beliefs within himself, and I shall now go on to show that all his feelings are turned in on himself.

Individualism is a word recently coined to express a new idea.[1] Our fathers only knew about egoism.

Egoism is a passionate and exaggerated love of self which leads a man to think of all things in terms of himself and to prefer himself to all.

Individualism is a calm and considered feeling which disposes each citizen to isolate himself from the mass of his fellows and withdraw into the circle of family and friends; with this little society formed to his taste, he gladly leaves the greater society to look after itself.

Egoism is a vice as old as the world. It is not peculiar to one form of society more than another.

Individualism is of democratic origin and threatens to grow as conditions get more equal.

Among aristocratic nations families maintain the same station for centuries and often live in the same place. A man almost always knows about his ancestors and respects them; his imagination extends to his great-grandchildren, and he loves them. He freely does his duty by both ancestors and descendants and often sacrifices personal pleasures for the sake of beings who are no longer alive or are not yet born.

---

1. [Tocqueville is widely credited with popularizing the word *individualism,* in the sense of a social doctrine or cultural ethos; the word's newness suited Tocqueville's desire to help European readers grasp what he observed to be the fundamental novelty of American character.]

Moreover, each citizen of an aristocratic society has his fixed station. There is always someone above him whose protection he needs and someone below him whose help he may require. So people living in an aristocratic age are almost always closely involved with something outside themselves. It is true that the general conception of *human fellowship* is dim and that men hardly ever think of devoting themselves to the cause of humanity, but men do often make sacrifices for the sake of certain other men.

In democratic ages, the bonds of human affection are wider but more relaxed.

New families continually rise from nothing while others fall, and nobody's position is quite stable. The woof of time is ever being broken and the track of past generations lost. Those who have gone before are easily forgotten, and no one gives a thought to those who will follow. All a man's interests are limited to those near himself.

As each class catches up with the next and gets mixed with it, its members do not care about one another and treat one another as strangers. Aristocracy links everybody, from peasant to king, in one long chain. Democracy breaks the chain and frees each link.

As social equality spreads there are more and more people who, though neither rich nor powerful enough to have much hold over others, have gained or kept enough wealth and understanding to look after their own needs. Such folk owe no man anything and hardly expect anything from anybody. They think of themselves in isolation and imagine that their whole destiny is in their own hands.

Thus, not only does democracy make men forget their ancestors, but also clouds their view of their descendants and isolates them from their contemporaries. Each man is forever thrown back on himself alone, and there is danger that he may be shut up in the solitude of his own heart.

3

HOW INDIVIDUALISM IS MORE PRONOUNCED AT THE END OF A DEMOCRATIC REVOLUTION THAN AT ANY OTHER TIME

JUST AT THE MOMENT when a democratic society is establishing itself on the ruins of an aristocracy, this isolation of each man from the rest and the egoism resulting therefrom stand out clearest.

Not only are there many independent people in such a society, but their number is constantly increasing with more who have just attained independence and are drunk with their new power. These latter, never imagining that they could ever need help again, have no inhibition about showing that they care for nobody but themselves.

There is usually a prolonged struggle before an aristocracy gives way, and in the course of that struggle implacable hatreds have been engendered between the classes. Such passions last after victory, and one can see traces of them in the ensuing democratic confusion.

Those who once held the highest ranks cannot forget their ancient greatness at once and regard all those whom society now makes their equals as oppressors. But those formerly at the bottom of the social scale cannot enjoy their newfound independence without some secret uneasiness: there is a look of fear mixed with triumph in their eyes if they do meet one of their former superiors, and they avoid them.

There is a tendency in democracy not to draw men together, but democratic revolutions make them run away from each other and perpetuate, in the midst of equality, hatreds originating in inequality.

The Americans have this great advantage, that they attained democracy without the sufferings of a democratic revolution and that they were born equal instead of becoming so.

4

HOW THE AMERICANS COMBAT
THE EFFECTS OF INDIVIDUALISM BY
FREE INSTITUTIONS

DESPOTISM SEES THE ISOLATION of men as the best guarantee of its own permanence. So it usually does all it can to isolate them. Of all the vices of the human heart egoism suits it best. A despot will forgive his subjects for not loving him, provided they do not love one another. He does not ask them to help guide the state; it is enough if they do not claim to manage it themselves. He calls those who try to unite to create a general prosperity "turbulent and restless spirits," and he calls those "good citizens" who care for none but themselves.

Thus vices originating in despotism are precisely those favored by equality. Equality puts men side by side without a common link to hold them firm. Despotism raises barriers to keep them apart. It disposes them not to think of their fellows and turns indifference into a sort of public virtue.

Despotism, dangerous at all times, is therefore particularly to be feared in ages of democracy. Liberty engenders particular hatreds, but despotism is responsible for general indifference. The Americans have used liberty to combat the individualism born of equality, and they have won.

The lawgivers of America did not suppose that a general representation of the whole nation would suffice to ward off a disorder at once so natural to democracy and so fatal.

The general business of a country keeps only the leading citizens occupied. It is only occasionally that they come together in the same places, and no lasting bonds form between them. But when the people who live there have to look after the particular affairs of a district, the same people are always meeting, and they are forced, in a manner, to know and adapt themselves to one another.

It is difficult to force a man out of himself and get him to take an interest in the affairs of the whole state, for he has little understanding of the way in which the fate of the state can influence his own lot. But if it is a question of taking a road past his property, he sees at once that this small public matter has a bearing on his greatest private interests, and there is no need to point out to him the close connection between his private profit and the general interest.

Thus, far more may be done by entrusting citizens with the management of minor affairs than by handing over control of great matters. Local liberties induce a great number of citizens to value the affection of their neighbors, bring men constantly into contact, despite the instincts which separate them, and force them to help one another.

It would seem as if in the United States every man's power of invention was on the stretch to find new ways of increasing the wealth and satisfying the needs of the public. The best brains in every neighborhood are constantly searching for new secrets to increase the general prosperity, and any that they find are at once at the service of the crowd.

If one takes a close look at the weaknesses and vices of many of those who bear sway in America, one is surprised at the growing prosperity of the people, but it is a mistake to be surprised. It is certainly not the elected magistrate who makes the American democracy prosper, but the fact that the magistrates are elected.

The free institutions of the United States and the political rights enjoyed there provide a thousand continual reminders to every citizen that he lives in society. At every moment they bring his mind back to this idea, that it is the duty as well as the interest of men to be useful to their fellows. Having no particular reason to hate others, since he is neither their slave nor their master, the American's heart easily inclines toward benevolence. At first it is of necessity that men attend to the public interest, afterward by choice. What had been calculation becomes instinct.

There are many men in France who regard equality of conditions as the first of evils and political liberty as the second. When forced to submit to the former, they strive at least to escape the latter. But for

my part, I maintain that there is only one effective remedy against the
evils which equality may cause, and that is political liberty.

5

ON THE USE WHICH THE AMERICANS
MAKE OF ASSOCIATIONS IN CIVIL LIFE

I DO NOT PROPOSE to speak of those political associations by which
men defend themselves against the despotic action of the majority.
I have treated that subject elsewhere. It is clear that unless each
citizen learned to combine with his fellows to preserve his freedom, tyranny would be bound to increase with equality. But here I
am only concerned with those associations in civil life which have
no political object.

Americans of all ages, stations, and dispositions are forever
forming associations. There are not only commercial and industrial associations, but a thousand different types—religious, moral,
serious, futile, very general and very limited, immensely large and
very minute. Americans combine to give fêtes, found seminaries,
build churches, distribute books, and send missionaries. Hospitals,
prisons, and schools take shape in that way. Finally, if they want to
proclaim a truth or propagate some feeling, they form an association. In any new undertaking, where in France you would find the
government or in England some territorial magnate, in the United
States you are sure to find an association.

Thus the most democratic country in the world now is that in
which men have carried to the highest perfection the art of pursuing
common desires and have applied this new technique to the greatest
number of purposes. Is this just an accident, or is there really some
necessary connection between associations and equality.

In aristocratic societies men have no need to unite for action, since they are held firmly together. But among democratic peoples all the citizens are independent and weak. They can do hardly anything for themselves, and none is in a position to force his fellows to help him. They would find themselves helpless if they did not learn to help each other voluntarily.

Unhappily, the same social conditions that render associations so necessary to democratic nations also make their formation more difficult there than elsewhere.

When several aristocrats want to form an association, they can easily do so. As each of them carries great weight in society, a very small number of associates may be enough. But in democratic nations, if the association is to have any power, the associates must be very numerous.

Many of my contemporaries claim that as the citizens become weaker and more helpless, the government must become proportionately more skillful and active, so that society should do what is no longer possible for individuals. They think that answers the whole problem, but I think they are mistaken.

A government could take the place of some of the largest associations in America, but what political power could ever carry on the vast multitude of lesser undertakings which associations daily enable American citizens to control? The more government takes the place of associations, the more will individuals lose the idea of forming associations and need the government to come to their help. That is a vicious circle of cause and effect. The morals and intelligence of a democratic people would be in as much danger as its commerce and industry if ever a government wholly usurped the place of private associations.

Feelings and ideas are renewed, the heart enlarged, and the understanding developed only by the reciprocal action of men one upon another.

I have shown how these influences are reduced almost to nothing in democratic countries; they must therefore be artificially created, and only associations can do that.

A government, by itself, is incapable of refreshing the circulation of feelings and ideas among a great people. Once it leaves the sphere of politics to launch out on this new track, it will exercise an intolerable tyranny. For a government can only dictate precise rules and it is never easy to tell the difference between its advice and its commands. Things will be even worse if the government supposes that its real interest is to prevent the circulation of ideas.

It is therefore necessary that it should not act alone.

Among democratic peoples associations must take the place of the powerful private persons whom equality of conditions has eliminated.

The first time that I heard in America that one hundred thousand men had publicly promised never to drink alcoholic liquor, I thought it more of a joke than a serious matter and for the moment did not see why these very abstemious citizens could not content themselves with drinking water by their own firesides.

In the end I came to understand that these hundred thousand Americans, frightened by the progress of drunkenness around them, wanted to support sobriety by their patronage. They were acting in just the same way as some great territorial magnate who dresses very plainly to encourage a contempt of luxury among simple citizens. One may fancy that if they had lived in France each of these hundred thousand would have made individual representations to the government asking it to supervise all the public houses throughout the realm.

Nothing, in my view, more deserves attention than the intellectual and moral associations in America. American political and industrial associations easily catch our eyes, but the others tend not to be noticed. And even if we do notice them we tend to misunderstand them, hardly ever having seen anything similar before. However, the latter are as necessary as the former to the American people; perhaps more so.

In democratic countries knowledge of how to combine is the mother of all other forms of knowledge; on its progress depends that of all the others. If men are to remain or to become civilized, the art of association must develop among them at the same speed as equality of conditions spreads.

6

ON THE CONNECTION BETWEEN
ASSOCIATIONS AND NEWSPAPERS

ONLY A NEWSPAPER CAN put the same thought at the same time before a thousand readers.

A newspaper is an adviser that need not be sought out, but comes of its own accord and talks to you briefly every day about the commonweal without distracting you from your private affairs.

So the more equal men become and more individualism becomes a menace, the more necessary are newspapers. We should underrate their importance if we thought they just guaranteed liberty; they maintain civilization.

A newspaper is not only able to suggest a common plan to many men; it provides them with the means of carrying out in common the idea that had occurred to them all simultaneously but separately. They all at once aim toward that light, and these wandering spirits, long seeking each other in the dark, at last meet and unite.

The newspaper brought them together and continues to be necessary to hold them together.

In a democracy an association cannot be powerful unless it is numerous. Those composing it must therefore be spread over a wide area. They need some means of talking every day without seeing one another and of acting together without meeting. So hardly any democratic association can carry on without a newspaper.

There is therefore a necessary connection between associations and newspapers. Newspapers make associations, and associations make newspapers. Thus, of all countries on earth, it is in America that one finds both the most associations and the most newspapers.

I should also attribute the increasing influence of the daily press to causes more general than those by which it is commonly explained.

A newspaper can only survive if it gives publicity to feelings or principles common to a large number of men. A newspaper therefore always represents an association whose members are its regular readers.

This association may be more or less strictly defined, more or less closed, more or less numerous, but there must at least be the seed of it in men's minds, for otherwise the paper would not survive.

That leads me to the final reflection with which I will end this chapter.

As equality spreads and men individually become less strong, they ever increasingly let themselves glide with the stream of the crowd and find it hard to maintain alone an opinion abandoned by the rest.

The newspaper represents the association; one might say that it speaks to each of its readers in the name of all the rest, and the feebler they are individually, the easier it is to sweep them along.

The power of newspapers must therefore grow as equality spreads.

7

RELATIONSHIPS BETWEEN CIVIL AND POLITICAL ASSOCIATIONS

THERE IS ONE COUNTRY in the world which, day in, day out, makes use of an unlimited freedom of political association. And the citizens of this same nation, alone in the world, have thought of using the right of association continually in civil life, and by this means have come to enjoy all the advantages which civilization can offer.

In civil life each man can, at a stretch, imagine that he is in a position to look after himself. In politics he could never fancy that.

So when a people has a political life, the idea of associations and eagerness to form them are part of everybody's everyday life. Whatever natural distaste men may have for working in common, they are always ready to do so for the sake of a party. A whole crowd of people who might otherwise have lived on their own are taught both to want to combine and how to do so.

So one may think of political associations as great free schools to which all citizens come to be taught the general theory of association.

But even if political association did not directly contribute to the progress of civil association, to destroy the former would harm the latter.

When citizens can only combine for certain purposes, they regard association as a strange and unusual procedure and hardly consider the possibility thereof. When they are allowed to combine freely for all purposes, they come in the end to think of association as the universal, one might almost say the only, means by which men can attain their various aims.

I do not assert that there can be no civil associations in a country in which political associations are forbidden, for men cannot live in society without undertaking some things in common. But I maintain that in such a country civil associations will always be few, feebly conceived, and unskillfully managed.

This naturally leads me to think that freedom of political association is not nearly as dangerous to public peace as is supposed and that it could happen that it might give stability to a state which for some time it had shaken.

In democratic countries political associations are, if one may put it so, the only powerful people who aspire to rule the state. When you see the Americans every day freely combining to make some political opinion triumph, to get some politician into the government, or to snatch power from another, it is hard to conceive that men of such independence will not often fall into the abuse of license.

But if, on the other hand, you come to think of the infinite number of industrial undertakings which are run in partnership in the United States, if you notice how on every side the Americans are working without relaxation on important and difficult designs which would be thrown into confusion by the slightest revolution, you will easily understand why these people who are so well occupied have no temptation to disturb the state or to upset the public calm by which they profit.

In this way, by the enjoyment of a dangerous liberty, the Americans learn the art of rendering the dangers of freedom less formidable.

By picking one moment in the history of a nation it is easy to prove that political associations disturb the state and paralyze industry. But if you take the life of a people as one complete whole it may prove easy to show that freedom of political association favors the welfare and even the tranquility of the citizens.

I said in the first part of this book: "One must understand that unlimited political freedom of association is of all forms of liberty the last which a people can sustain. If it does not topple them over into anarchy, it brings them continually to the brink thereof."

For these reasons I certainly do not think that a nation is always in a position to allow its citizens an absolute right of political association, and I even doubt whether there has ever been a nation in which it was wise not to put any limits to the freedom of association.

One hears it said that such and such a nation could not maintain internal peace, inspire respect for its laws, or establish a stable government if it did not set strict limits to the right of association. These are undoubtedly great benefits, and one can understand why a nation may agree for a time to impose galling restrictions on itself; but still a nation should know what price it pays for these blessings.

To save a man's life, I can understand cutting off his arm. But I don't want anyone to tell me that he will be as dexterous without it.

8

HOW THE AMERICANS COMBAT INDIVIDUALISM BY THE DOCTRINE OF SELF-INTEREST PROPERLY UNDERSTOOD

WHEN THE WORLD WAS under the control of a few rich and powerful men, they liked to entertain a sublime conception of the duties of man. It gratified them to make out that it is a glorious thing to forget oneself and that one should do good without self-interest, as God himself does. That was the official doctrine of morality at that time.

I doubt whether men were better in times of aristocracy than at other times, but certainly they talked continually about the beauties of virtue. Only in secret did they study its utility.

In the United States there is hardly any talk of the beauty of virtue. But they maintain that virtue is useful and prove it every day. American moralists do not pretend that one must sacrifice himself for his fellows because it is a fine thing to do so. But they boldly assert that such sacrifice is as necessary for the man who makes it as for the beneficiaries.

Montaigne said long ago: "If I did not follow the straight road for the sake of its straightness, I should follow it having found by experience that, all things considered, it is the happiest and the most convenient."[1]

So the doctrine of self-interest properly understood is not new, but it is among the Americans of our time that it has become popular. One finds it at the root of all actions. You hear it as much from the poor as from the rich.

The version of this doctrine current in Europe is much grosser

---

1. [Cf. Montaigne, *Essais*, Pléiade edition, p. 268; Tocqueville appears to paraphrase the first sentence of chapter 44.]

but at the same time less widespread and, especially, less adver-
tised.

The Americans, on the other hand, enjoy explaining almost every
act of their lives on the principle of self-interest properly understood.
It gives them pleasure to point out how an enlightened self-love leads
them to help one another and disposes them to give part of their
time and wealth for the good of the state. Sometimes in the United
States, as elsewhere, one sees people carried away by the disinterested,
spontaneous impulses natural to man. But the Americans prefer to
give the credit to their philosophy rather than to themselves.

Self-interest properly understood does not attempt to reach
great aims, but it does, without too much trouble, achieve all it sets
out to do. Being within the scope of everybody's understanding,
everyone grasps it and has no trouble in bearing it in mind. It is
wonderfully agreeable to human weaknesses, and so easily wins
great sway.

The doctrine of self-interest properly understood does not inspire great sacrifices, but every day it prompts small ones; by itself
it cannot make a man virtuous, but its discipline shapes a lot of orderly, temperate, moderate, careful, and self-controlled citizens. If
it does not lead the will directly to virtue, it establishes habits
which unconsciously turn it that way.

If the doctrine of self-interest properly understood ever came to
dominate all morality, no doubt extraordinary virtues would be
rarer. But I think that gross depravity would also be less common.
Such teaching may stop some men from rising far above the
common level of humanity, but many of those who fall below this
standard grasp it and are restrained by it. Some individuals it
lowers, but mankind it raises.

The doctrine of self-interest properly understood appears to me
the best suited of all philosophical theories to men in our time,
and I see it as their strongest remaining guarantee against themselves. Contemporary moralists therefore should give most of their
attention to it.

I do not think, by and large, that there is more egoism among
us than in America; the only difference is that there it is enlight-

ened, while here it is not. I see nothing but people bent on proving, by word and deed, that what is useful is never wrong. Who will make the public understand that what is right may be useful?

No power on earth can prevent increasing equality from disposing each citizen to get wrapped up in himself. One must therefore expect that private interest will more than ever become the chief if not the only driving force behind all behavior. But if citizens, attaining equality, were to remain ignorant and coarse, it would be difficult to foresee any limit to the stupid excesses into which their selfishness might lead.

I do not think that the doctrine of self-interest as preached in America is in all respects self-evident. But it does contain many truths so clear that for men to see them is enough to educate them. Hence it is all-important for them to be educated, for the age of blind sacrifice and instinctive virtues is already long past, and I see a time approaching in which freedom, public peace, and social stability will not be able to last without education.

9

HOW THE AMERICANS APPLY
THE DOCTRINE OF SELF-INTEREST PROPERLY
UNDERSTOOD TO RELIGION

IF THE DOCTRINE OF self-interest properly understood were concerned with this world only, that would not be nearly enough. For there are a great many sacrifices which can only be rewarded in the next. One therefore wants to know whether this doctrine can easily be reconciled with religious beliefs.

The philosophers who teach this doctrine tell men that to be happy in life they must watch their passions and restrain their excesses, that lasting happiness cannot be won except at the cost of a thousand ephemeral pleasures, and finally, that one must continually master oneself in order to serve oneself better.

The founders of almost all religions have used very much the same language. The way they point out is the same; only the goal is further off; instead of putting in this world the reward for the sacrifices demanded, they transpose it to the next.

Nevertheless, I refuse to believe that all who practice virtue from religious motives do so only in hope of reward. Christianity does, it is true, teach that we must prefer others to ourselves in order to gain heaven. But Christianity also teaches that we must do good to our fellows for love of God, expecting no other reward than the joy of contemplating it.

Hence I do not think that interest is the only driving force behind men of religion. But I do think that interest is the chief means used by religions themselves to guide men, and I have no doubt that that is how they work on the crowd and become popular.

I do not therefore see any plain reason why the doctrine of self-interest properly understood should drive men away from religious beliefs, but rather do I see ways in which it brings them close thereto.

Let us start from the assumption that in order to gain happiness in this world a man resists all instinctive impulses and deliberately calculates every action of his life, that instead of yielding blindly to his passions he has learned the art of fighting them, and that he habitually sacrifices the pleasure of the moment for the lasting interests of his whole life.

If such a man believes in the religion that he professes, it will hardly cost him anything to submit to such restrictions. Reason advises him to do so, and habits make it easy. Even if he does feel some doubt, he will think it wise to risk some of the good things of this world to save his claims to the immense inheritance promised in the next.

"If we make a mistake by thinking the Christian religion true," Pascal has said, "we have no great thing to lose. But if we make a mistake by thinking it false, how dreadful is our case."[1]

The Americans affect no vulgar indifference to a future state. They practice their religion without shame and without weakness. But in their zeal one generally sees something so quiet, so methodical, so calculated that it would seem that the head rather than the heart leads them to the foot of the altar.

Not only do the Americans practice their religion out of self-interest, but they often even place the interest here below. Preachers in America are forever pointing out how religious beliefs favor freedom and public order, and it is often difficult to be sure when listening to them whether the main object of religion is to procure felicity in the next world or prosperity in this.

10

THE TASTE FOR PHYSICAL COMFORT IN AMERICA

IN AMERICA THE TASTE for physical well-being is not always exclusive, but it is general. Everyone is preoccupied caring for the slightest needs of the body and the trivial conveniences of life.

Something of the same sort is more and more conspicuous in Europe.

Among the causes responsible for these similar results in the New and Old Worlds there are some so germane to my subject that they should be mentioned.

---

1.   [Tocqueville quotes Pascal's *Pensées* rather freely. Cf. Brunschvicg's edition, fragment 233.]

That which most vividly stirs the human heart is not the quiet possession of something precious but rather the imperfectly satisfied desire to have it and the fear of losing it again.

The rich in aristocratic societies, having never experienced a lot different from their own, have no fear of changing it. The comforts of life are by no means the aim of their existence; they are just a way of living. They enjoy them without thinking about them.

In nations where an aristocracy dominates society, the people finally get used to their poverty just as the rich do to their opulence. But when distinctions of rank are blurred and privileges abolished, and education and freedom spread, the poor conceive an eager desire to acquire comfort, and the rich think of the danger of losing it. A lot of middling fortunes are established. Their owners have enough physical enjoyments to get a taste for them, but not enough to content them. They never win them without effort or indulge in them without anxiety. They are therefore continually pursuing or striving to retain these incomplete and fugitive delights.

The passion for physical comfort is essentially a middle-class affair; it grows and spreads with that class and becomes preponderant with it. Thence it works upward into the higher ranks of society and thence spreads downward to the people.

In America I never met a citizen too poor to cast a glance of hope and envy toward the pleasures of the rich or whose imagination did anticipate good things that fate obstinately refused to him.

On the other hand, I never found among wealthy Americans that lofty disdain for physical comfort sometimes seen among aristocracies. Most of these rich men were once poor; they had long striven against fate, and now that they had won, they seemed drunk on the petty delights it had taken forty years to gain.

In the United States, as elsewhere, there are a fairly large number of rich men who, having inherited their property, effortlessly possess a wealth not gained. But even these people appear to be no less attached to the delights of the material world. Love of comfort has become the dominant national taste.

11

PARTICULAR EFFECTS OF THE LOVE
OF PHYSICAL PLEASURES IN DEMOCRATIC TIMES

IT MIGHT BE SUPPOSED, from what has just been said, that the love of physical pleasures would continually lead the Americans into moral irregularities, disturb the peace of families, and finally threaten the stability of society itself.

But it does not happen like that. The passion for physical pleasures produces effects very different from those in aristocratic societies.

It sometimes happens that boredom, excess wealth, decay of belief, and national decadence seduce an aristocracy to pursue nothing but sensual delights. At other times the power of a prince or the weakness of a people, without depriving the nobility of their wealth, forces them to avoid positions of power and leaves them restless. When the members of an aristocratic society thus turn exclusively to sumptuous depravity and startling corruption, they worship material things magnificently and seem eager to excel in the art of besotting themselves.

But love of physical pleasures never leads democratic peoples to such excesses. Among them love of comfort appears as a tenacious, exclusive, and universal passion, but always a restrained one. There is no question of sucking the world dry to satisfy one man's greed. It is more a question of adding a few acres to one's fields, enlarging a house, making life more comfortable, keeping irritations away, and satisfying one's slightest needs without trouble and almost without expense. These are petty aims, but the soul cleaves to them; and in the end they shut out the rest of the world and sometimes come between the soul and God.

This may apply to men of middling fortune; the opulent citizens of a democracy do not display tastes very different from those of the people. Public sensuality has adopted a moderate and tranquil shape to which all are expected to conform. Wealthy men living in democracies therefore think more of satisfying their slightest needs than seeking extraordinary delights. They are more prone to become enervated than debauched.

So in democracies the taste for physical pleasures takes special forms which are not opposed to good order; nor to moral regularity, for sound morals are good for public tranquility and encourage industry. It may even, not infrequently, combine with a type of religious morality; people want to do as well as possible in this world without giving up their chances in the next.

Some physical delights cannot be indulged without crime; from these they abstain strictly. There are others allowed by religion and morality; the heart and life itself are given up to these without reserve, until men lose sight of more precious goods which constitute the greatness and the glory of mankind.

12

WHY SOME AMERICANS DISPLAY ENTHUSIASTIC FORMS OF SPIRITUALITY

ALTHOUGH THE DESIRE TO acquire the good things of this world is the dominant passion among Americans, there are momentary respites when their souls seem suddenly to rush impetuously heavenward.

In every state of the Union, but especially in the half-peopled lands of the West, there are preachers hawking the word of God from place to place.

[The word *enthusiastic*, in early America, referred to Christian denominations and revival movements that today are often described as *evangelical*.]

Whole families, old men, women, and children, cross difficult country and come great distances to hear them. When they do arrive and listen, for several days and nights they neglect their affairs and even forget the most pressing needs of the body.

Here and there throughout American society you meet men filled with an enthusiastic, almost fierce spirituality such as cannot be found in Europe. Strange sects strive to open extraordinary roads to eternal happiness. Forms of religious madness are very common there.

We should not be surprised at this.

The soul has needs which must be satisfied. Whatever pains are taken to distract it from itself, it soon grows bored, restless, and anxious amid the pleasures of the senses.

If ever the great majority of mankind came to concentrate solely on the search for material blessings, there would be a colossal reaction in the souls of men. They would distractedly launch out into the world of spirits for fear of being held too tightly bound by the body's fetters.

It is therefore no cause for astonishment that in a society thinking about nothing but the world a few should want to look at nothing but heaven. I should be surprised if, among a people uniquely preoccupied with prosperity, mysticism did not soon make progress.

If their social condition, circumstances, and laws did not so closely confine the American mind to the search for physical comfort, it may well be that when they came to consider immaterial things they would show more reserve and keep themselves in check without difficulty. But they feel imprisoned within limits from which they are apparently not allowed to escape. Once they have broken through these limits, their minds do not know where to settle down, and they often rush far beyond the bounds of common sense.

13

WHY THE AMERICANS ARE OFTEN SO RESTLESS IN THE MIDST OF THEIR PROSPERITY

IN CERTAIN REMOTE CORNERS of the Old World you may stumble upon little places which seem to have stayed still while all around them moves. The inhabitants are mostly very ignorant and very poor; they take no part in affairs of government, and often governments oppress them. But yet they seem serene and often have a jovial disposition.

In America I have seen the freest and best educated of men in circumstances the happiest to be found in the world; yet a cloud habitually hung on their brow, and they seemed serious and almost sad even in their pleasures.

The chief reason for this is that the former do not give a moment's thought to the ills they endure, whereas the latter never stop thinking of the good things they have not got.

It is odd to watch with what feverish ardor the Americans pursue prosperity and how they are ever tormented by the shadowy suspicion that they may not have chosen the shortest route to get it.

Americans cleave to the things of this world as if assured that they will never die, and yet rush to snatch any that come within reach, as if expecting to stop living before they have relished them. They clutch everything but hold nothing fast, as they hurry after some new delight.

An American will build a house in which to pass his old age and sell it before the roof is on; he will plant a garden and rent it just as the trees are bearing; he will clear a field and leave others to reap the harvest; he will take up a profession and leave it, settle in one place and soon go off elsewhere with his changing desires. If his private business allows him a moment's relaxation, he will plunge into the whirlpool of politics. Then, if at the end of a year crammed with work he has a little spare leisure, his restless curiosity goes with him traveling up and down the vast territories of the United States. Thus he will travel five hundred miles in a few days as a distraction from his happiness.

Death steps in and stops him before he has tired of this futile pursuit of complete felicity, which always escapes him.

At first there is something astonishing in this spectacle of so many lucky men restless in the midst of abundance. But it is a spectacle as old as the world; all that is new is to see a whole people performing in it.

The taste for physical pleasures must be regarded as the first cause of this. A man who has set his heart on nothing but the good things of this world is always in a hurry, for he has only a limited time in which to find them, get them, and enjoy them. Apart from the goods he has, he thinks of a thousand others which death will prevent him from tasting if he does not hurry. This thought fills him with distress, fear, regret, and agitation, so that he is always changing his plans and his abode.

Add to this a social state in which neither law nor custom holds anyone in one place, and that is a further stimulus to restlessness. One will then find people continually changing path for fear of missing the shortest cut leading to happiness.

However, they are also easily discouraged. For as their ultimate object is enjoyment, the means to it must be prompt and easy, otherwise the trouble of getting the pleasure would be greater than the pleasure won. Hence the prevailing temper is at the same time ardent and soft, violent and enervated.

Equality leads by a still shorter path to the various effects I have just described.

When all professions are open to all and a man's own energies may bring him to the top, an ambitious man may think it easy to launch a great career. But that is a delusion which experience quickly corrects. The same equality which allows each man to entertain vast hopes makes each man by himself weak.

Not only are men powerless by themselves, but at every step they find immense obstacles which they had not at first noticed.

They have abolished the privileges of some of their fellows, but they come up against the competition of all. The barrier has changed shape rather than place. When men are more or less equal and follow the same path, it is very difficult for any of them to walk faster and get out beyond the crowd surrounding and hemming them in.

This constant strife between the desires inspired by equality and the means to satisfy them wearies the mind.

One can imagine men who have found a degree of liberty and enjoy independence without anxiety. But men will never establish an equality which will content them.

No matter how a people strives for it, all the conditions of life can never be perfectly equal. Even if, by misfortune, such an absolute dead level were attained, there would still be inequalities of intelligence which, coming directly from God, will ever escape the laws of man.

No matter, therefore, how democratic the social condition and political constitution of a people may be, one can be sure that each and every citizen will be aware of dominating positions near him. When everything is more or less level, the slightest variation is noticed. Hence the more equal men are, the more insatiable will be their longing for equality. Every instant they think they will catch it, and each time it slips through their fingers. They will be dead before they have fully relished its delights.

That is the reason for the strange melancholy often haunting inhabitants of democracies in the midst of abundance, and of that disgust with life sometimes gripping them in calm and easy circumstances.

In France we are worried about the increasing rate of suicides; in America suicide is rare, but I am told that madness is commoner than anywhere else.

Those are different symptoms of the same malady.

In democratic times enjoyments are more lively than in times of aristocracy, and immeasurably greater numbers taste them. But,

on the other hand, hopes and desires are much more often disappointed, minds are more anxious and on edge, and trouble is felt
more keenly.

14

HOW IN AMERICA THE TASTE FOR PHYSICAL PLEASURES IS COMBINED WITH LOVE OF FREEDOM AND ATTENTION TO PUBLIC AFFAIRS

I HAVE ALREADY POINTED out how men living in ages of equality
form associations in order to get the things they long for, and have
also shown how political freedom spreads the technique of association. Thus freedom in such ages is particularly favorable to the
production of wealth. One can see too that despotism is particularly hostile thereto.

Men in democratic times need to be free to provide themselves
with the physical pleasures for which they hanker.

Nevertheless, it sometimes happens that their excessive taste for
these same pleasures hands them over to the first master who
offers himself. Greed for prosperity then turns against itself.
Indeed there is a very dangerous phase in the life of democratic
peoples.

When the taste for physical pleasures has grown more rapidly
than either education or experience of free institutions, the time
comes when men are carried away and lose control of themselves
at sight of the new good things they are ready to snatch. Intent
only on getting rich, they find it a tiresome inconvenience to exercise political rights which distract them from industry. They
cannot waste their precious time in unrewarding work. Such folk

think they are following the doctrine of self-interest, but they have a very crude idea thereof. The better to guard their interests, they neglect the chief of them, that is, to remain their own masters.

If, at this critical moment, an able and ambitious man once gets power, he finds the way open for usurpations of every sort.

So long as he sees to it for a certain time that material interests flourish, he can easily get away with everything else. He must above all guarantee good order. People passionately bent on physical pleasures fear anarchy, and they are always ready to jettison liberty in the slightest storm.

Do not forget that it is through order that all peoples have reached tyranny. A nation which asks nothing from the government beyond the maintenance of order is already a slave to its prosperity, and the road is free for the man to tie the fetters.

The despotism of a faction is as much to be feared as that of a man.

When the great mass of citizens does not want to bother about anything but private business, even the smallest party need not give up hope of becoming master of public affairs.

Up to now the Americans have happily avoided all the reefs I have just charted, and one really must admire them for that.

There is perhaps no country in the world with fewer men of leisure than America, nor one in which all those who work are so keen on making themselves prosperous. But violent though the American passion for physical satisfactions may be, it is at least not blind, and reason, unable to restrain it, does direct it.

An American will attend to his private interests as if he were alone in the world; the moment afterward, he will be deep in public business as if he had forgotten his own. Sometimes he seems to be animated by the most selfish greed and sometimes by the most lively patriotism. But a human heart cannot really be divided in this way. Americans alternately display passions so strong and so similar, first for their own welfare and then for liberty, that one must suppose these urges to be united and mingled in their being. Americans in fact do regard their freedom as the best tool of and the firmest guarantee for their prosperity. They love them both for the sake of each other. They are therefore by no means inclined to suppose that it is no business of theirs to meddle in public affairs. On the contrary, they think it their most important concern to secure a government which will allow them to get the good things they want and which will not stop their enjoying those they have in peace.

15

HOW RELIGIOUS BELIEFS AT TIMES TURN THE THOUGHTS OF AMERICANS TOWARD SPIRITUAL THINGS

IN THE UNITED STATES, when the seventh day comes, trade and industry seem suspended throughout the nation. All noise stops. Solemn contemplation takes its place. At last the soul comes into its own and meditates upon itself.

On this day places of business are deserted; every citizen, accompanied by his children, goes to church; there he listens to strange language apparently hardly suited to his ear. He is told of the countless evils brought on by pride and covetousness. He is reminded of the need to check his desires and told of the finer delights which go with virtue alone.

When he gets home he does not hurry to his business ledgers. He opens the book of Holy Scripture and there finds accounts of the greatness and goodness of the Creator, of the infinite magnificence of the works of God, of the high destiny reserved for men, of their duties and claims to immortality.

Thus it is that the American in some degree from time to time escapes from himself, from the petty passions that trouble his life and the passing interests that fill it. He suddenly breaks into an ideal world where all is great, pure, and eternal.

Elsewhere in this book I have pointed to the causes helping to maintain American political institutions, among which religion seemed one of the most important. Now, when speaking of individuals, religion again comes into the picture.

By their practice Americans show that they feel the urgent necessity to instill morality into democracy by means of religion. What they think of themselves in this respect enshrines a truth which should penetrate deep into the consciousness of every democratic nation.

If you give democratic peoples education and freedom and leave them alone, they will easily extract from this world all the good things it has to offer. But while man takes delight in this legitimate quest for prosperity, there is a danger that he may lose his sublimest faculties and, bent on improving everything around him, degrade himself. That, and nothing else, is the peril.

In a democracy therefore it is ever the duty of lawgivers and of all upright educated men to raise up the souls of their fellow citizens and turn their attention toward heaven. When some of those pernicious theories are found in the intellectual climate of a democratic people, which tend to suggest that everything perishes with the body, the men who profess them must be regarded as the natural enemies of the people.

There are many things that offend me about the materialists. I think their doctrines pernicious, and their pride revolts me. When they think they have sufficiently established that they are no better than brutes, they seem as proud as if they had proved that they were gods.

In all nations materialism is a dangerous malady of the human spirit, but one must be particularly on guard against it among a democratic people, because the taste for physical pleasures, if it becomes excessive, soon disposes men to believe that nothing but matter exists. Materialism, in its turn, spurs them on to such delights with mad impetuosity. Such is the vicious circle into which democratic nations are driven.

Certainly the doctrine of metempsychosis is not more reasonable than that of materialism, but if it were absolutely necessary to make the choice between one or the other, I should think the citizens ran less danger of reducing themselves to the level of brutes by thinking that their soul would pass into a pig's body than by believing that it is nothing.

It is easy to see that it is particularly important in democratic times to make spiritual conceptions prevail, but it is far from easy to say what those who govern democratic peoples should do to make them prevail.

I have no belief in the virtue or the durability of official philosophies, and when it comes to state religions, though they may sometimes serve the interests of political power, they are always sooner or later fatal for the church.

Nor am I one of those who think that it is good to give its ministers indirectly a political influence which the laws refuse.

I am so deeply convinced of the almost inevitable dangers which face beliefs when their interpreters take part in public affairs, and so firmly persuaded that Christianity must be maintained among the new democracies, that I would rather shut priests up within their sanctuaries than allow them to leave them.

What means are then left to the authorities to lead men back toward spiritual opinions?

What I am going to say will certainly do me harm in the eyes of politicians. I think that the only effective means to make the doctrine of the immortality of the soul respected is to act as if they believed it themselves. It is only by conforming scrupulously to religious morality in great affairs that they can flatter themselves that they are teaching the citizens to understand and respect it in little matters.

16

HOW EXCESSIVE LOVE OF PROSPERITY
CAN DO HARM TO IT

THERE IS A CLOSER connection than is supposed between the soul's improvement and the betterment of physical conditions. A man can treat the two things as distinct and pay attention to each in turn. But he cannot entirely separate them without in the end losing sight of both.

Animals have the same senses as ourselves and much the same appetites. Why is it, then, that animals only know how to satisfy their primary and coarsest needs, whereas we can infinitely vary and increase our delights?

That which makes us better than brutes is that we employ our souls to find those material benefits to which instinct alone directs them. It is because man is able to raise himself above the things of the body and even to scorn life itself, a matter of which the beasts have not the least notion, that he can multiply these same good things of the body to a degree of which they have no conception.

Whatever elevates, enlarges, and expands the soul makes it more able to succeed even in those undertakings which are not the soul's concern.

On the other hand, whatever enervates and lowers it weakens it for every purpose, the least as well as the greatest. The soul must remain great, if only that it may from time to time put its strength at the service of the body.

If men ever came to be content with physical things only, it seems likely that they would gradually lose the art of producing them and would end up enjoying them without discernment and improvement, like animals.

17

WHY IN AGES OF EQUALITY AND SKEPTICISM IT IS IMPORTANT TO SET DISTANT GOALS FOR HUMAN ENDEAVOR

IN AGES OF FAITH the final aim of life is placed beyond life.

The men of those ages therefore grow accustomed to fix their eyes for years on some object toward which their progress is ever directed, and they learn to repress passing desires to satisfy the one great permanent longing which obsesses them. When these same men engage in worldly affairs, such habits influence their conduct. That is why religious nations have often accomplished such lasting achievements. In thinking of the other world, they found the secret of success in this.

Religions instill a general habit of behaving with the future in view. In skeptical ages, therefore, there is always a danger that men will give way to ephemeral desires and that, renouncing whatever cannot be acquired without protracted effort, they may never achieve anything great or lasting.

If, with a people so disposed, social conditions become democratic, this danger is increased.

When everyone is constantly striving to change his position, men think in terms of sudden fortunes easily won and lost, and chance in every shape and form. Social instability favors the natural instability of desires. The present looms large and hides the future, so that men do not want to think beyond tomorrow.

In such a country where unhappily skepticism and democracy exist together, philosophers and the men in power should always strive to set a distant aim as the object of human efforts; that is their most important business.

They must especially strive to banish chance, as much as possible, from the world of politics.

The sudden and undeserved promotion of a courtier in an aristocratic country causes no more than an ephemeral impression, because the whole complex of institutions and beliefs forces men to progress slowly along paths they cannot leave.

But such events give the worst possible example to a democratic people. Particular precautions are required to prevent the favor of prince or people, which comes and goes at random, from taking the place due to merit or duties performed. One must hope that all promotion will be seen as the reward of effort, so that men of ambition should be obliged to plan well ahead before they reach their goal.

Governments must study means to give men back that interest in the future which neither religion nor social conditions any longer inspire, and give daily practical examples to the citizens proving that wealth, renown, and power are the rewards of work, that great success comes when it has been long desired, and that nothing of lasting value is achieved without trouble.

18

WHY AMERICANS CONSIDER ALL HONEST CALLINGS HONORABLE

AMONG DEMOCRATIC PEOPLES WHERE there is no hereditary wealth, every man works for his living, or has worked, or comes from parents who have worked. Everything therefore prompts the assumption that to work is the necessary, natural, and honest condition of all men.

Not only is no dishonor associated with work, but among such peoples it is regarded as positively honorable; the prejudice is for, not against, it. A wealthy American feels he owes it to public opinion to devote his leisure to some public duties. He would expect his reputation to suffer if he just spent his life in living. It is to escape this obligation to work that so many rich Americans come to Europe; there they find the relics of aristocratic societies in which leisure is still honorable.

Equality makes not only work itself, but work specifically to gain money, honorable.

In aristocracies it is not exactly work itself which is despised, but work with an eye to profit. Work is glorious when inspired by ambition or pure virtue. However, he who works for honor is not insensible to greed for gain. In aristocratic countries there are hardly any public officials who do not claim to serve the state without interested motives. Their salary is a detail to which sometimes they give little thought and to which they always pretend to give none.

Thus the notion of profit remains distinct from that of work. The two may go together in fact, but tradition denies that.

But in democratic societies the two notions are always visibly united. As fortunes are middling and ephemeral, and everyone needs to increase his resources or create fresh ones for his children, all see quite clearly that it is profit which, if not wholly then at least partially, prompts them to work.

As soon as these two assumptions are made, that work is an honorable necessity and that it is always done, at least in part, for pay, the immense difference separating different professions in aristocratic societies disappears. If they are not all just the same, at least they have one characteristic in common. There is no profession at which a man works except for pay.

This serves to explain the views of Americans about different callings.

Americans do not feel degraded because they work, for everyone around them is working. There is nothing humiliating about the idea of receiving a salary, for the president of the United States works for a salary. He is paid for giving orders, as they are for obeying them.

In the United States professions are more or less unpleasant, more or less lucrative, but they are never high or low. Every honest profession is honorable.

19

WHAT GIVES ALMOST ALL AMERICANS A PREFERENCE FOR INDUSTRIAL CALLINGS

AGRICULTURE IS PERHAPS, OF all the useful arts, the one which improves most slowly in democratic nations. Almost all the tastes and habits born of equality naturally lead men in the direction of trade and industry.

Suppose a man to be active, educated, free, comfortably off, and full of desire. He is too poor to live in idleness; he is rich enough not to fear immediate want and is anxious to improve his lot. Our man has formed a taste for physical pleasures; he sees thousands around him enjoying them; he himself has tasted some too, and he is very keen to acquire the means to enjoy more. But life goes by, and time presses. What is he to do?

To cultivate the ground promises an almost certain reward, but a slow one. Agriculture only suits the wealthy, who already have a great superfluity, or the poor, who only want to live. His choice is made; he sells his field and takes up some risky but lucrative profession.

Now, democratic societies are full of people of this type. As equality spreads, it gives them a distaste for agriculture and directs them into trade and industry.[1]

---

1. It has often been noted that industrialists and merchants have an inordinate taste for physical pleasures, and trade and industry have been held responsible for this. I think that is to mistake the effect for the cause.

It is not trade and industry that give men the taste for physical pleasures, but rather the taste for them which induces men to go into trade and industry, so as to satisfy this taste more completely and quickly.

This turn of mind is manifest even among the wealthiest citizens.

In democratic countries, no matter how rich a man is, he is almost always dissatisfied, because he finds that he is less wealthy than his father was and is afraid that his son will be less wealthy than he. In this respect they share the poor man's instincts without his necessities, or rather they are driven by the most imperious of all necessities, that of not sinking.

The following observation applies to everyone in a democracy, rich or poor.

Chance is an element always present to the mind of those who live in the unstable conditions of a democracy, and in the end they come to love enterprises in which chance plays a part.

This draws them to trade not only for the sake of promised gain, but also because they love the emotions it provides.

It is only half a century since the United States escaped from the colonial dependence in which England held it; there are few great fortunes there and capital is still scarce. But no other nation has made as rapid progress in trade and industry. The Americans today are the second maritime nation in the world, and although their manufactures have to struggle against natural obstacles, they are daily making advances.

In the United States the whole population is engaged in industry; the poorest man as well as the most opulent gladly joins forces therein. One is in daily astonishment at the immense works carried through without difficulty by a nation which, one may say, has no rich men. The Americans arrived but yesterday in the land where they live, and they have already turned the whole order of nature upside down to their profit. They have joined the Hudson to the Mississippi and linked the Atlantic Ocean with the Gulf of Mexico across a continent of more than five hundred leagues. The longest railways yet constructed are in the United States.

I am even more struck by the multitude of little undertakings than by the extraordinary size of industrial enterprises.

Almost all the farmers in the United States have combined some trade with agriculture; most of them have made agriculture itself a trade.

Every year a swarm of people arrive from the North in the southern states and settle in the lands where cotton and sugar cane grow. These men cultivate the land in order to make it enrich them within a few years, when they will return to their native land to enjoy the fortune thus acquired. In such fashion the Americans carry over into agriculture the spirit of a trading venture, and their passion for industry is manifest there as elsewhere.

The Americans make great advances in industry because they are all at the same time engaged in it, and for this same reason they are subject to very unexpected and formidable industrial crises. Trade is affected by such various and complex causes that it is impossible to foresee what embarrassments may arise. At the least shock to business activity, all private fortunes are in jeopardy at the same time and the state is shaken.

I believe that the recurrence of these industrial crises is an endemic disease among all democratic nations in our day. It can be made less dangerous, but not cured, for it is not due to accident but to the essential temperament of these peoples.

20

HOW AN ARISTOCRACY MAY
BE CREATED BY INDUSTRY

WHEN A WORKMAN SPENDS every day on the same detail, the finished article is produced more easily, quickly, and economically.

Likewise, the larger the scale on which an industrial undertaking is conducted, the cheaper will its products be.

People had formed some inkling of these truths long ago, but it is in our day that they have been demonstrated. They have already been applied to several very important industries, and in due turn even the smallest will take advantage of them.

There is nothing in the world of politics that deserves attention more than these two new axioms of industrial science.

When a workman is constantly engaged in making one object, he ends by performing this work with singular dexterity. But at the same time, he loses the general faculty of applying his mind to the way he is working. Every day he becomes more adroit and less industrious, and one may say that the man is degraded as the workman improves.

What is one to expect from a man who has spent twenty years of his life making heads for pins? His thought is permanently fixed on the object of his daily toil; his body has contracted certain fixed habits which it can never shake off. In a word, he no longer belongs to himself, but to his chosen calling. An industrial theory stronger than morality or law ties him to a trade, and often to a place, which he cannot leave. He has been assigned a certain position in society which he cannot quit. In the midst of universal movement, he is stuck immobile.

As the principle of the division of labor is ever more completely applied, the workman becomes weaker, more limited, and more dependent. The craft improves, the craftsman slips back. Very rich and well-educated men come forward to exploit industries which, up to that time, had been left to ignorant and rough artisans. Thus, at the same time that industrial science constantly lowers the standing of the working class, it raises that of the masters.

While the workman confines his intelligence more and more to one single detail, the master daily embraces a vast field in his vision, and his mind expands as fast as the other's contracts. Soon the latter will need no more than bodily strength without intelli-

gence, while to succeed the former needs science and almost
genius. The former becomes more like the administrator of a
huge empire, and the latter more like a brute.

So there is no resemblance between master and workman, and
daily they become more different. There is no connection except
that between the first and last links in a long chain. One is in a
state of dependence on the other and seems to have been born to
obey, as the other was to command.

What is this, if not an aristocracy?

But that aristocracy is not at all like those that have preceded it.

Because it only flourishes in industry and in some industrial
callings, it is an exception, a monstrosity, within the general social
condition. Little aristocratic societies formed by certain industries
in the midst of democracy contain some very opulent men and a
multitude of wretchedly poor ones.

These poor men have few means of escaping from their condition and becoming rich, but the rich are constantly becoming poor or retiring from business when they have realized
their profits. Hence there is no true link between rich and
poor. The workman is dependent on masters in general, but
not on a particular master. These two men see each other at
the factory but do not know each other otherwise, and they
are not linked in any permanent fashion either by custom or
by duty.

A business aristocracy seldom lives among the manufacturing
population which it directs; its object is not to rule the latter but to
make use of it.

The aristocracy of past ages was obliged by law, or thought
itself obliged by custom, to come to the help of its servants and
relieve their distress. But the industrial aristocracy of our day,
when it has impoverished and brutalized the men it uses, aban-
dons them in time of crisis to public charity to feed them. This
is the natural result of what has been said before. Between workman and master there are frequent relations but no true association.

I think that, generally speaking, the manufacturing aristocracy which we see rising before our eyes is one of the hardest that have appeared on earth. But at the same time, it is one of the most restrained and least dangerous.

In any event, the friends of democracy should keep their eyes anxiously fixed in that direction. For if ever again permanent inequality of conditions and aristocracy make their way into the world, it will have been by that door that they entered.

PART III

Influence of Democracy on Mores Properly So Called

1

HOW MORES BECOME MORE GENTLE AS
SOCIAL CONDITIONS BECOME MORE EQUAL

WE SEE THAT FOR several centuries social conditions have been getting more equal and notice that at the same time mores have become more gentle. Did these two things simply take place at the same time, or is there some secret connection between them?

There are several causes which can concur in making a nation's mores less rough, but I think that the most potent of all is equality of conditions. So equality of conditions and greater gentleness of mores are not, in my view, things happening just by chance at the same time, but correlative facts.

Among an aristocratic people each caste has its opinions, feelings, rights, mores, and whole separate existence. Its members are not at all like members of all the other castes, and they hardly manage to think of themselves as forming part of the same humanity. Hence they cannot well understand what the others suffer, nor judge them by themselves.

When ranks are almost equal among a people, as all men think and feel in nearly the same manner, each instantaneously can judge the feelings of all the others. There is no misery that he cannot readily understand, and a secret instinct tells him its extent. It makes no difference if strangers or enemies are in question; his imagination at once puts him in their place.

In democratic ages men rarely sacrifice themselves for another, but they show a general compassion for all the human race. One never sees them inflict pointless suffering, and they are glad to relieve the sorrows of others when they can do so without much trouble to themselves. They are not disinterested, but they are gentle.

There is no country in which criminal justice is administered with more kindness than in the United States. While the English seem bent on carefully preserving in their penal legislation the bloody traces of the Middle Ages, the Americans have almost eliminated capital punishment.

North America is, I think, the only country on earth which has not taken the life of a single citizen for political offenses during the last fifty years.

There is a circumstance which conclusively shows that this singular mildness of the Americans is chiefly due to their social condition. That is the way they treat their slaves. The blacks there suffer terrible afflictions and are constantly subject to very cruel punishments.

It is easy to see that the lot of these unfortunates inspires very little compassion in their masters. They look upon slavery not only as profitable but also as an ill which scarcely touches them. Thus the same man who is full of humanity toward his equals becomes insensible to their sorrows when there is no more equality. It is therefore to this equality that we must attribute his gentleness, even more than to his civilization and education.

What I have just been saying about individuals applies to some extent to peoples too.

When each nation has its own opinions, beliefs, laws, and customs, it looks on itself as composing the whole of humanity and feels touched only by its own sorrows. If war breaks out between peoples of this disposition, it is sure to be conducted with barbarity.

But as people become more like one another, they show themselves reciprocally more compassionate, and the law of nations becomes more gentle.

HOW DEMOCRACY LEADS TO EASE AND SIMPLICITY IN THE ORDINARY RELATIONS BETWEEN AMERICANS

DEMOCRACY DOES NOT CREATE strong attachments between man and man, but it does put their ordinary relations on an easier footing.

Suppose two Englishmen meet by chance at the antipodes and are there surrounded by strangers whose language and manners they hardly understand.

First they will look at each other with great curiosity and a sort of secret anxiety; then they will turn away, or if they do address each other, they will take care to talk with a constrained and absent air about matters of little importance.

But there is no hostility between them; they have never met before, and each believes the other to be a perfectly respectable person. Why, then, do they take such trouble to avoid each other?

Aristocratic pride still being a very strong force with the English, and the boundaries of the aristocracy having become doubtful, each man is constantly afraid lest advantage be taken of his familiarity. Not being able to judge at first sight the social position of the people he meets, he prudently avoids contact with them. He is afraid that some slight service rendered may draw him into an unsuitable friendship.

Many people explain this strange unsociability and reserved disposition of the English by purely physical causes. Blood may count for something in the matter, but I think that social conditions count for much more. The example of the Americans serves to prove this.

In America, where privileges of birth never existed and where wealth brings its possessor no peculiar right, men unacquainted with one another frequent the same places and find neither danger nor advantage in telling each other freely what they think. Meeting by chance, their manner is natural, frank, and open. One sees that there is practically nothing that they either hope or fear from each other and that they are not concerned to show or to hide their social position.

In a foreign land two Americans are friends at once for the simple reason that they are Americans. There is no prejudice to hold them back, and their common fatherland draws them together. For two Englishmen the same blood is not enough; they must also have the same rank to bring them together.

The Americans notice this unsociable disposition of the English as much as we do and are just as surprised by it. Yet the Americans are close to the English in origin, religion, language, and partly also mores. Their social condition is the only difference. It therefore seems fair to assert that English reserve is due much more to the constitution of the country than of the citizens.

3

WHY THE AMERICANS ARE SO HARD TO OFFEND IN THEIR OWN COUNTRY AND SO EASILY OFFENDED IN OURS

THE AMERICANS, IN COMMON with all serious and thoughtful nations, have a vindictive temperament. They hardly ever forget an offense, but it is not easy to offend them, and their resentment is as slow to kindle as to abate.

In aristocratic societies, in which a few individuals manage everything, everyone has a precise conception of how to show respect or affability. Thus rules of politeness form a complicated code which it is difficult to master completely but which nonetheless it is dangerous to contravene.

But as distinctions of rank are obliterated and men of different education and birth mix and mingle in the same places, it is almost impossible to agree upon the rules of good manners. The code being uncertain, to contravene it is no longer a crime in the eyes even of those who do know it. So the substance of behavior comes to count for more than the form, and men grow less polite but also less quarrelsome.

There is a mass of little attentions to which an American attaches no importance; he thinks that they are not his due, or he supposes that people do not know they are due him. So he either does not notice that he has been slighted or forgives the slight; his formal behavior becomes less courteous but his manners simpler and more manly.

Scorning no man on account of his status, it does not occur to him that anyone scorns him for that reason, and unless the insult is clearly seen, he does not think that anyone wants to offend him. I have often noticed in the United States that it is not at all easy to make a man understand that his presence is unwelcome.

If I contradict every word an American says to show him that his conversation bores me, he will constantly renew his efforts to convince me. If I remain obstinately silent, he thinks that I am reflecting deeply on the truths he has put to me. If finally I get up abruptly and go, he supposes that I have some urgent business which I have not mentioned. Unless I tell him plainly, the man will not understand that he exasperates me, and I cannot escape from him except by becoming his deadly enemy.

It therefore seems surprising at first sight that this same man, transported to Europe, becomes suddenly so sensitive and touchy that it is as hard now to avoid offending him as it once was to cause offense. Both these very different results are due to the same cause.

Democratic institutions generally give men a grandiose opinion of their country and themselves.

The American leaves his country with a heart swollen with pride. He comes to Europe and at once discovers that we are not nearly so interested as he had supposed in the United States and the great nation that lives there. This begins to annoy him.

He had heard it said that conditions are not equal on our side of the world. He does in fact notice traces of rank, and some uncertain privileges which are as difficult to ignore as to define. Surprised and disturbed by all this, he has not the faintest notion what status he ought to enjoy in this half-ruined hierarchy. He is afraid of claiming too high a status and even more afraid of being ranked too low. This double peril is a constant worry and embarrassment to his every act and word. So he moves through a land full of traps. He is at pains himself to observe every tiny rule of etiquette, and he will not let any neglect to himself pass.

But that is not the whole story; here is another queer twist of human sensibility.

An American is constantly talking about the wonderful equality prevailing in the United States. He loudly proclaims his pride in this, but he likes to show that, in his own case, he is an exception to the rule he has extolled.

One hardly ever meets an American who does not want to claim some connection by birth with the first founders of the colonies, and as for offshoots of great English families, I think America is simply full of them.

When an opulent American lands in Europe, he is so much afraid that you may take him for the simple citizen of a democracy that he thinks up a hundred roundabout ways of calling fresh attention to his wealth every day. He usually takes up his quarters in the most fashionable part of the town and is always surrounded by his numerous servants.

We should not be astonished at such contrasts.

If the traces of ancient aristocratic distinctions had not been so completely wiped away in America, the Americans would be less simple and tolerant in their own country, less pretentious and affected in ours.

4

CONSEQUENCES DERIVING FROM
THE THREE PRECEDING CHAPTERS

WHEN MEN FEEL A natural compassion for the sufferings of others, when they are brought together in easy and frequent intercourse, it is easy to understand that they will give each other mutual support when needed. When an American needs the assistance of his fellows, it is very rare for that to be refused, and I have often seen it given spontaneously and eagerly.

Where there is an accident on the public road, people hurry from all sides to help the victim. When some unexpected disaster strikes a family, a thousand strangers willingly open their purses, and small but very numerous gifts relieve their distress.

It often happens in the most civilized countries of the world that a man in misfortune is almost as isolated in the crowd as a savage in the woods. That is hardly ever seen in the United States. The Americans, often coarse, are hardly ever insensitive. Though they may be in no hurry to volunteer services, they do not refuse them.

All this does not contradict what I have said about individualism.

Equality which makes men feel their freedom also shows them their weakness. They are free, but liable to a thousand accidents, and experience is not slow to teach them that although they may not usually need the help of others, a moment will almost always arrive when they cannot do without it.

The more similar conditions become, the more do people show this readiness of reciprocal obligation.

In democracies, though no one is presented with great benefits, constant acts of kindness are performed. A self-sacrificing man is rare, but all are obliging.

5

HOW DEMOCRACY MODIFIES
THE RELATIONS BETWEEN
MASTER AND SERVANT

AN AMERICAN WHO HAD traveled a lot in Europe once said to me: "We find the haughtiness . . . of the English toward their servants astonishing, but on the other hand, the French sometimes treat them with a friendliness and . . . politeness which we cannot understand. One would think they were afraid of giving orders. The position of superior and inferior is ill-maintained."

The observation is fair and I have often noticed it myself.

There has not yet been a society in which conditions were so equal that there was neither rich nor poor, and consequently neither masters nor servants.

Democracy in no way prevents the existence of these two classes, but it changes their attitudes and modifies their relations.

In aristocracies servants are a class apart, which changes no more than that of the masters. There are two societies imposed one on top of the other, always distinct, but with analogous principles. Men whose destiny is to obey certainly do not understand fame, virtue, honesty, and honor in the same way as their masters. But they have devised fame, virtues, and honesty suited to servants, and they conceive, if I may put it so, a sort of servile honor.[1]

However inferior the class may be, he who is first within it and has no thought of leaving it has an aristocratic position which prompts high thoughts, strong pride, and self-respect. It may be

---

1.   One is astonished to find among them, as among the most highly placed members of the feudal hierarchy, pride of birth, respect for ancestors and descendants, scorn for inferiors, a fear of contact, and a taste for etiquette, precedents, and antiquity.

imagined that he who occupies the lowest step in a hierarchy of valets is low indeed.

The French invented a word to designate this lowest of the servants of an aristocracy. They call him the lackey. Under the old monarchy, when one wanted to denote a vile and degraded creature, one said he had "the soul of a lackey."

In aristocratic societies the poor are trained from infancy to thoughts of obedience. All around, wherever they look, they see hierarchies of command. The master often exercises, even unconsciously, an immense power over the thoughts, habits, and mores of those who obey him, and his influence extends far beyond even his authority.

The servants, for their part, sometimes identify themselves so much with the master personally that they become an appendage to him in their own eyes as well as in his. In this extreme case the servant ends by losing his sense of self-interest; deserts himself, as it were, or rather he transports the whole of himself into his master's character. One still sometimes meets among us one of these old servants of the aristocracy; they are survivals from a race which will soon vanish.

Never in the United States have I seen anything to put one in mind of the trusted retainer whose memory still haunts us in Europe, but neither did I find the conception of the lackey. Both are lost without trace.

In democracies servants are not only equal among themselves, but one can say that in some fashion they are equal to their masters.

That needs some explanation to be fully understood.

The servant may at any time become the master, and he wants to do so. So the servant is not a different type of man from the master.

Why, then, has the latter the right to command, and what makes the former obey? A temporary and freely made agreement. By nature they are not at all inferior one to the other, and they only become so temporarily by contract. Within the terms of the contract, one is servant and the other master; beyond that, they are two citizens, two men.

No matter how wealth or poverty, power or obedience, accidentally put great distances between two men, public opinion, based on the normal way of things, puts them near the common level and creates a sort of fancied equality between them, in spite of the actual inequality of their lives.

This all-powerful opinion finally infuses itself into the thoughts even of those whose interest it is to fight against it; it both modifies their judgment and subdues their will. The master considers the contract the sole source of his power, and the servant thinks it the sole reason for his obedience. There is no dispute between them about their reciprocal position; each easily sees what is his and keeps to it.

I want to base all I have just said on the example of the Americans, but I cannot do so without making careful distinctions concerning persons and places.

In the South there is slavery, so all I have said cannot apply there.

In the North most servants are freed slaves or the sons of these. Such men hold a doubtful position in public esteem. The law brings them up close to their master's level. Mores obstinately push them back. They cannot see their own status clearly and are almost always either insolent or cringing.

But in these northern states, especially in New England, one does find a fairly large number of white men who agree for wages temporarily to perform the wishes of others. I have heard it said that these servants usually carry out the duties of their status without thinking themselves naturally inferior to those who give the orders.

The masters, for their part, do not expect more from their servants than the faithful and strict performance of the contract; they do not ask for marks of respect; they do not claim their love or devotion; it is enough if they are punctual and honest.

It would not therefore be true to say that in a democracy the relationship between master and servant is unorganized; it is organized in another way; the rule is different, but there is a rule.

6

INFLUENCE OF DEMOCRACY ON WAGES

MOST OF WHAT HAS been said above about masters and servants applies to masters and workmen.

As the rules of social hierarchy are less strictly observed, as great ones fall and the humble rise, as poverty as well as wealth ceases to be hereditary, the distance separating master from workman daily diminishes both in fact and in men's minds.

The workman conceives a higher idea of his rights, of his future, and of himself; new ambitions, new desires, fill his mind, and he constantly looks with covetous eyes at his master's profits. In striving to share them, he aims to up the price of his labor, and usually succeeds in this.

Most industry is carried on at small expense by men whose wealth and education do not raise them above the common level of those they employ. These industrial adventurers are very numerous, their interests differ, and so it is not easy for them to unite.

On the other hand, the workers have almost all got some sure resources which allow them to refuse their work if they cannot get what they consider the fair reward for their labor.

In France most agricultural wage earners themselves own some little plot of land which, at a pinch, will keep them alive without working for another man. When such as these offer to work for a great landlord or for a neighboring tenant farmer and are refused a certain wage, they go back to their little domain and wait for another opportunity.

[Originally chapter 7. Tocqueville's chapter 6, "How Democratic Institutions and Mores Tend to Raise Rents and Shorten the Terms of Leases," has been omitted.]

I think that, taking the whole picture into consideration, one can assert that a slow, progressive rise in wages is one of the general laws characteristic of democratic societies. As conditions become more equal, wages rise; and as wages rise, conditions become more equal.

But in our time there is one great and unfortunate exception.

I have shown in a previous chapter how aristocracy, chased out of political society, has taken refuge in some parts of industry and established its sway there in another shape.

That has a strong influence on the rate of wages.

As one must be very rich to embark on the great industrial undertakings of which I speak, the number of those engaged in them is very small. Being very few, they can easily league together and fix the rate of wages that pleases them.

Their workers, on the other hand, are very numerous, and their number is constantly on the increase. From time to time there are periods of extraordinary prosperity in which wages rise disproportionately and attract the surrounding population into industry. But once men have adopted this calling, as we have seen, they soon develop habits of body and mind which render them unsuited to any other work. Such men usually have little education, energy, or resources and are therefore at their master's mercy. When competition or any other circumstance reduces the master's profits, he can lower their wages at his pleasure and easily recover at their expense.

If by common accord they withhold their work, the master, who is rich, can easily wait without ruining himself until necessity brings them back to him. They must work every day if they are not to die, for they scarcely have any property beyond their arms. They have long been impoverished by oppression, and increasing poverty makes them easier to oppress. This is the vicious circle from which they cannot escape.

One must therefore not be surprised if wages, which have sometimes gone up suddenly, in this case fall permanently.

This state of dependence and poverty affecting part of the industrial population in our day is an exceptional fact running counter to conditions all around it. But for that very reason it is nonetheless serious and claims the particular attention of legislators. For it is hard when the whole of society is on the move to keep one class stationary.

7

INFLUENCE OF DEMOCRACY ON THE FAMILY

I HAVE JUST BEEN considering how among democratic peoples, particularly America, equality modifies the relations between one citizen and another. I want to carry the argument further and consider what happens within the family.

Everyone has noticed that in our time a new relationship has evolved between the different members of a family, that the distance formerly separating father and son has diminished, and that paternal authority, if not abolished, has at least changed form.

Something analogous, but even more striking, occurs in the United States.

In America the family, in its aristocratic sense, no longer exists. One only finds scattered traces thereof in the first years following the birth of children. As soon as the young American begins to approach man's estate, the reins of filial obedience are daily slackened. Master of his thoughts, he soon becomes responsible for his own behavior. In America there is in truth no adolescence. At the close of boyhood he is a man and begins to trace out his own path.

It would be wrong to suppose that this results from some sort of domestic struggle, in which the son had won the freedom which

_____

[Originally chapter 8.]

his father refused. The same habits and principles which lead the
former to grasp at independence dispose the latter to consider as
an incontestable right.[1]

When men are more concerned with memories of what has
been than with what is, and when they are much more anxious to
know what their ancestors thought than to think for themselves,
the father is the natural and necessary link between the past and
the present, the link where these two chains meet and join. In aristocracies, therefore, the father is not only the political head of the
family but also the instrument of tradition, the interpreter of
custom, and the arbiter of mores. He is heard with deference, he
is addressed always with respect, and the affection felt for him is
ever mingled with fear.

When the state of society turns to democracy and men adopt
the general principle that it is good and right to judge everything
for oneself, paternal opinions come to have less power over the
sons, just as his legal power is less too.

Perhaps the division of patrimonies which follows from democracy does more than all the rest to alter the relations between
father and children.

I am not certain, generally speaking, whether society loses by
the change, but I am inclined to think that the individual gains.
I think that as mores and laws become more democratic the relations between father and sons become more intimate and
gentle; there is less of rule and authority, often more of confidence and affection, and it would seem than the natural bond
grows tighter.

A perusal of the family correspondence surviving from aristocratic ages is enough to illustrate the difference between the two
social states in this respect. The style is always correct, ceremoni-

---

1. It has, however, never occurred to the Americans to do what we have done in
France and take away from fathers one of the chief elements of their power by refusing them the right to dispose of their possessions after their death. In the United
States testamentary powers are unlimited. It is easy to see that while American political legislation is much more democratic than ours, our civil legislation is infinitely
more democratic than theirs.

ous, rigid, and cold, so that natural warmth of heart can hardly be felt through the words.

But among democratic nations every word a son addresses to his father has a tang of freedom, familiarity, and tenderness all at once, which gives an immediate impression of the new relationship prevailing in the family.

An analogous revolution changes the relations between the children.

In the aristocratic family the eldest son, who will inherit most of the property and almost all the rights, becomes the chief and to a certain extent the master of his brothers. The eldest usually takes trouble to procure wealth and power for his brothers, and the younger sons try to help the eldest in all his undertakings, for the greatness and power of the head of the family increase his ability to promote all the branches of the family. So their interests are connected and their minds are in accord, but their hearts are seldom in harmony.

Democracy too draws brothers together, but in a different way.

Under democratic laws the children are perfectly equal, and consequently independent; nothing forcibly brings them together, but also nothing drives them apart. Having a common origin, brought up under the same roof, and treated with the same care, scarcely anything can break the bond thus formed at the start of life. Brotherhood daily draws them together, and there is no cause for friction.

I may be able to sum up in one phrase the whole sense of this chapter and of several others that preceded it. Democracy loosens social ties, but it tightens natural ones. At the same time as it separates citizens, it brings kindred closer together.

8

EDUCATION OF GIRLS IN
THE UNITED STATES

THERE HAVE NEVER BEEN free societies without mores, and as I observed in the first part of this book, it is woman who shapes these mores. Therefore everything which has a bearing on the status of women, their habits, and their thoughts is, in my view, of great political importance.

In almost all Protestant nations girls are much more in control of their own behavior than among Catholic ones.

This independence is even greater in those Protestant countries, such as England, which have kept or gained the right of self-government. In such cases both political habits and religious beliefs infuse a spirit of liberty into the family.

In the United States, Protestant teaching is combined with a very free Constitution and a very democratic society, and in no other country is a girl left so soon or so completely to look after herself.

Long before the young American woman has reached marriageable age, she already thinks for herself, speaks freely, and acts on her own. All the doings of the world are plain for her to see; far from trying to keep this from her sight, she is taught to look thereon with firm and quiet gaze. So the vices and dangers of society are soon plain to her, and she judges them without illusion and faces them without fear, for she is full of confidence in her own powers.

Thus you can hardly expect an American girl to show that virgin innocence and those artless graces which in Europe go with the

[Originally chapter 9.]

stage between childhood and youth. Seldom does an American girl, whatever her age, suffer from shyness or childish ignorance; her morals are pure rather than her mind chaste.

I have often been surprised and almost frightened to see the skill and audacity with which young American women steer their thoughts and language through the traps of sprightly conversation. She enjoys all permitted pleasures without losing her head about any of them, and her reason never lets the reins go, though it may often seem to let them flap.

In France, we often give girls a timid, almost cloistered education, as was done under the aristocracy, and then leave them unguided amid all the disorder inseparable from democratic society.

The Americans realize that there must be a great deal of individual freedom in a democracy; youth will be impatient, paternal authority weak, and a husband's power contested.

They have calculated that there was little chance of repressing in woman the passions of the human heart and that it was a safer policy to teach her to control them herself. Unable to prevent her chastity from being often in danger, they want her to know how to defend herself. Far from hiding the world's corruption from her, they are more anxious to ensure her good conduct than to guard her innocence too carefully.

Although the Americans are a very religious people, they have not relied on religion alone to defend feminine chastity; they have tried to give arms to her reasoning powers. In this they are using the same approach that they have employed in many other circumstances.

I know that such an education tends to develop judgment at the cost of imagination and to make women chaste and cold rather than tender and loving companions of men. But we no longer have a choice; a democratic education is necessary to protect women against the dangers with which the institutions and mores of democracy surround them.

9

THE YOUNG WOMAN AS A WIFE

IN AMERICA A WOMAN loses her independence forever in the bonds of matrimony. While there is less constraint on girls there than anywhere else, a wife submits to stricter obligations. For the former, her father's house is a home of freedom and pleasure; for the latter, her husband's is almost a cloister.

Religious peoples and industrial nations take a particularly serious view of marriage. The former consider the regularity of a woman's life the best guarantee of her morals. The latter see in it the surest safeguard of the order and prosperity of the house.

The Americans are both a Puritan and a trading nation. Both their religious beliefs and their industrial habits demand much abnegation on the woman's part and a sacrifice of pleasure for the sake of business, which is seldom expected in Europe. Thus in America inexorable public opinion carefully keeps woman within the little sphere of domestic interests and duties.

When she is born into the world the young American girl is soon convinced that she cannot for a moment depart from the usages accepted by her contemporaries without immediately putting in danger her peace of mind, her reputation, and her very social existence. She finds the strength required for such an act of submission in the firmness of her understanding and the manly habits inculcated by her education.

One may say that it is the very enjoyment of freedom that has given her the courage to sacrifice it without complaint when the time has come for that.

Moreover, the American woman never gets caught in the bonds of matrimony as in a snare. She knows beforehand what will be

---

[Originally chapter 10.]

expected of her and has freely accepted the yoke. She suffers her new state bravely, for she has chosen it.

Because in America paternal discipline is very lax and the bonds of marriage very tight, a girl is cautious and wary in agreeing thereto. Precocious weddings hardly occur. So American women only marry when their minds are experienced and mature, whereas elsewhere women usually only begin to mature when they are married.

When the time has come to choose a husband, her cold and austere powers of reasoning, which have been educated by a free view of the world, teach the American woman that a free spirit within the bonds of marriage is an everlasting source of trouble, not of pleasure. A girl's amusements cannot become the recreation of a wife, and for a married woman, the springs of happiness are inside the home. Seeing clearly the only path to domestic felicity, from the first step she sets out in that direction and follows it to the end without seeking to turn back.

This same strength of will is no less manifest in all the great trials of their lives.

In no country of the world are private fortunes more unstable than in the United States. It is not exceptional for one man in his lifetime to work up from poverty to opulence and then come down again.

American women face such upheavals with quiet, indomitable energy. Their desires seem to contract with their fortune as easily as they expand.

Most of the adventurers who yearly go west belong, as noted in my earlier book, to the old Anglo-American stock of the North. Many who launch out so boldly have already gained a comfortable living in their own land. They take their wives and make them share dangers and privations. In the utmost confines of the wilderness I have often met young wives, brought up in the refinement of life of New England, who have passed almost without transition from their parents' prosperous houses to leaky cabins in the forest. Fever, solitude, and boredom had not broken the resilience of their courage. Their features were changed and faded, but their looks were firm. They seemed both sad and resolute.

I am sure that it was the education of their early years which built up that inner strength on which they were later to draw.

So, in America the wife is still the same person that she was as a girl; her part in life has changed, and her ways are different, but the spirit is the same. (See Appendix, [p. 403].)

10

HOW EQUALITY HELPS TO MAINTAIN GOOD MORALS IN AMERICA

SOME PHILOSOPHERS AND HISTORIANS have stated or implied that women's morals are more or less strict in accordance with the distance at which they live from the equator. I am not denying that in certain climates the passions arising from the reciprocal attraction of the sexes may be particularly intense. But I think that this natural intensity may always be excited or restrained by social conditions and political institutions.

Travelers who have visited North America all agree that mores are infinitely stricter there than anywhere else. In that respect the Americans are greatly superior to their fathers, the English. A superficial glance at the two nations is enough to show that.

In England, as in all other European countries, malicious gossip constantly attacks the frailties of women. Philosophers and statesmen complain that mores are not strict enough, and the country's literature constantly suggests that this is so.

In America all books, not excepting novels, suppose women to be chaste, and no one there boasts of amorous adventures.

[Originally chapter 11.]

No doubt this great strictness of American mores is due partly to the country, the race, and the religion. But all those causes, which can be found elsewhere, are still not enough to account for the matter. To do so one must discover some particular reason.

I think that reason is equality and institutions deriving therefrom.

The Americans regard marriage as a contract which is often burdensome but every condition of which the parties are strictly bound to fulfill, because they knew them all beforehand and were at liberty not to bind themselves to anything at all.

The same cause which renders fidelity more obligatory also renders it easier.

The object of marriage in aristocratic lands is more to unite property than persons; so it can happen sometimes that the husband is chosen while at school and the wife at the breast. It is not surprising that the conjugal tie which unites the fortunes of the married couple leaves their hearts to rove at large. That is the natural result of the spirit of the contract.

But when each chooses his companion for himself without any external interference or even prompting, it is usually nothing but similar tastes and thoughts that bring a man and a woman together, and these similarities hold and keep them by each other's side.

Almost all the men in a democracy practice some calling, whereas limited incomes oblige the wives to stay at home and watch over the details of domestic economy.

These separate and necessary occupations form natural barriers which, by keeping the sexes apart, make the solicitations of the one less frequent and less ardent and the resistance of the other easier.

Not that equality of conditions could ever make man chaste, but it gives the irregularity of his morals a less dangerous character. As no man has leisure or opportunity to attack the virtue of those who wish to defend themselves, there are at the same time a great number of courtesans and a great many honest women.

Such a state of affairs leads to deplorable individual wretchedness, but it does not break up families and does not weaken national morality. Society is endangered by prostitution much less than intrigues.

The constantly harassed life which equality makes men lead not only diverts their attention from lovemaking by depriving them of leisure but also turns them away by a more secret but more certain path.

Everyone living in democratic times contracts, more or less, the mental habits of the industrial and trading classes; their thoughts take a serious turn, calculating and realistic. Equality does not destroy the imagination, but clips its wings and only lets it fly touching the ground.

No men are less dreamers than the citizens of democracy; one hardly finds any who indulge in such leisurely and solitary moods of contemplation as generally produce great agitations of the heart.

They do, it is true, set great store on obtaining that type of deep, regular, and peaceful affection which makes life happy and secure. But they would not willingly chase violent and capricious emotions which disturb life and cut it short.

11

HOW THE AMERICAN VIEWS THE EQUALITY OF THE SEXES

I HAVE SHOWN HOW democracy destroys or modifies various inequalities which are in origin social. But is that the end of the matter? May it not ultimately come to change the great inequality between man and woman which has up till now seemed based on the eternal foundations of nature?

[Originally chapter 12.]

I think that the same social impetus which brings nearer to the same level father and son, master and servant, and generally every inferior to every superior does raise the status of women and should make them more and more nearly equal to men.

But in this I need more than ever to make myself clearly understood. For there is no subject on which the crude, disorderly fancy of our age has given itself freer rein.

In Europe there are people who, confusing the divergent attributes of the sexes, claim that man and woman are not only equal, but actually similar. They would attribute the same functions to both, impose the same duties, and grant the same rights; they would have them share everything—work, pleasure, public affairs. Equality forced on both sexes degrades them both and that could produce nothing but feeble men and unseemly women.

That is far from being the American view of the democratic equality between man and woman. They think that nature, which created such great differences between the physical and moral constitution of men and women, clearly intended to give their diverse faculties a diverse employment; and they consider that progress consists not in making dissimilar creatures do roughly the same things but in giving both a chance to do their job as well as possible. The Americans have applied to the sexes the great principle of political economy which now dominates industry. They have separated the functions of man and woman so that the great work of society may be better performed.

In America, more than anywhere else in the world, care has been taken to trace distinct spheres of action for the two sexes, and both are required to keep in step, but along paths that are never the same. You will never find American women in charge of the external relations of the family, managing a business, or interfering in politics; but they are also never obliged to undertake rough laborer's work or any task requiring hard physical exertion. No family is so poor that it makes an exception to this rule.

If the American woman is never allowed to leave the quiet sphere of domestic duties, she is also never forced to do so.

As a result, American women, who are often manly in their intelligence and energy, usually preserve great delicacy of personal appearance and always have the manners of women, though they sometimes show the minds and hearts of men.

Nor have the Americans ever supposed that democratic principles should undermine the husband's authority and make it doubtful who is in charge of the family. In their view, every association, to be effective, must have a head, and the natural head of the conjugal association is the husband. They therefore never deny him the right to direct his spouse. They think that in the little society composed of man and wife, just as in the great society of politics, the aim of democracy is to regulate and legitimatize necessary powers and not to destroy all power.

That is by no means an opinion maintained by one sex and opposed by the other.

I have never found American women regarding conjugal authority as a usurpation of their rights or feeling that they degraded themselves by submitting to it. On the contrary, they seem to take pride in the free relinquishment of their will, and it is their boast to bear the yoke themselves rather than to escape it. That, at least, is the feeling expressed by the best of them; the others keep quiet, and in the United States one never hears an adulterous wife noisily proclaiming the rights of women while stamping the most hallowed duties under foot.

In Europe a certain contempt lurks in the flattery men lavish on women; although a European may often make himself a woman's slave, one feels that he never sincerely thinks her his equal.

In the United States men seldom compliment women, but they daily show how much they esteem them.

Americans constantly display complete confidence in their spouses' judgment and deep respect for their freedom. They hold that woman's mind is just as capable as man's of discovering the naked truth, and her heart as firm to face it. They have never sought to place her virtue, any more than his, under the protection of prejudice, ignorance, or fear.

It would seem that in Europe, where men so easily submit to the despotic sway of women, they are regarded as seductive but incomplete beings. The most astonishing thing of all is that women end by looking at themselves in the same light and that they almost think it a privilege to be able to appear futile, weak, and timid. The women of America never lay claim to rights of that sort.

It may, moreover, be said that our moral standards accord a strange immunity to man, so that virtue is one thing in his case and quite another for his spouse, and that the same act can be seen by public opinion as a crime in the one but only a fault in the other.

The Americans know nothing of this unfair division of duties and rights. With them the seducer is as much dishonored as his victim. In America a young woman can set out on a long journey alone and without fear.

American legislators, who have made almost every article in the criminal code less harsh, punish rape by death; and no other crime is judged with the same inexorable severity by public opinion. There is reason for this: as the Americans think nothing more precious than a woman's honor and nothing deserving more respect than her freedom, they think no punishment could be too severe for those who take both from her against her will.

In France, where the same crime is subject to much milder penalties, it is difficult to find a jury that will convict. Is the reason scorn of chastity or scorn of woman? I cannot rid myself of the feeling that it is both.

To sum up, the Americans do not think that man and woman have the duty or the right to do the same things, but they show an equal regard for the part played by both and think of them as beings of equal worth, though their fates are different.

Thus, then, while they have allowed the social inferiority of woman to continue, they have done everything to raise her morally and intellectually to the level of man. In this I think they have wonderfully understood the true conception of democratic progress.

For my part, I have no hesitation in saying that although the American woman never leaves her domestic sphere and is in some respects very dependent within it, nowhere does she enjoy a higher station. And now that I come near the end of this book in which I have recorded so many achievements of the Americans, if anyone asks me what I think the chief cause of the extraordinary prosperity and growing power of this nation, I should answer that it is due to the superiority of their women.

<h1 style="text-align:center">12</h1>

HOW EQUALITY NATURALLY DIVIDES THE AMERICANS INTO A MULTITUDE OF SMALL PRIVATE CIRCLES

IT MIGHT BE SUPPOSED that the result of democratic institutions would be to jumble all the citizens together in private as well as in public life and compel them all to lead a common existence.

That would be giving a very coarse interpretation to the equality produced by democracy.

No social system and no laws can ever make men so similar that education, fortune, and tastes can put no differences between them; and though men who are different may sometimes find it to their interest to do the same things and do them together, one must suppose that they will never make it their pleasure. So they will always slip through the legislator's fingers, whatever he does, and establish little private societies held together by similar conditions, habits, and mores.

In the United States the citizens all get together to deal with matters which affect the common destiny, but I have never heard anyone suggest that they should all be brought together to entertain

---

[Originally chapter 13.]

themselves in the same way and take their pleasures jumbled together in the same places. Each freely recognizes every other citizen as equal, but he only accepts a very small number as his friends or guests.

That strikes me as very natural. As the extent of political society expands, one must expect the sphere of private life to contract. When neither law nor custom is at pains to bring particular men into frequent and habitual contact, their opinions and inclinations decide the matter, and that leads to an infinite variety of private societies.

In democracies, where there is never much difference between one citizen and another and where there is always a chance of their all getting merged in a common mass, a multitude of artificial and arbitrary classifications are established to protect each man from being swept along in spite of himself with the crowd.

This will always be the case. For one can change human institutions, but not man. However energetically society in general may strive to make all the citizens equal and alike, the personal pride of each individual will always make him try to escape from the common level, and he will form some inequality somewhere to his own profit.

In aristocracies men are separated by high, immovable barriers. In democracies they are divided by a lot of almost invisible little threads, which are continually getting broken and moved from place to place.

Therefore, whatever the progress toward equality, in democracies a large number of little private associations will always be formed within the great political society. But none of these will resemble in manners the upper class which rules in aristocracies.

13

SOME REFLECTIONS ON
AMERICAN MANNERS

NOTHING SEEMS LESS IMPORTANT than the external formalities of human behavior, yet men can get used to anything except living in a society which does not share their manners. Manners, speaking generally, have their roots in mores; they are also sometimes the result of an arbitrary convention agreed between certain men. They are both natural and acquired.

True dignity in manners consists in always taking one's proper place, not too high and not too low; that is as much within the reach of a peasant as of a prince. In democracies everybody's status seems doubtful; as a result, there is often pride but seldom dignity of manners.

There is too much mobility in the population of a democracy for any definite group to be able to establish a code of behavior and see that it is observed. So everyone behaves more or less after his own fashion, and a certain incoherence of manners always prevails, because they conform to the feelings of each individual rather than to an ideal example provided for everyone to imitate.

In democracies manners are never so refined as among aristocracies, but they are also never so coarse. One misses both the crude words of the mob and the elegant and choice phrases of the high nobility. There is much triviality of manner, but nothing brutal or degraded.

Democratic manners are neither so well thought out nor so regular, but they often are more sincere. They form a thin, transparent veil through which the real feelings and personal thoughts of each man can be easily seen. Hence there is frequently an intimate

[Originally chapter 14.]

connection between the form and the substance of behavior; we
see a less decorative picture, but one truer to life. One may put the
point this way: democracy imposes no particular manners, but in a
sense prevents them from having manners at all.

Sometimes the feelings, passions, virtues, and vices of an aristocracy may reappear in a democracy, but its manners never. They are
lost and vanish past return when the democratic revolution is completed. The manners of the aristocracy created a fine illusion
about human nature; though the picture was often deceptive, it
was yet a noble satisfaction to look on it.

14

ON THE GRAVITY OF THE AMERICANS AND WHY IT OFTEN DOES NOT PREVENT THEIR DOING ILL-CONSIDERED THINGS

IN ARISTOCRATIC SOCIETIES THE people freely let themselves go in
bursts of tumultuous, boisterous gaiety, which at once make them
forget all the wretchedness of their lives. But in democracies it is
always a cause of regret if they lose sight of themselves. To frivolous delight they prefer staid amusements which are more like
business and which do not drive business entirely out of their
minds.

Instead of dancing gaily in the public square as many people of
the same social status in Europe still delight to do, an American
may prefer quietly drinking in his own house. Such a man enjoys
two pleasures at once: he thinks about his business affairs and gets
drunk decently at home.

[Originally chapter 15.]

I used to think that the English were the most serious-minded people on earth, but having seen the Americans, I have changed my mind.

I am not denying that temperament is an important element in the American character, but I think that political institutions count for even more.

The gravity of Americans is partly due to pride. In democratic countries even a poor man has a high idea of his personal worth. This disposes them to measure their words and their behavior carefully and not to let themselves go, lest they reveal their deficiencies. They imagine that to appear dignified they must remain solemn.

But I see another, more intimate and more powerful, cause from which this astonishing American gravity results.

Peoples under despotism burst out from time to time in mad fits of gaiety, but usually they are sad and constrained through fear. But all free peoples are serious-minded because they are habitually preoccupied with some dangerous or difficult project. Those who are not ambitious to control the commonwealth devote all their energies to increasing their private fortunes. Among such a people gravity is not a characteristic peculiar to certain men, but becomes a national trait.

But no one must suppose that, for all their labors, the inhabitants of democracies think themselves objects of pity; quite the contrary. No men are more attached to their own way of life, which would lose its savor if they were relieved from the anxieties which harass them. They love their cares more than aristocrats love their pleasures.

I am led to inquire why these same serious-minded democratic peoples sometimes act in such an ill-considered way.

The Americans, who almost always seem poised and cold, are nonetheless often carried away, far beyond the bounds of common sense, by some sudden passion or hasty opinion. They will in all seriousness do strangely absurd things.

One should not be surprised by this contrast.

Under despotisms men do not know how to act because they are told nothing; in democratic nations they often act at random because there has been an attempt to tell them everything. The former do not know; the latter forget. The main features of each picture become lost in a mass of detail.

In democracies men never stay still; there is almost always something unforeseen, something provisional about their lives. Hence they are often bound to do things which they have not properly learned to do and to say things which they scarcely understand; they have to throw themselves into actual work unprepared by a long apprenticeship.

In aristocracies every man has but one sole aim which he constantly pursues; but man in democracies has a more complicated existence; it is the exception if one man's mind is not concerned with several aims at the same time. Unable to be an expert in all, a man easily becomes satisfied with half-baked notions.

In a democracy, if necessity does not urge a man to action, longing will do so, for none of the good things around him are completely beyond his reach. Therefore he does everything in a hurry, is always satisfied with a "more or less," and never stops for more than one moment to consider each thing he does.

His curiosity is both insatiable and satisfied cheaply, for he is more bent on knowing a lot quickly than on knowing anything well.

He hardly has the time, and he soon loses the taste, for going deeply into anything.

Hence democratic peoples are serious-minded because social and political circumstances constantly lead them to think about serious matters, and their actions are often ill-considered because they give but little time and attention to each matter.

Habitual inattention must be reckoned the great vice of the democratic spirit.

15

WHY AMERICAN NATIONAL PRIDE HAS A MORE RESTLESS AND QUARRELSOME CHARACTER THAN THAT OF THE ENGLISH

IN THEIR RELATIONS WITH strangers the Americans are impatient of the slightest criticism and insatiable for praise. They are at you the whole time to make you praise them, and if you do not oblige, they sing their own praises. One might suppose that, doubting their own merits, they want an illustration thereof constantly before their eyes. Their vanity is not only greedy but also restless and jealous. It is both mendicant and querulous.

I tell an American that he lives in a beautiful country; he answers: "That is true. There is none like it in the world." I praise the freedom enjoyed by the inhabitants, and he answers: "Freedom is a precious gift, but very few peoples are worthy to enjoy it." I note the chastity of morals, and he replies: "I suppose that a stranger, struck by the immorality apparent in all other nations, must be astonished at this sight." He will not stop till he has made me repeat everything I have said. One cannot imagine a more obnoxious or boastful form of patriotism. Even admirers are bored.

The English are not like that. Your Englishman quietly enjoys the real or supposed advantages he sees in his country. He is not in the least disturbed by a foreigner's criticism, and hardly flattered by his praise. His pride needs no nourishment, living on itself.

That two peoples, sprung so recently from the same stock, should feel and talk in ways so diametrically opposite is in itself remarkable.

The great men in aristocratic countries do not think of boasting about prerogatives which all can see and none question. They

---

[Originally chapter 16.]

stand unmoved in solitary grandeur, knowing that the whole world sees them without their needing to show themselves and that no one will attempt to drive them from their position.

But when, on the contrary, there is little difference in social standing, the slightest advantage tells. When each sees a million others around him all with the same or similar claims to be proud of, pride becomes exacting and jealous; it gets attached to wretched trifles and doggedly defends them.

In democracies, with their constant ebb and flow of prosperity, men have almost always acquired the advantages they possess recently. For that reason they take infinite pleasure in vaunting them; and, as at any moment these advantages may slip from them, they are in constant anxiety to show that they have them still.

The inhabitants of democracies love their country after the same fashion as they love themselves, and what is habitual in their private vanity is carried over into national pride. This restless and insatiable vanity of democracies is entirely due to equality and the precariousness of social standing.

16

HOW THE ASPECT OF SOCIETY IN THE UNITED STATES IS AT ONCE AGITATED AND MONOTONOUS

ONE MIGHT HAVE THOUGHT the aspect of the United States peculiarly calculated to arouse and feed curiosity. Fortunes, ideas, and laws are constantly changing. Immutable nature herself seems on the move, so greatly is she daily transformed by the works of man.

[Originally chapter 17.]

In the long run, however, the sight of this excited community becomes monotonous, and the spectator who has watched this pageant for some time gets bored.

All men are alike and do roughly the same things. They are subject to great vicissitudes, but as the same successes and reverses are continually recurring, the name of the actors is all that changes, the play being always the same. American society appears animated because men and things are constantly changing; it is monotonous because all these changes are alike.

Men living in democratic times have many passions, but most of these culminate in love of wealth or derive from it. That is not because their souls are narrower but because there is hardly anything left but money which makes very clear distinctions between men or can raise some of them above the common level. Distinction based on wealth is increased by the disappearance or diminution of all other distinctions.

So one usually finds that love of money is either the chief or a secondary motive at the bottom of everything the Americans do. This recurrence of the same passion is monotonous; so, too, are the details of the methods used to satisfy it.

Though industry often brings in its train great disorders and great disasters, it cannot prosper without exceedingly regular habits and the performance of a long succession of small uniform motions. One may say that it is the very vehemence of their desires that makes the Americans so methodical. It agitates their minds but disciplines their lives.

What I say about the Americans applies to almost all men nowadays. Variety is disappearing from the human race; the same ways of behaving, thinking, and feeling are found in every corner of the world. This is not only because nations are more in touch with each other and able to copy each other more closely. The men of each country, discarding the ideas peculiar to one caste, profession, or family, are getting closer to what is essential in man, and that is everywhere the same. In that way they grow alike, even without imitating each other. One could compare them to travelers dispersed throughout a huge forest, all the tracks in which lead to the same point. If all at the same time notice where the central point is and direct their steps thither, in the end they will be surprised to find that they have all assembled at the same place. All those peoples who take not any particular man but man in himself as the object to study and imitate are tending in the end toward similar mores, like the travelers converging on the central point in the forest.

17

CONCERNING HONOR IN THE UNITED STATES AND DEMOCRATIC SOCIETIES[1]

PUBLIC OPINION EMPLOYS TWO very different standards in judging the actions of men: in the one case it relies on notions of right and wrong, which are common to all the world; in the other it assesses them in accordance with notions peculiar to one age and country. The two standards never completely coincide or completely oust each other.

Nothing is so unproductive for the human mind as an abstract idea. So I hasten to consider the facts. An example will make my meaning clear.

I will choose the most extraordinary type of honor which has ever been seen in the world and the one which we know best, aristocratic honor sprung up within a feudal society.

[Originally chapter 18.]

1.   The word *honor* is not always used in the same sense either in French.

   a. The first sense is the esteem, glory, or reputation which a man enjoys among his fellows; it is in that sense that one is said *to win honor*.

   b. Honor includes all those rules by which such esteem, glory, and consideration are obtained. Thus we say that a man *has always strictly conformed to the laws of honor* and that he has *forfeited his honor*.

In the feudal world actions were by no means always praised or blamed with reference to their intrinsic value, but were sometimes appreciated exclusively with reference to the person who did them or suffered from them, which is repugnant to the universal conscience of mankind. Some actions could thus have no importance if done by a commoner but would dishonor a noble.

That honor or shame should attach to a man's actions according to his condition—that same phenomenon appears in every country which has had an aristocracy. As long as there is any trace of it left, these peculiarities will remain: to debauch a Negro girl hardly injures an American's reputation; to marry her dishonors him.

Among opinions current among Americans[2] one still finds some scattered notions detached from the old European aristocratic conception of honor, but they have no deep roots or strong influence. It is like a religion whose temples are allowed to remain but in which one no longer believes.

Amid these half-effaced notions of an exotic honor some new opinions have made their appearance, and these constitute what one might call the contemporary American conception of honor.

I have shown the Americans are continually driven into trade and industry. They now form an almost exclusively industrial and trading community placed in the midst of a huge new country whose exploitation is their principal interest. That is the characteristic trait which now distinguishes the Americans from all other nations.

Therefore all those quiet virtues, which tend to regularity in the body social and which favor trade, are sure to be held in special honor by this people. So no stigma attaches to love of money in America, and provided it does not exceed the bounds imposed by public order, it is held in honor. The American will describe as noble and estimable ambition which our medieval ancestors would have called base cupidity. He would consider as barbarous frenzy that ardor for conquest which led the latter every day into new battles.

---

2. In this context I am speaking of those Americans who live in the parts of the country where there is no slavery. It is they alone who provide a complete picture of a democratic society.

In the United States fortunes are easily lost and gained again. The country is limitless and full of inexhaustible resources. For a people so situated the danger is not the ruin of a few, which is soon made good, but apathy and sloth in the community at large. Boldness in industrial undertakings is the chief cause of their rapid progress, power, and greatness. To them industry appears as a vast lottery in which a few men daily lose but in which the state constantly profits. Such a people is bound to look with favor on boldness in industry and to honor it. But any bold undertaking risks the fortune of the man who embarks on it and of all those who trust him. The Americans, who have turned rash speculation into a sort of virtue, can in no case stigmatize those who are thus rash.

That is the reason for the altogether singular indulgence shown in the United States toward a trader who goes bankrupt. An accident like that leaves no stain on his honor. In this respect the Americans are different not only from the nations of Europe, but from all trading nations of our day; their position and needs are also unlike those of all the others.

In the United States martial valor is little esteemed; the type of courage best appreciated is that which makes a man brave the fury of the ocean to reach port more quickly, and face the privations of life in the wilds and that solitude which is harder to bear than any privations, the courage which makes a man almost insensible to the loss of a fortune laboriously acquired and prompts him instantly to fresh exertions to gain another. It is chiefly courage of this sort which is needed to maintain the American community and make it prosper, and to betray a lack of it brings certain shame.

One last trait will serve to make the idea underlying this chapter stand out clearly.

In a democratic society such as that of the United States, where fortunes are small and insecure, everybody works, and work opens all doors. That circumstance has made honor do an about turn against idleness.

In America I have sometimes met rich young men temperamentally opposed to any uncomfortable effort and yet forced to enter a profession. Their characters and their wealth would have allowed them to stay idle, but public opinion imperiously forbade that. But among European nations where an aristocracy is still struggling against the current that carries it away, I have often met men whose inclinations constantly goaded them to action, who yet remained idle so as not to lose the esteem of their equals who found boredom easier to face than work.

No one can fail to see that both these contradictory obligations are rules of conduct originating in notions of honor.

Honor plays a part in democratic as well as aristocratic ages, but not only are its injunctions different, they are fewer, less precise, and more loosely obeyed. In such a country as America, where all the citizens are on the move, society changes its opinions with changing needs. In such a country men have glimpses of the rules of honor, but they seldom have leisure to consider them with attention.

There are indeed for such a people certain national needs which give rise to common opinions concerning honor, but such opinions never present themselves at the same time, in the same manner, and with equal intensity to the mind of every citizen; the law of honor exists, but it is often left without interpreters.

Honor among democratic nations, being less defined, is of necessity less powerful, for it is hard to apply an imperfectly understood law with certainty and firmness. Public opinion, which is the natural and supreme interpreter of the law of honor, not seeing clearly to which side to incline in the distribution of praise and blame, always hesitates in giving judgment. Sometimes public opinion is self-contradictory; often it remains undecided and lets things slide.

Where all are jumbled together in the same constantly fluctuating crowd, there is nothing for public opinion to catch hold of; its subject matter is ever vanishing from sight and escaping. In such circumstances honor must always be less binding and less urgently pressing.

The reader who has followed my argument so far will see that there is a close and necessary connection between what we call honor and inequality of conditions, a connection which, if I am not mistaken, has never been clearly pointed out before.

If one can further suppose that all races should become mixed, and all the peoples of the world should reach a state in which they all had the same interests and needs, and there was no characteristic trait distinguishing one from another, the practice of attributing a conventional value to men's actions would then cease altogether. Everyone would see them in the same light. The general needs of humanity, revealed to each man by his conscience, would form the common standard. Then one would see nothing in the world but simple, general notions of good and bad, to which nature and necessity would attach conceptions of praise and blame.

Thus, to conclude, compressing my essential thought into a single sentence, it is the dissimilarities and inequalities among men which give rise to the notion of honor; as such differences become less, it grows feeble; and when they disappear, it will vanish too.

18

WHY THERE ARE SO MANY MEN OF AMBITION IN THE UNITED STATES BUT SO FEW LOFTY AMBITIONS

THE FIRST THING THAT strikes one in the United States is the innumerable crowd of those striving to escape from their original social condition; and the second is the rarity of any lofty ambition. Every American is eaten up with longing to rise, but hardly any of them

_____

[Originally chapter 19.]

seem to entertain very great hopes or to aim very high. All are constantly bent on gaining property, reputation, and power, but few conceive such things on a grand scale. That, at first sight, is surprising, since there is no obvious impediment in the mores or laws of America to put a limit to ambition.

Equality of conditions hardly seems a sufficient explanation of this strange state of affairs. For when this same equality was first established in France, it gave birth at once to almost unlimited ambitions. Nevertheless, I think that we may find the chief reason for this in the social conditions and democratic manners of the Americans.

Every revolution increases men's ambition, and that is particularly true of a revolution which overthrows an aristocracy.

When the barriers that formerly kept the multitude from fame and power are suddenly thrown down, there is an impetuous universal movement toward those long-envied heights of power which can at last be enjoyed. In this first triumphant exaltation nothing seems impossible to anybody.

Thus ambitions are on the grand scale while the democratic revolution lasts; the hope of easy success lives on after the strange turns of fortune which gave it birth. Longings on a vast scale remain, though the means to satisfy them become daily less. Little by little the last traces of the battle are wiped out and the relics of aristocracy finally vanish. Peace follows war, and order again prevails in a new world. Longings once more become proportionate to the available means. Wants, ideas, and feelings again learn their limits. Men find their level, and democratic society is finally firmly established.

When we come to take stock of a democratic people which has reached this enduring and normal state, we easily come to the conclusion that although high ambitions swell while conditions are in process of equalization, that characteristic is lost when equality is a fact.

Ambition becomes a universal feeling, but equality, though it gives every citizen some resources, prevents any from enjoying resources of great extent. Desires must of necessity be confined within fairly narrow limits. Hence in democracies ambition is both eager and constant but not very high. For the most part life is spent in eagerly coveting small prizes within reach.

It is not so much the small scale of their wealth as the efforts requisite to increase it which chiefly diverts men in democracies from high ambitions. They strain their faculties to the utmost to achieve paltry results, and this inevitably limits their range of vision and circumscribes their powers.

In a democratic society, as elsewhere, there are only a few great fortunes to be made. As the careers leading thereto are open without discrimination to every citizen, each man's progress is bound to be slow. The rules of advancement become more inflexible and advancement itself slows. From hatred of privilege and embarrassment in choosing, all men, whatever their capacities, are finally forced through the same sieve. All without discrimination are made to pass a host of petty preliminary tests, wasting their youth and suffocating their imagination. When at last they reach a position in which they could do something out of the ordinary, the taste for it has left them.

Equality produces the same results everywhere. Even where no law regulates and holds back advancement, competition has this effect.

Hence great and rapid promotion is rare in a well-established democracy. Such events are exceptions to the general rule. Their very singularity makes men forget how seldom they occur.

The inhabitants of democracies do at length appreciate that while the law opens an unlimited field before them, and while all can make some easy progress there, no one can flatter himself that his advance is swift. They see a multitude of little intermediate obstacles, all of which have to be negotiated slowly, between them and their ultimate desires. The very anticipation of this prospect tires ambition and discourages it. They therefore discard such distant and doubtful hopes, preferring to seek delights less lofty but easier to reach. No law limits their horizon, but they do so for themselves.

I have said that high ambitions were rarer in democratic ages than under aristocracies. I must add that when they do appear, they wear another face.

Under aristocracies the career open to ambition is often wide, but it does have fixed limits. In democratic countries its field of action is usually very narrow, but once those narrow bounds are passed, there is nothing left to stop it. As a result, when ambitious men have once seized power, they think they can dare to do anything. When power slips from their grasp, their thoughts at once turn to overturning the state in order to get it again.

This gives a violent and revolutionary character to great political ambitions, a thing which is seldom seen, to the same extent, in aristocratic societies.

I think that ambitious men in democracies are less concerned than those in any other lands for the interests and judgment of posterity. The actual moment completely occupies and absorbs them. They carry through great undertakings quickly in preference to erecting long-lasting monuments. They are much more in love with success than with glory. What they most desire is power. Their manners almost always lag behind the rise in their social position. As a result, very vulgar tastes often go with their enjoyment of extraordinary prosperity, and it would seem that their only object in rising to supreme power was to gratify trivial and coarse appetites more easily.

I think that nowadays it is necessary to purge ambition, to control and keep it in proportion, but it would be very dangerous if we tried to confine it beyond reason.

I confess that I believe democratic society to have much less to fear from boldness than from paltriness of aim. What frightens me most is the danger that, amid all the trivial preoccupations of private life, ambition may lose both its force and its greatness, with the result that the progress of the body social may become daily quieter and less aspiring.

I therefore think that the leaders of the new societies would do wrong if they tried to send the citizens to sleep in a state of happiness too uniform and peaceful, but that they should sometimes give them difficult and dangerous problems to face, to rouse ambition and give it a field of action.

Moralists are constantly complaining that the pet vice of our age is pride.

There is a sense in which that is true; everyone thinks himself better than his neighbor and dislikes obeying a superior. But there is another sense in which it is very far from the truth. The same man who is unable to put up with either subordination or equality has nonetheless so poor an opinion of himself that he thinks he is born for nothing but the enjoyment of vulgar pleasures. Of his own free will he limits himself to paltry desires and dares not face any lofty enterprise; indeed, he can scarcely imagine such a possibility.

Thus, far from thinking that we should council humility to our contemporaries, I wish men would try to give them a higher idea of themselves and of humanity; humility is far from healthy for them; what they most lack, in my view, is pride. I would gladly surrender several of our petty virtues for that one vice.

19

CONCERNING PLACE-HUNTING IN SOME DEMOCRATIC COUNTRIES

IN THE UNITED STATES, when a citizen has some education and some resources he tries to enrich himself either by trade and industry or by buying a field covered in forest and turning into a pioneer. All he asks from the state is not to get in his way while he is working and to see that he can enjoy the fruit of his labor.

But in most of the countries of Europe, as soon as a man begins to feel his strength and extend his ambitions, the first idea that occurs to him is to get an official appointment. Place-hunting attracts more recruits than any other trade.

[Originally chapter 20.]

There is no need for me to say that this universal and uncontrolled desire for official appointments is a great social evil, that it undermines every citizen's sense of independence and spreads a venal and servile temper throughout the nation, that it stifles manly virtues; nor need I note that such a trade only leads to unproductive activity and unsettles the country without adding to its resources. All that is obvious.

But I do want to point out that a government favoring this tendency risks its own peace and puts its very existence in great danger.

In democratic countries, as in all others, there must be some limit to the number of public appointments. But the number of men of ambition is not limited, but rather constantly increases as equality becomes greater; the only check is the number of the population.

So, then, if administration is the only road open to ambition, the government faces a permanent opposition. It is bound to try and satisfy, with limited means, demands which multiply without limit. Of all the peoples in the world, a nation of place-hunters is the hardest to restrain and direct. However hard its leaders try, it can never be satisfied, and there is always a danger that it will eventually overthrow the Constitution and give new shape to the state simply for the purpose of cleaning out the present officeholders.

It would have been both safer and more honest to have taught their subjects the art of looking after themselves.

20

WHY GREAT REVOLUTIONS
WILL BECOME RARE

IT SEEMS NATURAL TO suppose that in a democratic society ideas, things, and men must eternally be changing shape and position and that ages of democracy must be times of swift and constant transformation.

But is this in fact so? Does equality of social conditions habitually and permanently drive men toward revolutions? Does it contain some disturbing principle which prevents society from settling down and inclines the citizens constantly to change their laws, principles, and mores? I do not think so. The subject is important, and I ask the reader to follow my argument closely.

Almost every revolution which has changed the shape of nations has been made to consolidate or destroy inequality. Either the poor were bent on snatching the property of the rich, or the rich were trying to hold the poor down. So, then, if you could establish a state of society in which each man had something to keep and little to snatch, you would have done much for the peace of the world.

I realize that among a great people there will always be some very poor and some very rich citizens. But the poor, instead of forming the vast majority of the population as in aristocratic societies, are but few, and the law has not drawn them together by the link of an irremediable and hereditary state of wretchedness. As there is no longer a race of poor men, so there is not a race of rich men; the rich daily rise out of the crowd and constantly return thither.

In democratic societies, between these two extremes is an innumerable crowd who are much alike and, though not exactly

_____
[Originally chapter 21.]

rich nor yet quite poor, who have enough property to want order and not enough to excite envy.

Such men are the natural enemies of violent commotion; their immobility keeps all above and below them quiet, and assures the stability of the body social.

I am not suggesting that they are themselves satisfied with their actual position or that they would feel any natural abhorrence toward a revolution if they could share the plunder without suffering the calamities. On the contrary, their eagerness to get rich is unparalleled, but the same social condition which prompts their longings restrains them within necessary limits. It gives men both greater freedom to change and less interest in doing so.

Not only do men in democracies feel no natural inclination for revolutions, but they are afraid of them.

Any revolution is more or less a threat to property. If one studies each class of which society is composed closely, it is easy to see that passions due to ownership are keenest among the middle classes.

Men whose comfortable existence is equally far from wealth and poverty set immense value on their possessions. As they are still very close to poverty, they see its privations in detail; nothing but a scanty fortune keeps them therefrom. The constant care which it occasions daily attaches them to their property; their continual exertions to increase it make it even more precious to them. The idea of giving up the smallest part of it is insufferable to them, and the thought of losing it completely strikes them as the worst of all evils. Now, it is just the number of the eager and restless small property owners which equality of conditions constantly increases.

Hence the majority of citizens in a democracy do not see clearly what they could gain by a revolution, but they constantly see a thousand ways in which they could lose by one.

I have shown elsewhere in this work how equality naturally leads men to go in for industry and trade and that it tends to increase and distribute real property. I pointed out that it inspires every man with a constant and eager desire to increase his well-being. Nothing is more opposed to revolutionary passions than all this.

Moreover, I know nothing more opposed to revolutionary morality than the moral standards of traders. Trade is the natural enemy of all violent passions. Trade loves moderation, delights in compromise, and is most careful to avoid anger. It is patient, supple, and insinuating, only resorting to extreme measures in cases of absolute necessity. Trade makes men independent of one another and gives them a high idea of their personal importance; it leads them to want to manage their own affairs and teaches them how to succeed therein. Hence it makes them inclined to liberty but disinclined to revolution.

In a revolution the owners of personal property have more to fear than all others, for their property is often both easy to seize and capable of disappearing completely at any moment. Owners of land have less to fear on this score, for although they may lose the income from it, they can hope at least to keep the land itself through the greatest vicissitudes.

Therefore the more widely personal property is distributed and increased and the greater the number of those enjoying it, the less is a nation inclined to revolution.

Moreover, whatever a man's calling and whatever type of property he owns, one characteristic is common to all.

No one is fully satisfied with his present fortune, and all are constantly trying a thousand various ways to improve it. Consider any individual at any period of his life, and you will always find him preoccupied with fresh plans to increase his comfort. Do not talk to him about the interests and rights of the human race; that little private business of his for the moment absorbs all his thoughts, and he hopes that public disturbances can be put off to some other time.

This not only prevents them from causing revolutions, but also deters them from wanting them. Violent political passions have little hold on men whose whole thoughts are bent on the pursuit of well-being. Their excitement about small matters makes them calm about great ones.

It is true that from time to time in democratic societies aspiring and ambitious citizens do arise who are not content to follow the beaten track. Such men love revolutions and hail their approach.

But they have great difficulty in bringing them about unless extraordinary events play into their hands.

I am not making out that the inhabitants of democracies are by nature stationary; on the contrary, I think that such a society is always on the move and that none of its members knows what rest is. Daily they change, alter, and renew things of secondary importance, but they are very careful not to touch fundamentals. They love change, but they are afraid of revolutions.

Although the Americans are constantly modifying or repealing some of their laws, they are far from showing any revolutionary passions. In no other country in the world is the love of property keener or more alert than in the United States, and nowhere else does the majority display less inclination toward doctrines which in any way threaten the way property is owned.

If there ever are great revolutions there, they will be caused by the presence of the blacks upon American soil. That is to say, it will not be the equality of social conditions but rather their inequality which may give rise thereto.

I am far from asserting that democratic nations are safe from revolutions; I only say that the social state of those nations does not lead toward revolution, but rather wards it off. I must again make it perfectly clear that a nation is not safe from revolution simply because social conditions are equal there. But I do think that, whatever institutions such a people may have, great revolutions will be infinitely less violent and rarer than is generally supposed. I can vaguely foresee a political condition, combined with equality, which might create a society more stationary than any we have ever known in our western world.

I do not think it as easy as is generally supposed to eradicate the prejudices of a democratic people, to change its beliefs, to substitute new religious, philosophical, political, and moral principles for those which have once become established, in a word, to bring about great or frequent mental revolutions. Not that there the human mind is lazy; it is constantly active, but it is more concerned with the consequences to be derived from known principles, and in finding new consequences, than in seeking new principles.

It must, I think, be rare in a democracy for a man suddenly to conceive a system of ideas far different from those accepted by his contemporaries; and I suppose that, even should such an innovator arise, he would have great difficulty in making himself heard to begin with, and even more in convincing people.

As men grow more like each other, a dogma concerning intellectual equality gradually creeps into their beliefs, and it becomes harder for any innovator whosoever to gain and maintain great influence over the mind of a nation. In such societies sudden intellectual revolutions must therefore be rare. Taking a general view of world history, one finds that it is less the force of an argument than the authority of a name which has brought about great and rapid changes in accepted ideas.

Even when one has won the confidence of a democratic nation, it is a hard matter to attract its attention. It is very difficult to make the inhabitants of democracies listen when one is not talking about themselves. They do not hear what is said to them because they are always very preoccupied with what they are doing. The fire they put into their work prevents their being fired by ideas.

I think it is an arduous undertaking to excite the enthusiasm of a democratic nation for any theory which does not have a visible, direct, and immediate bearing on the occupations of their daily lives. Such a people does not easily give up its ancient beliefs. For it is enthusiasm which makes men's minds leap off the beaten track and brings about great intellectual, as well as political, revolutions.

Whenever conditions are equal, public opinion brings immense weight to bear on every individual. It surrounds, directs, and oppresses him. The basic constitution of society has more to do with this than any political laws. The more alike men are, the weaker each feels in the face of all. Not only does he doubt his own judgment, he is brought very near to recognizing that he must be wrong when the majority hold the opposite view. There is no need for the majority to compel him; it convinces him.

Therefore, however powers within a democracy are organized and weighted, it will always be very difficult for a man to believe what the mass rejects and to profess what it condemns.

This circumstance is wonderfully favorable to the stability of beliefs.

When an opinion has taken root in a democracy and established itself in the minds of the majority, it afterward persists by itself, needing no effort to maintain it since no one attacks it. Those who at first rejected it as false come in the end to adopt it as accepted, and even those who still at the bottom of their hearts oppose it keep their views to themselves, taking great care to avoid a dangerous and futile contest.

We live in a time that has witnessed the swiftest changes in men's minds. But perhaps some of the main opinions of mankind may be soon more stable than ever before in the centuries of our history. Such a time has not yet come, but it may be at hand.

The more closely I examine the needs and instincts natural to democracies, the more am I convinced that if ever equality is established generally and permanently in the world, great intellectual and political revolutions will become much more difficult and much rarer.

Can I safely say this amid the surrounding ruins? What I most fear for succeeding generations is not revolutions.

If the citizens continue to shut themselves up in the little circle of petty domestic interests and keep themselves constantly busy therein, there is a danger that they may become practically out of reach of those great and powerful public emotions which perturb peoples but which also make them grow. Seeing property change hands so quickly, and love of property become so anxious and eager, I cannot help fearing that men may reach a point where they look on every new theory as a danger, every innovation as a toilsome trouble, every social advance as a first step toward revolution. The prospect really does frighten me that they may finally become so engrossed in a cowardly love of immediate pleasures that their interest in their own future and in that of their descendants may vanish, and that they will prefer tamely to follow the course of their destiny rather than make a sudden energetic effort necessary to set things right.

21

WHY DEMOCRATIC PEOPLES NATURALLY WANT PEACE BUT DEMOCRATIC ARMIES WAR

THE SAME INTERESTS, THE same fears, the same passions that deter democratic peoples from revolutions also alienate them from war. The military and revolutionary spirit grows feeble at the same time, and for the same reasons. Among civilized nations warlike passions become rarer and less active as social conditions get nearer to equality.

Yet war is a hazard to which all nations are subject, democracies as well as the rest. No matter how greatly such nations may be devoted to peace, they must be ready to defend themselves if attacked, or in other words, they must have an army.

Fortune, which has showered so many peculiar favors on the United States, has placed them where one can almost say that they have no neighbors. For them a few thousand soldiers are enough, but that is something peculiar to America, not to democracy.

Equality of conditions and the mores and institutions deriving therefrom do not rescue a democracy from the necessity of keeping up an army, and their armies always exercise a powerful influence over their fate. It is therefore important to discover what are the natural instincts of those who compose these armies.

In aristocracies, especially where birth alone decides rank, there is the same inequality in the army as elsewhere in the nation; officers are nobles, soldiers serfs; the one is necessarily called on to command and the other to obey. In aristocratic armies, therefore, the soldier's ambition has very narrow limits.

[Originally chapter 22.]

In democratic armies all the soldiers may become officers, and that fact makes desire for promotion general and opens almost infinite doors to military ambition.

Desire for promotion is almost universal in democratic armies; it is eager, tenacious, and continual. All other desires serve to feed it, and it is only quenched with life itself. Promotion in times of peace must be slower in democratic armies than in any other armies, as the number of commissions is naturally limited, while the number of competitors is almost innumerable.

Therefore all the ambitious minds in a democratic army ardently long for war, because war makes vacancies available and at last allows violations of the rule of seniority, which is the one privilege natural to a democracy.

We thus arrive at the strange conclusion that of all armies those which long for war most ardently are the democratic ones, but that of all peoples those most deeply attached to peace are the democratic nations. And the most extraordinary thing about the whole matter is that it is equality which is responsible for both these contradictory results.

These contrary inclinations of nation and army cause great hazards to democratic societies.

When a nation loses its military spirit, military men drop down to the lowest rank among public officials. It is not the leading citizens, but the least important who go into the army. A man only develops military ambitions when all other doors are closed. That forms a vicious circle, from which it is hard to escape. The elite avoid a military career because it is not held in honor, and it is not held in honor because the elite do not take it up.

There is therefore no reason for surprise if democratic armies are found to be restless, prone to complaint, and ill-satisfied with their lot, although their physical condition is generally much better and discipline less strict than in all other armies. The army finally becomes a little nation apart, with a lower standard of intelligence and rougher habits than the nation at large. But this little uncivilized nation holds the weapons and it alone knows how to use them.

One can therefore make this generalization, that although their interests and inclinations naturally incline democracies to peace, their armies exercise a constant pull toward war and revolution.

I do not wish to speak ill of war; war almost always widens a nation's mental horizons and raises its heart. In some cases it may be the only antidote for certain inveterate diseases to which democratic societies are liable.

War has great advantages, but we must not flatter ourselves that it can lessen the danger I have just pointed out. It only puts the danger off, to come back in more terrible form when war is over.

There are two things that will always be very difficult for a democratic nation: to start a war and to end it. Any long war always entails great hazards to liberty in a democracy. War does not always give democratic societies over to military government, but it must invariably and immeasurably increase the powers of civil government; it must almost automatically concentrate the direction of all men and the control of all things in the hands of the government. If that does not lead to despotism by sudden violence, it leads men gently in that direction by their habits.

For my part, I think that a restless, turbulent spirit is an evil inherent in the very constitution of democratic armies, and beyond hope of cure. In the nation, not in the army itself, one must seek the remedy for the army's vices.

Democratic peoples are naturally afraid of disturbances and despotism. All that is needed is to turn these instincts into considered, intelligent, and stable tastes. The general spirit of the nation, penetrating the spirit peculiar to the army, tempers the opinions and desires engendered by military life or, by the all-powerful influence of public opinion, actually represses them. Once you have educated, orderly, upstanding, and free citizens, you will have disciplined and obedient soldiers.

Therefore any law which in repressing this turbulent spirit of the army should tend to diminish the spirit of freedom in the nation and to cloud conceptions of law and rights would defeat its object. It would do much more to increase than to impede the dangers of military tyranny.

After all, whatever one does, a large army in a democracy will always be a serious danger, and the best way to lessen this danger will be to reduce the army. But that is not a remedy which every nation can apply.

22

SOME CONSIDERATIONS CONCERNING WAR IN DEMOCRATIC SOCIETIES

WHEN THE PRINCIPLE OF equality spreads, as in Europe now, at the same time among several neighboring peoples, the inhabitants of these various countries, despite different languages, customs, and laws, always resemble each other in an equal fear of war and love of peace. Their interests become so mixed and entangled that no nation can inflict on others ills which will not fall back on its own head. So that in the end, all come to think of war as a calamity almost as severe for the conqueror as for the conquered.

Therefore, on the one hand it is difficult in democratic ages to draw nations into hostilities, but on the other, it is almost impossible for two of them to make war in isolation. The interests of all are so much entwined, that no one of them can stay quiet when the rest are in agitation. So wars become rarer, but when they do come about, they spread over a vaster field.

According to the law of nations adopted by civilized countries, the object of war is not to seize the property of private individuals

---

[Originally chapter 26. Tocqueville's chapter 23, "Which Is the Most Warlike and Revolutionary Class in Democratic Armies;" chapter 24, "What Makes Democratic Armies Weaker Than Others at the Beginning of a Campaign but More Formidable in Prolonged Warfare;" and chapter 25, "Of Discipline in Democratic Armies," have been omitted.]

but simply to get possession of political power. Private property is only occasionally destroyed for the purpose of attaining the latter object.

When an aristocratic nation is invaded after the defeat of its army, the nobles prefer to go on defending themselves individually rather than submit, for if the conqueror remains master of the land, he will take away their political power, which they prize even more highly than their property. They therefore prefer to fight than be conquered, and they easily carry the people with them.

But where equality of conditions prevails in a nation, each citizen has but a small share of political power, and often none at all; on the other hand, all are independent and have property to lose; as a result, they are much less afraid of conquest and much more afraid of war than the inhabitants of an aristocratic land. It will always be very difficult to make a democratic people decide to take up arms when hostilities have reached its own territory. That is why it is so necessary to provide such a people with the rights and the political spirit which will endow each citizen with some of those interests which influence the behavior of nobles in aristocratic lands.

The princes and other leaders of democracies should remember that it is only passion for freedom, habitually enjoyed, which can do more than hold its own against a habitual absorption in well-being.

I shall add only a few words about civil wars for fear of exhausting the reader's patience.

Most of what I have said about foreign wars applies with even greater force to civil wars. The inhabitants of democracies do not naturally have any military spirit; they sometimes develop it when they have been dragged onto the battlefield; but to rise spontaneously in a body and voluntarily expose themselves to the miseries of war, especially civil war, is not a course of action inhabitants of democracies are likely to follow. Only the most adventurous of their citizens would be prepared to run such risks. The bulk of the population would stay quiet.

The only case in which a civil war could take place is if the army were divided, one part raising the standard of revolt and the other remaining loyal. The war might be bloody, but it would not be long. For either the rebellious army would bring the government over to its side by a simple demonstration of its power or by its first victory, and then the war would be over; or else a struggle would take place, and the [rebellious] army would soon either disperse of its own accord or be destroyed.

One can therefore accept the general proposition that in ages of equality civil wars will become much rarer and shorter.[1]

---

1.   I must make it clear that I am here referring to *unitary* democratic nations and not to confederations. In confederations the predominant power always resides, in spite of all political fictions, in the state governments, and not in the federal government. So civil wars are really foreign wars in disguise.

PART IV

On the Influence
of Democratic Ideas and Feelings
on Political Society

I COULD NOT PROPERLY fulfill the purpose of this book if, having pointed out the ideas and feelings prompted by equality, I did not in conclusion indicate the influence which these ideas and these feelings may exercise upon the government of human societies.

For this purpose it will often be necessary to go back over old ground. But I trust that the reader will not refuse to follow me when familiar paths may lead to some new truth.

1

EQUALITY NATURALLY GIVES MEN
THE TASTE FOR FREE INSTITUTIONS

EQUALITY, WHICH MAKES MEN independent of one another, makes them suspicious of all authority and soon suggests the notion and the love of political liberty. Men living at such times have a natural bias toward free institutions.

This love of independence is the most striking political effect of equality, and the one which frightens timid spirits most. Nor can it be said that they are completely wrong, for anarchy does have a more terrible aspect in democratic countries than elsewhere. As the citizens have no direct influence on one another, as soon as the central power begins to falter, it would seem that disorder must reach a climax and that the fabric of society must fall into dust.

Nevertheless, anarchy is not the greatest of the ills in democratic times, but the least.

Two tendencies in fact result from equality; the first leads men directly to independence and could push them over into anarchy; the other, by a more roundabout but also more certain road, leads them to servitude.

Nations easily see the former tendency and resist it. But they let themselves be carried along by the latter without seeing it. So it is most important to point it out.

For my part, far from blaming equality for the intractability it inspires, I praise it just for that. I admire the way it insinuates deep into the heart and mind of every man. Some instinctive inclination toward political freedom thereby prepares the antidote for the ill which it has produced. That is why I cling to it.

2

WHY THE IDEAS OF DEMOCRATIC PEOPLES ABOUT GOVERNMENT NATURALLY FAVOR THE CONCENTRATION OF POLITICAL POWER[1]

THE IDEA OF SECONDARY powers, between the sovereign and his subjects, was natural to the imagination of aristocratic peoples, because such powers were proper to individuals or families distinguished by birth, education, and riches, who seemed destined to command. Opposite reasons naturally banish such an idea from the minds of men in ages of equality.

Democratic peoples are put off by complicated systems and like to picture a great nation in which every citizen resembles one set type and is controlled by one single power and by uniform legislation. As each sees himself little different from his neighbors, he

---

1.   [In this chapter and throughout the remainder of the book, Tocqueville builds a convoluted argument that may be summarized as follows: Looking back on the French Revolution, the bloody "Terror," and the oppressive regimes that followed, he suggests that the demise of the aristocracy and its privileges had unintended negative consequences. With its entitlements and independence, the aristocracy stood as a "secondary" power between the sovereign and the people, providing a bulwark against both tyranny from above and anarchy from below. The aristocracy was more a guardian of its own prerogatives than of general liberties, but its displacement (and that of other intermediate powers, such as corporations and the Church) contributed to what Tocqueville sees as an unprecedented and dangerous centralization of power peculiar to democracies. Because the sovereign was now "the people," unchecked by secondary powers with special privileges, democratic tyrants ruling in the name of "the people" were more likely to arise and harder to restrain. Such tendencies were exacerbated, he adds, by individualism and political apathy among a population newly preoccupied with equality and with getting ahead. Tocqueville links these new ingredients of "democratic" despotism to the postrevolutionary violations of property and human rights in France. Tocqueville's analysis of that history, and his reactions to the revolution of 1830 in France, prompt his warnings that despotism is a particular hazard of democratic ages. "The American example," he argues, is in certain ways an exception that proves this new rule.]

cannot understand why a rule applicable to one man should not be applied to all the rest. The slightest privileges are therefore repugnant to his reason and legislative uniformity strikes him as the first condition of good government.

But this notion of a uniform rule imposed equally on all members of the body social seems so blind, in that individuals seem of less and society of greater importance. Every citizen, having grown like the rest, is lost in the crowd, and nothing stands out conspicuously but the great and imposing image of the people itself.

The Americans believe that in each state supreme power should emanate directly from the people, but once this power has been constituted, they can hardly conceive any limits to it. As for particular privileges granted to towns, families, or individuals, they have forgotten the possibility of such things. The idea of intermediate powers is obscured and obliterated. The idea of the omnipotence and sole authority of society at large is coming to fill its place.

In France, where the revolution of which I speak has gone further than in any other European country, these opinions have got complete hold of the public mind. Most think that the government is behaving badly, but all think that the government ought constantly to act and interfere in everything. Even those who attack each other most vehemently are nevertheless agreed on the omnipotence of the social power and the uniformity of its rules. If such ideas arise spontaneously in the minds of private individuals, they strike the imagination of princes even more forcibly.

While the ancient fabric of European society is changing and dissolving, sovereigns acquire new conceptions about the scope of their action and duties. For the first time they learn that the central power which they represent can and should administer directly, according to a uniform plan, all affairs and all men. This opinion, which I am sure no king in Europe before our time ever thought of, has now sunk deeply into the minds of princes and stands firm amid the agitation of more unsettled thoughts.

Our contemporaries therefore are much less divided ьhan is commonly supposed. They do argue constantly about who should have sovereign power, but they readily agree about the duties and rights of that power. They all think of the government as a sole, simple, providential, and creative force.

3

HOW BOTH THE FEELINGS AND THE THOUGHTS OF DEMOCRATIC NATIONS ARE IN ACCORD IN CONCENTRATING POLITICAL POWER

WHILE IN TIMES OF equality men readily conceive the idea of a strong central power, both their habits and their feelings predispose them to accept and help it forward. I can very briefly make the point clear, as most of the reasons for it have been given already.

The inhabitants of democracies think it always an effort to tear themselves away from their private affairs and pay attention to those of the community; the natural inclination is to leave the only visible and permanent representative of collective interests, that is to say, the state, to look after them. Not only are they by nature lacking in any taste for public business, but they also often lack the time for it.

I am certainly not the one to say that such inclinations are invincible, for my chief aim in writing this book is to combat them. I am only asserting that in our time a secret force constantly fosters them in the human heart, and they give the citizen of a democracy extremely contradictory instincts. He is full of confidence in his independence among his equals, but from time to time his weakness makes him feel the need for some outside help which he cannot expect from any of his fellows. In this extremity he naturally turns his eyes toward that huge entity which alone stands out above the universal level, and he ends by regarding it as the sole and necessary support of his individual weakness.

In democratic societies the central power alone has both some stability and some capacity to see its undertakings through. All the citizenry is ever-moving and changing around. Now, it is in the nature of every government to wish continually to increase its sphere of action. Moreover, it is almost bound ultimately to succeed in this, for it acts with fixed purpose and determination on men whose position, ideas, and desires change every day.

Often the citizens, without intending to, play into its hands.

All that helps one to understand a frequent phenomenon in democracies, that men who are restive under any superior patiently submit to a master, proving themselves both proud and servile.

Men's hatred of privilege increases as privileges become rarer and less important. Amid general uniformity, this ever-fiercer hatred against the slightest privileges singularly favors the gradual concentration of all political rights in those hands which alone represent the state. The sovereign, being of necessity and incontestably above all the citizens, does not excite their envy, and each thinks that he is depriving his equals of all those prerogatives which he concedes to the state.

In democratic ages a man is extremely reluctant to obey his neighbor who is his equal; he refuses to recognize that the latter knows more than he; he mistrusts his fairness and regards his power with jealousy; he fears and despises him; he likes to make him feel the whole time their common dependence on the same master.

Democratic peoples often hate those in whose hands the central power is vested, but they always love that power itself.

Thus two different paths have led me to the same conclusion. I have pointed out how equality prompts men to think of one sole uniform and strong government. I have just shown how equality gives them the taste for it.[1]

---

1. [For clarity, the two paragraphs that follow are interpolated from Tocqueville's appendix, from his endnote referring to this point in the text.]

Not only is a democratic people led by its own tastes to centralize government, but the passions of all its rulers constantly urge it in the same direction.

It may easily be foreseen that ambitious men in a democratic country will labor constantly to increase the scope of social power, for they all hope sooner or later to control it themselves. It is a waste of time to demonstrate to such men that extreme centralization may be harmful to the state, for they are centralizing for their own interests.

It must therefore be toward governments of this kind that nations nowadays are tending provided only that they do not hold themselves in check. I think that in the dawning centuries of democracy individual independence and local liberties will always be the products of art. Centralized government will be the natural thing.

4

CONCERNING CERTAIN PECULIAR AND ACCIDENTAL CAUSES WHICH EITHER LEAD A DEMOCRATIC PEOPLE TO COMPLETE THE CENTRALIZATION OF GOVERNMENT OR DIVERT THEM FROM IT

ALTHOUGH ALL DEMOCRATIC PEOPLES are instinctively drawn toward centralization of power, this attraction is uneven. It depends on particular circumstances which may promote or restrain the natural effects of the state of society. There are many such circumstances, and I shall mention only a few.

When equality starts developing among a people who have never known or long forgotten what freedom is, as one sees it happen on the continent of Europe, all powers seem spontaneously to rush to the center. They accumulate there at an astonishing rate and the state reaches the extreme limits of its power all at once, while private persons allow themselves to sink in one moment down to the lowest degree of weakness.

The English who emigrated three centuries ago to found a democratic society in the wilds of the New World were already accustomed in their motherland to take part in public affairs; they knew trial by jury; they had liberty of speech and freedom of the press, personal freedom, and the conception of rights and the practice of asserting them. They carried these free institutions and virile mores with them to America, and these characteristics sustained them against the encroachments of the state.

Thus, in America it is freedom that is old, and equality is comparatively new.

I have said that among democratic nations the only form of government which comes naturally to mind is a sole and central power and that they are not familiar with the notion of intermediate powers. This applies particularly to those democratic nations which have seen the principle of equality triumph with the help of a violent revolution. The classes that managed local affairs were suddenly swept away, and the confused mass which remains has as yet neither the organization nor the habits to take the administration in hand. The state alone seems capable of taking upon itself all the details of government. Centralization becomes a fact, and in a sense, a necessity.

One must not praise or blame Napoleon for concentrating administrative powers in his own hands, for with the nobility and the upper ranks of the middle classes abruptly brushed aside, these powers fell automatically into his hands; it would have been almost as difficult for him to reject as to assume them. No such necessity has ever faced the Americans, for being from the beginning accustomed to govern themselves, they never had to call upon the state to act temporarily as guardian.

Hence centralization does not spread in a democracy simply in step with equality, but also depends on the way in which that equality was established.

At the beginning of a great democratic revolution, when war between the various classes is just starting, the people centralize the government so as to snatch control of local affairs from the aristocracy. But toward the end of such a revolution it is generally the defeated aristocracy which tries to put the control of everything into the hands of the state, dreading the petty tyranny of the common people who have become its equal and often its master.

So it is not always the same class of citizens that is eager to increase the prerogatives of power. But while a democratic revolution is in progress there is always a class in the nation, powerful through its numbers or its wealth, which is led by special and particular interests to centralize administration, notwithstanding that hatred of being ruled by one's neighbor which is a general and permanent sentiment in democracies.

These observations suffice to explain why the social power is always stronger and individuals weaker in a democracy which has reached equality after a long and painful social struggle than in one where the citizens have been equal from the beginning. The American example completely proves that.

No privilege has ever kept the inhabitants of the United States apart. They have never known the mutual relationship between master and servant, and as they neither fear nor hate each other, they have never felt the need to call in the state to manage the details of their affairs. The American destiny is unusual; they have taken from the English aristocracy the idea of individual rights and a taste for local freedom, and they have been able to keep both these things because they have had no aristocracy to fight.

At no time, therefore, is a people more disposed to increase the functions of the central power than when it has emerged from a long and bloody revolution, which, having snatched their property from the former owners, has filled the nation with fierce hatreds, conflicting interests, and contending factions. The taste for public tranquility then becomes a blind passion, and the citizens are liable to conceive a most inordinate devotion to order.

For half a century Europe has been shaken by many revolutions and counterrevolutions which have led it in opposite directions.

But in one respect all these movements are alike: they have all undermined or abolished secondary powers.

The point I want to make is that all these various rights which have been successively wrested in our time from classes, corporations, and individuals have not been used to create new secondary powers on a more democratic basis, but have invariably been concentrated in the hands of the government. Everywhere it is the state itself which increasingly takes control of the humblest citizen and directs his behavior even in trivial matters.

If the reader thinks that I have exaggerated the progress of the social power or that I have underestimated the sphere in which individual independence still operates, I beg him to put this book down for a moment and take a look for himself at the facts I have been trying to point out. Let him look attentively at what is daily happening among us and in other lands. Let him ask his neighbors, and finally look at himself. Unless I am much mistaken, he will reach, unguided and by other roads, the conclusion to which I have pointed.

He will see that in the last half century centralization has increased everywhere in a thousand different ways. Wars, revolutions, and conquests have aided its advance; all men have labored to increase it. In this same period, while men have succeeded one another at a tremendous rate at the head of affairs and while their ideas, interests, and passions have shown infinite variety, yet all have desired centralization in one way or another. The instinct for centralization has proved the one permanent feature amid the unusual mutability of their lives and their thoughts.

For my part I have no confidence in the spirit of liberty which seems to animate my contemporaries. The nations of this age are turbulent, but it is not clear to me that they are freedom-loving. And I fear that at the end of all these agitations which rock thrones, sovereigns may be more powerful than ever before.[1]

---

1.   [The last five paragraphs are taken from Tocqueville's chapter 5, "How the Sovereign Power Is Increasing Among the European Nations of Our Time Although the Sovereigns are Less Stable," which has otherwise been omitted.]

5

WHAT SORT OF DESPOTISM
DEMOCRATIC NATIONS HAVE TO FEAR

I NOTICED DURING MY stay in the United States that a democratic society similar to that found there could lay itself peculiarly open to despotism. And on my return to Europe I saw how far most of our princes had made use of the ideas, feelings, and needs engendered by such a state of society to enlarge the sphere of their power.

I was thus led to think that the nations of Christendom might perhaps in the end fall victims to the same sort of oppression as formerly lay heavy on several of the peoples of antiquity.

More detailed study of the subject and the new ideas which came into my mind during five years of meditation have not lessened my fears but have changed their object.

In past ages there had never been a sovereign so powerful that he could by himself, without the aid of secondary powers, administer every part of a great empire. No one had ever tried to subject all his people indiscriminately to the details of a uniform code, nor personally to lead every single one of his subjects. It had never occurred to the mind of man to embark on such an undertaking, and had it done so, inadequate education, imperfect administrative machinery, and above all the natural obstacles raised by unequal conditions would soon have put a stop to so grandiose a design.

When the power of the Roman emperors was at its height, the different peoples of the empire still preserved various customs and mores. Although they obeyed the same monarch, most provinces had a separate administration. The whole government empire was

---

[Originally chapter 6.]

concentrated in the hands of the emperor alone and he could, if necessary, decide everything, yet the details of social life and personal everyday existence normally escaped his control.

It is true that the emperors had immense and unchecked power, so that they could use the whole might of the empire to indulge any strange caprice. They often abused this power to deprive a man arbitrarily of life or property. The burden of their tyranny fell most heavily on some, but it never spread over a great number. It had a few main targets and left the rest alone. It was violent, but its extent was limited.

But if despotism should be established among the democratic nations of our day, it would probably have a different character. It would be more widespread and milder; it would degrade men rather than torment them.

Doubtless, in such an age of education and equality as our own, rulers could more easily bring all public powers into their own hands alone, and they could impinge deeper and more habitually into the sphere of private interests than was ever possible in antiquity. But that same equality which makes despotism easy tempers it. We have seen how, as men become more alike and more nearly equal, public mores become more humane and gentle. When all fortunes are middling, passions are naturally restrained, imagination limited, and pleasures simple. Such universal moderation tempers the sovereign's own spirit. Democratic governments might become violent and cruel at times of great excitement and danger, but such crises will be rare and brief.

Taking into consideration the trivial nature of men's passions now, the softness of their mores, the extent of their education, the purity of their religion, their steady habits of patient work, and the restraint which they all show in the indulgence of both their vices and their virtues, I do not expect their leaders to be tyrants, but rather schoolmasters.

Thus I think that the type of oppression which threatens democracies is different from anything there has ever been in the world before. I have vainly searched for a word which will exactly express the whole of the conception I have formed. Such old words as "despotism" and "tyranny" do not fit. The thing is new, and as I cannot find a word for it, I must try to define it.

I am trying to imagine under what novel features despotism may appear in the world. In the first place, I see an innumerable multitude of men, alike and equal, constantly circling around in pursuit of the petty and banal pleasures with which they glut their souls. Each one of them, withdrawn into himself, is almost unaware of the fate of the rest. Mankind, for him, consists in his children and his personal friends. As for the rest of his fellow citizens, they are near enough, but he does not notice them. He touches them but feels nothing. He exists in and for himself, and though he still may have a family, one can at least say that he has not got a fatherland.

Over this kind of men stands an immense, protective power which is absolute, thoughtful of detail, orderly, provident, and gentle. It would resemble parental authority if, fatherlike, it tried to prepare its charges for a man's life, but on the contrary, it only tries to keep them in perpetual childhood. It is not at all tyrannical, but it hinders, restrains, enervates, stifles, and stultifies so much that in the end each nation is no more than a flock of timid and hardworking animals with the government as its shepherd.

I have always thought that this brand of orderly, gentle, peaceful slavery which I have just described could be combined, more easily than is generally supposed, with some of the external forms of freedom, and that there is a possibility of its getting itself established even under the shadow of the sovereignty of the people.

Our contemporaries are ever a prey to two conflicting passions: they feel the need of guidance, and they long to stay free. Unable to wipe out these two contradictory instincts, they try to satisfy them both together. Their imagination conceives a government which is unitary, protective, and all-powerful, but elected by the people. Centralization is combined with the sovereignty of the people. They console themselves for being under schoolmasters by thinking that they have chosen them themselves.

Under this system the citizens quit their state of dependence just long enough to choose their masters and then fall back into it.

A great many people nowadays very easily fall in with this brand of compromise between administrative despotism and the sovereignty of the people. They think they have done enough to guarantee personal freedom when it is to the government that they have handed it over. That is not good enough for me. To create a national representation of the people in a very centralized country does diminish the extreme evils which centralization can produce, but it does not entirely abolish them.

Those democratic peoples which have introduced freedom into the sphere of politics, while allowing despotism to grow in the administrative sphere, have been led into the strangest paradoxes. It really is difficult to imagine how people who have entirely given up managing their affairs could make a wise choice of those who are to do that for them. One should never expect a liberal, energetic, and wise government to originate in the votes of a people of servants.

One cannot state in any absolute or general way whether the greatest danger at the present time is license or tyranny, anarchy or despotism. Both are equally to be feared, and both could spring from one and the same cause, that is, the general apathy, the fruit of individualism.[1]

---

1.   [For clarity, this paragraph is interpolated from Tocqueville's appendix, from his endnote referring to this point in the text.]

6

CONTINUATION OF THE PRECEDING CHAPTERS

I BELIEVE THAT IT is easier to establish an absolute and despotic government among a people whose social conditions are equal than among any other. I also believe that such a government once established in such a people would not only oppress men but would, in the end, strip each man there of several of the chief attributes of humanity.

I therefore think that despotism is particularly to be feared in ages of democracy.

I think that at all times I should have loved freedom, but in the times in which we live, I am disposed to worship it.

There is therefore no question of reconstructing an aristocratic society, but the need is to make freedom spring from that democratic society in which God has placed us.

These two basic truths appear to me simple, clear, and fertile. They naturally lead one to consider how a free government can be established among a people with equality of conditions.

It is both necessary and desirable that the central power of a democratic people should be both active and strong. One does not want to make it weak or casual, but only to prevent it from abusing its agility and force.

What most helped to secure the independence of private people in ages of aristocracy was that the ruler did not govern or administer the citizens by himself. He was bound to leave part of this task to the members of the aristocracy. In this way the social power was always divided.

[Originally chapter 7.]

I well understand that one cannot now employ that method, but I do see some democratic procedures to replace it.

Instead of entrusting all the administrative powers taken away from the nobility to the government alone, some of them could be handed over to secondary bodies temporarily composed of private citizens. In that way the freedom of individuals would be safer without their equality being less.

I am firmly convinced that one cannot found an aristocracy anew in this world, but I think that associations of plain citizens can compose very rich, influential, and powerful bodies, in other words, aristocratic bodies.

By this means many of the greatest political advantages of an aristocracy could be obtained without its injustices and dangers. An association, be it political, industrial, commercial, or even literary or scientific, is an educated and powerful body of citizens which cannot be twisted to any man's will or quietly trodden down, and by defending its private interests against the encroachments of power, it saves the common liberties.

In aristocratic ages each man is always bound by close ties to many of his fellow citizens, so that he cannot be attacked without the others coming to his help. In times of equality each man is naturally isolated. He can call on no hereditary friends for help nor any class whose sympathy for him is assured. He can easily be set upon alone and trodden underfoot. Nowadays an oppressed citizen has only one means of defense: he can appeal to the nation as a whole, and if it is deaf, to humanity at large. The press provides his only means of doing this. Equality isolates and weakens men, but the press puts each man in reach of a very powerful weapon which can be used even by the weakest and most isolated of men. The press is, par excellence, the democratic weapon of freedom.

Something analogous may be said of judicial power.

It is of the essence of judicial power to be concerned with private interests and gladly to pay attention to trivial subjects submitted to its consideration. Another essential element in judicial power is never to volunteer its assistance to the oppressed, but always to be at the disposal of the humblest when they solicit it. However weak a man may be, he can always compel a judge to listen to his complaint and give him an answer. The power of the courts has been at all times the securest guarantee which can be provided for individual independence, but this is particularly true in ages of democracy.

It is especially necessary in our own democratic age for the true friends of liberty and of human dignity to be on the alert to prevent the social power from lightly sacrificing the private rights of some individuals while carrying through its general designs. No citizen is so insignificant that he can be trodden down without very dangerous results, and no private rights are of such little importance that they can safely be left subject to arbitrary decisions. To infringe such a right deeply corrupts the mores of the nation and puts the whole of society in danger, because the very idea of this kind of right tends constantly among us to be impaired and lost.

There are some habits, some ideas, and some vices which are peculiar to a state of revolution and which any prolonged revolution cannot fail to engender and spread, whatever may be in other respects its character, object, and field of action.

When in a brief space of time any nation has repeatedly changed its leaders, opinions, and laws, ordinary ideas of equity and morality are no longer enough to explain and justify all the innovations daily introduced by revolution. Men fall back on the principle of social utility, political necessity is turned into a dogma, and men lose all scruples about freely sacrificing particular interests and trampling private rights beneath their feet in order more quickly to attain the public aim envisaged. There is always a danger that revolutionary instincts will mellow and assume more regular shape without entirely disappearing, but will gradually be transformed into mores of government and administrative habits.

Hence, I know of no country in which revolutions are more dangerous than in a democracy, because apart from the ephemeral ills which they are ever bound to entail, there is always a danger of their becoming permanent, and one may almost say, eternal.

I think that resistance is sometimes justified and that rebellion can be legitimate. I cannot therefore lay it down as an absolute rule that men living in times of democracy should never make a revolution. But I think that they, more than others, have reason to hesitate before they embark on such an enterprise and that it is far better to put up with many inconveniences in their present state than to turn to so dangerous a remedy.

I shall conclude with one general idea which comprises not only all the particular ideas with which this chapter treats but also most of those which this book is intended to expound.

Other dangers and other needs face the men of our own day.

In most modern nations the sovereign, whatever its origin or constitution or name, has become very nearly all-powerful, and private persons are more and more falling down to the lowest stage of weakness and dependence.

We should lay down extensive but clear and fixed limits to the field of social power. Private people should be given certain rights and the undisputed enjoyment of such rights. The individual should be allowed to keep the little freedom, strength, and originality left to him. His position in face of society should be raised and supported. Such, I think, should be the chief aim of any legislator in the age opening before us.

Two contrary ideas are current among us, both equally fatal.

There is one lot of people who can see nothing in equality but the anarchical tendencies which it engenders. They are frightened of their own free will; they are afraid of themselves.

Others, who are fewer but more perceptive, take a different view. Beside the track which starts from equality and leads to anarchy, they have in the end discovered another road, which seems to lead inevitably to servitude. They shape their souls beforehand to suit this necessary servitude, and despairing of remaining free, from the bottom of their hearts they already worship the master who is bound soon to appear.

The former surrender liberty because they think it dangerous and the latter because they think it impossible.

If I shared this latter belief, I never should have written the book which you have just read, but would have contented myself with mourning in secret over the fate of my fellows.

I have sought to expose the perils with which equality threatens human freedom because I firmly believe that those dangers are both the most formidable and the least foreseen of those which the future has in store. But I do not think that they are insurmountable.

The men living in the democratic centuries into which we are entering have a natural taste for freedom. By nature they are impatient in putting up with any regulation. They get tired of the duration even of the state they have chosen. They love power but are inclined to scorn and hate those who wield it, and they easily escape its grasp by reason of their very insignificance and changeableness.

These instincts will always recur because they result from the state of society, which will not change. For a long time they will prevent the establishment of any despotism, and they will furnish fresh weapons for each new generation wanting to struggle for human liberty.

Let us, then, look forward to the future with that salutary fear which makes men keep watch and ward for freedom, and not with that flabby, idle terror which makes men's hearts sink and enervates them.

7

GENERAL SURVEY OF THE SUBJECT

BEFORE I FINALLY BRING to an end the subject I have discussed, I should have liked to take one last look at all the various features of the New World and to form some considered view of the general influence which equality is likely to have over the fate of mankind. But the difficulty of such an undertaking holds me back. Faced by so vast a subject, I feel my vision hazy and my judgment hesitant.

This new society which I have tried to portray and would like to evaluate has only just begun to come into being. Time has not yet shaped its definite form. The great revolution which brought it about is still continuing, and of all that is taking place in our day, it is almost impossible to judge what will vanish with the revolution itself and what will survive thereafter.

The world which is arising is still half buried in the ruins of the world falling into decay, and in the vast confusion of all human affairs at present, no one can know which of the old institutions and former mores will continue to hold up their heads and which will in the end go under.

The revolution that is taking place in the social condition, laws, ideas, and feelings of men is still far from coming to an end, yet its results are already incomparably greater than anything which has taken place in the world before. Working back through the centuries to the remotest antiquity, I see nothing at all similar to what is taking place before our eyes. The past throws no light on the future, and the spirit of man walks through the night.

Nevertheless, in this vast prospect, both so novel and so confused, I can make out some salient features which I will point out.

_____

[Originally chapter 8.]

I find that good things and evil in the world are fairly evenly distributed. Great wealth tends to disappear and the number of small fortunes to increase; desires and pleasures are multiplied, but extraordinary prosperity and irremediable penury are alike unknown. Everyone feels some ambition, but few have ambitions on a vast scale. Each individual is isolated and weak, but society is active, provident, and strong; private persons achieve insignificant things, but the state immense ones.

Mores are gentle and laws humane. Though heroic devotion and other exalted and pure virtues may be rare, habits are orderly, violence rare, and cruelty almost unknown. Men tend to live longer, and their property is more secure. Life is not very glamorous, but extremely comfortable and peaceful. There is seldom great refinement or gross vulgarity in men's pleasures, little polish in their manners but little brutality in their tastes. One hardly ever finds men of great learning or whole communities steeped in ignorance. Genius becomes rarer but education more common. The spirit of man is advanced by the tiny efforts of all combined, and not by the powerful impulse given by the few. In the works of man there is less perfection but greater abundance. All the ties of race, class, and country are relaxed. The great bond of humanity is drawn tighter.

Seeking for the most general and striking of all these various characteristics, I notice that almost all extremes are softened and blunted. Almost all salient characteristics are obliterated to make room for something average, less high and less low, less brilliant and less dim, than what the world had before.

When I survey this countless multitude of beings, shaped in each other's likeness, among whom nothing stands out or falls unduly low, the sight of such universal uniformity saddens and chills me, and I am tempted to regret that state of society which has ceased to be.

When the world was full of men of great importance and extreme insignificance, very wealthy and very poor, very learned and very ignorant, I turned my attention from the latter to concentrate on the pleasure of contemplating the former. But I see that this pleasure arose from my weakness. It is because I am unable to see at once all that is around me that I thus select and separate the objects of my choice from among so many others. It is not so with the Almighty and Eternal Being, who surveys distinctly and simultaneously all mankind and each single man.

It is natural to suppose that not the particular prosperity of the few, but the greater well-being of all, is most pleasing in the sight of the Creator and Preserver of men. What seems to me decay is thus in His eyes progress; what pains me is acceptable to Him. Equality may be less elevated, but it is more just, and in its justice lies its greatness and beauty.

I therefore do all I can to enter into understanding of this divine view of the world and strive from thence to consider and judge the affairs of men.

No man on earth can affirm, absolutely and generally, that the new state of societies is better than the old, but it is already easy to see that it is different.

Some vices and some virtues were so inherent in the constitutions of aristocratic nations and are so contrary to the genius of modern peoples that they can never be introduced therein. One must therefore be very careful not to judge the nascent societies on the basis of ideas derived from those which no longer exist. To do so would be unfair, for these societies are so immensely different that direct comparison is impossible.

It would be just as unreasonable to expect from men nowadays the particular virtues which depended on the social condition of their ancestors, since that state of society has collapsed, bringing down in the confusion of its ruin all that it had of good and bad.

But these matters are still badly understood in our day.

The task is no longer to preserve the particular advantages which inequality of conditions had procured for men, but to secure those new benefits which equality may supply. We should not strive to be like our fathers but should try to attain that form of greatness and of happiness which is proper to ourselves.

For myself, looking back now from the extreme end of my task, I am full of fears and of hopes. I see great dangers which may be warded off and mighty evils which may be avoided or kept in check; and I am ever increasingly confirmed in my belief that for democratic nations to be virtuous and prosperous, it is enough if they will to be so.

I am aware that many of my contemporaries think that nations on earth are never their own masters and that they are bound to obey some insuperable and unthinking power, the product of pre-existing facts of race, or soil, or climate.

These are false and cowardly doctrines which can only produce feeble men and pusillanimous nations. Providence did not make mankind entirely free or completely enslaved. Providence has, in truth, drawn a predestined circle around each man beyond which he cannot pass; but within those vast limits man is strong and free, and so are peoples.

The nations of our day cannot prevent conditions of equality from spreading in their midst. But it depends upon themselves whether equality is to lead to servitude or freedom, knowledge or barbarism, prosperity or wretchedness.

Appendix

EXCERPT FROM TOCQUEVILLE'S TRAVEL DIARY

Tocqueville's appendixes to his twelfth edition of Democracy in America *included discursive notes to both volumes, keyed to specific pages of the general text. Among these, only one entry is quoted from Tocqueville's journal of his American tour, and since the book itself includes little in the nature of raw observations, that single entry is retained here.*

I FIND THE FOLLOWING passage in my travel diary,[1] and it will serve to show what trials are faced by those American women who follow their husbands into the wilds. The description has nothing but its complete accuracy to recommend it.

"From time to time we came to new clearings. As all these settlements are exactly like one another, I will describe the place at which we stopped tonight. It will provide a picture of all the others.

"The bells which the pioneer is careful to hang round his beasts' necks, so as to find them again in the forest, warned us from afar that we were getting near a clearing. Soon we heard the sound of an ax cutting down the forest trees. The closer we got, the more signs of destruction indicated the presence of civilized man. Our path was covered with severed branches; and tree trunks, scorched by fire or cut about by an ax, stood in our way. We went on farther and came to a part of the wood where all the trees seemed to have been suddenly struck dead. In full summer their withered branches seemed the image of winter. Looking at

---

1.   [Tocqueville's travel diary has been published under the title *Journey to America*, ed. by J. P. Mayer, New Haven, 1962.]

them close up, we saw that a deep circle had been cut through the bark, which by preventing the circulation of the sap had soon killed the trees. We were informed that this is commonly the first thing a pioneer does. As he cannot, in the first year, cut down all the trees that adorn his new property, he sows corn under their branches, and by striking them to death, prevents them from shading his crop. Beyond this field, itself an unfinished sketch, or first step toward civilization in the wilds, we suddenly saw the owner's cabin. It is generally placed in the middle of some land more carefully cultivated than the rest, but where man is yet sustaining an unequal fight against the forest. There the trees have been cut, but not grubbed up, and their trunks still cover and block the land they used to shade. Around these dry stumps wheat and oak seedlings and plants and weeds of all kinds are scattered pell-mell and grow together on rough and still half-wild ground. It is in the midst of this vigorous and variegated growth of vegetation that the planter's dwelling, or as it is called in this country, his log house, stands. Just like the field around it, this rustic dwelling shows every sign of recent and hasty work. It is seldom more than thirty feet long and fifteen high; the walls as well as the roof are fashioned from rough tree trunks, between which moss and earth have been rammed to keep out the cold and rain from the inside of the house.

"As the night was coming on, we decided to go and ask the owner of the log house to put us up.

"At the sound of our steps the children playing among the scattered branches got up and ran to the house, as if frightened at the sight of a man, while two large, half-wild dogs, with ears prickled up and outstretched muzzles, came growling out of the hut to cover the retreat of their young masters. Then the pioneer himself appeared at the door of his dwelling; he looked at us with a rapid, inquisitive glance, made a sign to the dogs to go indoors, and set them the example himself, without showing that our arrival aroused either his curiosity or apprehension.

"We went into the log house; the inside was quite unlike that of the cottages of European peasants; there was more that was super-

fluous and fewer necessities; a single window with a muslin cur-
tain; on the hearth of beaten earth a great fire which illuminated
the whole interior; above the hearth a good rifle, a deerskin, and
plumes of eagles' feathers; to the right of the chimney a map of
the United States, raised and fluttering in the draft from the cran-
nies in the wall; near it, on a shelf formed from a roughly hewn
plank, a few books; a Bible, the first six cantos of Milton, and two
plays of Shakespeare; there were trunks instead of cupboards
along the wall; in the center of the room, a rough table with legs
of green wood with the bark still on them, looking as if they grew
out of the ground on which they stood; on the table was a teapot
of English china, some silver spoons, a few cracked teacups, and
newspapers.

"The master of this dwelling had the angular features and lank
limbs characteristic of the inhabitants of New England. He was
clearly not born in the solitude in which we found him. His physical constitution by itself showed that his earlier years were spent in
a society that used its brains and that he belonged to that restless,
calculating, and adventurous race of men who do with the utmost
coolness things which can only be accounted for by the ardor of
passion, and who endure for a time the life of a savage in order to
conquer and civilize the backwoods.

"When the pioneer saw that we were crossing his threshold, he
came to meet us and shake hands, as is their custom; but his face
was quite unmoved. He opened the conversation by asking us what
was going on in the world, and when his curiosity was satisfied, he
held his peace, as if he was tired of the importunities and noise of
the world. When we questioned him in our turn, he gave us all the
information we asked and then turned, with no eagerness, but me-
thodically, to see to our requirements. Why was it that, while he was
thus kindly bent on aiding us, in spite of ourselves we felt our sense
of gratitude frozen? It was because he himself, in showing his hospitality, seemed to be submitting to a tiresome necessity of his lot and
saw in it a duty imposed by his position, and not a pleasure.

"A woman was sitting on the other side of the hearth, rocking a
small child on her knees. She nodded to us without disturbing

herself. Like the pioneer, this woman was in the prime of life; her appearance seemed superior to her condition, and her apparel even betrayed a lingering taste for dress; but her delicate limbs were wasted, her features worn, and her eyes gentle and serious; her whole physiognomy bore marks of religious resignation, a deep peace free from passions, and some sort of natural, quiet determination which would face all the ills of life without fear and without defiance.

"Her children cluster around her, full of health, high spirits, and energy; they are true children of the wilds; their mother looks at them from time to time with mingled melancholy and joy; seeing their strength and her weariness, one might think that the life she has given them exhausted her own, and yet she does not regret what they have cost her.

"The dwelling in which these immigrants live had no internal division and no loft; its single room shelters the whole family in the evening. It is a little world of its own, an ark of civilization lost in a sea of leaves. A hundred paces away the everlasting forest spreads its shade, and solitude begins again."

A NOTE ON THE ABRIDGMENT

READABILITY HAS BEEN MY main criterion in streamlining Tocqueville's masterpiece. In deciding what, how, and how much to remove from George Lawrence's graceful translation, I have aimed to create the shortest and clearest version possible without omitting any of the author's main arguments or topics of inquiry.

Mostly, this has been accomplished by condensing and combining paragraphs and by eliminating repetition. In part because it was published as two books and in part because of its author's style, *Democracy in America* is very repetitive. Constructing an argument point by point, Tocqueville tended to repeat earlier points at each new step, even within a single sentence. I have broken up long paragraphs or sentences, occasionally, and sometimes have transposed words for readability; but I have not reordered sentences or paragraphs.

I have also tightened many a run-on sentence by cutting words or clauses and by inserting punctuation. Tocqueville's penchant for indefinite pronouns and compound adjectives not only annoys but often confuses modern readers. I have tried to trim sentences and paragraphs without losing the nineteenth-century tone. Occasionally, I have added a small word or changed the conjugation of a verb in the interests of syntax. Because brackets and ellipses can be distracting, especially in excess, I have made almost all such emendations silently. Brackets appear around a very few words I have changed for clarity or brevity.

Comparatively few whole pages, sections, or chapters have been cut. All chapters of volume 1 remain in some form, as do all but nine of the seventy-five chapters that comprise volume 2. The omitted chapters are ones that I deemed either redundant ("Concerning the Progress of Roman Catholicism in the United States"), digressive ("How Democratic Institutions and Mores Tend to Raise Rents and Shorten the Terms of Leases"), or elusive ("How the Sovereign Power Is Increasing Among European Nations of Our Time, Although the Sovereigns Are Less Stable"). I have renumbered the remaining chapters.

Prefatory material has been minimized. I have condensed J. P. Mayer's foreword to the 1966 edition and have omitted a second foreword he added in 1975, as well as his acknowledgments of colleagues, librarians, and grantors who assisted him nearly fifty years ago.

The unabridged book included three appendixes, containing the author's explanatory notes, his review of a book about Swiss democracy, and a parliamentary speech he made in 1848. I have dispensed with all of this, except for three of Tocqueville's explanatory notes. Two brief notes were incorporated into the main text of volume 2, part 4, to make the author's argument easier to follow (these passages are identified by footnotes). Tocqueville's Appendix I included a single extract from his travel diary, which I have retained as a brief appendix.

All told, this edition contains not quite 40 percent of the 1966 volume, in hopes of following the novelist Elmore Leonard's famous dictum, "Try to leave out the parts that people skip." For the same reason, I have kept my introduction to a minimum of background facts and themes that I think general readers need to know before judging for themselves. Ditto the few bracketed footnotes I have added as points of information to supplement J. P. Mayer's bracketed bibliographic footnotes in the full edition. Footnotes without brackets are Tocqueville's.

Readers may skip the acknowledgments but I cannot omit a few names. Susan Spellman reformatted the electronic text and made the cuts from my marked-up paperback. After Susan, I owe thanks to Hugh Van Dusen, Marie Estrada, and Rob Crawford at HarperCollins for their patience, to Martha Cameron for copyediting, to Judy Lyon Davis for indexing, to Seymour Drescher for an e-mail, to Katherine Lynch for a translation, to Matt Mancini for a phone call, to Anthony Kaye for a referral, and to Greg Cherpes for everything.

Index

Adams, John Quincy, 75
administrative decentralization,
    51–52, 139–40
adultery, as crime, 32*n*, 32–33
advantages of American
        democracy, 123–31
    federal system, 87–89, 92–93
    political activity and
        involvement, 129–31
    public spirit, 125–27
    respect for the law, 128–29
    rights, importance of, 127–28
    serving greatest good for
        greatest number, 123–25,
        129–31,
        305–7, 401
Aesop, 181*n*
African Americans
    colony in Liberia, 192–93
    compared with Indians, 165
    condition of, 14*n*
    as danger to whites, 180–95,
        370
    education of, 194
    free, 166, 189–90, 332
    intermarriage of, 190
    in Northern states, 182, 191, 332
    oppression of, 165–68, 180–95
    in Southern states, 182–95. *see
        also* slavery
    voting rights of, 34*n*, 134–35*n*,
        182

agriculture
    in the English colonies, 26
    in France, 333
    interdependence among
        states in, 198–99
    industry preferred to, 314–16
    slavery and. *see* slavery
    trade combined with, 316
Alabama
    Indians in, 167–68, 173*n*
    tariff affair of 1820 and, 208
alcohol
    abuse of, 33, 120, 130, 288
    temperance and, 130, 130*n*,
        288
Allegheny Mountains, 19, 20
ambition, 361–65
American Colonization Society,
    192–93
American democracy
    advantages of, 123–31
    arts and, 246–49, 253–56
    as basis of social conditions,
        38–41
    corruption in, 77, 83, 117–18,
        125
    envy in, 109–10, 117–18, 298,
        302–5, 354–55
    expenses under monarchy
        versus, 114–17
    foreign policy in, 121–23,
        132*n*

American democracy (*cont.*)
  future prospects for, 134–35,
    195–213
  love of war, 373–76
  maintenance of. *see*
    maintaining American
    democracy
  majority rule in. *see* majority
    rule
  mistakes, ease of correcting,
    119–20, 124–25
  opposing tendencies in, 61–
    63, 69, 83–85, 204–11, 384–
    86
  as philosophical method,
    235–37, 243
  public spirit in, 125–27
  science and, 246–53
  self-control in, 119–20
  source of beliefs in, 237–39
  sovereignty in. *see* sovereignty
    of the people
  strength of, 134–35
  as true democracy, 118–19
American exceptionalism, 382*n*
American Indians. *see* Indians or
    name of tribe
American Revolution
  causes of, 46
  compared with French
    Revolution, 62
  contradictions in, 61–63, 197
  impact of, 39, 98
  Indians fighting in, 179
  leaders of, 39, 137
  political parties and, 98, 99
American Union. *see* United
    States

anarchy, fear of, 306, 381, 397
Andrus, Silas, 32*n*
Anti-Masonic Party, 100*n*
apprenticeships, 40–41, 215
Archimedes, 251
archives, lack of public, 113–14,
    114*n*
aristocracy
  actions in war, 377
  associations in, 276
  bail and, 37–38
  bank directors as, 207
  bias toward mediocrity, 125
  corruption and, 117, 299
  craftsmanship in, 254–55,
    317–19
  desire for status quo, 115,
    245–46, 254, 282
  feudal society and, 9–10, 357–
    58
  foreign policy under, 122
  history and, 265, 270, 271
  industry in creating, 316–19,
    334–35
  inequality in army, 373
  inheritance laws and, 39–40,
    248, 298, 336, 336*n*, 337
  lack of, and professions,
    40–41
  language of, 261
  legal profession as American,
    140–41, 143
  leisure as honorable in, 313
  literature and, 258–59, 260,
    265, 267, 269, 270
  manners and, 326–28, 350–51
  marriage in, 343
  nature of, 213

overthrow of, 362, 382*n*, 388.
  see also democratic
  revolutions
parliamentary eloquence and,
  273, 275
patriarchy in, 335–37
physical pleasures and, 298,
  299, 304–5
poetry and, 265, 267
political parties and, 101
pride in, 325, 326, 354–55
public opinion and, 239
rejection of, in the New
  World, 26, 40–41, 160, 248
royal power and, 10–12
as secondary power, 382*n*
servants in, 330–31
social advantages of, 11
in the South, 39, 188
Tocqueville as member of, ix
upper classes versus, 248
vices and virtues of, 401
views of science, 251–52
see also monarchy
Arkansas, 177–78, 205*n*
army
  democratic, love of war,
    373–76
  lack of standing, 52, 118,
    197*n*
  see also militias; war
arts
  craftsmanship and, 254–55
  democratic peoples' interest
    in, 246–49
  public monuments, 256
  utility versus beauty in,
    253–55

associations
  in civil life, 286–88, 290–92
  newspapers and, 289–90
  political. *see* political
    associations
  power of, 395
  private societies, 348–49
  for religious causes, 153
  right of association, 106–8
Athens, 35, 262
attorneys. *see* legal profession
Australia colony, 28
authority
  liberty versus, 36
  moral, 132–33, 136
  of religious faith, 244
  respect for laws and, 128–29

Bacon, Francis, 236
bail, 37–38
Baltimore, in the War of 1812,
  134*n*
Bank of the United States, 207–
  10
bankruptcy law, 63*n*, 65*n*, 119–
  20, 359
barbarians, 213, 253
Beaumont, Gustave de, ix–x, xii,
  14*n*, 180*n*
beliefs
  source of democratic, 12,
    237–39
  stability under majority rule,
    371–72
Bellah, Robert N., xii
Bering Straits, 21*n*
bison, 169*n*, 170
Blacks. *see* African Americans

blasphemy, as crime, 32
bombastic speeches, 268–69
bribery, 117
British Empire. *see* England
buffalo, 169n, 170
Burns, Ken, xii
Byron, George Gordon, 268,
    268n

Calhoun, John C., 208
Canada
    French colonies in, 218
    restlessness as strength in,
        147–48
capital punishment, 33, 324
    under Massachusetts laws, 32n
    public execution, 136, 136n
    for rape, 347
Carey, Matthew, 188
Caribbean colonies, 20–21
Cass, Lewis, 169n, 170, 172n,
    173n
Catholic Church. *see* Roman
    Catholic Church
censorship, 102
centralization of power, 104–5,
    211, 382–89
    decentralization versus, 51–52
chance, 315
character. *see* individual
    character; national
    character
Charles I, 30, 31
Charles II, 31
chastity
    of men, 32–33, 343–44
    of women, 32–33, 339, 347
Chauteaubriand, François-René,

    vicomte de, 268, 268n
Cherokees, 173–80
Chickasaws, 173n
children, 29
Choctaws, 171, 173n
Christianity
    equality and, 12, 242–44
    evangelical groups, 300–301
    independence of women and,
        338–39
    liberty and, 150–54
    politics and, 150–56, 212,
        241–44, 309
    Puritans and, 26, 28–30, 144,
        153, 247
    self-interest and, 295–97
    slavery and, 195
    see also Roman Catholic
        Church
circuit courts, 80n
civil laws
    bail, 37–38
    juries and, 142–43
    in Massachusetts, 31n, 32n
civil wars, 194, 377–78
Clark, William, 169n, 170, 172n
classes. *see* social classes
clergy, 151, 154–56, 244
colonies
    of England. *see* English
        colonies
    of France, 26, 147–48, 187n,
        218
    Liberia, 192–93
    of Russia, 219, 220
    of Spain, 20–21, 26, 145, 160,
        179–80, 219
commerce. *see* industry; trade

communication systems, 64–65, 158
communitarianism, xii
compassion, 323–24, 329
competition, 361–65
Connecticut, 27*n*, 29*n*, 31, 32–34, 92, 157
conscription, 118
Constitution of the United States
  advantages of, 87–89, 92–93
  compared with others, 85–87, 90–93
  executive powers, 68–78
  judicial powers, 56–58, 78–83
  legislative powers, 65–67, 84
  history of, 61–63
  nullification doctrine and, 208–10
  prerogatives of federal government, 64–65, 81, 85–87
  Seventeenth Amendment, 67*n*
  state adoption of, 63, 63*n*, 197, 201, 205–6
  state powers, 50, 81
  summary of, 63–64
  superiority over state constitutions, 83–85
  Thirteenth Amendment, 187*n*
corn, 198
corruption, 77, 83, 117–18, 125, 299, 339
cotton, slavery and, 187, 198
counties, 44, 47, 51
  as administrative centers, 48–49

decentralization of, 53
courtesans, 343–44
courts. *see* judicial powers
craftsmanship, 215, 254–55, 317–19
Creator. *see* God
Creeks, 167–68, 173–80
Creoles, 167–68
criminal laws, 31*n*, 32-33, 54, 120
  bail, 37–38
  juries and, 142
  in other countries, 324
crisis
  assisting others in times of, 329
  election of president as, 72, 75–76
  political rights in times of, 128
curiosity, 240–41, 353
customs, tariff affair of 1820, 207–10

Darby, William, 202*n*
death
  inheritance laws and, 39–40, 248, 298, 336, 336*n*, 337
  prosperity and, 303, 304
  suicide rate, 304
  see also capital punishment
decentralization, 51–54, 139–40
Delaware, 66
Democratic Party, 99, 101, 206
Democratic-Republican Party, 99
democratic revolutions
  centralization of power at beginning of, 388–89

democratic revolutions (*cont.*)
  in Europe, ix, vii–viii, xvii,
    xvii*n*, 9, 118, 231–32, 382*n*,
    388–89
  as fated, 9–14
  individualism at end of, 283
  lack of, in the United States,
    237, 283
Descartes, René, 235, 236
descriptive poetry, 265–67
despotism, 306, 352–53
  administrative, 392–93, 395
  of the American majority,
    134*n*, 136, 137, 149, 390–93.
    see also tyranny of the
    majority
  as defender of oppressed, 128
  liberty versus, 162–64, 284–
    86, 375, 390–98
district assemblies, 51
district courts, 79, 80*n*
District of Columbia, 256
division of labor
  in industry, 215, 316–18, 334
  in marriage, 340–42, 343,
    345–48
draft, military, 118
drama, 269–70
drunkenness, 33, 120, 130, 288
duels, in the Southwest, 120

East (eastern states)
  Indian tribes of, 168–69
  democracy in, 161
  see also New England
education
  of African Americans, 194
  democracy and, 157–59, 308

equality and, 40–41
jury duty as source of, 143
middling standards for, 40–41
in New England, 28, 35, 157
official appointments, 365–66
religion and, 26
of women, 338–39, 340–41
see also arts; literature; science
egoism
  despotism and, 284
  in Europe, 294–95
  individualism versus, 271
electoral college system, 73–75
employment. *see* work
England
  colonies of. *see* English
    colonies
  as commercial center, 216
  Constitution of, 56
  emigrants to North America,
    28–30
  financial state of, 118
  freedom of thought in, 105
  influence on the United
    States, 53–54
  inheritance laws of, 39–40
  pride of aristocracy in, 325, 326
  religion and politics in, 30
  right of association in, 107
  seriousness of citizens, 352
  as source of literature for the
    United States, 257–58, 261
  War of Independence and. *see*
    American Revolution
English colonies
  first arrivals in America, 22–30
  history of federal Constitution
    and, 61–63

New England, 27–30, 33, 35, 153, 236–37, 247
 ownership of lands, 30–31, 219–21
 religion and, 28–30, 33, 35, 153, 236–37, 247
 sovereignty of the people in, 42–43
 Virginia, 26–27
enlightenment, 154, 156–59, 216
envy, 109–10, 117–18, 298, 302–5, 354–55
Epstein, Joseph, xii
equality of conditions, 9–14, 235–46, 311—12, 325–28, 381
 associations and, 286–88, 348–49
 central power and, 382–89
 Christianity and, 12, 26, 242–44
 in colonies, 26, 33–37
 as danger in war, 376–78
 despotism and, 284–85, 390–98
 education and, 40–41
 Indians and, 22–23
 individualism and, 271
 liberty versus, 279–80
 limits on ambition and, 361–65
 in maintaining democracy, 144–49
 in master-servant relationships, 331–32
 in the political sphere, 41–42
 preference for industry over

 agriculture and, 314–16
 private societies and, 348–49
 public opinion and, 371
 religion and, 12, 242–44
 revolutions as rare event and, 367–72
 softening of mores in, 323–24
 weakness of individual and, 276, 329
 well-being and, 110, 243–44, 285–86, 303–4
 women and, 342–48
 see also majority rule; sovereignty of the people; tyranny of the majority
Europe
 American trade with, 213–16
 area of, 202*n*
 attitude toward criminals, 54
 centralization in, 52
 democracy in, 162–64
 democratic revolutions in. *see* democratic revolutions
 equality of conditions in, 9, 13
 monarchy in. *see* monarchy
 place-hunting and, 365–66
 political jurisdiction in, 59–60
 political parties in, 108
 political tribunals in, 60
 restlessness as danger in, 147–48
 revolutions of 1848, xvii, xvii*n*
 servant class in, 330–31
 taste for pleasures in, 297–98
 women in, 338–39, 342, 346–47
 see also colonies *and names of specific European countries*

evangelical religions, 300–301
Everett, Edward, 172*n*
executive powers
  concentration of, 77–78
  dangers of, 70–72
  at federal level, 68–78
  impeachment process, 59–60,
    67
  of legislative branch, 67, 68
  of state governments, 50–52
  see also president of the
    United States

factions, 76, 100, 107, 306.
  see also political parties
failure, attitudes toward, 110,
    245–246, 312, 356, 359.
  see also success
family
  democracy and, 335–37
  paternal authority in, 335–37,
    339, 341, 346
  see also marriage
famine, among the Indians,
    170–71
fate, belief in, 9–13, 53, 272
federal government
  Constitution and. *see*
    Constitution of the United
    States
  dissolution of, and end to
    slavery, 191–92
  division of power with states,
    43–44, 64–65, 195–97
  foreign policy role of, 82,
    121–23, 132–33
  judicial powers, 55–59, 64,
    78–83

legislative powers, 65–67, 84
  in maintaining democracy,
    149
  merging tendencies of states
    in, 191–92, 195–211, 216–17
  patriotism attached to, 195–97,
    204
  prerogatives of, 64–65, 85–87
  secession of states from, 191–
    92, 195–211, 216–17
  taxes and, 65, 86
  see also federal system
Federalist, The, 63*n*, 64*n*, 138
Federalist Party, 98, 99
federal system, 90–93
  advantages of, 85–89, 92–93
  in large republics, 87–89
  opposing tendencies in, 61–
    63, 69, 83–85, 204–11, 384–
    86
  see also federal government
feudal system
  destruction of, 9–10
  honor within, 357–58
  see also aristocracy
Florida, slavery and, 187
food, 148, 170–71
foreign policy, 82, 121–23, 132–
    33
foreign trade. *see* trade
France
  agricultural workers in, 333
  comparison of U.S.
    presidency with monarchy,
    69–70, 118
  crimes against women in, 347
  democratic revolutions in, ix,
    xvii, 9, 118, 382, 382*n*, 383

education of girls in, 339
equality in, 279–80, 362
immutability of Constitution, 56
July Revolution of 1830, ix, xvii
under monarchy, xvii–xviii, 69–70
New World colonies of, 26, 147–48, 187n, 218
religion versus freedom in, 154
servants in, 331
suicide rate in, 304
Franklin, Benjamin, xi, 50
free African Americans, 166, 189–90, 332
freedom. *see* liberty
freedom of assembly, 106–7
freedom of association, 11, 107, 108, 292
freedom of the press, 102–5
free laborers, slaves versus, 184–87
French Revolution, viii, 382n
American sympathies with, 122–23
compared with American Revolution, 62
Fulton, Robert, 157

generalizations, American desire for, 240–41, 263–64, 271–72
geographic characteristics, of North America/United States, 19–24, 92, 144–46, 159–62, 202, 247

Georgia
Indians in, 173n, 176n, 179
shipping in, 202n
slavery and, 187, 188n
tariff affair of 1820 and, 208
German Empire, federal system of, 85
God, 13, 134, 401
in general conceptions of men, 241–43, 307
in legal swearing-in, 152–53, 153n
see also Christianity; religion
gold, 26–27, 27n
governors (state), 50–51
Greeks, 35, 262

"habits of the heart," 150, 156–59. *see also* mores
half-breeds, 190
Hamilton, Alexander, 63n, 64n
happiness
of married women, 341
restless search for, 302–5
historical writing, 270–72
honor
of employment, 312–13, 359–61
importance of, 357–61
House of Representatives, federal
election of, 111–12, 203
legislative powers of, 65–67
political jurisdiction of, 59–60, 67
role in presidential elections, 75
House of Representatives, state, 49

humility, 365
Hutchinson, Thomas, 31*n*, 32*n*

idleness, 27, 33, 37, 184–186,
    188, 359, 360
Illinois, 48*n*, 147, 169*n*
immigrants , 146, 151, 183.
    see also colonies
immortality of the soul, 309
impeachment process, 59–60,
    67
improvement
    innovation and, 215–16, 251–
    52
    thirst for, 115–16, 215–16,
    245–49
Indiana, as northwestern state,
    48*n*
Indians, 21–24, 166–80
    compared with African
        Americans, 165
    equality and, 22–23
    forced migrations of, 170–80
    hunting by, 169–70, 172–73*n*
    intermarriage of, 190
    language of, 21, 23, 171, 174
    nomadic nature of, 23–24,
        145–46, 169
    oppression of, 166–68, 170–
        80
    population of, 168*n*, 173*n*
    religion of, 23
    treaties with United States,
        172–73*n*, 177*n*
    voting rights of, 34*n*
    war and, 22–23
individual character
    of officials, 111–12, 124–25

seriousness of Americans,
    351–53
studies of, 109–10
individualism, xi–xii, 235–36,
    281–86, 293–95
    benefits of associations for,
        287
    defined, 271
    egoism versus, 271
    free institutions to mitigate,
        284–86
    isolation and, 282, 283, 284
    popularizing of term, 281*n*
    tyranny of the majority versus,
        136
industry
    in American character, 358–
        61
    American prejudice against
        mechanical arts, 157
    aristocracy created from, 316–
        19, 334–35
    associations and, 291–92
    division of labor in, 316–18,
        334
    industrial expansion, 131, 205
    influence of democracy on
        wages, 333–35
    innovation and, 157, 215–16
    marriage and, 340
    mental habits and, 344, 356,
        358
    in North versus South, 186,
        193–94, 202–3, 207–8, 216–
        17
    preferred to agriculture, 314–16
    revolution as threat to, 368–
        69

science and, 157, 252–53
spirit of, in literature, 260
inheritance laws, 39–40, 248,
   298, 336, 336*n*, 337
innovation, 115–16, 157, 215–
   16, 251–52
   new words and ideas, 261–62
   rejection of, 372
   science and, 246–49, 251–52
intellectual activity and
   movements
   American philosophical
      method, 235–39, 243
   arts, 246–49, 253–55
   enlightenment, 154, 156–59,
      216
   generalizations, American
      desire for, 240–41, 263–64,
      271–72
   literature. *see* literature
   science, 246–53
   tyranny of the majority over
      thought, 135–37
   see also religion
intermarriage, 182, 190
international laws, 82
Irish emigrants, 151
Irons, Jeremy, xii
Islam, 242–43

Jackson, Andrew, x, 101*n*, 210
Jacksonian Democratic Party,
   100*n*, 101, 101*n*
jargon, 262
Jay, John, 64*n*
Jefferson, Thomas, xvi, 22*n*, 71,
   75, 99, 121–22, 138–39,
   190*n*, 203*n*

Jeffersonian party, 99, 99*n*
Jesus Christ, authority of, 149
journalism, 258
judges, 55, 56, 58–59, 140–41
   as aristocracy in America, 143
   other powers of, 58–59
   see also judicial powers; legal
      profession
judicial powers, 55–56, 395–96
   district courts, 79, 80*n*
   federal, 55–59, 64, 78–83
   freedom of the press and, 103
   function of juries, 142–43
   impeachment, 59–60, 67
   legal profession and, 140–41,
      143
   of legislative branch, 59–60,
      67
   local and state, 47, 55–59, 79
   in maintaining democracy,
      150
   of the Supreme Court, 64,
      79–83
   see also Constitution of the
      United States
July Revolution of 1830, ix, xvii
juries, 134, 142–43

Kent, James, 63*n*
Kentucky, slavery and, 183–86

lackey, as term, 331
La Fayette, Marquis de, 271
Lamartine, Alphonse de, 268,
   268*n*
language
   American changes in, 260–64
   of African Americans, 165

language (*cont.*)
  of bombastic speakers, 268–
    69
  of the English colonists, 25,
    161
  of immigrant populations,
    146
  of the Indians, 21, 23, 171,
    174
  judicial analysis of, 103
  of the legal profession, 141
  personification of words, 263
  of politics, 141
  vagueness of, 263–64
Lawrence, George, xv
laws
  African Americans and, 182
  bankruptcy, 63*n*, 65*n*, 119–20,
    359
  Constitution versus, 56–58
  democracy and, 13, 14, 39–40,
    53, 123–25, 149–50, 159–62,
    163, 400
  father-son relationship and,
    336
  Indians and, 172–73*n*, 173–80
  inheritance, 39–40, 248, 298,
    336, 336*n*, 337
  international, 82
  limits on ambition, 361–65
  mores and, 36, 159–62, 163
  in New England, 32–34
  patent, 65*n*
  peculiarities of American, 37–38
  respect for, 128–29
  township, 44–49, 53
  see also civil laws; criminal
    laws; legal profession

lawyers. *see* legal profession
Ledeen, Michael A., xi–xii
legal profession, as American
    aristocracy, 140–41, 143.
    see also judges
legislative activity and powers,
    55, 57
  concentration of, 84
  division of, 49–50, 65–67, 84
  of the English colonies, 32
  of federal government, 65–
    67, 84
  legal profession and, 141
  parliamentary eloquence,
    273–75
  political agitation and, 130
  of state governments, 49–50,
    84
  of townships, 47
  tyranny of the majority and,
    60, 84–85, 138–39
leisure
  curiosity versus, 240–41
  as honorable in aristocracy,
    313
  of slave holders, 185–86
  see also aristocracy; work
Lenapes, 168
Lévy, Bernard-Henri, xiii
Liberia, 192–93
libertarianism, xi–xii
liberty
  abuses of, 84
  American Revolution and, 46
  authority versus, 36
  centralization of power and,
    389
  Christianity and, 150–54

to combat individualism, 284
courts and, 81–82
despotism of one man versus, 162–64, 284–86, 375
of the English colonists, 25, 31*n*
equality versus, 279–80, 381, 398
freedom of association, 11, 107, 108, 292
freedom of the press, 102–5
judicial powers and, 57, 58
mores and, 12
opposing tendencies in, 61–63, 69, 83–85
physical pleasures and, 305–7
religion and, 36–37, 161
sacrifices for, 118–19, 280, 281, 293–96
spirit of, 36–37
surrender of, 397–98
literature, 257–75
American bias against, 156–57
aristocracy and, 258–59, 260, 265, 267, 269, 270
democratic peoples' interest in, 246–49
England as source of American, 257–58, 261
historical writing, 270–72
industrial spirit of, 260
journalism, 258. *see also* newspapers
language modifications in American democracy, 260–64
poetry, 264–68
speeches, 268–69, 273–75

theater, 269–70
local government, 25–26, 34–35
counties in, 44, 47, 49, 51, 53
taxes and, 35
townships in, 44–49
"Loco Foco" Democrat Party, 100*n*
Louisiana, slavery and, 185*n*
Louis XIV, 263
Louis XVI, ix
lower classes
alcohol abuse in, 120
compared with upper classes, 109–12, 115–17
good qualities and, 109–10
jury duty and, 142
poetry and, 265
power in democracy, 129
sacrifices for democracy, 118–19
servants in Europe, 330–31
taxes and, 115, 116, 119
thirst for improvement and, 115–16
see also poverty; slavery; universal suffrage
Luther, Martin, 236
lying, as crime, 33

Madison, James, 63*n*, 64*n*, 138, 203*n*
Maine
as New England state, 27*n*
slavery and, 188
maintaining American democracy, 144–63, 211–13
accidental causes in, 144–49
enlightenment in, 156–59

maintaining American (*cont.*)
  geographic circumstances in,
      144–46, 159–62, 202, 247
  laws in, 149–50, 159–62
  mores in, 150, 159–62
  practical experiences in, 156–
      59
  in relation to Europe, 162–64
  religion in, 150–56, 212, 241–
      44
majority rule, 97, 136, 239
  in republics, 211–13
  stability of beliefs under, 371–72
  see also public opinion;
      sovereignty of the people;
      tyranny of the majority
Malte-Brun, Conrad, 202*n*
Mancini, Matthew, xii
manners, 326–28, 350–51, 364.
  see also mores
manufacturing. *see* industry;
      trade
Man Without a Country, A
      (Vonnegut), vii
*Marie; or, Slavery in the United
      States* (Beaumont), xii, 14*n*,
      180*n*
marriage
  division of labor in, 340–42,
      343, 345–48
  among races, 182, 190
  women and, 340–42, 343
Marshall, 27*n*
Marx, Karl, xv
Maryland, 30*n*, 31*n*
  slavery and, 186, 188
  in the War of 1812, 134*n*
Massachusetts, 27*n*

charter granted by Charles I,
      31, 31*n*
  education of citizens, 157
  laws of, 31*n*, 32*n*
  shipping in, 202*n*
  slavery and, 188
  townships in, 45–47, 48
  in the War of 1812, 92
master-servant relationships
  in aristocracy, 330–31, 388
  in democracy, 331–32
  in slavery, 324, 332
Masur, Louis P., xii–xiii
materialism, 12
  of aristocracy, 299
  dangers of, 308–9
  love of prosperity in, 310
  restlessness in, 302–5
  revolution as threat to, 367–72
  of slaveholders, 185
  see also physical pleasures;
      prosperity
Mather, Cotton, 36*n*
Mayer, Jacob-Peter, xv–xvii
mechanical arts, 157
men
  of ambition in America, 361–65
  chastity and, 32–33, 343–44
  equality of the sexes and,
      344–48
  master-servant relationships,
      324, 330–31
  morality of women versus, 343–
      44, 347
  prostitution and, 343–44
  white manhood suffrage and,
      34*n*, 109, 109*n*
  see also paternal authority

Index

425

metempsychosis, 309
Mexico
  federal system of, 90
  slavery and, 187*n*
  Texas as province of, 219
Michigan, 48*n*, 205*n*
Middle Ages, punishments in,
  58–59, 324
middle class
  in the English colonies, 26–
    27, 28–30
  revolution as threat to, 367–
    72
  taste for physical pleasures
    and, 298
militias
  formation of, 34
  lack of permanent armed
    forces, 52, 118, 197*n*
  right to call up, 91–92
  see also army; war
Mill, John Stuart, x
Minnesota, as northwestern state,
  48*n*
minority, majority versus, 133,
  138
Mississippi
  Indians in, 173*n*
  tariff affair of 1820 and, 208
Mississippi River, 19–20
Mississippi Valley, exploration
  of, 40
Moeurs, translation of, 150*n.*
  see also mores
Mohicans, 168
Molière, Jean Baptiste Poquelin,
  136–37

monarchy, xvii–xviii, 25–26, 69–
  70, 135–36, 162–64
  comparison of president of
    the United States and, 69–
    70, 71
  foreign policy under, 122
  public expenses under
    democracy versus, 114–17
  sovereignty of the people
    versus, 41–42, 138–39
  see also aristocracy; democratic
    revolutions
money
  love of, 40, 117, 356, 358
  notes of the Bank of the
    United States, 207
  regulating value of, 64
  working to gain, 312–13
Monroe, James, 203*n*
Montaigne, 293
monuments, public, 256
morality
  Christian, respect for, 152
  corruption in democracy,
    117–18
  liberty and, 12
  physical pleasures and,
    300
  pride as vice, 364–65
  rationality as basis of, 200
  revolution as threat to, 369
  tyranny of the majority and,
    132–33, 136
  United States influences in
    New World, 216
  of women, 338–39, 342–44,
    347
  see also honor; religion; virtue

mores
 defined, 150
 democracy and, 12, 13, 148,
  150, 159–62, 163, 211, 400
 education of women, 338–39,
  340–44
 of immigrant populations,
  146
 laws and, 36, 159–62, 163
 limits on ambition, 361–65
 manners and, 326–28, 350–
  51, 364
 in New England, 32–33
 patriarchy and, 335–37
 softening of, 323–24
 translation of *moeurs,* 150*n*
Morris, Gouverneur, 63*n*
Morris, Robert, 63*n*
Morton, Nathaniel, 29, 29*n*
Muhammad, 242–43
mulattos, 190
murder, in the Southwest, 120
mysticism, 301

Napoleon, ix, 387
Narragansetts, 168
National Archives, 114*n*
national character, 25
 impact of tyranny of the
  majority on, 137–38
 thirst for improvement and,
  115–16, 215–16, 245–49
 trade and industry as part of
  American, 358–61
National Republican Party, 100*n*
Native Americans. *see* Indians
Negroes. *see* African Americans
Netherlands, federal system of, 85

New England, 27–30
 as American exception, viii
 characteristics of colonists, 28–
  29, 35, 157
 connection to mother
  country, 31–32
 equality of conditions in, 33–
  37
 foundations of, 27–28, 236–37
 founding of colonies in, 30–
  31
 Indian tribes of, 168–69
 laws in, 32–34
 master-servant relationship in,
  332
 population growth of, 30
 social contracts of, 29–30
 sovereignty of colonies, 31–32
 states of (list), 27*n*
 townships in, 45–47, 48
 women in, 341
New Hampshire, 27*n*
New Haven, Connecticut
 founding of, 29*n*, 31
 laws of, 33
New Jersey, 30*n*
newspapers, 101, 102–5
 associations and, 289–90
 Cherokee, 174
 as historical records, 113–14
 journalists as writers, 258
 nationwide distribution of,
  104
 power of, 104–5, 395
 public opinion and, 105,
  289–90
New World colonies. *see* colonies
New York state

inheritance laws in, 40
public expenditures in, 116*n*
religious beliefs in legal
  swearing-in, 152–53, 153*n*
representatives in Congress,
  66
separation of church and state,
  155*n*
slavery and, 188
North (northern states)
African Americans separated
  from society in, 182, 191,
  332
character of citizens, 201
compared with South, 186–
  89, 193–94, 198, 200–204,
  207–8, 216–17
interdependence with other
  parts of U.S., 198–99
master-servant relationship in,
  332
tariffs and, 100
North America
discovery of, 145–46
geographic situation of, 19–
  24, 92, 144–46, 159–62, 202,
  247
population growth of, 30,
  146, 188–89, 201–2, 202*n*,
  220
westward expansion in, 146–
  48, 218–19, 341–42
wilderness of. *see* wilderness of
  North America
North Carolina, 30*n*
shipping in, 202*n*
slavery and, 188*n*
tariff affair of 1820 and, 208

northwest
  expansion into, 218–19
  states in (list), 48*n*
Northwest Territory, 48*n*
Notes on the State of Virginia
  (Jefferson), 22*n*
nullification doctrine, 208–10

officials, public. *see* public
  officials
Ohio
  as northwestern state, 48, 48*n*
  slave state of Kentucky
    compared with, 183–86
  westward movement of
    population and, 146–47
Ohio River, as slavery dividing
  line, 183–86
oppression
  of African Americans, 165–68,
    180–95
  in despotism of equality of
    conditions, 284–85, 390–98
  of Indians, 166–68, 170–80
  see also democratic revolutions
oration. *see* speeches
Osage, 172*n*

pamphlets, political, 257
papers. *see* newspapers
parties. *see* political parties
Pascal, Blaise, 251, 297, 297*n*
passions
  for equality, 110
  freedom of the press and, 103
  see also tyranny of the majority
passports, lack of, 54
patent laws, 65*n*

paternal authority, 335–37, 339,
    341, 346
  in master-servant relationship,
    324, 330–32
  weakness of American, 335–
    37, 339, 341
patriotism
  as motivator of action, 53
  in pursuit of public affairs,
    306–7
  as sort of religion, 125–26,
    354
  state versus federal, 195–97,
    204
  in townships, 45
peace, democratic peoples and
    love of, 373–76. *see also* war
Penn, William, 168
Pennsylvania, 30*n*
  single-assembly experiment
    in, 50
  slavery and, 186, 188
Pequots, 168
physical pleasures
  aristocracy and, 298, 299,
    304–5
  combined with public affairs,
    305–7, 387
  dangers of materialism and,
    308–9
  liberty and, 305–7
  love of prosperity and, 310,
    372
  preference for industry over
    agriculture and, 314
  prosperity and, 145, 303
  well-being and, 297–300, 301
  see also materialism

Pilgrims, 28–30
Plutarch, 251, 252*n*
Plymouth, 29, 29*n*, 31
poetry, 264–68
police regulations, 52, 54
politeness, 326–28
politics
  bias toward action in, 129–31
  legal profession and, 140–41
  religion in, 150–56, 212, 241–
    44, 309
  trader's habits in, 148–49
political associations
  civil associations versus, 286,
    288, 290–92
  freedom of assembly and,
    106–7
  political pamphlets and, 257
  power of, 106
  universal suffrage in
    moderating violence of, 108
political jurisdiction
  defined, 59
  in Europe, 59–60
  at federal level, 67
  at state level, 59–60
political parties, 98–101, 273–75
  aristocracy and, 101
  in Europe, 108
  freedom of association and,
    107, 108
  language of, 141
  legal profession and, 141
  in presidential elections, 76
  press and, 101, 102–5, 257
  as threat to future of the
    United States, 99–100
political powers

centralization of, 104–5, 211,
382–89
of judges, 56, 141
secondary, 382, 382*n*, 389,
395
political science, need for new,
10
political tribunals, in Europe, 60
population size
growth of North American,
30, 146, 201–2, 202*n*, 220
House of Representatives
and, 66, 66*n*, 203
Indian, 168*n*, 173*n*
of Russia, 221*n*
slavery and, 66*n*, 183–86, 188–
91, 193*n*, 203
westward movement and,
146–47
postal service, 64, 158*n*, 204–5
poverty
bail and, 37–38
decline in wages and, 334–35
in the English colonies, 27, 28
equality and, 26
move westward and, 158
physical pleasures and, 298
see also lower classes
power
abuses of, 306
of associations, 106
centralization of, 104–5, 382–89
corruption and, 117–18
limits on ambition and, 364
of the press, 105
pursuit of wealth versus, 113
president of the United States,
68–78

appointment of Supreme
Court justices and, 79–80
compared with king, 69–70,
71
as dependent power, 69–73
in disputes between state and
federal government, 210
election of, 70–76
foreign policy and, 121–23
impeachment process, 59–60,
67
reelection of, 68, 76–78
salary of, 68–69, 313
South as source of, 203, 203*n*
tariff affair of 1820 and, 209–
10
term length, 68
veto powers of, 77–78
war powers of, 91–92
press, freedom of, 102–5.
see also newspapers
pride
of American people, 200,
327–28, 350, 352–53, 354–
55
in aristocracy, 325, 326, 354–
55
as vice, 364–65
primogeniture, 39, 337
private property
principle of, xviii, 40
revolution as threat to, 368–
69, 376–77
see also property rights
privilege, hatred of, 385
professions
apprenticeships, 40–41, 215
flexibility of, 254, 303, 313

professions (*cont.*)
  legal profession, 140–41, 143
  writing and, 258–59
profit
  wage levels and, 334
  working for, 313
property rights, 30–31, 219–21
  importance of, 148–49
  Indians and, 172–73*n*, 175,
    177
  inheritance laws and, 39–40,
    248, 298, 336, 336*n*, 337
  ownership as voting
    qualification, 42, 109*n*
  recognition of, 127–28, 148–
    49
  revolution as threat to, 367–
    72
  see also private property
prosperity, 12, 52, 305, 310, 372
  attitudes toward death and,
    303, 304
  bias toward action in, 302–5
  as danger for the United
    States, 203–11
  as general tendency of
    American laws, 124–25
  instability of private fortunes
    in America, 341, 355, 359
  limits on ambition and, 361–65
  marriage and, 340
  physical pleasures and, 145,
    303. *see also* physical
    pleasures
  power over political behavior,
    148–49
  restlessness in midst of, 302–5
  stability of government and,145

wages and, 334
prostitution, 343–44
providence, belief in, 272
Providence, Rhode Island, 29*n*,
  31
provincial banks, 207
public affairs, self-interest in,
  306–7, 387
public execution, 136, 136*n*
public expenses
  under democracy versus
    monarchy, 114–17
  salaries of public officials, 68–
    69, 80, 116–17, 313
public monuments, 256
public officials
  in aristocracies, 275, 313
  concern for political parties
    versus constituents, 273–75
  merit of, 111–13, 124–25
  military men as, 374
  place-hunting and, 365–66
  salaries of, 68–69, 80, 116–17,
    313
  see also executive powers;
    judicial powers; legislative
    activity and powers
public opinion
  on centralization of powers,
    211
  of clergy in America, 244
  of crimes against women, 347
  equality of conditions and,
    371
  honor and, 357–61
  importance of, 70
  of intermarriage, 182
  majority rule and, 238–39

master-servant relationship
    and, 332
newspapers and, 105, 289–90
power of, 133, 134, 238–39
role of women, 340
public spirit, 125–27
Purdon, John W., 48*n*
Puritans, 28–30, 144, 153, 247

Quapaws, 172*n*

races in the United States, 164–
    95
    hierarchy of, 165
    intermarriage among, 182,
        190
    see also African Americans;
        Indians
rape, 32–33, 347
rationality
    in educating girls, 338–39,
        340–41
    as source of morality, 200
    tyranny of the majority and,
        133–35
reason. *see* rationality
Reeve, Henry, xi, xv–xvi
religion
    African Americans and, 182
    Catholic Church and, 151
    civil liberty and, 36–37
    education of girls and, 338,
        339
    evangelical, 300–301
    focus on the future in, 311–12
    freedom and, 36–37, 161
    of immigrant populations,
        146

of the Indians, 23
Islam, 242–43
legal swearing-in, 152–53,
    153*n*
marriage and, 340
as motivator of action, 53
need for external ceremonies
    and, 243–44
in the New England colonies,
    28–30, 33, 35, 153, 236–37
patriotism as sort of, 125–26, 354
as political institution, 150–
    56, 212, 241–44, 309
power of, 154–56, 199, 236–
    37, 239
Puritanism and, 28–30, 144,
    153, 247
purpose of, 242, 243–44
religious liberty and, 33
self-interest and, 295–97
separation of church and
    state, 154–56, 244, 309
spiritual beliefs and, 300–301,
    307–9
universal respect for, 100
    see also Christianity
representative government, 31*n*
Republican (Democratic-
    Republican) Party, 99, 99*n*
Republican (modern) Party, 99,
    99*n*
restlessness, 352–57
    as danger in Europe, 147–48
    of democratic armies, 373–76
    in prosperity, 302–5
    revolutions and, 369–70
    as strength in America, 147–
        48

Rhode Island, 27*n*, 29*n*, 31, 34*n*
rice, slavery and, 187*n*, 198
rights
    idea of, 127–28
    patriotism in exercise of, 126–
        27
    see also property rights; voting
        rights
Rocky Mountains, 19
Roman Catholic Church, 243*n*
    clergy in the United States,
        151, 154–56
    Irish immigrants, 151
    separation of church and
        state, 154–56, 244, 309
Romans, 22*n*, 213, 217, 253,
    262, 390–91
royal power, 10–12
Russia
    as destined for greatness,
        221–22
    New World colonies of, 219,
        220
    population size of, 221*n*

salaries
    influence of democracy on
        wage levels, 333–36
    of public officials, 68–69, 80,
        116–17
San Domingo colony, 28
science
    applications versus theory in,
        247, 250–53
    beliefs and, 12
    democratic interest in, 246–
        49
    industry and, 157, 252–53

innovation and, 246–49, 251–
    52
secondary powers, 382, 382*n*,
    389, 395
self-control, 119–20
self-interest
    in, 305–7, 387
    religion and, 295–97
    virtue and, 293–95, 296
self-reliance, 235–36. *see also*
    success
Senate, federal
    election of members, 67*n*,
        111–12, 121*n*
    foreign policy and, 121–23
    legislative powers of, 65–67
    membership requirements,
        84
    political jurisdiction of, 59–
        60, 67
    role of president and, 68, 79–80
    in Supreme Court justice
        selection, 79–80
Senate, state, 49
servants, 330–32
Seventeenth Amendment, 67*n*
shipping
    navigation and, 246
    in North versus South, 202*n*
    steamships, 204–5, 205*n*
    trade based on, 202*n*, 204–5,
        213–17, 246, 315
silver, 26–27, 27*n*
skepticism, 265, 311–12
slang, 262
slavery
    abolition of, 181–83, 186–92,
        187*n*

American Colonization
Society colony in Liberia,
192–93
in antiquity, 181, 181*n*, 194
aristocratic principles and, 39
Christianity and, 195
dishonoring of labor through,
27
federal government and, 191–
92, 195–211
free labor versus, 184–85,
185*n*, 187
justification of, 193–94
master-servant relationship in,
324, 332
materialism of slaveholders,
185
oppression of, 165–67
population size in
determining number of
representatives, 66*n*
population trends under, 66*n*,
183–86, 188–91, 193*n*, 203
in South versus North, 186–88
treatment of slaves, 324
in Virginia colony, 27, 27*n*
see also African Americans
social classes
capacity for improvement
and, 245–46
confusion of, 254–55, 282
of jurors, 142
language changes and, 261–64
master-servant relationships
and, 324, 330–32, 388
poetry and, 265, 267
pride in aristocracy and, 325,
326, 354–55

revolutions as rare event and,
367–72
see also aristocracy; lower
classes; middle class; upper
classes
social conditions
democracy as basis of, 38–41
political consequences of, 41–
43
societies, private, 348–49
sorcery, as crime, 32
South (southern states)
aristocracy and, 39, 188
African Americans in society
of, 182–95. *see also* slavery
character of citizens, 201
climate of, 187–88, 200–201
compared with North, 186–
88, 193–94, 198, 200–204,
207–8, 216–17
first colonies in, 26–27
free trade and, 100
Indians of, 167–68, 173–80
industry in North versus, 186,
202–3, 207–8
interdependence with other
parts of U.S., 198–99
nullification doctrine and,
208–10
secession question for, 191–
92, 195–211, 216–17
tariff affair of 1820 and, 208
South America
agriculture in, 145
colonies in, 20–21, 145, 160
native peoples of, 145
slavery and, 187*n*
South Carolina, 30*n*

South Carolina (*cont.*)
  shipping in, 202*n*
  slavery and, 188, 188*n*
  tariff affair of 1820 and, 208–9
sovereignty of the people
  absolute power versus, 41–42,
    138–39
  choice of the people in, 109–11
  and despotism of equality of
    conditions, 284–85, 390–98
  first Constitution of the
    United States and, 62
  freedom of association and,
    11, 106–8, 292
  freedom of the press and,
    102–5
  in New England, 31–32
  political parties and, 98
  principle of, xviii, 42–43
  in republics, 211–13
  second Constitution of the
    United States and, 63, 85
  in state versus federal
    government, 43–44, 61–63,
    69, 83–85, 195–96, 204–11
  true power and, 52–53
  see also majority rule
Spain, New World colonies of,
    20–21, 26, 145, 160, 179–80,
    219
speeches
  bombastic, 268–69
  parliamentary eloquence and,
    273–75
spirituality
  evangelical forms of, 300–301
  religious beliefs in, 307–9. *see
    also* religion

state governments, 43–54
  adoption of Constitution of
    the United States, 63, 63*n*,
    197, 201, 205–6
  counties and, 44, 47, 49, 51, 53
  disputes with federal
    government, 210
  division of power between
    federal government and,
    64–65, 195–97
  effects of administrative
    decentralization, 51–54
  executive power of, 50–52
  interdependence among,
    195–201
  judicial powers, 55–59, 79
  laws extended to cover Indian
    tribes, 178–79
  legislative power of, 49–50, 84
  patriotism and, 195–97, 204
  role of, 132*n*
  secession and, 191–92, 195–
    211, 216–17
  superiority of federal over
    state constitutions, 83–85
  townships and, 44–49, 53
  tyranny of the majority and,
    138*n*
  see also names of specific states
steamships, 204–5, 205*n*
Stith, William, 27*n*
Story, Joseph, 80*n*
success, attitudes toward, 110,
    117–118, 240, 265, 311-312,
    356, 362, 364
suffrage. *see* voting rights
sugar, slavery and, 185*n*, 187,
    198

suicide rate, 304
Supreme Court
  appointment of justices, 79–80
  creation of, 64
  in determining competence of federal courts, 80–81
  high standing as tribunal, 81–83
Switzerland, federal system of, 85, 86n, 90

Tanner, John, 174–75n
tariffs
  North and, 100
  tariff affair of 1820, 207–10
taxes
  federal government and, 65, 86
  local government and, 35
  social class and, 115, 116, 119
  as voting qualification, 109n
temperance, 130, 130n, 288
Tennessee, Indians in, 171, 173n
Terence, 181n
testamentary powers, 336n
Texas, under Mexican rule, 219
theater, 269–70
theoretical discoveries, American prejudice against, 156–57
Thirteenth Amendment, 187n
thought, tyranny of the majority over, 135–37. *see also* intellectual activity and movements
tobacco
  slavery and, 186n, 187, 198

use of, 33
Tocqueville, Alexis de
  biography of, ix–x
  concept of individualism, xi–xii, 281n
  first publication of *Democracy in America*, vii, x
  itinerary in the United States, ix–x
  misjudgments of, viii–ix
  study of U.S. prisons, ix, x
  travel diary, excerpt, 403–6
townships, 44–49
  daily duties of, 45–46
  decentralization of, 53
  in New England, 45–47, 48
trade
  in American character, 358–61
  combined with agriculture, 316
  with Europe, 213–16
  habits of traders in politics, 148–49
  mental habits of industrial and trading classes, 344, 356, 358
  in North/South relations, 100, 198, 216–17
  nullification doctrine and, 208–10
  revolution as threat to, 368–69
  shipping industry and, 202n, 204–5, 213–17, 246, 315
  Supreme Court role in, 82
  tariff affair of 1820, 207–10

treaties
  in European settlement of the
    New World, 219
  making, 121*n*
  with the North American
    Indian tribes, 172–73*n*,
    177*n*
  Supreme Court role in
    interpreting, 82
Tudor monarchy, 25–26
Twain, Mark, xi
tyranny of the majority, 132–43
  centralization and, 139–40
  dangers of, 60, 84–85, 107
  despotism in, 134*n*, 136, 137,
    149, 390–93
  effects on national character,
    137–38
  freedom of association and,
    11, 107, 108, 292
  legislative powers and, 60, 84–
    85, 138–39
  modifying factors in, 139–43
  moral authority and, 132–33,
    136
  nature of, 133–35
  as source of danger, 138–39
  over thought, 135–37

Union. *see* United States
Union Party, 208*n*
United States
  archives of, 113–14
  attitude toward criminals, 54
  as destined for greatness,
    203–4, 217, 221–22
  first immigrants, 25–30
  future prospects for, 195–213

  geographic situation of, 19–
    24, 92, 144–46, 159–62, 202,
    247
  moral influences in the New
    World, 216
  national character of, 25
  political influence of England
    on, 53–54
  political jurisdiction in, 59–60
  prosperity as danger for, 203–11
  state government in. *see* state
    governments
universal suffrage, 43
  censorship versus, 102
  choices of the people and,
    109–11
  in federal Senatorial
    elections, 112
  introduction of, 115
  in moderating violence of
    political associations, 108
  for white men, 34*n*, 109, 109*n*
upper classes
  aristocracy versus, 248
  compared with lower classes,
    109–12, 115–17
  good qualities and, 109–10
  jury duty and, 142
  loss of power in democracy,
    129
  taxes and, 115, 116, 119

Vermont, 27*n*
veto powers
  of the president, 77–78
  of state governors, 50
Virginia
  as first English colony, 26–27

shipping in, 202*n*
slavery and, 27, 27*n*, 186,
   186*n*, 188, 188*n*
tariff affair of 1820 and, 208
virtue
   aristocracy and, 401
   in politics, 127–28
   prosperity and, 12
   regular habits, 356, 358
   self-interest and, 293–95, 296
Volney, Constantin, 169*n*
Voltaire, 236
Vonnegut, Kurt, vii, xii
voting rights
   of African Americans, 34*n*,
      134–35*n*, 182
   of Indians, 34*n*
   respect for laws and, 128–29
   sovereignty of the people and,
      42–43
   universal suffrage and, 43,
      102, 108, 109–11, 115
   voting qualification, 34*n*, 42,
      109
   white manhood suffrage, 34*n*,
      109, 109*n*
   of women, 34*n*

wages
   influence of democracy on,
      333–36
   salaries of public officials and,
      68–69, 80, 116–17
war
   advantages of, 375
   civil, 194, 377–78
   considerations in democratic
      societies, 376–78

democratic armies and love
   of, 373–76
ending, difficulty of, 375
federal system and, 88
Indians and, 22–23
lack of conscription in the
   United States, 118
object of, 376–77
powers of government in, 91–
   92
starting, difficulty of, 375
see also militias *and names of
   specific wars*
War of 1812
   despotism of the majority in,
      134*n*
   militia in, 92
War of Independence. *see*
   American Revolution
Washington, D.C., 256
Washington, George, 63, 63*n*,
   121, 122–23, 176, 203*n*
Watson, Harry, xii
wealth
   corruption and, 117–18
   distrust of, 140
   employment and, 359–61
   hierarchy of, 148–49
   inheritance laws and, 39–40,
      248, 298, 336, 336*n*, 337
   instability of private fortunes
      in America, 341, 355, 359
   lack of influence of, 40, 244
   liberty and, 305
   limits on ambition and, 361–
      65
   pursuit of power versus, 113
   slavery and, 185–92

wealth (*cont.*)
  see also aristocracy; upper
    classes
Weber, Max, xv
well-being
  in equality of conditions, 110,
    243–44, 285–86, 303–4
  pleasures in, 297–300, 301
  revolution as threat to, 367–72
  in serving greatest good for
    greatest number, 123–25,
    129–31, 305–7, 401
West (western states)
  evangelical religions in, 300–
    301
  interdependence with other
    parts of U.S., 198–99
  rough habits of residents in,
    120, 161
  slavery as fatal to masters in,
    183–86
West Indies, colonies in, 20–21
westward movement, 146–48,
  341–42
wheat, 198
Whig Party, 100*n*
white manhood suffrage, 34*n*,
  109, 109*n*
wilderness of North America
  descriptive poetry and, 266–
    67
  destruction of Indian tribes
    in, 168–80
  development of, 146–48,
    205*n*, 218–21, 341–42
  education of Anglo-
    Americans in, 157–58
  immigrants in, 146

  slavery as fatal to masters in,
    183–86
  westward movement and,
    146–48, 218–19, 341–42
  women in, 341–42, 403–6
Williams, Edwin, 214*n*
Wisconsin, as northwestern
  state, 48*n*
women
  attendance at public
    meetings, 130
  African American, 165
  chastity and, 32–33, 339, 347
  crimes against, 32–33, 347
  education of, 338–39, 340–41
  equality of conditions and,
    338–39, 342–44
  equality of the sexes and,
    344–48
  frailty of European, 338–39,
    342, 346–47
  independence of American,
    338–39
  Indian, 172*n*
  in marriage, 340–42, 343,
    346–48
  morality of, 338–39, 342–44,
    347
  in the New England colonies,
    29
  personal appearance and, 346
  voting rights of, 34*n*
  in wilderness, 341–42, 403–6
work
  changing of occupations in
    America, 215, 254, 303, 313
  of free laborers compared
    with slaves, 184–85, 185*n*

honor of employment, 312–13, 359–61

influence of democracy on wages, 333–35

master-servant relationship and, 330–32

place-hunting and, 365–66

salaries of public officials, 68–69, 80, 116–17, 313

see also leisure